THE GOSPEL OF MARK AS MIDRASH ON EARLIER JEWISH AND NEW TESTAMENT LITERATURE

Dale Miller
and
Patricia Miller

Studies in the Bible and Early Christianity
Volume 21

The Edwin Mellen Press
Lewiston/Queenston/Lampeter

Library of Congress Cataloging-in-Publication Data

Miller, Dale, 1923-
The gospel of Mark as Midrash on earlier Jewish and New Testament literature / Dale Miller and Patricia Miller.
p. cm. -- (Studies in the Bible and early Christianity ; v. 21)
Includes bibliographical references.
ISBN 0-88946-621-1
1. Bible. N. T. Mark--Criticism, interpretation, etc. 2. Bible. N. T. Mark--Relation to the Old Testament. 3. Bible. O. T.--Quotations in the New Testament. 4. Aramic literature--Relation to the New Testament. 5. Rabbinic literature--Relation to the New Testament. 6. Midrash. I. Miller, Patricia, 1950- . II. Title. III. Series.
BS2585.2.M55 1990
226.3'06--dc20 90-32887
CIP

This is volume 21 in the continuing series
Studies in the Bible and Early Christianity
Volume 21 ISBN 0-88946-621-1
SBEC Series ISBN 0-88946-913-X

A CIP catalog record for this book
is available from the British Library.

The Edwin Mellen Press
Box 450
Lewiston, New York
USA 14092

The Edwin Mellen Press
Box 67
Queenston, Ontario
CANADA L0S 1L0

The Edwin Mellen Press, Ltd.
Lampeter, Dyfed, Wales
UNITED KINGDOM SA48 7DY

Printed in the United States of America

CONTENTS

PREFACE

The Gospel of Mark has been at the center of attention for New Testament scholarship for some time now and justifiably so. We are convinced, nevertheless, that much of its message has been missed because the essential clues for interpreting the intent of its author have gone unnoticed. Mark is a book with a consistent development from beginning to end. Its author used already existing Jewish sacred literature in great detail to shape both his overall point of view and the details of particular narratives and teachings of Jesus. Attention to the particulars of Mark's use of scripture unlocks the secret of the continuity of the Gospel. A recent effort in that same direction is Wolfgang Roth's *Hebrew Gospel: Cracking the Code of Mark*. Roth's subtitle could well be ours because we believe that we have indeed discovered how Mark intended his book to be read. The ability to read Mark in turn makes it possible to discover the flow of thought in John and Luke-Acts. Thus, our intention is to open up for biblical scholars and others a new era in Gospel interpretation.

We envision this book as the first of three, the second focusing on John, the third on Luke-Acts. The primary skill needed for research on all three is close reading of the text in order to unearth as much as possible the intent of each author as it has come down to us through the best available manuscripts. Close reading of the text requires intensive effort on the part of the reader. The book is therefore not intended as casual reading. Close reading is the art which has been largely lost in Gospel scholarship during this century because of a highly productive but overly narrow concern for historical analysis. We have intentionally erred in the opposite direction by ignoring most historical questions. In the long run the two sides of criticism will have to be brought back into balance. The result, we predict, will be a dramatically revised view of the origins of Christianity and its sacred literature.

The research behind our book began in 1954 but proceeded spasmodically until we recently became a mutually stimulating father-daughter team. As frequent references will attest, we are indebted in particular to the writings of James A. Sanders, Howard Clark Kee, and Samuel Sandmel. Professor Sanders has also supplied valuable commentary in advance of publication. We express our appreciation to C. L. Smith for his expertise in identifying the etymologies of key words from Hebrew, Greek, and Aramaic, to Maurice LaBelle for providing valuable support in shaping the book manuscript, and to Walden Miller for copy editing.

Readers will note that this book seeks to persuade other scholars and also to be readable as an introduction for ordinary students and church people. This reflects our bias that good scholarship should be available to the laity and to students in particular as instantly as possible. It also demands that our interests be centered on a balance between purely technical information and the spiritual ideas which motivated the author to write a Gospel in the first place.

Dale Miller
Patricia Miller

CHAPTER ONE

MIDRASH

Midrash is an ancient biblical form of interpreting and updating scripture, long recognized as important in Judaism, but only recently discovered to be relevant to study of the New Testament. The main stream of New Testament scholarship has been dominated for most of the twentieth century by the conviction that the authors of the four gospels collected bits and pieces of information about Jesus and pasted them together in hodgepodge sequences, with the consequence that none of the books could profitably be studied by devoting primary attention to the flow of thought in the text. Martin Dibelius, an early exponent of that position, was convinced that Mark and Matthew are "unliterary writings" which "should not be compared with 'literary' works," but are instead "collections of material. The composers are only to the smallest extent authors. They are principally collectors of tradition, editors. Before all else their labour consists in handing down, grouping, and working over the material which has come to them."[1] In this type of scholarship, some of the content of the Gospels is presumed to have gone back to Jesus himself, some to have been created by the church. That which is attributed to Jesus can be known only by highly technical procedures for separating the two strands of material. The methodology to support these conclusions was initiated largely by Dibelius in *The Form Criticism of the Gospels* and Rudolf Bultmann in *The History of the Synoptic Tradition*, and has been continued with modifications by schools of thought associated with their names. William G. Doty ascribes to Bultmann the title of "'father of contemporary NT studies,' if 'father' can be understood as indicating immediate progenitor."[2] Bultmann's successors, often known as Neo-Bultmannians, include two giants of the American scene, the late Norman Perrin and Howard Clark Kee. Bultmann and Dibelius developed Form Criticism, a methodology through which the components of the Gospels are studied in their pre-Gospel forms. Willi Marxsen adapted the Bultmann-Dibelius methodology as Redaction Criticism,[3] which involves tracing the history of sayings of Jesus which were moving toward their final form in the Gospels, including any editing by the evangelists themselves.[4] Perrin and Duling summarize the generally accepted position of gospel scholars today:

> Though it is virtually impossible to say very much about the life of Jesus on the basis of the New Testament, the same is not true of his message. Here our resources are greater, and historical scholarship has arrived at satisfactory criteria for determining the authenticity of material attributed to the Jesus of the New Testament....
>
> The New Testament writers present us with material put on the lips of the Jesus of the gospels by the church. But this Jesus is not the historical Jesus and the material attributed to him in fact had a long and complex history of transmission in the tradition of the church before it reached the form in which we find it. It came in part from Jesus himself, but also from anonymous prophets and scribes in the community, and even from the evangelists themselves. It had constantly been edited and interpreted in response to the changing needs and insights of the communities of Christians through which it passed. Our problem is, therefore, twofold: we have to find a way of working

> back through the tradition to the earliest form of the material we can reach, and then we have to devise criteria for determining whether in that form it can be attributed to the historical Jesus.[5]

Bultmann, late in his career, pointed to the dilemma of the New Testament scholar who was sure that there had been a historical Jesus but who could know little or nothing about him. Bultmann was certain that "the doubt as to whether Jesus existed is unfounded and not worth refutation. No sane person can doubt that Jesus stands behind the historical movement whose first distinct stage is represented by the oldest Palestinian community."[6] Bultmann admitted, however, that "we can now know almost nothing concerning the life and personality of Jesus, since the early Christian sources show no interest in either, are moreover fragmentary and legendary; and other sources about Jesus do not exist."[7]

Composition Criticism, a study which focuses on the author more as creator rather than as collector or editor, is an alternative to Form Criticism. The Composition analyst looks at each separate book as having its own integrity, searching for the author's development of imagery, plot, character, theme, etc., as one would in studying any significant literary work. Some of the better scholars have sought to combine Form and Composition Criticism. Both Kee and Perrin, for example, have moved considerably toward the possibility that Mark was more of an innovator than a gatherer. This is especially evident in Perrin's *A Modern Pilgrimage in New Testament Christology*, but even here he still was wrestling with the question as to whether Mark wrote each passage, edited it, or copied it in its inherited form. Robert Fowler cites Perrin as having observed that the "evangelists are genuinely authors, authors using traditional material but nevertheless authors; they write for a definite purpose, they give their work a distinct and individual structure, they have thematic concerns which they pursue...."[8] Kee suggests Mark's activity as composer by identifying three components in his Gospel: "units of oral tradition, small collections of narratives and/or sayings, and the Jewish prophetic-apocalyptic practices of eschatological exegesis, which include reworking prophetic tradition *in the light of the immediate, critical needs of his community*."[9]

A methodology for studying the gospels which is an extension of Composition Criticism is now available. James A. Sanders, its foremost advocate, calls it Comparative Midrash. It addresses the possibility that the Gospels were created through the use of a distinctively Jewish literary device known as midrash.[10] Midrash is broadly defined as the interpretation of present events and teachings as sacred through the use of texts already accepted as sacred. Midrash is akin to a distinction made by Jaroslav Pelikan: "Tradition is the living faith of the dead. Traditionalism is the dead faith of the living."[11] Midrashic interpretation is always the living faith of the past, reclothed in the flesh and blood of the interpreter's time. It is never the wooden repetition of what once was true. This applies equally to predictive and non-predictive aspects of tradition.

Two helpful guides on the subject of midrash are Samuel Sandmel, a Jew whose field of expertise was the century in which most of the New Testament was written, and James A. Sanders, a Christian who is now the most widely known exponent of the Canonical Criticism school of biblical study.[12] Both recognize the importance of midrash for understanding the Old and New Testaments. Sandmel wrote in 1978 that three articles on midrash in the 1904 *Jewish Encyclopedia* "are a treasury of information, not significantly superseded."[13] S. Horovitz, in the first of the three articles, defines midrash in terms of the root "to study" or "to investigate," and denoting "exposition" and "exegesis," especially that of the scriptures.[14] He differentiates *peshat* and midrash as two levels of exegesis. *Peshat* refers to discovery of the literal meaning of the text; midrash, by "going more deeply than the mere literal sense, attempts to penetrate into the spirit of the Scriptures, to examine the text from all sides, and thereby to derive interpretations which are not immediately obvious."[15] Horovitz notes that "the divergence between midrash and *peshat* increased steadily,"[16] and that "the first traces of midrashic exegesis are found in the Bible itself."[17]

Horovitz treats midrash primarily as a phenomenon of the rabbinic period, from 200 BCE (Before the Common Era) to 200 CE.[18] The rabbinic period was a transitional time in Judaism when the office of "rabbi" emerged to provide leadership to congregations no longer able to organize their religious life around the temple, either because of Jewish dispersion or the destruction of the temple. Jews were using the word "midrash" both to designate a method of interpreting scripture and as the name of a particular collection of scriptural interpretations. Horovitz identifies three kinds of midrashic literature produced in the rabbinic period: verse by verse commentaries on biblical books; collections of teachings arranged by topics, known as the Mishna; and supplements to the Mishna which supplied explanations and specific scriptural references for it. The latter two were put into written form by about 175 CE[19] All three began as oral tradition and were promulgated by the Pharisees. Rabbis claimed that the oral midrashic interpretations of scripture which they produced were as authoritative as scripture itself. Midrash, according to Horovitz, took three forms during the rabbinic period: *haggadah*, *halakah*, and *pesiqta*..[20] *Halakah* refers to a midrashic interpretation of a legal passage from scripture, either a law or teaching. *Haggadah* refers to a midrashic interpretation of a non-legal passage of scripture, a story, particularly in a "moralizing or edifying manner."[21] *Pesiqta* refers to whole sermons or homilies written midrashically.

Sandmel, despite his praise for Horovitz' article, disagreed with his tendency to limit midrash to the rabbinic period. He was convinced, as is Sanders, that much of the Bible was written midrashically.[22] Creating scripture by means of a midrashic process is significantly different from interpreting scripture midrashically, even though the two have much in common. Compare, for example, the styles of an interpretative midrash from the *Mechilta on Exodus* and a midrashically written biblical passage.

> Why was the Torah not given in the land of Israel? In order that the nations of the world should not have the excuse for saying: Because it was given in Israel's land, therefore we have not accepted it. Another reason: To avoid causing dissension among the tribes. Else one might have said: In my territory the Torah was given. And the other might have said: In my territory the Torah was given. Therefore, the Torah was given in the desert, publicly and openly, in a place belonging to no one.[23]

Midrash in the *Mechilta* passage presents an argument through which an original detail from the Torah is retained and applied to a new situation. By contrast, the story of the stoning of Stephen is creative narration. The Stephen account can be seen as a midrashic reformulation of Jesus' baptism and crucifixion merged into one event. Acts 7.54-60, with emphasis added[24] to point out its midrashic parallels to Luke, reads:

> Now when they heard these things they were enraged, and they ground their teeth against him. But he [Stephen], *full of the Holy Spirit,* gazed into heaven and saw the glory of God...and he said, "Behold, *I see the heavens opened,* and the *Son of man standing at the right hand of God.*" ... Then they cast him *out of the city* and stoned him; and the witnesses *laid down their gar-*

> *ments* at the feet of a young man named Saul. And as they were stoning Stephen, he prayed, "Lord Jesus, *receive my spirit.*" And he knelt down and cried with a loud voice, "*Lord, do not hold this sin against them.*" And when he had said this, *he fell asleep.*

The opened sky linked with reception of spirit comes from Lk. 3.21-22: "When Jesus also had been baptized and *was praying, the heaven was opened,* and the *Holy Spirit descended upon him.*" A stronger midrashic source for Stephen's statement about spirit comes from Lk. 23.46: "Then Jesus, crying with a loud voice, said, '*Father, into thy hands I commit my spirit.*' And having said this *he breathed his last.*" Jesus' "breathed his last" parallels Stephen's "fell asleep" as a quiet death. The reference to garments and the prayer of forgiveness for one's executioners originates in Lk. 23.33-34: "And when they came to the place which is called The Skull, there they crucified him, and the criminals, one on the right and one on the left. And Jesus said, '*Father forgive them, for they know not what they do.*' And they cast lots to *divide his garments.*" Two of the sayings of Stephen in Acts closely parallel Luke's sayings of Jesus from the cross; both stories refer to garments; both Jesus and Stephen are taken outside the city to be executed; both men pray. Stephen sees into heaven and is filled with the Holy Spirit, like Jesus at his baptism. The original details are resignified to create a new sacred story.

The confusion between midrashic creation of new scripture and midrashic interpretation of old texts is illustrated by an attempt to define midrash as a literary genre. Addison Wright refers to it as a "literature about a literature,"[25] an analysis from outside the literature being examined. He nevertheless admits that the interpreter may rewrite the original text as well as comment upon it. Roger Le Deaut, a Targum specialist, objects that Wright's definition is too narrow. He argues that new texts can be created from generally accepted facts of history quite apart from a source text, and that it is the use of a more "complex meaning" of midrash "which will assure penetration into the thought world of the New Testament writers."[26] Le Deaut desists from even trying to define midrash because any definition would exclude some creative way in which a New Testament author had made use of the method.[27] A purist could well argue that Le Deaut's "more complex meaning" stretches the limits of the term midrash too far. If that is true, what would be needed would be some other as yet unknown term to cover the wide range of creative ways New Testament authors wrote new scripture by making use of the old.

Confusion between midrash as interpretation of an old text and as creation of a new one is exemplified in a long treatment of "Son of Man" by Perrin. In the process of showing that there was an independent pre-New Testament tradition based on Dan. 7.13, Perrin delineates the ways in which I Enoch made use of Daniel and other biblical books. He argues that "the Enoch saga is a major development in Jewish apocalyptic, inspired by the cryptic references to Enoch in the Old Testament." He compares the "call" of Enoch in I Enoch 70-71 with the imagery of Ezek. 1, Dan. 7, and Gen. 5.24, which says "Enoch walked with God; and he was not, for God took him." Perrin continues:

> From Ezekiel 1 come the chariots of the spirit (70.2), the flaming cherubim (71.7), the fire which girdles the house (71.6; in Ezekiel fire surrounds the cherubim); and Enoch, like Ezekiel, falls to the ground when confronted by the vision (71.11; Ezek. 1.28). From Daniel 7 come the streams(s) of fire (71.2), the Head of Days (71.10) and, above all, the use of the Son of Man in connection with Enoch. It is easy enough to see what has happened: the seer has interpreted the translation of Enoch in terms of the call of Ezekiel and

> of the appearance before the Ancient of Days of the Son of Man.[28]

Perrin's analysis gives clear examples of I Enoch's use of narrative midrash. Perrin, however, refers to such passages as *pesher*, a term which in his usage is close to midrash except that he limits it to apocalyptic contexts only.[29] He reserves "midrash" only for the portions of the Mishna which interpret biblical passages. For example, a text in the Mishna cites Rabbi Alexander as saying "R. Joshua opposed two verses: it is written 'and behold, with the clouds of heaven one like a Son of Man came' [Dan 7.13]; while it is written, 'lowly, and riding upon an ass' [Zech 9.9]. If they are meritorious [the Messiah will come] 'with the clouds of heaven' if not 'lowly, and riding upon an ass.'"[30]

Leo Baeck also recognizes the dependence of one text on another without using the term "midrash." Sandmel and Sanders would refer to his comments on Daniel as illustrating haggadic or narrative-style midrash. Baeck wrote:

> The Book of Daniel is nothing less than the apocalypse *par excellence*; and one of its important elements is the apparition of him "who is like unto a Son of Man and comes with the clouds of heaven and steps before God." Wherever in later works "that Son of Man," "this Son of Man," or "the Son of Man" is mentioned, it is the quotation from Daniel that is speaking.... Yet these two sentences, in which the old meaning is still evident, are overshadowed by the many others which show time and time again that the word [Son of Man] has received a new sense in the Gospels and has become a very specific term. It is no longer the ancient apocalyptic image that appears in it; it has become an independent theological concept.[31]

Thus the biblical writers used midrash to create texts as the early rabbis concomitantly used midrash to analyze them.

The source of the confusion between interpretative midrash and creative midrash is the failure to recognize that the latter is also explanatory. Kee, without using the term "midrash," shows how creation and explanation were combined in Mark's style of merging and blending scripture rather than giving precise quotations:

> As E.E. Ellis [*Paul's Use of the New Testament*] has noted, in the *pesher* quotations found in abundance in the Dead Sea Scrolls, 'the interpretation or exposition is incorporated into the body of the text itself, thereby determining its text form.' Not only does Mark not hold to a single authoritative version of the text or scripture, but he is not concerned about the literal details or the original import of the text which he finds fulfilled in Jesus. J.A. Fitzmyer[32] has observed that in what he calls 'accommodated texts' the original meaning has been 'modified to meet the new situation' in the interpreter's own time.[33]

What is said about Mark applies to midrashic writers in general and is even more true of their modification of texts when they are not quoting at all. They interpret each traditional text by claiming that its truth is in the new version quite apart from the intent of the original author. Thus the characteristics of interpretative midrash in the style of the rabbinic period should be seen as applying to creative midrash by biblical authors as well.

Horovitz notes that midrashic explanations could be disciplined or highly imaginative and that early rabbinical midrash on biblical laws was likely to be more restrained while midrash on non-legal portions of scripture, such as narratives, was less so. J. Theodor, in another of the articles commended by Sandmel, identifies Leopold Zunz[34] as "the master of midrash study," and quotes him in support of Horovitz' position as follows:

> Definite rules were as impossible for this exegesis as rules of rhetoric for the Prophets.... For the power of this exegesis lay not in literal interpretation and in natural hermeneutics...but in the unhampered application of the contents of the Bible to contemporary views and needs: everything that was venerated and beloved by the present generation was connected with the sacred though limited field of the past. This method of free exegesis was manifested in many ways: the obvious sense of the Biblical passage was followed; or the inner meaning of the text, to the exclusion of the literal sense, was considered; or recourse was had to the traditional haggadah; or the results of the Masorah were taken into account.... But this liberty wished neither to falsify scripture nor to deprive it of its natural sense, for its object was the free expression of thought.[35]

Zunz' point is that through the midrashic process everything venerated in the present is connected with the sacred past. Both in the rabbinic schools of thought and in the New Testament, the authors affirmed the sacredness of their own time and its concerns by midrashic connections to texts already accepted as holy. Only on this ground could the rabbis claim that their oral tradition was as religiously valid as the written scripture itself. New Testament authors claimed on the same basis that their interpretations of Jesus were equal or superior to the original biblical passages for which they were the midrashic interpretation.

Zunz' judgment that definite rules were impossible for midrashic exegesis did not prevent early rabbis from proposing them. The most widely known set was composed by Rabbi Hillel shortly before the Christian era and applied only to midrash on law. Hillel's rules are interesting, nevertheless, for the wide range of interpretations which they permitted beyond the literal statement of a law. His standards for legitimate explanation of scriptural laws included:

1. A deduction from a simple rule to a more rigorous one, e.g., if theft is prohibited, so is burglary.
2. A deduction from equal decrees so that two rules have the same intent if similar words appear in both.
3. A deduction of a general rule from an example once stated.
4. A deduction of a general rule from the combination of two verses.
5. A deduction either of a specific regulation from a general principle, or of a general principle from a specific regulation.
6. A deduction in one situation from a specific regulation in another.
7. A deduction from a context, in contrast to a deduction from a statement.[36]

Those rules apply only to *halakah*. Zunz' judgment that *haggadah* was even more loose and imaginative in its possibilities would justify adaptations of original texts even less restrained than Hillel's rules permit. Such freedom enabled New Testament authors on occasion to use a scriptural detail in two ways, one consistent with its original meaning and the other diametrically opposite to the original, e.g., fishing for men as both hunting them for punishment, as in Jeremiah 16.16, and recruiting them for service.

James A. Sanders, without disagreeing with the above, correctly carries the definition of midrash one step further. He distinguishes between midrash and comparative midrash:

> A new method of approach to the question of the relation between the Old and New Testaments is called

> comparative midrash. If one studies the various ways in which Second Temple Judaism contemporized OT traditions, one can actually trace the history of such midrashic tendency back into OT itself. In fact, since the older discipline of tradition criticism has begun to include in its purview the question of *why* a tradition would be repeated, or taken up again in another form, it has begun to sound more and more like the study of midrash.[37]

Sanders presents comparative midrash as a tool for relating any tradition or text, its historical and sociological context, and its interpretation to each other: "Canonical criticism [using comparative midrash as a primary tool] not only looks for all the traditions, texts, and precursors that flow into a passage studied but it also seeks to determine exactly how that tradition functioned in the text and the hermeneutics by which it did so."[38] Midrash thus takes three essentially different forms: original creation, interpretation, and comparative study.

Sanders shows the relevance of creative midrash to comprehension of the Jewish and Christian canons. In his insightful essay "Torah and Christ" he identifies *halachah* with laws, ethics, life style, and *ethos*; and *haggadah* with story, identity, gospel, and *muthos* [myth].[39] The distinction is important throughout the Old Testament and into the New. Sanders rightly states that the Torah is constitutive for both Judaism and Christianity, that "the Torah is primarily a story and not primarily a set of laws," and that the laws in the Torah "derive their authority from the story." He explains that "through the Torah, Israel passed from a nation in destitution to a religious community in dispersion which could never be destroyed. But this remarkable force not only defined the Jerusalem community, it defined forever all Jewry as Judaism. From Ezra on, Torah was Judaism and Judaism was Torah."[40]

Sanders notes that stories captivate people in all ages and determine how they think about their own identities, and that each religion is based on an accepted history in narrative form. The distinct difference between Judaism, for which Torah was its sufficient story, and Christianity is the addition of the life of Jesus and particularly the crucifixion as a necessary basis for every new statement of faith. It was a daring act for a Jew such as Paul to declare that "Christ is the climax of the Torah for all who believe in the righteousness of God."[41] For Mark to interpret Christ as going beyond the limits of Torah was even more courageous.

The primacy of the Torah in biblical Judaism is inherently connected with the reason for Jews to use midrash. To the extent that their religion is defined by the Torah, it is possible for Jews to relive its insights in new situations, but it is not possible for them to live new truths which contradict the old ones. Jews, in order to identify with their spiritual heritage, must find in the Torah that which is the latent form of each new experience. Either by *haggadah* or *halakah*, they must retell the teachings or the story of Judaism in such a way that the present is linked literarily to the past. To do so is to practice midrash.

Sanders argues persuasively in *Torah and Canon* that Moses, rather than the laws of the Torah, became the midrashic model for the rest of the Old Testament. He became the prototype for Joshua, Eli, Samuel, David, Solomon, Elijah, and Elisha, each of whom exemplified one or more aspects of the Moses story. Sanders' position is illustrated by Exod. 14.21-22 as a model:

> "Then Moses stretched out his hand over the sea; and the Lord drove the sea back by a strong east wind all night, and made the sea dry land, and the waters were divided. And the people of Israel went into the midst of the sea on dry ground, the waters being a wall to them on their right hand and on their left." When Joshua

> brought the people to the Jordan River, "the waters coming down from above stood and rose up in a heap far off," and all Israel passed "over on dry ground" (Josh. 3.14-17).

This also happened to Elijah and Elisha when they came to the Jordan. Elijah and Elisha "were both standing by the Jordan. Then Elijah took his mantle, and rolled it up, and struck the water, and the water was parted to the one side and to the other, till the two of them could go over on dry ground" (2 Kgs. 2.7-8). After Elijah's ascension, Elisha struck the water with Elijah's mantle; "the water was parted to the one side and to the other; and Elisha went over" (2 Kgs. 2.14). The story line in each instance enhances the sacredness of Joshua, Elijah, and Elisha by their similarity to Moses. Other examples of midrash on Moses include both Moses and Joshua sending spies into Canaan (Numb. 13.1-2; Josh. 2.1), Caleb and Moses both having undiminished strength in old age (Deut. 34.7; Josh. 14.10-11), and God speaking through forces of nature to both Moses and Elijah at Mt. Horeb (Deut. 4.11-12; 1 Kgs. 19.8, 19.11-12). Josephus reports that two first century messianic candidates emulated Moses: Theudas by claiming that he had stopped the flow of the Jordan River, and Festus by asking people to follow him into the wilderness for miraculous relief.[42]

Midrash about Moses is closely connected to midrash about Jacob, whose name was both a synonym for Israel as a people in that the tribes of Israel were descended from Jacob's sons, and a symbol of someone supplanting another who had a legal right to some benefit or position. The latter imagery originates in the tale of Jacob finessing his brother Esau out of both his blessing and his birthright. Esau observed: "Is he not rightly named Jacob? For he has supplanted me these two times" (Gen. 27.36). The name Jacob functions in parts of the Old Testament as a symbol of God's preference for the younger over the legally preferable first-born. By extension, Jacob symbolizes any person or group elected by God to replace one previously chosen. Israel as an entity, according to Mal. 1.2-3, is the chosen people precisely because of the supplanting motif: God should have chosen Edom, but he chose Israel instead. The Jacob motif of a second replacing the first was often used midrashically, as is shown by analysis of the relationships of important Old Testament pairs, such as Moses-Joshua, David-Solomon, and Elijah-Elisha. God gave the first-mentioned, Moses-like hero in each pair one or more tasks to perform, part of which he did not complete. The second person succeeded him to do the unfinished work: Joshua led Moses' people into the Promised Land; Elisha anointed the kings whose anointing had been assigned to Elijah; and Solomon built the temple which David had wanted to construct. Josh. 11.15 states that Joshua "left nothing undone of all that the Lord had commanded Moses." Each of the three successors is midrashically a new Jacob.

Midrash can be mistakenly confused with casual allusion to older texts. This has has occurred, for example, with Paul's view of Jesus as a new Adam (1 Cor. 15.45), the portrait of Jesus as a lamb slain for the sins of the world in Rev. 5.12, and Mark's use of details from the Psalms as part of the story of Jesus' trial and death (Mk. 15.23 ff.). Kee and Young interpret Mark's crucifixion account without referring to details from the Psalms; Perrin and Duling list the Psalmic passages and then ignore them in their interpretation of the crucifixion.[43] To treat such references as merely incidental, without much significance for the overall interpretation of the biblical books, is an error for both a general and a specific reason. The general reason is that in well-written narratives, including midrashic ones, there are no incidental details. Hans Frei, in *The Eclipse of Biblical Narrative*, insists that the meaning of an account is not illustrated but is constituted through all the particulars, "the indispensable narrative web," of a given story.[44] Gary

Comstock correctly interprets Frei's intention: "The meaning of the gospel [or any other narrative] cannot be paraphrased or rendered in any other way except as it is constituted by the writers themselves."[45] Each specific is constitutive of the narrative and cannot be replaced by some other one without changing the meaning as a whole. When a narrative is midrashic, discounting a source passage as an incidental allusion is more specifically an error because the intention of the author is inextricably related to corresponding details in the source from which the new pericope was created.

A clear illustration of the Frei-Comstock point as it relates to midrash is Luke's John-Jesus infancy narrative. Mary's "Magnificat" speech (Lk. 1.46-55) paraphrases a statement by Hannah, the mother of Samuel (1 Sam. 2.1-10). John's mother, Elizabeth, is miraculously pregnant in old age (as Hannah was); God answers Hannah's and Zechariah's prayer for a child at the temple; Jesus increases in wisdom and stature (as Samuel did); Hannah had five additional children (compared to Mary's six or more additional ones); and John the Baptizer was predicted to be a Nazarite (as Samuel was). One such parallel might constitute an incidental allusion but many parallels require the reader to conclude that Luke's narrative must be interpreted at least in part in the context of 1 Samuel. Luke wanted his readers to ponder the decision of God to send his son into the world through a potentially scandalous pregnancy of a young woman when he had available as a model the sensational miracle of the pregnancy of an aged woman who was perfect in Judaism, as Luke says of Elizabeth. He did so by the midrash on details from 1 Samuel.

Another example of significant parallel details between biblical stories is found in the exegesis of Acts 13.6-12. Paul, while still named Saul, visits a proconsul, Sergius Paulus. He meets Bar-Jesus ("Son of Jesus"), whose alternative name is Elymas the Magician. In the midst of the story, Saul is referred to as Paul and never again as Saul (like the Saul of 1 Sam. 10 being "turned into another man"). Paul labels Son of Jesus as son of the devil (as Jesus was accused of casting out demons by Satanic means), causes Son of Jesus to become blind (like Saul-Paul on the road to Damascus), and reproaches him for making straight paths crooked. Saul-Paul had regained his own sight on "Straight" street in Damascus. Each such parallel serves in comparative midrashic interpretation to alert the reader to look to the earlier story as a key to understanding the second one. In virtually all midrash on narratives the more in-depth interpretations of the story, such as in Paul's name change, are hidden in the relationships between its details and the tradition to which it is related. Sanders refers to such relationships as "the unrecorded hermeneutics that lie between the lines of Scripture."[46]

The fact that narrative details are indispensable does not mean that there is only one correct interpretation of a narrative. Sanders insists that he does not know of a "biblical passage of substance" with only a single correct interpretation.[47] The "multivalence" of meanings, to use his term, which Sanders sees in scripture is like what we are accustomed to in interpreting poetry, in which there are often multiple "layers" of significance with only the most superficial level showing on the surface.

Midrash can also be confused with fulfilling prophecies as if they had been intended only as predictions. In the Old Testament, prophecies often include predictions, but never apart from a much broader context of meaning. Prophecy at its best is akin to incisive critical analysis, penetration to the core of meaning of certain events. As a result of such critiques, prophets occasionally predicted some event which actually occurred. Prophecy at its worst is royal cheerleading, nationalistic flag waving, submissive yea-saying to those in power. Note for example the contrast between Micaiah and the false prophets in I Kgs 22: Micaiah alone sees disaster and death as the inevitable result of proposed military ventures; the others insist that easy victory is guaranteed. They are "false" because they parrot what the powerful want them to say, not only because Micaiah's prediction turns out to be more correct than theirs. The issue is critical analysis, not prediction.

Study of a prophetic prediction as midrash differs considerably from dealing with predictions in a straightforward manner. Scholars, in doing the latter, seek to evaluate as accurately as possible the intention of a prophet in his or her total situation and then render a judgment based on subsequent history as to the senses in which the prognostication was or was not accurate. When predictions are used midrashically, all that changes. The midrashic author begins from what is perceived to be fulfillment and works backward to the forecast itself, reinterpreting the original to mean whatever its completion requires. Isa. 7.14-17 serves as an example of the two approaches. It portrays a woman who will become pregnant and give birth to a child. Before the child is old enough to distinguish between good and evil (an unspecified age), two kings will have lost their power to terrify. Within Isaiah, the prediction is accurate. The book tells nothing about the woman or her child but chronicles the death of both kings. The woman could be anyone, perhaps even the prophet's wife. Her act of giving birth in a terrifying time was seen by the prophet as a vote of confidence that the future would be tolerable for her child. Her story was a way of saying that things are going to get better soon, symbolized by the child's name, Emmanuel ("God Is With Us"). R.B.Y. Scott summarizes the scholarly analysis of the story:

> The king and his counselors are still wavering; they have not yet finally rejected the prophet's word and appealed to Tiglath-pileser. So Isaiah goes further and offers them a **sign**, i.e., an event which will soon happen and prove to them that the Lord has indeed spok-

> en by his prophet. The sign is thus firmly anchored to the historical situation in which it was given.[48]

Matthew midrashically transformed this story in his gospel. The woman becomes a virgin; the child becomes the baby Jesus; the dreaded kings become Herod; and the story becomes a messianic prediction. For Matthew, the "fact" that the Messiah was virgin-born was sufficient to establish the authenticity of a fulfilled predictive prophecy. "God Is With Us" was Jesus' alternate name, another proof that "all this took place to fulfil what the Lord had spoken by the prophet" (Mt. 1.22-23). Matthew's midrashic treatment grates on rationalist scholarly sensitivities. His fulfillment formula, used also in 2.15; 8.17; 12.17; 13.35; and 21.04, is factually false. In each instance Matthew disregarded the original context and read the passage to mean what he wanted it to mean. Factuality, however, is beside the point in midrash. Matthew's midrashic interpretation embodied his faith in the nature of Jesus and Jesus' connection to sacred texts. Any midrashist who concurred with Matthew's beliefs about Jesus would not find the fulfillment formula offensive. Since Matthew found the analogy in Isaiah, the analogy is "really" there as one among the multivalent levels of interpretation.

A familiar form of midrash is a doublet, the second of two narratives or teachings in a single work which are sufficiently similar to each other that they appear to be the same account told twice. It is well illustrated in the Torah, written over a period of several hundred years by different authors who are usually referred to as J, E, D, and P.[49] The later authors often wrote a new version of an earlier account or law without removing the original from the text. In the Torah, for example, Abraham twice presented his wife as his sister; Moses went up Mt. Sinai more than once to get the Ten Commandments; there are two creation stories; and some parts of the flood story are told twice. From a rationalist vantage point, the pairs of stories can be seen as a double tradition, two authors reporting the same event. In late biblical times, however, probably everyone thought that Moses himself had written the entire Torah. What appears to us as the work of two authors would have appeared to Mark or Isaiah, for example, as two versions of the same story written by the same author. Whether written by one person or two, the second telling of the story would be both a doublet and midrash. Either a writer was doing midrash on the work of an earlier one, or was doing internal midrash on an account previously written by himself or herself. Recognizing that an author could write midrash on his own earlier passage both broadens the meaning of the term and facilitates deeper levels of comprehension as to what the gospel authors were doing, for example, in pairs of accounts of feeding the multitudes, crossing the lake, entering Jerusalem, etc.

The purpose of a doublet is to enable an author to register a change of meaning from one setting to another without having to create an entirely new story to express the altered meaning. Acts provides excellent examples of doublets in its pair of imprisonment accounts, its repeated narrative of the descent of the holy spirit, and its multiple use of the names "Ananias" and "Simon." In Acts 12, Peter is miraculously rescued from incarceration by angelic intervention under cover of night, with the result that his guards are put to death and his associates apparently placed in such jeopardy that he will not even stay with them after his release. In the Acts 16 doublet, a miracle enables Paul to be freed from another prison. He and other prisoners are so protective of the jailer that they remain in their cells lest the man should be executed. He even refuses to leave the next day until a trial is convened and his right to be free is legalized and publicly announced. The doublet reflects the author's general distinction between the Jerusalem church and Gentiles, the former opting for safety (symbolized by

Peter's miraculous rescue even at the cost of other's lives) whereas the Gentiles are willing to suffer versions of the voluntary death of Christ (symbolized by Paul's refusal to be rescued as Peter was).

A second example from Acts concerns the descent of the Holy Spirit. At Pentecost in Jerusalem the spirit comes down upon the twelve apostles as "tongues of fire" with the result that they can "speak in tongues" (Acts 2.1-13). The doublet in Acts 19.5-7 is less well known: "On hearing this, they were baptized in the name of the Lord Jesus. And when Paul laid his hands upon them, the Holy Spirit came on them; and they spoke with tongues and prophesied. There were about twelve of them in all." In the aftermath of each story, Peter and Paul, respectively, perform sensational miracles, in which some people are healed by having Peter's shadow fall upon them (Acts 5.12-16), and others are healed by touching cloth which Paul had touched (Acts 19.11). The doublet is integral to Luke's hypothesis that the Jerusalem church had been replaced by Gentile churches as the core of the new religion which was supplanting Judaism.

A doublet might be as simple as the repetition of a name in a context which affects the meaning. In Acts 5, Ananias ("God Is Gracious") lies to the church about giving all his property to the common treasury and, as a consequence, dies immediately. In Acts 9, a second Ananias risks his life to accept Saul, whom Ananias knows to be a potential murderer. In another example, from Acts 10, Simon Peter stays in the house of Simon the Tanner, a man whose occupation makes him ritually unclean. Simon Peter is convinced in a vision there that no food or person is unclean. Thus Simon the Tanner points to Simon Peter's previous preoccupation with superficial rather than internal cleanness (Mk. 7.14-23). Each second story in these examples is a midrash on the first. The first story in turn may have been a midrash on a previously written text or on a tradition. That does not affect the fact that the second story is a midrash from within the author's book, justified generally by the perception that Moses had rewritten stories in the Torah.

A peculiar characteristic of midrash is that it is possible for a second author to quote an earlier one exactly, but dramatically transform the meaning of any cited passage by changing its context. Four parables which Matthew adapts from Mark are examples. In Mk. 3-4, Jesus has appointed the Twelve, expecting them to understand what the crowds cannot because parables (in Mark's usage) hide the truth from everyone except those few who live according to the truth. The Twelve, however, consistently show that they have no better "sight" than the spiritually blind crowds. Jesus decides to risk, despite their failure, that they have some now-hidden capacity which will enable them to "see" later. In Mk. 4.21-32, Jesus announces this decision in four consecutive pericopes—a lamp to be used later, an axiom that he who has a little will get more, an invisible seed-to-harvest growth, and a mustard seed. The function of the four "parables" is to illustrate Jesus' expectation of the disciples' ultimate success. Matthew, by contrast, rejected Mark's assumption that the Twelve do not understand. He cited Ps. 78.2-4 midrashically to prove that Jesus intended parables as revealing that which "has been hidden from the foundation of the world" (Mt. 13.35) and implying that the Twelve understand with or without a brief explanation by Jesus. Matthew copied three of the parables exactly, separating them from each other (5.15; 10.26; 13.31-32), and rewrote the one about invisible growth (13.24-30). By so doing, he turned all of them into general teachings about the kingdom of God. Thus even the three parables which are verbatim with Mark are midrashic on Mark's originals because their interpretation is changed by virtue of their different contexts in Matthew. The same generalization would be true in the improbable case that Matthew was the original gospel and Mark was quoting Matthew.

Midrashic creation of a parable from a non-parable source is well illustrated by James Sanders' interpretation of the Parable of the Prodigal Son. Sanders refers to it as the parable of the two sons and makes it a critical piece of evidence that the Central Section of Luke (9.51--18.30) is midrashic on Deuteronomy. Interpretation of the central section occupies the attention of Gospel scholars because in it Luke abandoned his previous style of quoting entire Markan pericopes to report teachings of Jesus not found in Mark. Most scholars, including Kee and Perrin, ascribe those teachings to a hypothetical collection of sayings of the historical Jesus usually alluded to as "Q." By Sanders' logic there was no Q because Luke was doing midrash on Deuteronomy throughout as he was in this parable:

> The parable of the two sons in Luke 15.11-32 lies opposite the legislation in Deut. 21.18-21 about the stubborn and rebellious son who becomes a glutton and a drunkard. The law provides that if the son refuses to repent he may be brought to court and sentenced to death by stoning. The Lukan parable gives a beautiful illustration of the case where the son does indeed seek reconciliation, as the law, of course, allows.[50]

None of the practitioners of creative midrash in the Bible ever elaborate on their method of composition. Proof is never as simple as having an author inform the reader that the work is based on midrash. The superb storyteller conveys the impression that what is on the page is what really happened in the lives of characters in the story. A significant problem in interpreting New Testament stories is that there are no validated historical sources outside the New Testament itself with which one can compare. No non-biblical records written by contemporaries of Jesus, Peter, or Paul are extant. That does not signify that the New Testament accounts are not historical; it merely means that scholars have no access to the kind of sources needed in order to check their historicity.

The only criterion for establishing with certainty that an author has made midrashic use of some particular source is the presence of so many significant parallels between the two texts that they cannot be accounted for by coincidence. That criterion distinguishes between a midrashic motif and an isolated midrash, the latter being one in which an author has made use of only a single detail from a work of sacred literature. An analyst who recognizes an isolated parallel between two texts will be unable to provide evidence that it was not coincidental. By contrast, the criteria for literary motifs, including midrashic ones, are well defined by William Freedman.[51] He proposes that the two indispensable factors are frequency and avoidability: the more often a usage occurs and the greater extent to which its occurrence seems unnecessary. Three supplemental factors are appearance of the usage in the more significant contexts in the work, relevance of the usage to the whole of the text, and the appropriateness of any symbols used.

An easily understood example of a New Testament literary motif is the use of "my hour" which the author of the Gospel of John adapted midrashically from references to "hour" in 1 John and Mark's crucifixion story. The expression "my hour" (or "my time") appears in John in eighteen different contexts. Before the Last Supper, "my hour" has not yet come (2.4; 7.8) or is coming (12.27; 13.1). The hour begins (12.23-24) when Jesus analaogizes himself to a kernel which must die in order to produce fruit and (13.31) when Judas leaves the Last Supper to betray Jesus. From that moment Jesus begins to instruct the disciples about his death and the new commandment to love one's brothers. The hour is finished on the cross (19.30). John's resurrection stories point backward to the hour. The "my hour" motif makes sense out of one otherwise incomprehensible story. Jesus, in Jn. 7.3-14, tells his brothers to go to Jerusalem because it is always their time for doing so. He says that he will not go because it is not yet his time, but having said that he goes to Jerusalem. The explanation provided by the entire series of references to "my time" is that the Jerusalem to which Jesus cannot yet go is the Jerusalem of the hour of his death; he can and does go at any other time to the "tourist Jerusalem" of his brothers. By such evidence the existence of the "my hour" motif in John is proved.

Identification of a midrashic motif requires more proof than an ordinary motif. In addition to demonstrating some or all of the literary characteristics specified by Freedman, one must demonstrate that a midrashic motif is paralleled in considerable detail in one or more earlier sacred texts. In order to identify any work as midrashic, one must have access to the sources from which it was adapted. A good example is The Protevangelium of James, a virgin birth story, probably from the second century, which is midrashically dependent on the Gospels and other New Testament books. It converts into simple miracle tales the much more sophisticated material from Luke's and Matthew's virgin birth accounts. It is important for study of the New Testament because it documents that at least some Christians in the second century were close enough to their Jewish roots to understand midrash and to continue to write midrashically.

Perrin recognized that interpretation of Mark was central to study of the entire New Testament.[52] Study of New Testament midrash likewise revolves around the Gospel of Mark. Midrashic composition was the characteristic style of all the early New Testament authors, but it was Mark who imbued the method with qualities of genius and set the pattern for John, Luke-Acts, and Matthew.[53] Mark's gospel was also the first distinctively Christian writing in that it introduced into history the conviction that the crucifixion is essentially different from the Torah and not merely a reflection of its insights. James/Jacob,[54] I John, I Peter, Galatians, I and II Corinthians, Romans, and Hebrews[55] prepared the way for Mark by midrashically presenting Jesus as a Messiah like the Suffering Servant in Isaiah and the paschal lamb of the Torah. Each was based on the authority of the Torah, interpreting Jesus and religion in light of it. Mark, to the contrary, while accepting the sacredness of the Jewish Bible, rejected its adequacy as the core story of his religion and insisted on viewing Jesus in light of the crucifixion rather than interpreting him according to any earlier sacred writings. Mark's unique midrashic task was to create a life-of-Jesus narrative using a mass of details from Jewish sacred literature at the same time he was arguing the insufficiency of all major ideals and models in that scripture.

ENDNOTES FOR CHAPTER ONE

[1]M. Dibelius, *From Tradition to Gospel* (London: 1935), Second Edition, as cited in H.C. Kee, *Community of the New Age* (Philadelphia: Westminster, 1977) 5.

[2]William G. Doty, *Contemporary New Testament Interpretation* (Englewood Cliffs, N.J.: Prentice-Hall, 1972) 28.

[3]Willi Marxsen, *Mark the Evangelist: Studies on the Redaction History of the Gospels* (Nashville: Abingdon, 1969, in English edition; original 1956).

[4]Good descriptions of Form Criticism and Redaction Criticism are provided in N. Perrin and D. C. Duling, *The New Testament, An Introduction* (New York: Harcourt Brace Jovanovich, 1982), II Edition; and William Doty, *Contemporary New Testament Interpretation* (Englewood Cliffs: Prentice-Hall, 1972).

[5]Perrin and Duling, 400-401.

[6]Rudolf Bultmann, *Jesus and the Word* (New York: Scribner's, 1958) 13.

[7]Bultmann, *Jesus and the Word* , 8.

[8]Robert Fowler, "Using Literary Criticism on the Gospels," *Christian Century*, 99/19:626-629, 1982.

[9]Howard Clark Kee, *Community of the New Age: Studies in Mark's Gospel* (Philadelphia: Westminster, 1977) 49.

[10]Jacob Neusner's *What is Midrash?* (Philadelphia: Fortress, 1987) was published after our work was mostly done. His word "midrash" means no more and no less than exegesis, but is limited to exegesis on the Bible done by Jews. He illustrates well the Jewishness of the New Testament in this regard.

[11]Jaroslav Pelikan, *History of the Christian Tradition* (Richmond: University of Virginia, 1973) I, 9.

[12]Canonical Criticism is a methodology for studying the Bible in the form in which the church or synagogue canonized it without primary attention to the process by which the Bible came to exist in that form.

[13]Samuel Sandmel, *Judaism and Christian Beginnings* (New York: Oxford UP, 1978) 434, f.n.109. Sandmel was recommending three articles: "Midrash," "Midrash Haggadah," and "Midrash Halacha."

[14]S. Horovitz, "Midrash,"*The Jewish Encyclopedia* (New York: Funk and Wagnalls, 1904) 548.

[15]Horovitz, 548.

[16]Horovitz, 548.

[17]Horovitz, 548.

[18]The designations "Common Era" and "Before the Common Era" are used in lieu of the traditional Christian use of "BC" and "AD" as ways of identifying historical dates.

[19]Horovitz, 458. Sandmel, in *Judaism and Christian Beginnings*, dates the written form of the Mishna and its supplements, the Talmud, in the 450-500 CE period.

[20]Transliteration spelling of Hebrew words in English varies widely.

[21]J. Theodor, "Midrash Haggadah," *Jewish Encyclopedia* (New York: Funk and Wagnalls, 1904) 550.

[22]Jacob Neusner, *What Is Midrash?* makes an even stronger case for this position and uses the Gospel of Matthew for much of his New Testament evidence.

[23]As translated by Kee, *The Origins of Christianity: Sources and Documents* (Englewood Cliffs: Prentice-Hall, 1973) 144.

[24]Unless indicated otherwise, emphasis added in a scriptural quotation will be for the purpose of calling to the attention of the reader a portion of the quotation which has special significance or which is used midrashically.

[25]Addison Wright, *The Literary Genre Midrash* (Staten Island: Alba House, 1967) 74.

[26]Roger Le Deaut, "Apropos a Definition of Midrash," *Interpretation*, 271, Spr., 1971.

[27]Le Deaut, 281-282.

[28]Norman Perrin, *A Modern Pilgrimage in New Testament Christianity* (Philadelphia: Fortress, 1974) 28.

[29]Richard Longnecker, *Biblical Exegesis in the Apostolic Period* (William B. Eerdmans, 1975) uses the term *pesher* in a more restricted way as a text claiming that "this is that," i.e., that a current event is the fulfillment counterpart of a sacred text. Le Deaut notes efforts of scholars to distinguish between

midrash and *pesher*, and their failure to agree, footnote # 64, p. 277. He recognizes a similar confusion between midrash and targum, p. 278.

[30]Perrin, *Modern Pilgrimage*, 33, cited from bSanh 98a.

[31]Perrin, *Modern Pilgrimage*, 40, cited from Baeck, *Judaism and Christianity*, 28-29.

[32]J. A. Fitzmyer, "The Use of Explicit Old Testament Quotations," *New Testament Studies*, 7, 1960-61, 319-21.

[33]Kee, *Community of the New Age*, 46-47.

[34]Leopold Zunz was a nineteenth century European Jewish scholar. The article about him in the *Jewish Encyclopedia* says that his influence was so great in Judaism that all schools of thought in Judaism were claiming his support within a short time after his death.

[35]Horovitz, *Jewish Encyclopedia*, 554.

[36]Paraphrased from Hillel's norms as translated by Sandmel, *Judaism and Christian Beginnings*, 114.

[37]James A. Sanders, *From Sacred Story to Sacred Text* (Philadelphia: Fortress, 1987) 20-21.

[38]Sanders, *Canon and Community*, 67.

[39]The essay "Torah and Christ" first appeared in *Interpretation*, Oct., 1975, 372-390. Sanders emphasized the distinction between Torah and law in *From Sacred Story to Sacred Text*, 49: "But whether the Torah signifies the Pentateuch only or all authoritative tradition, it does not primarily mean law; ...it means revelation. In fact, it came to mean Judaism—the whole covenant of God's relation to his people."

[40]Sanders, *Torah and Canon* (New York: Fortress Press, 1972) 51.

[41]Sanders' translation, "Torah and Christ," 383.

[42]Josephus, *Antiquities* , XX, 1.

[43]Howard Clark Kee and Franklin W. Young, *Understanding the New Testament* (Englewood Cliffs: Prentice-Hall, 1957) 172-74; Perrin and Duling, II, 253-54.

[44]Hans Frei, *The Eclipse of Biblical Narrative* (New Haven: Yale UP, 1974) 280.

[45]Gary Comstock, "Truth or Meaning: Ricouer versus Frei on Biblical Narrative," *Interpretation*, Apr., 1986. The quoted sentence comes from the longer pre-publication version of the article.

[46]Sanders, *Canon and Community*, 62.

[47] Sanders, *Canon and Community*, 67.

[48]R. B. Y. Scott, "Isaiah," *The Interpreter's Bible* (New York: Abingdon, 1956) V, 217.

[49]John T. Greene, "Balaam: Prophet, Diviner, and Priest...," *SBL Seminar Papers* (1989) 76-77, says that most scholars "assign the dates ca. 950, 850, 650, and 550 BCE respectively to" J, E, D, and P. He cites Richard Friedman as disagreeing. Friedman held that all of J, E, JE, P, and part of D were produced before 609 BCE. What is not at issue is whether there were midrashic rewritings of the Torah.

[50]Sanders, *Canon and Community*, 64.

[51]William Freedman, "The Literary Motif," *Novel*, 4 (1971): 123-131.

[52]Perrin, *A Modern Pilgrimage in New Testament Christianity*.

[53]Our present research indicates that the order of composition of the Gospels was Mark, John, Luke-Acts, and Matthew. In Comparative Midrash the key criterion is literary dependence. Our contention is that Mark can stand alone among the Gospels, that John must have known Mark but did not have to have known the others, and that Luke-Acts needed both Mark and John.

[54]The name "James" is one Anglicized version of Jacob. The New Testament name "James" is identical to the LXX version of the Old Testament name "Jacob." Because the name "Jacob" in the Old Testament is rich with meanings which are consistently used by the New Testament authors, the New Testament name should also be "Jacob," both for the Letter and the characters named James. To avoid confusion, the name "Jacob" will be reserved henceforth for Old Testament references to Jacob; and the designation "James/Jacob" (abbreviated as Jas./Jac.) will be used for New Testament references.

[55]Pre-Markan dates for the original writing of each of these books is a working hypothesis based on four criteria. First, the eight books contain no detailed information about Jesus as presented in the Gospels. Second, they accept the authority of Jewish Bible without question, in contradistinction to Mark and Luke. In addition, they interpret the crucifixion and resurrection of Jesus, insofar as they mention them at all, only in light of Jewish scripture or as a parallel to experiences in the life of the author. Finally, each of the eight contains passages which logically are likely to have served as midrashic sources for Mark.

CHAPTER TWO

MARK'S INTRODUCTORY SENTENCE

One of the most important set of decisions which translators have had to make about any one specific biblical passage concerns the opening words of Mark:

> 1.1 The beginning of the gospel of Jesus Christ, the Son of God. 1.2 As it is written in Isaiah the prophet, 'Behold I send my messenger before thy face, who shall prepare thy way [Mal. 3.1]; 1.3 the voice of one crying in the wilderness: Prepare the way of the Lord, make his paths straight' [Isa. 40.3].

Minor problems for the translator relate to the fact that half of the quotation ascribed to Isaiah is from Malachi and that the original in Isa. 40.3 has the voice crying: "In the wilderness prepare the way of the Lord." The more important translation problems, however, are rooted in the fact that Mark was written in Greek at a time when punctuation, spaces between words, or distinctions between upper and lower case to assist readers in discerning an author's intentions had not yet been invented . Thus the first sentence, when printed in English, would have looked somewhat like this:

> thebeginningofthegospelofjesuschristthesonofgodasitiswritt
> eninisaiahtheprophetbeholdisendmymessengerbeforethyfac
> ewhoshallpreparethywaythevoiceofonecryinginthewildernes
> spreparethewayofthelordmakehispathsstraight

The text could have been written entirely in upper case letters instead of lower case, which adds to the confusion. Upper and lower case, however, were never mixed.

The shape and meaning of the first sentence of Mark cannot be properly determined until the translator has mastered its entire context in Mark. Thus the translator has to ask to be taken on trust, with the promise that the gradually emerging context will justify the translation decisions at the beginning of the book.

If Mk. 1.1 and 1.2-3 are read as separate sentences, then 1.1 appears to be the title of the book, implying that Mark as a whole can be seen as good news about Jesus Christ, the Son of God. It is so translated in most English Bibles, including the Revised Standard Version (RSV). Mk. 1.1-3, however, should be translated as a single sentence:

> The beginning of the gospel of Jesus Christ, the son of God, as it is written in Isaiah the prophet, "Behold, I send my messenger before thy face, who shall prepare thy way: the voice of one crying in the wilderness, 'Prepare the way of the Lord; make his paths straight.'"

This alternative translation converts two grammatically incomplete sentences into one grammatically incomplete sentence, and changes the usual capital "S" in Son of God to lower case son of God. The latter conforms to Mark's thesis that all human beings are children of God, with the result that no one child of God can rescue the others. The single-sentence translation implies that the subject matter for the work is the good news about Jesus which began in the book of Isaiah rather than a "beginning of the gospel [good news] of Jesus Christ, the Son of God" in Jesus' time. That means that the Jesus story did not begin in the first century of the common era; it began centuries earlier. Furthermore, it began in Jewish scripture, the ultimate source of Jewish midrash. The statement that the gospel of Jesus began in Isaiah is as close as Mark comes to having a "master paradigm in order to accommodate within it other models"—the claim which Roth mistakenly makes for the Elijah-Elisha cycle of 1-2 Kings.[1]

One way to test the single-sentence translation is to explore Isaiah in order to discover what Mark could have found in it relating to the four specifics in the sentence: gospel, Jesus, messiah, and son of God. If the "gospel" about "Jesus," "the messiah," and "son of God" began in Isaiah, it should be possible to find in Isaiah the details which would have justified Mark in making such an assertion.

The name Jesus is not used in Isaiah. The names Jesus and Isaiah, however, share an affinity of meaning. The name Jesus means "God Is Salvation" or "God Saves"; the name Isaiah means "The Salvation of God." Thus the entire book of Isaiah could be viewed as being the story of Jesus, i.e., an account of God's saving activity. This is confirmed by such passages in the book as "The Lord is our king; he will save us" (Isa. 33.22); "Behold, your God will come with vengeance, with the recompense of God. He will come and save you" (Isa. 35.4); "So now, O Lord our God, save us from his hand" (Isa. 37.20); "For I [the Lord] will defend this city to save it" (Isa. 37.35); "They have no knowledge who carry about their wooden idols, and keep on praying to a god that cannot save" (Isa. 45.20); "I will save your children" (Isa. 49.25); "Behold, the Lord's hand is not shortened, that it cannot save" (Isa. 59.1); "In returning and rest you shall be saved; in quietness and in trust shall be your strength" (Isa. 30.15); "But Israel is saved by the Lord with everlasting salvation" (Isa. 45.17); "For he [the Lord] said, 'Surely they are my people, sons who will not deal falsely;' and he became their Savior. In all their affliction he was afflicted, and the angel of his presence saved them; in his love and in his pity he redeemed them" (Isa. 63.8-9); "It will be a sign and a witness to the Lord of hosts in the land of Egypt; when they cry to the Lord because of oppressors he will send them a savior, and will defend and deliver them" (Isa. 19.20); "Then all flesh shall know that I am the

Lord your Savior, and your Redeemer" (Isa. 49.26); "I, I am the Lord, and besides me there is no savior" (Isa. 43.11); "And there is no other God besides me, a righteous God and a Savior" (Isa. 45.21). Mark did not need to find the name "Jesus" in Isaiah in order to affirm that the story of "God Saves" began there. Indirect confirmation of Mark's statement that the gospel of Jesus Christ began in Isaiah comes from Acts 8.30-35, in which Philip interprets an Isaiah Suffering Servant passage as "the good news of Jesus."

By declaring that the gospel about "God Saves" began in scripture, Mark made available to himself a rich Old Testament literature. The names Joshua ("God Saves"), Elisha ("God Saves"), and Hosea ("The Salvation of God") bear witness to God's saving activity via their etymology; much of the attention of the Old Testament text is focused on the possibility of God saving the Jews from their various historical predicaments. Extension of the "God Saves" imagery was Mark's midrashic justification in including the sentence from Malachi in his Isaiah quotation. The overall question in Malachi is whether the Jews as children of God will be saved from their estrangement from the Father God.

Mark wrote within the Jewish tradition of playing on the meaning of words and of naming people to express meanings which are integral to their lives. Quite apart from Mark's particular midrashic sources, one cannot understand Mark without keeping in mind that Jesus' name means "God Saves." Philippians 2.5-11 states that Jesus Christ received the name "Jesus" as a consequence of his emptying himself of godhood and dying voluntarily. The Philippians passage, like Mark, encourages its readers to regard "Jesus" as a theological name, expressing the meaning that "God saves."

> Have this in mind among yourselves, which you have in Christ Jesus, who, though he was in the form of God, did not count equality with God a thing to be grasped, but emptied himself, taking the form of a servant, being born

> in the likeness of men. And being found in human form he humbled himself and became obedient unto death, even death on a cross. *Therefore God has* highly exalted him and *bestowed on him the name* which is above every name, that at the name of *Jesus* every knee should bow, in heaven and on earth, and every tongue confess that Jesus Christ is Lord....

The Mk. 1.2 citation of Mal. 3.1 as belonging to Isaiah supports the reading "son of God" by calling attention to similar treatment of "sons" in the introductions of both books. Isa. 1.2-4 quotes God as referring to those rebellious "sons who deal corruptly" whom he "reared and brought up," but who are now "utterly estranged." Isaiah's hope for such sons is general well-being for Israel: "It shall come to pass in the latter days that the mountain of the house of the Lord shall be established" (Isa. 2.2).

The thesis of Mal. 1.2-6 is similar to Isaiah's. It begins with reference to the Jacob motif: "'I have loved you,' says the Lord. But you say, 'How hast thou loved us?' 'Is not Esau Jacob's brother?' says the Lord. 'Yet I have loved Jacob but I have hated Esau." It continues by identifying the Jews as God's sons: "A son honors his father, and a servant his master. If then I am a father, where is my honor" (1.6)? In the complete text, Israel is represented by Jacob and Edom by Esau. The Jacob-Esau story is widely used in the Jewish Bible as evidence of God's preference for second sons, successors to the heroes, etc. Malachi used it to affirm God's love for the Jews rather than the Edomites as children of God. Paul, in Rom. 9.12-13, used it similarly: "'The elder will serve the younger.' As it is written, 'Jacob I loved, but Esau I hated.'" Paul's midrash is that God could love or reject anyone whom he chose, thus making grace or rejection God's free choice.

Malachi's charge that the sons do not honor the father is addressed first to the priests and then, by inference, to the remainder of Israel. Malachi proposes that the Levites can be reconciled to the Father by following the example of Levi, their founder, and that the masses can be reconciled by obeying Elijah's instructions when he reappears. Thus Malachi predicted that God "will send you Elijah the prophet before the great and terrible day of the Lord comes. And he will turn the hearts of fathers to their children and the hearts of children to their fathers, lest I come and smite the land with a curse" (Mal. 4.5-6). The need for the children of God to be reconciled to the Father functions in Mark as the implied background of many stories about children and parent, e.g., the sons of Zebedee, Simon and his mother-in-law, Jairus and his daughter, Jesus and his mother. Various levels of success and failure in the agenda Mark set for Jesus are revealed by parent-child relationships in each new context and by the efforts of tempters to persuade Jesus to announce himself as the only holy Son of God.

There is no suggestion in the latter half of Isaiah (2 Isaiah) that the unnamed suffering servant in chapter 53 or the "anointed" messenger bringing the gospel in 61.1 is a "son of God" or the "Son of God." However, Wisd. 2.10—5.24,[2] in an unmistakable midrash on Isa. 52.13—54.3 and 56.3-5, refers to an unnamed "suffering" "virtuous man" who "boasts of having God for his father" (2.16). He is "condemned to a shameful death" (2.20). "He has sought to please God, so God has loved him; as he was living among sinners, he has been taken up" (4.10) while "people look on, uncomprehending" (4.14). He is not the only Son of God or a unique son of God; the author says that he has "come to be counted as one of the sons of God" (5.5). Mark utilized other material from the Wisdom of Solomon; therefore he was familiar with the book. He (and some others of his time) may have regarded Isaiah in the light of its midrash in Wisdom, interpreting its relevant sections as being about the gospel that God saves, in part through a suffering servant who is God's son.

Mark certainly could have noted in LXX[3] Isaiah the word *euangellion* from which "gospel" or "good news" is translated. The

Greek term is transliterated in English as "evangel," "evangelism," etc. *Euangellion* appears in the following sentences in Isaiah, here translated as "gospel" to clarify the point: "How beautiful upon the mountain are the feet of *him who brings the gospel*, who publishes peace, *who brings the gospel of good, who publishes salvation*"[4] (Isa. 52.7); "I have first declared it to Zion, and I give Jerusalem a *herald of the gospel*" (Isa. 41.27, but the word "gospel" is not in the LXX version); "The spirit of the Lord is upon me, because *the Lord has anointed me* [i.e., designated me as Messiah or Christ]; *to bring the gospel* to the afflicted (Isa. 61.1); "Get you up to a high mountain, *O Zion, herald of the gospel*; lift up your voice with strength, *O Jerusalem, herald of the gospel*" (Isa. 40.9).

Mark would have been justified in writing that good news about the "messiah" (in Greek, "Christ") began in Isaiah because of several messianic references. The word "messiah" is ordinarily translated in RSV as "anointed one" because its associated ritual involves anointing a leader with oil as an act of inauguration into office. Each Jewish king was a messiah in that sense of the term. When Jewish kings no longer reigned in Israel, the concept was expanded to refer to future messiahs who might be kings or who might occupy other leadership positions such as priest or prophet. Isaiah used the term in this broader sense. For example, Isa. 45.1 names King Cyrus as the Lord's messiah: "Thus says the Lord to his anointed [his messiah], to Cyrus." Isa. 61.1-2 conceives of the messiah as one who brings the gospel to the poor and afflicted: "The Spirit of the Lord God is upon me, because *the Lord has anointed me [named me Messiah] to bring good tidings [gospel]* to the afflicted; he has sent me to bind up the brokenhearted, to proclaim liberty to the captives, and the opening of the prison to those who are bound; to proclaim the year of the Lord's favor, and the day of vengeance of our God; to comfort all who mourn." Isaiah's herald of the gospel is messianic, but there is no strong evidence in the text that the suffering servant is a messiah or is the same person or group of people as the herald. Paul, in Rom. 15.12, cites Isa. 11.10 as messianic in an expanded manner: "The root of Jesse shall come, he who rises to rule the Gentiles; in him shall the Gentiles hope." Given that much breadth in the meaning of messiah, Mark would certainly have been justified in asserting in his introductory sentence that the gospel about Jesus as messiah began in Isaiah.

"Jesus" as the specific name for the messiah was derived from the Greek version of Zechariah. Zerubbabel and Jesus (Joshua in Hebrew) are designated in Zech. 4.14 as messiahs. Of the two, Jesus is clearly the one preferred by God. He is to be called "the Branch," a messianic title (Zech. 3.8; 6.11-12). In the day when Jesus is made the leader, "every one of you will invite his neighbor under his vine and under his fig tree" and thus fulfill a traditional messianic expectation (Zech. 3.10). Assuming that the "one whom they have pierced" in Zech. 12.10 is the same person as the Jesus/Joshua of Zech. 3-4, the messiah of Zechariah would be a savior who is killed and who removes sin from people in one day (Zech. 3.9; 13.1). Jer. 23.5-6 and 33.14-16 also refer to a messianic "righteous Branch to spring forth for David" who "will be called 'The Lord is our righteousness' [or salvation].'" Jer. 23.6 in Greek says that he will be called "Josedec among the prophets"; in LXX Zech. 5.11, the messiah "Jesus" is "son of Josedec."

In recent centuries, Christians have read versions of the Old Testament which are translated primarily from the Hebrew. Thus in Zechariah we read of the messiah "Joshua" rather than "Jesus," which is how the name was read by ancient Jewish and Christian readers of the LXX. Mark's first sentence, however, clearly leaves open the possibility that the good news of Jesus as the messiah, the Christ, began in the LXX, in which "Joshua" was "Jesus." One must not overstate this point. Mark's sources are sometimes identifiably either from the LXX or the Hebrew Masoretic text, but usually from passages which convey the same thought in either the Greek or Hebrew text.

The most important test of the single-sentence translation is that it fits compatibly into the whole context of Mark. Interpreters can best evaluate that claim by exegesis of critical parts of Mark which are thematically related, such as the following. When Jesus is on trial for his life, the priests hear him affirm that he is both messiah and son of God (Mk. 14.61-62), but they distort the meaning of both terms to fit their preference for a supernatural military liberator Messiah. After the death, a Roman military officer sees Jesus as a son of God because of the manner of his dying (15.39). The primary issue at the cross is whether God will play the role delineated for him in Jewish scripture and save Jesus from death. The drama of the whole Gospel centers in Mark's disagreement with the Old Testament tradition advocating God's salvation, substituting for it the positive example of Jesus as a child of God who yields his life voluntarily and is consequently reconciled to the Father. Throughout Mark, significant variations on "son of God" and "saving" themes substantiate the single-sentence reading and its contention that the gospel began in Isaiah.

The single-sentence translation enables readers to understand some otherwise obscure passages. For example, Mark's inclusion of Mal. 3.1, "I send my messenger to prepare the way before me," in his opening citation from Isa. 40.3 is not an error. Mal. 3-4 portrays Elijah as a preacher demanding obedience to the Lord. Isa. 40.3 is correctly punctuated to read: "A voice cries: 'In the wilderness prepare the way of the Lord'." In Isaiah's context, the intended audience is the exiles in Babylon who are to prepare the way of the Lord in the wilderness on their way home. In Mark, the same words are correctly punctuated to read "A voice cries in the wilderness, 'Prepare the way of the Lord.'" Mark's "voice" itself was in the wilderness, lonely and unheard, but the preparation for the way of the Lord could be accomplished anywhere. Mark presented

John the Baptizer[5] as Elijah the messenger fulfilling the Malachi predictions and as the voice crying in the Gospel wilderness. Hence, for Mark, the gospel which began in Isaiah included Malachi's Elijah model.

The linking of Malachi with Isaiah was not original with Mark. Kee perceives a linkage in Jesus Ben Sirach between the Elijah figure of Malachi and the servant-redeemer in Isaiah.[6] The Ben Sirach passage to which Kee calls attention is midrashic on the Elijah, Malachi, and Isaiah passages which follow it:

> How terrible wast thou, Elijah! And he who is like thee shall be glorified. Who didst *raise up a dead man from death*, and from Sheol, according to the good pleasure of Jahveh; who broughtest down kings to the Pit, and them that were honoured from their beds [of sickness]; who heardest rebukes in Sinai, and judgments of vengeance in Horeb; who anointedst kings for retribution, and a prophet as successor in thy place; who wast *taken upwards in a whirlwind, and by fiery troops to the heavens*; who art *ready for the time*, as it is written, to still wrath before the fierce anger of God, to *turn the heart of the fathers unto the children*, and to *restore the tribes of Israel* (Sir. 48.4-10).[7]

The concluding clause refers to the Elijah of Malachi, who will return "on the great and terrible day of the Lord" to "turn the hearts of fathers to their children and the hearts of children to their fathers" (Mal. 4.5-6). Kee sees Sirach's reference to restoring the tribes of Israel as coming from: "It is too light a thing that you should be my servant to raise up the tribes of Jacob and to restore the preserved of Israel" (Isa. 49.6). Ben Sirach used several Elijah references midrashically, among them: "And as they still went on and talked, behold, a chariot of fire and horses of fire separated the two of them [Elijah and Elisha]" (2 Kgs. 2.11); "And the Lord hearkened to the voice of Elijah; and the soul of the child came into him again, and he revived" (1 Kgs. 17.22). One cannot prove that Mark had read Ben Sirach, but it is unlikely that a first century author writing about Jesus would have ignored or have been uninformed about a book whose title included the name Jesus.

A second advantage of the single-sentence translation is that it facilitates understanding of motifs which develop in Mark. Different uses of the concept "wilderness" serve as an example. John appears preaching in a wilderness, after which Jesus is baptized in that particular wilderness. The Holy Spirit then drives him to a different wilderness to be tempted. In Mk. 2, Jesus becomes the new Moses of the Exodus wilderness. In Mk. 3, the disciples are called in that wilderness to become a New Israel. In Mk. 6, the disciples are expected to become the Suffering Servant remnant in a wilderness of self-discipline—the original meaning of Isa. 40.3, the passage in which Mark claimed the gospel had begun. The variations of wilderness underscore Mark's word "beginning." The gospel began in one kind of wilderness, but did not end there. So it was with Mark's initial interpretations of Jesus as son of God and messiah, which were to increase in depth throughout the Gospel. The gospel which began in Isaiah did not end there. Mark's developing motifs support the single-sentence translation.

A third advantage of the single-sentence translation is illustrated below.

Mark 1.2	**Exod. 23.20 (LXX)**	**Mal. 3.1**
"Behold, I send my messenger before thy face, who shall prepare thy way."	"And, behold, I send my angel [messenger] before thy face, that he may keep thee in the way, that he may bring thee into the land which I have prepared for thee."	"Behold, I send my messenger to prepare the way before me."

The single sentence translation links the beginning of the gospel to Moses as well as to Isaiah and Malachi's Elijah. Most Elijah stories and themes are ultimately midrashic on Moses ones because it was important for biblical authors to present Elijah as a new Moses. Mark's sentence is midrashic on both Exod. 23.20 and Mal. 3.1. Exod. 23.20-21 was also later used by Mark in his transfiguration account, in which God orders the disciples to listen to his son. Exod. 23.21 (LXX) reads: "Take heed to thyself and hearken to him...for my name is on him."

An additional strong confirmation of the one-sentence translation is the likelihood that Mark's first sentence was patterned after the first sentence of Romans:

> Paul, a servant of Jesus Christ, called to be an apostle, set apart for the gospel of God which he promised beforehand through his prophets in the holy scriptures, the gospel concerning his Son, who was...designated Son of God in power according to the Spirit of holiness by his resurrection from the dead, Jesus Christ our Lord (Rom. 1.1-4).

Paul's sentence contains all the elements which are in the first sentence of Mark: the gospel beginning in the prophets, Jesus as messiah, and Jesus as Son/son of God. The fact that Mark at other significant points relied on Paul's letters as source material for his midrash strengthens the conclusion that Mark meant his introductory statement as a variation on Rom. 1.1-4.

Mark's first sentence, properly translated and understood, prepares the reader to expect that the entire Gospel will portray a gradual development of motifs relating to "gospel," "Jesus," "Christ (Messiah)," and "son/Son of God." It furthermore enables the reader to focus attention from the beginning on the dimensions of the good news which originate in Isaiah as modified by the Elijah quotation from Malachi.

ENDNOTES FOR CHAPTER TWO

[1]Roth, *Hebrew Gospel*, 87.

[2]Wisdom of Solomon is a Jewish book written before the New Testament period.

[3]LXX is the usual abbreviation for the Septuagint, an excellent translation of the Jewish Bible into koine Greek two or three centuries prior to the usually accepted time of Jesus. It has been a long-established fact of Markan scholarship that Mark often quoted Jewish scripture from the LXX translation. LXX is so named because of a legend that it was translated by seventy scholars sent from Israel to Egypt for that purpose. There is more than one version of the LXX text.

[4]Virtually the same sentence appears in Nahum, a relevant fact in the investigation of the role of Capernaum in Mark.

[5]By long usage John has been known as John the Baptist. The correct translation of the term is John "the Baptizer." See Kee and Young, *Understanding the New Testament*: "John--called 'the Baptizer' (John the Baptist)," p. 77; and "The fact that John was called "the Baptizer" indicates the importance of baptism in his mission," p. 81. The difference between John the Baptist and John the Baptizer is not significant except that the principle of accurate translation militates toward consistent use of the less familiar John the Baptizer.

[6]Kee, *Community of the New Age*, 28.

[7]Jesus Ben Sirach is a Jewish book which was written at least a century before the common era, ostensibly for Hellenized Jews in Egypt. It is, as far as we know, the first writing outside the LXX to refer to the name Jesus in its Greek form.

CHAPTER THREE

MIDRASH ON ELIJAH AND THE CROWDS OF OLD ISRAEL

The Gospel of Mark is divided into four major sections, each with its separate midrashic emphases. The first, primarily concerned with crowd reaction in traditional Israel, has three sub-sections, one in which John the Baptizer is the new Elijah-Moses figure, one in which Jesus succeeds John as Elijah-Elisha, and another in which Jesus succeeds John as Moses-Levi-Joshua. Each sub-section functions as a unit, a set of materials unified around a single theme.

The combination of Elijah and Moses themes stems from Malachi, in which the crowds and priests could be reconciled to God by obeying Elijah's preaching or by following the example of Levi, the progenitor of Moses' priestly tribe. Mark brought Elijah and Moses together on the Mount of Transfiguration by referring to "Elijah with Moses." The phraseology points to the Old Testament fact that Elijah was midrashically a Moses figure. Mark often deals with Elijah in a way which suggests Elijah's midrashic sources in Moses and the Torah. 2 Kings quite clearly deals with Elisha as a midrashic counterpart of Elijah, so much so that for Mark the two figures are interchangeable.

This chapter focuses on the model of Elijah for Mark's portrayal of John the Baptizer and Jesus. Mark's midrashic use of the Elijah-Elisha motif is proved by the consistency with which Elijah and Elisha sources are used in Mk. 1, both in the story of John the Baptizer and of Jesus. A comprehensive list of Elijah-Elisha details used in Mk. 1 is presented here to show the overall shape of Mark's pattern of usage. Each of the references will later be discussed in detail.

Elijah-Elisha Parallels in Mark

John's role as the wilderness messenger (Mk. 1.2,4).	Behold I send my messenger to prepare the way (Mal. 3.1).
John's tasks, to baptize, preach repentance, offer forgiveness (Mk. 1.4)	Elijah's tasks, to anoint Hazael, Jehu, and Elisha (1 Kgs. 19.15-16).
John succeeds at one task, but not the other two (Mk. 1.4-5).	Elijah anoints Elisha but not the two kings (1 Kgs. 19.17-21).
Jesus (God Saves) is John's successor (Mk. 1.7, 9).	Elisha (God Saves) is Elijah's successor (2 Kgs. 2).
Jesus 2 tasks: offer repentance and forgiveness (Mk. 1.14-2.17).	Elisha 2 tasks: anoint Hazael and Jehu (2 Kgs. 8.8-15; 9.1-3).
John wears a camel's hair garment (Mk. 1.6).	Elijah is known by his unique haircloth garment (2 Kgs. 1.8).
Jesus succeeds John at the Jordan River (Mk. 1.9).	Elisha succeeds Elijah at the Jordan River (2 Kgs. 2.9-14).
Jesus receives holy spirit at the Jordan (Mk. 1.10).	Elisha receives Elijah's spirit at the Jordan (2 Kgs. 2.9).
Jesus hears the voice of God (implied) in the silence of spirit (Mk. 1.11).	Elijah hears the voice of God in the silence (1 Kgs. 19.11-12).
The heavens open at the Jordan for Jesus (Mk. 1.10).	Elijah goes up into heaven from the Jordan (2 Kgs. 2.11).
God announces his love for Jesus (Mk. 1.11).	God loves his children and is to be loved by them (Mal. 1.2-6).
Jesus is tempted during forty days in a wilderness (Mk. 1.12-13).	Elijah is tempted during 40 days in a wilderness (1 Kgs. 19.1-18, especially 19.8).
Angels minister to Jesus in that wilderness (Mk. 1.13).	An angel ministers to Elijah in that wilderness (1 Kgs. 19.5-7).
Jesus preaches repentance when the time is fulfilled (Mk. 1.15).	Elijah is to return to earth to preach repentance (Mal. 3-4).
Jesus encourages first disciples to leave without farewells to parents (Mk. 1.20).	Elijah urges Elisha to follow him after saying farewell to parents (1 Kgs. 19.19-21).

Jesus calls followers away from fishing and mending nets (Mk. 1.18-20).	Elijah calls Elisha away from plowing (1 Kgs. 19.19-20).
Jesus is accused by the unclean spirit of being destructive (Mk. 1.24).	Both Elijah and Elisha destroyed people; in Malachi, Elijah is predicted to do so (e.g., 1Kgs. 18.40, 2 Kgs. 1.9-12, 2.23-24, Mal. 3.2, 4.5).
Jesus heals Peter's mother-in-law miraculously (Mk. 1.30-31).	Both Elijah and Elisha perform miracles for an old woman (1 Kgs. 17.8-24, 2 Kgs. 4.1-37.
Jesus heals a leper (Mk. 1.40-42).	Elisha heals Naaman's leprosy (2 Kgs. 5.1-14).
Jesus sends the healed leper to the Levitical priests for rituals (Mk. 1.43-44).	Elijah performs priestly role in context with Ba'al priests (1 Kgs. 18.20-40).

John the Baptizer As a Midrashic Figure: Mk. 1.4-8

Detailed comparison of John the Baptizer and Elijah clearly confirms that John was Elijah crying in the wilderness. Elijah was given three tasks in 1 Kgs. 19.15-16, to anoint two kings, Jehu and Hazael, and to recruit Elisha as his successor. He accomplished only the latter; Elisha anointed the two kings. John likewise is given three tasks to perform: baptizing, demanding repentance, and offering or proclaiming forgiveness. His baptizing is a phenomenal success: every inhabitant of Jerusalem plus others from all over Judah come for the ritual, each confessing his/her sins. The text, however, is silent about anyone repenting (changing one's way of life) or receiving forgiveness. The judgment that John failed depends in part upon the distinction between confession and repentance. Confession involves admitting guilt, whereas repentance means changing one's life so as to do something about that to which one has confessed. John does no more than persuade people to confess. His failure is confirmed by his own tribute to Jesus' role: "After me comes he who is mightier than I, the thong of whose sandals I am not worthy to stoop down and untie. I have baptized you with water; but he will baptize you with the Holy

Spirit" (1.7). Jesus was to begin his career preaching repentance and offering forgiveness, the two tasks at which John had failed.

A second important midrashic source for Mark's portrayal of John the Baptizer is a combination of passages from the early epistles. The content of John's tasks and the audience response to them are suggested by 1 Jn. 1.9: "If we confess our sins, he is faithful and just, and will forgive our sins and cleanse us from all unrighteousness." This sentence in 1 John has the elements of confession (but not repentance), forgiveness and cleansing (baptism). John's distinction between baptism with spirit and superficial washing with water follows the logic of 1 Pet. 3.21 that baptism "now saves you, not as a removal of dirt from the body but as an appeal to God for a clear conscience." Jas./Jac. 4.8 presents the point tersely: "Cleanse your hands, you sinners, and purify your hearts, you men of double mind." Alongside 1 Pet. 3.21 and Jas./Jac. 4.8, 1 Jn. 1.9 takes on extraordinary importance for understanding Mark's midrashic mind. The three passages together contain the key elements of the Baptizer's agenda plus a criterion for judging external cleansing to be a failure in comparison to the inner purification of holy spirit.

The combination of passages from 1 John, James/Jacob, and 1 Peter provide the first hint that Mark could have created John, name and all, from those sources and imbued him with other characteristics garnered from Elijah. In support of that possibility, John the Baptizer is not referred to in any book known to have been written earlier than Mark. He is not mentioned in Paul's letters, where there could have been good reason for doing so had a John movement existed alongside the early churches.[1] Mark's use of Elijah-Elisha materials for additional facets of his picture of John is consistent with his literary style, which was to create biography from previously accepted sacred literature.

John's three tasks also have counterparts in the Elijah section of Malachi. John's baptism corresponds to Malachi's purification: "For he [Elijah] is like refiner's fire and like fuller's soap; he will sit as a refiner and purifier of silver, and he will purify the sons of Levi and refine them like gold and silver, till they present right offerings to the Lord" (Mal. 3.2-3). Malachi does not use the specific term "repentance," but the general concept of demanding radically changed behavior is inferred in the admonition to "bring the full tithes into the storehouse" rather than robbing God "in your tithes and offerings" (Mal. 3.7-10). John's message of forgiveness corresponds to the promises of "an overflowing blessing" (Mal. 3.10) and the rise of the sun of righteousness "with healing in its wings" (Mal. 4.2).

Mark dressed John in an attire of camel's hair and a leather girdle in order to clarify for anyone aware of the Elijah-Elisha cycle that John was Elijah. In 2 Kgs. 1.7-8, King Ahab asked, "'What kind of man was he who came to meet you and told you these things?' They answered him, 'He wore a garment of haircloth, with a girdle of leather about his loins.' And he said, 'It is Elijah the Tishbite.'" The identification of Elijah by the clothing he wore is corroborated by a prediction in Zech. 13.4, alluding to a time when similar garb had become the standard uniform of some or all who claimed to be prophets: "On that day every prophet will be ashamed of his vision when he prophesies; he will not put on a hairy mantle in order to deceive."

The desert site for John's baptizing is likely to have been influenced by Mark's reading of Isaiah. The author refers to exiles in Babylon going into the desert for their own purification, not to purify others: "Depart, depart, go out thence, touch no unclean thing; go out from the midst of her, purify yourselves..." (Isa. 52.11). Isa. 40.3 alludes to preparing "the way of the Lord...in the desert."

The midrashic details identifying John as Elijah were necessary for Mark to establish the existence of a "Jesus theme" in the Jewish Bible. The Jesus theme appears in scripture whenever a figure whose name means "God Is Salvation" completes the God-given tasks of a leader who has failed to do so. In this instance, Mark introduced Jesus as Elisha ("God Is Salvation"), the successor to Elijah-John. The Jesus theme was first presented in the Jewish Bible in terms of repeating and completing in the relationship between Moses and Joshua. When Moses was assigned to lead the Hebrew slaves "out of the affliction of Egypt" and into "a land flowing with milk and honey" (Exod. 3.17), he accomplished only one of the two tasks. The other was accomplished by Joshua, whose name, like that of Jesus, means "God is Salvation" and whose name was consistently written as "Jesus" in the Greek Bible used by many ancient Jews and Christians. The passages describing his appointment emphasize spirit. Moses said, "'Let the Lord...appoint a man over the congregation...who shall lead them....' And the Lord said to Moses, 'Take Joshua [in Greek, Jesus] the son of Nun, a man in whom is the spirit, and lay your hand upon him.... You shall invest him with some of your authority, that all of the congregation of the people of Israel may obey'" (Num. 27.15-20); "And Joshua [Jesus] the son of Nun was full of the spirit of wisdom, for Moses had laid his hands upon him; so the people of Israel obeyed him, and did as the Lord had commanded Moses" (Deut. 34.9). Joshua was commissioned to complete Moses' unfinished work:

> After the death of Moses the servant of the Lord, the Lord said to Joshua [Jesus] the son of Nun, Moses' minister, 'Moses my servant is dead; now therefore arise, go over this Jordan, you and all this people, into the land which I am giving to them, to the people of Israel. Every place that the sole of your foot will tread upon I have given to you, as I promised to Moses' (Josh. 1.1-3).

Thus the first full section of Mark is built around the Jesus theme that just as when the original heroes Moses and Elijah failed, each was replaced by a man named "God Is Salvation," so also John was replaced by Jesus who took over the roles of the successors to Elijah and Moses.

A different and somewhat more complicated support for the contention that Mark created John the Baptizer midrashically relates to the five brothers of the Hasmonean dynasty, popularly known as the Maccabees. 1-2 Maccabees does not use messianic language but praises the five brothers as if they were Davidic leaders. There is too much overlap between names in Mark and in 1-2 Maccabees to be explained simply as coincidence. One of the duplications is the name "John." Two of the five brothers were named John and Jonathan. John Hyrcanus was the son of another brother, Simon. Turner refers to John Hyrcanus (135-105 BCE) as the "probable hero" of "messianic psalms."[2] The messianic tradition about John Hyrcanus could have drawn Mark's attention to that John, with Mark naming the forerunner of the messiah after John Hyrcanus as well as after the author of 1 John. That possibility, weak as it is, is strengthened by more substantial midrashic connections between 1-2 Maccabees and particular events in Jesus' story.

Blending the four Gospels together has resulted in much confusion about the relationship between John the Baptizer and Jesus. Matthew and John insisted that John the Baptizer knew in advance who Jesus was, that Jesus would be John's successor, and that John was publicly announcing Jesus' superiority. Mark, in contrast, presented John as not knowing Jesus' identity. He knew only that his successor would be mightier than himself and would baptize with "Holy Spirit" in contradistinction to John baptizing with water only. John knew that spiritual cleansing is superior to water baptism, which is a purification of skin only, a superficial act unrelated to any change in behavior by those who go through the ritual. Furthermore, Elijah-John knew midrashically that because he was Elijah there had to be a coming Elisha, a successor who would perform that more spiritual role. He did not know that the new Elisha would be named Jesus.

The distinction between inner and outer cleanness continues through Mk. 1.1—10.52 in a variety of ways not limited to baptism. Baptism itself was a ritual practiced by Jews for at least several centuries before Mark wrote.[3] Mark did not have to invent it in order to describe John as a baptizer. He did, however, midrashically develop a distinction between different kinds of cleanliness as suggested in Ezek. 36.25-27: "I will sprinkle clean water upon you, and you shall be clean from all your uncleannesses, and from all your idols I will cleanse you. A new heart I will give you and a new spirit I will put within you.... And I will put my spirit within you...." Ps. 51.2, 10 reads: "Wash me...from my iniquity and cleanse me from my sin! Create in me a clean heart, O God, and put a new and right spirit within me."

The term "Holy Spirit" in "he will baptize you with the Holy Spirit" (Mk. 1.8) presents a translation problem. Most English translations capitalize both words as if John was referring to the third person of the Trinity. The context in Mark, as in each of Mark's probable sources, requires a reading much more like "he will purify you inwardly, spiritually, in a really holy manner, in contrast to the external cleansing of water only." To capitalize Holy Spirit here is to mislead readers by confusing the third person of the Trinity with John's lament about his own failure and his expectation of a spiritual successor. To avoid that confusion, the grammatically correct phrase "holy spirit" should be translated, with or without the capital letters, as "godly spirit" or "spirit of holiness."

It would be a mistake to conclude from the non-capitalization of "holy spirit" and "son of God" that Mark was denying the divinity of Jesus as it is affirmed in the doctrine of the Trinity. The trinitarian formula, approved in its mature form only at the Council of Chalcedon in 456 CE, was then and is now a valid solution to a Greek philosophical problem which arose decades after the New

Testament was finished. The problem emerged when Greek-speaking Christians no longer understood the Semitic cultural roots of biblical affirmations. By the canons of Greek logic, Jesus could not be both human and divine. Hellenized Christians sought for centuries to contrive compromises by means of which they could combine the real humanness of Jesus in the Gospels and the perfect divinity of Jesus in a theological version of Plato's philosophy. The trinitarian formula was a way of stating that Jesus is as fully divine as God and as fully human as all other persons, and that the meaning of that apparent contradiction is true in a theological-historical sense despite offending Greek logic. The formula is an extension of New Testament insights which themselves were pre-trinitarian. Thus there is no conflict between believing in the Trinity and accepting Mark's particular affirmation of Jesus as a lower case "s" son of God who baptized with "holy spirit" and who demonstrated by his life what is necessary for any son or daughter of God to do in order to be reconciled to the Father. Mark was addressing a wholly different issue.

Mark's purpose in the 1.9-45 unit, after having John admit his failure as a new Elijah, was to demonstrate the inadequacy of the Elijah repentance model by showing both its inherent failure and its temptative qualities. The unit follows naturally after introducing Jesus as a new Elisha, succeeding Elijah-John. Mark's midrash here is based on Malachi and on the Elijah-Elisha cycle from 1 Kgs. 17 to 2 Kgs. 13, in which Elisha often relives events already narrated about Elijah. Both divide the waters of the Jordan River, miraculously provide food for a woman, and resurrect a woman's son after being blamed for his death. Some who oppose Elisha are soon dead, as is the case with Elijah. Elijah ascends to heaven in a fiery chariot pulled by fiery horses; at Elisha's death the king exclaims, "the chariots of Israel and its horsemen" (2 Kgs. 13.14)! Elisha is simultaneously a mirror image of Elijah and the one who succeeds where Elijah fails. Mark, well aware of that, presented Jesus in an even more complicated reflection as the supplanter of both Elijah and John, at the same time that he is beginning to develop a new agenda of his own. In Jesus' case, Mark finally rejected the picture of Jesus as Elijah-Elisha because of inadequacies in the original model.

John Baptizing Jesus at the Jordan: Mk. 1.9-11

Jesus comes to John at the River Jordan. After being baptized by John, Jesus sees a vision in the sky and receives a spirit of holiness which John had earlier forecast as a characteristic of his successor. The story parallels the receiving of spirit by Elisha on the occasion of Elijah's death after he had followed Elijah from Gilgal to Bethel to Jericho to the River Jordan (2 Kgs. 2.1-18). At the river, Elijah struck the water with his mantle; the water divided and the two men crossed on dry land. On the other side, Elijah asked Elisha what he wanted, to which he replied: "I pray you, let me inherit a double share[4] of your *spirit*" (2.9). Elijah promised that the spirit would be given if Elisha could see him as he was ascending "into heaven" in "a chariot of fire and horses of fire" (2.10-11). Elisha ripped his own clothes, then put on Elijah's fallen mantle, striking the Jordan River with it and walking over on dry land. "Sons of the prophets" seeing him said, "The *spirit of Elijah rests on Elisha.*" (2.15).

The account of the transfer of spirit from Elijah to Elisha is likely in turn to have been midrashic on a narrative in Numb. 11 in which Moses had complained about the burden of leadership. God told him to appoint seventy men as assistants; God would "take some of the *spirit* which is upon you and *put it upon them*; and they shall bear the burden of the people with you, that you may not bear it yourself alone" (Num. 11.17). The descent of the spirit on Jesus is related to the spirit resting on Elisha and God putting the spirit upon Moses' assistants.

Mark had other midrashic sources available for the descent of spirit upon Jesus. Isaiah related spirit to messianic themes in several passages: "The *Spirit* of the Lord God is upon me because he has *anointed* me [named me Messiah]" (Isa. 61.1); "I have put *my spirit upon him* [my chosen one]" (Isa. 42.1); desolation is predicted "until the *Spirit is poured upon us from on high*, after which "justice will dwell in the *wilderness*" (Isa. 32. 14-16); "And the *Spirit of the Lord shall rest upon him* [a shoot from the stump of Jesse]" (Isa. 11.1-2). It would be consistent with Mark's blending of Malachi with Isaiah for him to have merged the spirit themes in Isaiah with the spirit themes in the Elijah-Elisha cycle. Assuming that Mark intended to present the baptismal experience of Jesus as a vision, Joel 2.28 would be relevant: "I will *pour out my spirit* on all flesh; your sons and your daughters shall prophesy, your old men shall dream dreams, and your *young men shall see visions*."

A passage in The Testament of the Twelve Patriarchs, a Jewish book with one section each for the twelve sons of Jacob, presents a special problem in its midrashic relationship to Mark: "The *heavens will be opened*, and from the temple of glory will come *his call* to his sacred office with *the Father's voice*, as from Abraham Isaac's father. And the glory of the Most High will be uttered over him, and *the spirit* of understanding and holiness will *rest upon him in the water*" (Test. of Levi 18.6-7). There are so many parallels with Mark's account of Jesus' baptism (the opened heavens, the call to a sacred office, the Father's voice, the spirit resting upon him, in the water) that Mark must have been using the Testament of Levi midrashically, or vice versa. Kee dates the Testament as first century BCE, thus supporting the premise that Mark was using Levi, but correctly cautions that Christians sometimes added passages to older Jewish books for polemic purposes.[5] That does not appear to have been so in this instance. Mark could have been impressed with the connection between Isaiah and the passage in Testament of Levi because the clause "from the temple of glory will come his call to his sacred office" is midrashic on Isaiah's vision in the temple (Isa. 6).

John may not have known that in baptizing Jesus he was doing more than wetting a body with water. The baptismal event is most plausibly read as an inner vision of Jesus only. The grammar of Mark's text cannot be stretched further than that Jesus alone saw the heavens opened and the spirit descend; the voice spoke directly to him; and he alone was aware that God had communicated to him in a special way the Father's love for a son: "He saw the heavens opened and the spirit descending upon him like a dove; and a voice came from heaven, 'Thou art my beloved son; with thee I am well pleased'" (Mk. 1.11). Luke and Matthew are more amenable to the possibility that others present could either see the spirit-dove or hear the spirit-voice.

Mark presented Jesus as a son of God, that is, a child of God, not as The Only Son. The spirit message conveying God's love for Jesus is consistent with the introductions to Isaiah and Malachi, especially in the latter in which the love of God for all his children is proved by Jacob being preferred to Esau. The basic issue in Malachi and Mark is how God's children should respond. Mark reformulated Malachi's thesis to ask questions appropriate for Mark's time. Assuming that Jesus is one of many children of God and that all others have responded inadequately to God's love, what would be an adequate response? Should believers in Jesus respond in the same way as he did? The question about Jesus involves an inherent contradiction between his etymological identity as the divine rescuer for others and his opportunity as a child of God to do whatever is necessary for himself to be reconciled to the Father. This contradiction provides much of the dramatic power of Mark's sequence of events.

The "beloved son" motif in the baptism story is likely to have been underscored for Mark by Paul's introduction in Romans 1.4 in which Jesus was designated as "son" according to the "Spirit of holiness." Other probable sources include Gen. 22.2, 2 Sam. 12, Ps. 2.7, and Gen. 37.3. Psalm 2 presumably refers to David as "the Lord's anointed": "You are my son, today I have begotten you." 2 Sam. 12 is particularly relevant to Mark because it combines the implied messianic title "son of David" with specific reference to a beloved son. When Solomon, son of David, was born, "the Lord loved him", "so he called his name Jedidiah [Beloved of the Lord]" (2 Sam. 12.24-25). In 2 Sam. 7.14-15, God had said of a son of David, "I will be his father and he shall be my son.... I will not take my steadfast love from him." Mark later used "son of David" as a messianic title for Jesus. Gen. 37.3 reports that "Jacob [Israel] loved Joseph more than all his sons." This is midrashically relevant to Mark because Mark's resurrection story is partially constructed from Joseph material; Joseph was alive after being thought to be dead. In Gen. 22.2, God instructs Abraham to take "your only son Isaac, whom you love," to a mountain where the boy was to be sacrificed as a burnt offering. Abraham's willingness to trust and obey God by killing his own son, for whom he had waited nearly a century, is one of the most powerful biblical models for God's willingness to have his son Jesus be killed on the cross. This puts particular emphasis on "the son whom you love" as a midrashic source for Mark.

The fact that all four of the passages cited above are midrashically used only once in the baptism story with no other nearby uses of closely related material in Mark's context illustrates the difficulty of providing proof for midrashic possibilities. Unlike the demonstrable proof of nineteen consecutive Elijah-Elisha midrashic details in Mk. 1, there is only one identifiable reference each in Mk. 1 to the psalm, to 2 Samuel, to Solomon as son of David, to Joseph, or to Abraham and Isaac. This means that the student of comparative midrash must be very cautious in claiming that Mark was or was not conscious of any or all of the passages. The most that can be said is that each is consistent with the possibility that

Mark used it, and that the combination of significant ideas in his Gospel was already available to him in Jewish tradition, regardless of whether or not in fact he made use of these particular sources. Sanders hints at a similar difficulty in his suggestion that midrashic resignification be ordered on a scale of one to ten because some passages are much more identifiable with the original than others.[6]

The Jordan site for the baptism was probably of greater midrashic importance for Mark than merely being the place where Elisha had succeeded Elijah. Joshua (Josh. 3.14-17), Elijah (2 Kgs. 2.8), and Elisha (2 Kgs. 2.14) had each parted the Jordan. Moses and Elijah died in unique ways near the Jordan (Deut. 34.1-8; 2 Kgs. 2.6-11). The site thus implicitly identified Jesus with Moses and Joshua as well as with Elijah and Elisha. An additional meaning may relate to Isa. 9.1-7, in which a messianic event is specified as occurring "beyond the Jordan."

The baptismal story specifies that Jesus came from Nazareth of Galilee. Both names are important. A significant reference to Galilee in Isa. 9.1 refers to it as "the land beyond the Jordan, Galilee of the nations [i.e., Gentiles]." The book of Jesus (Joshua) refers to Galilee three times, twice identifying Kedesh as a city of refuge in Galilee (20.7; 21.32), and once in connection with a "king of goi-im," a word which has come to mean non-Jews (12.23). Marxsen, after reviewing the literature about Galilee, concluded that Mark was uncertain about its geographical boundaries but that Galilee had "special significance" for him.[7] The midrashic sources above indicate that this special significance should be Galilee's reputation as a dwelling place for Gentiles, but Mark developed a theological geography in which Galilee was a Jewish area separated from Gentile Transjordan by the Sea of Galilee.

Jesus is referred to in Mark as being from Nazareth (1.9; 1.24; 10.47; 16.6) and as a Nazarene (14.67). The reference to Nazarene facilitates understanding of "Nazareth" and opens up an interesting dimension of Mark's style. The two words have often been discussed in terms of Mark's incompetence in Greek, on the assumption that Nazarene has no true etymological root in any known language. Taylor notes a debate about whether Mark was a poor grammarian or whether he wrote "in a relatively simple and popular form of Greek which has striking affinities with the spoken language of everyday life" of his time.[8] Matthew amended Mark's *Nazarenos* to *Nazoraios* to make it more obvious that the town name "Nazareth" and the adjectival form "Nazarene" were both related to the biblical designation of a particular type of holy men as Nazarites. Eduard Schweizer's comment on Matthews' usage, summarized by Longnecker, is somewhat appropriate for Mark:[9]

> E. Schweizer has cogently argued that there is in the reference to Jesus as a *Nazoraios* in Matt. 2.23 both a typological correspondence to the Nazarite Samson ...[Judg. 16.17]—which LXX^B translates as *hagios* [holy one], but LXX^A as *naziraios* [Nazarite]—and a wordplay on the village named Nazareth; and that the understanding of Jesus in light of the Nazirite Samson probably was original, to which was added the factor of Nazareth as Jesus' home village—thereby making him doubly a *Nazi(o)raios*.[10]

Kee holds Schweizer's solution to be "untenable" despite concurring with his LXX^B reading of *hagios*.[11] Their essential difference is that Kee insists on grammatical precision while Schweizer correctly permits sound-alike wordplay. Mark used the latter regardless of etymological incorrectness. By doing so, he followed an ancient biblical tradition which is illustrated by E. A. Speiser's pointing to the "continuing but unsuccessful efforts" to discover the etymology of the God name "Yahweh": "All such ventures start out with the Bible's own explication in Exod. 3.14 ["I am who I am"]. Yet that name gloss should not be adduced as a technical etymology. It is manifestly a case of sound symbolism no less than the instances in Gen. 2.3, 4.1, 11.9, and many other passages."[12] What Speiser called "sound symbolism" is the conscious use of words which sound alike in the absence of technically correct etymology. Mark intentionally used that style in his references to Nazareth and Nazarene to connect Jesus with the tradition of holy men, Nazarites. The problem in translating *nazaraios* is complicated by the fact that Acts 24.5 refers to Paul as "ringleader of the sect of Nazarenes." In that context it cannot possibly mean a sect of people from Nazareth, and must be given a more spiritual interpretation.

Mark portrayed Jesus as coming from Nazareth because of the possibility of the messiah being a holy man, a Nazarite. Jesus' identification as a holy man is found only on the lips of his enemies, especially the unclean spirits (1.24; 3.11; 5.7). For Mark, Jesus was *from* Nazareth, but was not *of* Nazareth. He was not the holy one. John the Baptizer played the role of a Nazarite in a limited way, for example his spartan diet and clothing. Luke (1.15) recognized this characterization in Mark and made it specific that John was to be a Nazarite from birth. The comments concerning Mark's use of ungrammatical etymology are not intended to indicate that he did not also use grammatical ones. He did so beautifully with such names as Jesus, Capernaum, Bethsaida, Jacob, Gethsemane, etc.

Jesus' Temptation in Elijah 's Wilderness: Mk. 1.12-13

The same spirit of holiness which, at the baptism, informed Jesus that God loved him as a son also drove Jesus into a wilderness to be tempted by Satan. The fact that the baptism and temptation stories are both closely modeled after a series of events in the life of Elijah and are continuous in Mark provides the essential clues for interpreting the event. Jesus' temptation is patterned on that of Elijah in 1 Kgs. 19, in which Elijah is in a wilderness for forty days and forty nights without food, with a ministering angel.

Elijah's experience was in turn rooted in three different accounts of Moses' forty-day stays on a mountain. In one, Moses "was on the mountain forty days and forty nights" (Exod. 24.17-18), perhaps accompanied by Joshua (Jesus). In Exod. 34.28 and Deut. 9.9, Moses was on a mountain "with the Lord forty days and forty nights," fasting the entire time.

During Elijah's contest with the priests of the false gods, he said, "*I, even I only, am left* a prophet of the Lord; but Ba'al's prophets are four hundred and fifty men" (1 Kgs. 18.22). Elijah thought of himself as the only prophet still alive, although Obadiah had told him about a hundred others hidden in a cave (1 Kgs. 18.13). After Elijah had executed Ba'al's prophets, he twice lamented: "*I, even I only, am left;* and they seek my life, to take it away" (1 Kgs. 19.10; 19.14). Paul's midrashic use of this story emphasizes the inappropriateness of Elijah's view of himself as being alone (Rom. 11.3-4). In 1 Kgs. 19.4, Elijah went into a wilderness to pray, saying, "It is enough; now, O Lord, take away my life, for I am no better than my fathers." Elijah's "I alone" midrashically reformulates Moses' self-concern in the context of his sense of being overwhelmed by the responsibilities of leading the ex-slaves in a wilderness: "*I am not able to carry all this people alone,* the burden is too heavy for me. If thou wilt deal thus with me, kill me at once, if I find favor in thy sight, that I may not see my wretchedness" (Num. 11.14-15). Both Elijah and Moses wished to die because they felt alone and their situations seemed overwhelming. Moses recruited seventy helpers, each imbued with part of his spirit. The parallels between Elijah and Moses are increased when in Num. 11.18 the Lord gives the people meat to eat, and in 1 Kgs. 19.21 when Elijah's successor, Elisha, slays his oxen so that the people have meat to eat.

Jesus' version of Elijah's "I, even I only" temptation is to think of himself as the only child loved by God. Mark may have been influenced by Paul's admonition to every one "not to think of himself more highly than he ought to think" (Rom. 12.3-5). Both Mark and Paul were keenly aware that all are children of God, that Jesus was not the only child of God. Malachi (2.10) said it most clearly: "Have we not all one father? Has not one God created us?"

To create the baptism-spirit-temptation sequence, Mark midrashically combined the Malachi passage with Paul's assertion that "*all who are led by the Spirit of God are sons of God.* For you did not receive the spirit of slavery to fall back into fear, but you have received the spirit of sonship. When we cry, 'Abba! Father!' it is the Spirit himself bearing witness with our spirit that we are children of God" (Rom. 8.14-17). Mark could also have noted Paul's repeated affirmation that people "shall be called 'sons of the living God'" (Rom. 9.25-26), that "you are all sons of God, through faith" (Gal. 3.26), and that "because you are sons, God has sent the Spirit of his Son into our hearts, crying, 'Abba! Father'" (Gal. 4.4-6)! Mark was to use the "Abba! Father" expression in his Gethsemane story.

The ambiguity of the term "son of God," coupled with not thinking of oneself more highly than one should, raised the issue of temptation for Jesus. Was he to think of himself as the Only Child of God loved by the Father, or was he to think of himself as one of the many children of God, as one who had received the spirit of sonship? For Mark, denial that all are children of God loved by God was a Satanic, jealous, Elijah-like temptation, as suggested in James/Jacob's statement that "God tempts no one; but each person is tempted when he is lured and enticed by his own desire" (Jas./Jac. 1.13-14).

The detail of the "wild beasts" being with Jesus during the temptation may be midrashic on the Leviticus warning to sinners that "I will bring more plagues upon you sevenfold as many as your sins. And I will let loose wild beasts among you" (Lev. 26.21-22). The Test. of Issachar 7.3 suggests that wild beasts have power only over those who sin. Thus Jesus' resistance to temptation would give him power over the wild beasts. If Mark had the Test. of Issachar passage in mind, a remarkable midrashic pun is possible. Issachar means "Son of Zakar." Zakar means "Man of Hire." Issachar sounds like Iscariot. Judas Iscariot hired himself to the priests to betray Jesus. Thus, Jesus could have been "tempted by Satan," "with the wild beasts" of Issachar and thus be with Iscariot. Such a reading, despite stretching midrash to the limit, would justify the Markan thesis that Jesus, by being the beloved son of God, is immediately subject to the temptation which leads to his being betrayed on the cross.

The holy spirit which descended on Jesus at the baptism "drove him out into the wilderness" of temptation where Satan waited (Mk. 1.12). The driving force was not the devil, as one would expect, but the spirit of holiness. Allurement comes from Satan and is identified with him but is not initiated by him. It stems rather from a very great "good," from God's spirit-voiced pronouncement of his love for Jesus. The critical distinction, according to Mark, is always the difference between a moral alternative with higher or lesser merit; it is not the difference between good and evil. For Mark, the possibility of the lesser choice is always inherent in the greater. Analogously, the Satanic always implicitly accompanies the spirit of holiness. Whenever that spirit offers a higher choice, Satan waits to promote the option of lower merit. Mark's examples are abundant: Jesus choosing between being a physician for sinful hearts or paralyzed bodies, cleansing the inner person or the leprous skin, permitting the disciples to develop faith at their own pace or intervening to do their tasks for them miraculously, etc.

Mark's insight was not new. Plato had observed in *The Meno* that all choices are between "goods," that it is not possible for anyone to choose what would be evil for him, however evil it might seem to an outsider.

A more extreme version of lesser good coming from greater is found in Paul:

> What then shall we say? That the law is sin? By no means! Yet, if it had not been for the law, I should not have known sin.... The very commandment which promised life proved to be death to me. For sin, finding opportunity in the commandment, deceived me and by it killed me. So the law is holy, and the commandment is holy and just and good. Did that which is good, then, bring death to me? By no means! It was sin, *working death in me through what is good*, that sin might be shown to be sin.... So I find it to be a law that when I want to do right, evil lies close at hand (Rom. 7.7-21).

Paul held that sin, while working through the good, finds opportunity through rules to kill people. Mark's most obvious midrashic use of this insight was in 3.9, that Jesus would be crushed by the crowds if he were to give in to the lesser goods they so avidly desired.

Mark pictured Jesus as having a clear choice. God's spirit, speaking out of the midrashic context of 1 Kings and Romans, implicitly urges Jesus within his own spirit to say that "God loves all his children, and I now know as a fact in my life that I am loved." According to Mark, love's inherent jealousy automatically transforms being loved into seeing oneself as the *only one* who is loved. This provides the opportunity for Satan and the unclean spirits to urge upon Jesus the sentiment that he is the only one whom God loves, that he is special, the only begotten Son of God, the Holy One.

Mark told stories about unclean spirits and the holy spirit as if they were living entities which can exist outside of persons. Such a view would be accepted by many of his contemporaries. Jubilees 10.1-14 writes about unclean spirits existing outside of persons, causing diseases and various evils, and originating as offspring of the Watchers (angels). Most of such unclean spirits were imprisoned until the end of time, but a tenth were allowed to roam. Such references to unclean spirits pervade Jubilees and I Enoch. Mark, however, was not explicit that the spirits exist in a form in which anyone other than Jesus ever heard their voices; he was interested in Jesus' personal, inner experience of temptation.

A model for Mark's treatment of spirit voices which is an alternative to external spirits is found in Elijah's experience in his wilderness of temptation:

> And behold, the Lord passed by, and a great and strong wind rent the mountains...but the Lord was not in the wind; and after the wind an earthquake, but the Lord was not in the earthquake; and after the earthquake a fire, but the Lord was not in the fire; and after the fire *a still small voice [a sound of gentle stillness*[13]]. And when Elijah heard it, he wrapped his face in his mantle...[as Moses had when God spoke to him at the burning bush] (1 Kgs. 19.11-13).

Mark midrashically personified the silent sound of spirit as if Jesus were being spoken to by invisible creatures. It was as if Jesus knew God's love for him as a child of God, but was also keenly aware of the temptation automatically involved. Thus, two spirit voices were speaking to him simultaneously.

Mark's role for unclean spirits is considerably at variance from the Wrede tradition[14] that they were supernatural figures who recognized the divine Jesus because of previous acquaintance with him in heavenly realms. Thus, for Wrede, when demons were later to say, "We know who you are," they were correct; the reader would know Jesus' true identity through the testimony of unclean spirits. Mark, to the contrary, viewed unclean spirits as tempters. For Mark, their every utterance was of a temptative nature and could not be fully right. In each confrontation with Jesus, such spirits represent a lesser version, a distortion of some genuine truth, a new version of the Elijah temptation."I, only I."

Jesus' Mission of Preaching Repentance: Mk. 1.14-15

After Elijah's forty-day stay in a wilderness of temptation, God gave him work to do. An implied "crowd" task was for Elijah to find and preach to "seven thousand in Israel, all the knees that have not bowed to Ba'al, and every mouth that has not kissed him" (1 Kgs. 19.18). Malachi envisioned Elijah returning just before "the great and terrible [judgment] day of the Lord" (4.5). He was to provide guidelines for the masses to follow in order to be reconciled to the Father, and to threaten those who disobeyed with virtually instant destruction: "For behold, the day comes, burning like an oven, when all the arrogant and all evildoers will be stubble" (Mal. 4.1). Malachi did not use the term "repentance," but Elijah's sermons were to be consistent with the idea of turning a life around and going in the opposite direction.

Most Jewish prophetic books had some version of such a Day of the Lord, differing primarily in whether it was far off, or near at hand. Mark proposed a midrashically similar agenda for Jesus. Bratcher and Nida suggest that his message was "The time is fulfilled: now is when God is going to rule; repent and believe the good news."[15] An acceptable paraphrase would be: "The Day of Judgment is at hand. It is time for you to obey God, to let God be sovereign in your lives right now! Change your lives and believe that this is good news." The good news which began in Isaiah (Mk. 1.1-2) had been that "God reigns" (52.7), that the Jews can return home from Babylon; that war is ended (40.1-9); that God's servant will bring forth justice (41.27--42.1); and that the afflicted and captives will be cared for. Mark midrashically transformed Isaiah's "gospel" to make it applicable to his own time and to the Elijah-Malachi agenda of judgment day at hand.

Mark portrayed Jesus as preaching repentance, but not baptizing. This follows Paul's description of himself: "For Christ did not send me to baptize but to preach the gospel, and not with eloquent wisdom, lest the cross of Christ be emptied of its power" (1 Cor. 1.17). In 2 Cor. 6.17--7.1, Paul midrashically adapted Isa. 52.11 and Hos. 1.10 to urge people to "come out from among [unbelievers] and be separate from them." Such repentance apart from baptism would be a cleansing "from every defilement of body and spirit" with the reconciliatory consequence that God "will be a father to you, and you shall be my sons and daughters." A ritual baptism would be superfluous for such a reconciliation. For Mark, John-Elijah had completed the baptismal task; his Elisha-Jesus successor did not have to do that.

Preaching repentance because something like the Day of Judgment is at hand is sometimes interpreted as the theme of the whole of Mark. Kee, for example, refers to Mk. 1.15 as "the summary statement" of Jesus' mission.[16] It is in fact the theme of this unit, 1.9-45, only. Both repentance and judgment figure in the unit, although Jesus affirms the first while denying the second. After this unit, Jesus never again focuses on repentance or the advocacy of final judgment, although there are scattered references to both.

Jesus waits to begin his ministry of preaching repentance until after John is arrested. No details of the arrest are given until Mk. 6. The details are of little importance in the Elijah-Elisha midrash. All that matters is that Jesus could not begin his Elisha-like career until Elijah-John was out of the way. The passing note "after John was arrested" made that possible.

A fascinating set of alternatives for translators emerges from the fact that the Greek verb "paradidomai" rendered here as "arrested" is read as "betrayed" in the relationship between Judas Iscariot and Jesus, and as "handed over to the authorities" in 1 Cor. 11.23. None of the translations are necessarily wrong, but there are sufficient nuances of different meaning to lead interpreters to be cautious in drawing conclusions from any one English version. Mark's repeated use of the verb calls attention to the possibility that he was conscious or its variety of meanings and their potential midrashic interrelationships.

Calling the First Four Disciples: Mk. 1.16-20

Jesus' specific Elijah-like task was to recruit followers to assist him, just as Elijah found Elisha plowing and recruited him as his first act outside the wilderness (1 Kgs. 19.19-21). Mark used that type-scene for calling the first four disciples, although he called four rather than one and changed from plowing to fishing.[17] Having more than one disciple is midrashically justified by the fact that Elijah also had followers called "sons of the prophets" who subsequently attached themselves to Elisha.

"Fishers of men" is usually interpreted as meaning "recruiters of followers." Mark's context requires that fishers of men be read as a midrash on Jer. 16.16-18 in which God sends out fishers and hunters to bring home dispersed Jewish sinners so that they can be punished for their evil: "Behold, I am sending for many fishers, says the Lord, and they shall catch them; and afterwards I will send for many hunters, and they shall hunt them from every mountain and every hill, and out of the clefts of the rocks. For my eyes are upon all their ways; they are not hid from me, nor is their iniquity concealed from my eyes. And I will doubly recompense their iniquity and their sin." A supplementary midrashic source is Amos 4.2, in which people are threatened with being taken away on fishhooks in order to induce repentance. In Mark's context, Jesus has initially been depicted as a preacher of repentance in the terrifying Malachi-Elijah model of repent-or-be-punished, as in the prediction of Mal. 4.1 that "the day comes, burning like an oven, when all the arrogant and all evildoers will be stubble; the day that comes shall burn them up." In Mark's next pericope[18], a spirit-possessed man will assume that Jesus has come to destroy sinners. Mark's "fishers" of men" were thus originally intended as gatherers of sinners-to-be-punished rather than as recruiters. Jesus, having explored the adequacy of this concept, soon rejects it altogether.

One reason for Mark to shift imagery from plowing to fishing was to make use of the Sea of Galilee shoreline to communicate meaning in his Gospel. Mark used the western shore of that sea as a symbolic divider between Jews and Gentiles. On the beach, where the four disciples are called, Jesus stands on the borderline between the two worlds. Each time he crosses that shoreline he always moves away from Judaism toward some more Gentile orientation. By returning westward across the shore, he comes back to traditional Judaism. The borderline character of the seashore on which Jesus called the four disciples is confirmed by their names: James/Jacob and John, both Hebrew; Andrew, Greek; and Simon, Hellenized Hebrew.

Peter, James/Jacob, and John were undoubtedly historical people in that Paul refers to them in historical contexts. Despite that fact, Mark develops the Gospel details of their lives out of his midrashic identification of them with texts from the books bearing their names. James/Jacob and John are names associated with the epistles of James/Jacob and I John. Simon is Mark's name for the author of I Peter; Mark reserves "Peter" as a surname to be bestowed by Jesus upon Simon later. Mark's style is to treat the three books as a group and to draw midrashic details from all for any one of the three disciples. It will be appropriate later to examine all the passages in Paul's letters alluding to them: Gal. 1.18-19; 2.6-14; 1 Cor. 1.12, 3.21-23; 9.5-6; 15.3-8. From them, Mark used midrashically only the details that the three were pillars of the church, that Simon was married, that Simon had a special preeminence, and that Jesus had a brother named James/Jacob. For information about them as historical persons, one should trust only the books which they themselves wrote and Paul's statements about them.

Mark's phraseology in describing the pairs of brothers is conspicuously strange. This is especially so because Paul gave no hint that any one was brother to another. Mark wrote "Simon and Andrew the brother of Simon" and "James/Jacob the son of Zebedee and John his brother." The latter is repeated in Mk. 3.17.

The primacy of Simon Peter over Andrew[19] in Mark is clear, but the preference for James/Jacob over John must be justified. Mark's reason for referring to them this way may be in the etymology of their names.[20] John means "God Is Gracious"; Jacob means "Israel" or "He Who Supplants His Brother"; Zebedee means "Gift of God." The original Jacob was doubly a gift of God, first as the son of Isaac who had been a gift of God to Abraham and Sarah in old age and secondly as one who received the blessing and birthright which legally belonged to Esau. Zebedee as father of James/Jacob is midrashically in the role of Isaac, the "Gift of God" who was father of a son whose supplanting symbolized the gift of God. John's "God Is Gracious" meaning serves as a commentary on the gifts of God. Just as Jesus has supplanted John the Baptizer, so now in the list of the first four followers is another John with a brother whose name alludes to supplanting.

Mark is likely to have had an additional sound-alike midrash in mind with the name Zebedee. One of the twelve sons of Jacob was Zebulon. Deut. 33.18-19 links Zebulon with Issachar:

> And of Zebulon he said, "Rejoice, Zebulon, in your going out; and Issachar, in your tents. They shall call peoples to their mountain; there they offer right sacrifices; for they suck the affluence of the seas and the hidden treasures of the sand."

Jacob's blessing of Zebulon had earlier emphasized that "Zebulon shall dwell at the shore of the sea; he shall become a haven for ships..." (Gen. 49.13). The Test. of Zebulon describes Zebulon as catching fantastic amounts of fish, as in the miracle stories in John and Luke associated with the sons of Zebedee (Jn. 21.1-14; Lk. 5.1-11). Furthermore, the Test. of Zebulon begins with a statement that Zebulon considers himself to be a "good gift," close to the etymology for Zebedee. It is thus possible that Mark intended the sound-alike linkage of Zebedee and Zebulon, and virtually certain that John and Luke read Mark as having intended it.

Both James/Jacob and 1 John emphasize the obligation to love one's brother. Mark's James/Jacob may also be particularly a son of the gift of God in that God's gifts are a major theme throughout the letter of Jacob/James: "If any of you lacks wisdom, let him ask *God who gives to all men generously*:...and it will be given him" (1.5); restoration from illness is a gift (5.14-15); "*Every perfect gift is from above*, coming down from the Father of lights" (1.17). The author of the epistle goes on to discuss God's gifts of the "implanted word" (1.21), the "perfect law" (1.25), and the "wisdom from above" (3.15). 1 John equally emphasizes God's gifts: "See what *love the Father has given us*, that we should be called children of God" (3.1); "He loved us and *sent his son* to be the expiation for our sins" (4.10); "He has *given us of his own Spirit*" (4.13); "*God gave us eternal life* and this life is in his Son" (5.11); "If we ask anything according to his will *he hears us*" (5.14).

Mark structured the story of the calling of the brothers so as to emphasize the word "immediately." Mark previously had used the word in a peculiar way in the baptism-temptation pair of stories: "And when Jesus came up out of the water, immediately he saw the heavens opened" (1.10), and "the Spirit immediately drove him out into the wilderness" (1.12). In the calling of the brothers, the first pair "immediately left their nets and followed him" (1.18). Jesus then "immediately called" the second pair (1.20). In the first calling, Jesus observes the immediacy in the action of Simon and Andrew, but in the second calling it is Jesus, not James/Jacob and John, who acts immediately .

Mark used the term "immediately" thirty-five times in seventeen pericopes, according to the RSV, almost always twice to a story. The paired usage is the clue for decoding Mark's meaning. In most pericopes in which "immediately" occurs twice, Mark intended a sequence in which an event happens quickly with the result that Jesus is promptly and inevitably tempted. In the baptism-wilderness sequence, the meaning would be that *as soon as* Jesus comes up out of the water he sees the heavens opened; as a result, he is driven *automatically* into a wilderness of temptation. Likewise, earlier, *as soon as* Jesus calls Simon and Andrew they follow him; as a result, Jesus is *automatically* tempted to demand authoritatively that John and Jacob follow him. In each pair one "immediately" has a straight-forward "as soon as" meaning, and the other carries with it the implication of an automatic temptation inherent in the first.

When the word "immediately" appears more than once in a pericope, there is usually a greater-good/lesser-good dichotomy in the context. When Jesus called two pairs of brothers, the second pair were called immediately, with the result that they were separated from their father, Zebedee ("The Gift of God"). Mark's midrash on Malachi had already established that Jesus' sole goal was to enable the children of the Father to be reconciled to the Father. In this case, the calling has the opposite result: "they *left their father* Zebedee in the boat with the hired servants, and followed Jesus." The midrashic source for abandoning Zebedee is Elisha leaving home in order to run after Elijah (1 Kgs. 19.19-21). Elisha said, "Let me kiss my father and my mother, and then I will follow you." Elijah responded, "Go back again; for what have I done to you?" Elisha returned from following Elijah, killed the oxen, boiled the meat, and "gave it to the people, and they ate. Then he arose and went after Elijah, and ministered to him" (1 Kgs. 19.19-21). Elijah appeared at first to have demanded instant obedience, expecting Elisha to leave without saying good-bye to his parents.

Elijah relented long enough for Elisha to kill and roast the oxen and serve a feast to a crowd. The text does not say that he said good-bye to his parents. An alternative interpretation is that Elijah repented that he had deprived Elisha of an opportunity to tell his parents good-bye and gave him permission to do so. Either way, the result is a final separation from father and mother. In Malachi and Mark, the opposite is supposed to be true. The overall goal is for people to be reconciled to fathers, especially God as Father, not to be parted from them. Often in Mark the failure of a traditional spiritual model is indicated by a division between parents and a child.

Mark's account of James/Jacob and John abandoning the parent whose name stands for the Gift of God unambiguously disclosed for the first time that he intended to criticize Old Testament models rather than to affirm them. He did not, like Paul, argue that God's truth is established merely by being in the Bible. Rather, he implied that the Old Testament model of Elijah's calling of Elisha had not been good enough. James/Jacob, the namesake of all the children of God according to Malachi, is separated from his father instead of being reunited to him by Jesus' use of the Elijah model.

The Unclean Spirit in the Synagogue: Mk. 1.21-28

The first specified occasion on which Jesus preaches repentance is when he *immediately* enters the Capernaum synagogue and "teaches with authority." An unclean spirit is *immediately* there to accuse him of "coming to destroy us" and is convulsed by Jesus' reply. This suggests Mark's midrashic reliance on James/Jacob: "You believe that God is one; you do well. Even the demons believe—and *shudder*" (Jas./Jac. 2.19). The immediacy of coming to the synagogue and the convulsion is likely to be rooted in the threat of Mal. 3.1-2 that "the Lord whom you seek will *suddenly come to his temple*," but no one will be able to "*stand* when he appears." Mark stressed Jesus' authoritative utterance and action, thus tying it to the sequence which began with his *immediate* demand that the second pair of brothers follow him. First he "taught them as one who had *authority*, and not as the scribes" (1.22). His reputation for authoritativeness grew when the crowd noted that "*with authority he commands* even the unclean spirits" (1.27). In calling the four disciples Jesus' self-confidence was only implicit. Now it is mentioned explicitly in the context of a paired use of "immediately" and a conversation with an unclean spirit, both indicators of temptation.

The unclean spirit calls Jesus "the Holy One of God." Is. 43.14-15 may imply that God alone is holy: "the Holy One of Israel" says "I am the Lord, your Holy One." 2 Kgs. 4.9, however, refers to Elisha as "a *holy man of God*." This latter reference was determinative for Mark's midrash in this initial confrontation with an unclean spirit. Here Jesus is not tempted to think of himself as God, but as Elijah/Elisha, the only holy one.

The unclean spirit's accusation that Jesus of Nazareth is destructive is midrashic on 1-2 Kings. Assuming that the demon's reference to Nazareth is Mark's sound-alike way of referring to Jesus as a Nazarite-like "holy one," the demon's fears center on the predicted destructiveness of Elijah as the holy one of God on the occasion of his return. Elijah's threatening reputation had been well earned. A widow in 1 Kgs. 17.18 addressed him as "man of God. Have you come to bring my sins to remembrance and to slay my son?" Elijah ordered the execution of the priests of the false gods (1 Kgs. 18.40). When King Ahab sought Elijah, he beckoned fire from heaven to consume two troops of fifty soldiers (2 Kgs. 1.9-12). Elisha, repeating and completing Elijah's career, cursed small boys who jeered at him, with the result that a bear "tore forty-two of the boys" (2 Kgs. 2.24). The cry of the demon in the presence of Elijah-Jesus is understandable: "Have you come to destroy us?"

The story of Jesus' confrontation with the synagogue spirit can be interpreted in at least three ways and can hence be referred to as multivalent.[21] At a superficial level, the crowd sees an apparently disturbed person interrupting a guest speaker in the synagogue, and interprets his rude behavior in terms of spirit possession, probably what we would label as emotional disturbance. When the disrupter is silenced and collapses at Jesus' order, witnesses are amazed at the authoritativeness of the act and exclaim, "What is this? A new teaching! With authority he commands even the unclean spirits and they obey him" (Mk. 1.27). The audience assumes that it has seen Jesus perform a miraculous exorcism.

At a second level, the man sees himself as a sinner and sees Jesus as Elijah returned from the dead to preach to sinners. He knows Elijah's reputation for immediate destruction of the ungodly and knows the predictions in Malachi that Elijah will return to destroy those who do not repent. When Jesus orders him to be silent, he collapses in stark terror because he sees death staring him in the face. In that respect he is midrashically like the demons of Jas./Jac. 2.19; he believes "and shudders!"

At a spiritual level, the story concerns a raging temptation within Jesus himself. He is confronted with a crowd which both adores him for his charisma and fears him for his Elijah-like power.[22] The temptation to *announce himself* as the Holy One of God, which had begun at the baptism and continued through forty days in the wilderness, is still with him. The temptation is accentuated by the fact that he had just performed his first miracle, exorcising a demon in full view of the congregation. There was no better platform from which to launch a campaign to have himself accepted as the Only Holy One. In that context Jesus' words to the demon have their deepest meaning. When he says "Be silent, and come out of him," it is as if he is saying "Spirit within me, shut up! Give no hint to this crowd that I expect to be treated as the *only* child of God. I am calling all these people to repentance so that they can be reconciled to the Father. I am not just trying to elevate my own reputation."

The event occurs in Capernaum ("City of Nahum"), a village not mentioned in the Old Testament. Mark used the name of the town as a midrash on Nah. 1.15, the only sentence in the Old Testament outside of Isaiah to use the word "gospel" in a spiritual sense. Mk. 1.1-2 says that the gospel began in Isaiah. Mk. 1.21-28 implies, in a different way, that the gospel began in Capernaum. This apparent confusion is justified by the similarity of Nah. 1.15 to Isa. 52.7: "Behold, on the mountains the feet of him who brings the gospel, who proclaims peace" (Nah. 1.15); "How beautiful upon the mountains are the feet of him who brings the gospel, who publishes peace, who brings the gospel of good, who publishes salvation" (Isa. 52.7). Nahum's "good news of peace" was ironically the destruction of Nineveh and restoration of "the majesty of Jacob" (Nah. 2.2). Capernaum is the first named place where Jesus preached the gospel. Later it is to be the place where Jesus begins the Moses-Levi-forgiveness stage of the gospel. Thus it serves as a symbol for beginnings.

Jesus' First Miraculous Healing of Disease: Mk. 1.29-31

Mk. 1.29-31 and the next two pericopes are concerned primarily with the midrashic fact that Elijah was a sensational healer as well as a preacher and destroyer. Mark develops the midrashic imagery in connection with his already established temptation motif; healing diseased people is good, but not nearly as good as reconciling people to God the Father. *Immediately* upon leaving the synagogue, Jesus goes to the home of Simon and Andrew with Jacob and John. The four *immediately* tell him that Simon's mother-in-law is in bed with a fever. Jesus does nothing to her other than to "lift her up," but the fever subsides. The pair of *immediately* references in the story implies that temptation is involved, but the pericope itself does not overtly identify the nature of the temptation. Interpretation of the story centers on the question as to what kind of a miracle occurred. Did Jesus intend to perform a healing or did the miracle merely happen to him? Did he discover in this event a power to perform miracles that he had not previously possessed? That appears to be the implication of the text, but it is not a necessary conclusion in order to follow the flow of thought in the story.

The fact that Peter is or has been married and hence has a mother-in-law is rooted midrashically in 1 Cor. 9.5: "Do we not have the right to be accompanied by a wife, as the other apostles and the brothers of the Lord and Cephas?" Mark connected Peter's mother-in-law with accounts of two women and their sons in the Elijah-Elisha cycle. Elijah, in 1 Kgs. 17, saves a woman and her son from starvation by creating a miraculous supply of food, in return for which the woman serves him. He later resurrects her son when he dies. Elisha, in 2 Kgs. 4, saves two children from slavery by creating for their mother a miraculous supply of oil. Another woman serves him, and he later resurrects her son when he dies. Peter's mother-in-law is miraculously healed of her fever, after which she serves Jesus. The unstated portion of the parallel raises a question about whether Peter, "the son," will "die" and be "resurrected," and if so in what sense? The statements of both women prefigure the testimony to Jesus which was given by the synagogue unclean spirit in Mark. The woman in 1 Kgs. 17.24 says of Elijah, "Now I know that you are a man of God'; the woman in 2 Kgs. 4.9 perceives that Elisha is "a holy man of God." Both are parallel to Jesus the Nazarite, the Holy One of God.

Opening the Floodgates of Miracle: Mk. 1.32-34

Jesus' reputation as a miraculous healer in the midrashic tradition of Elijah and Elisha comes to its first climax as soon as the sabbath ends and it becomes religiously legal for people to bring their sick to him. "The whole city" gathers at a house where

Jesus is. Mark implies that residents of Capernaum had heard about the exorcism miracle in the synagogue and the healing miracle in Simon's home. Hence they bring demoniacs and the ill to be cured. Jesus willingly accedes to their requests on his own authority, without regard to any expectation of repentance, thus manifesting the extent to which he has been tempted to abandon his original goal of preaching repentance as the means of achieving Father-children reconciliation. That morning he had gone to the synagogue to be a preacher. By the end of the sabbath, he had become a locally famous master-healer, a miraculous physician in the lineage of both Elijah and Elisha. Public belief in Jesus as the new Elijah was sufficient to support the belief that he could heal any kind of disease.

Rapidly developing authoritativeness had lead Jesus to this juncture. When Jesus had preached repentance, he had called Simon and Andrew and they had obeyed *immediately*. He then *immediately* called Jacob and John and they had obeyed. He next taught with authority in the synagogue, after which he authoritatively exorcised an unclean spirit there. He authoritatively lifted Simon's mother-in-law to her feet and healed her fever, perhaps unintentionally. Finally he intentionally healed all who were brought to his door. Authoritativeness in preaching had gradually became unintentional miracle and then intentional, authoritative miracle. Mark must have intended the entire sequence because he raised the issue of authoritativeness and because the unit is so logically consistent. Not permitting "the demons to speak because they knew him" is a generalization from the instance of the synagogue unclean spirit who was told to be silent when he claimed to know Jesus. Jesus' refusal to permit the unclean spirits to speak is the author's narrative way of saying that Jesus is resisting the Satanic temptation to announce himself to the public as the Only Holy One, the only beloved son of God. Mass miracles made the temptation even stronger for Jesus than it had been before, metaphorically creating many more unclean spirits to silence.

"Healing many who were sick with various diseases" is significantly different from "casting out many demons." Curing diseases is a type of miracle which Jesus does only in the Elijah-repentance unit of Mark. After this unit, Jesus will never again be depicted by Mark as healing diseases in general. Resisting temptation by exorcising demons is an activity of Jesus which goes on intermittently until the last one is cast out and commanded never to return in Mk. 9.25. Mark expected his readers to distinguish between miraculous healing in general and resistance to temptation as expressed by unclean spirits.

Physician or Preacher of Repentance? Mk. 1.35-39

Jesus' response to the swiftly increasing temptation to act authoritatively is to go off by himself to a "lonely place" where he prays for much of the night. The unspecified subject matter of his prayer is clarified by the context. Simon and the others have followed him and inform him that everyone is looking for him. Jesus replies that he should "'go on to the next towns, that I may *preach* there also; *for that is why I came out*.' And he went throughout Galilee, preaching in their synagogues and casting out demons" (Mk. 1.38-39). Going to the rest of Galilee implies leaving Capernaum, the place associated with the beginning of the gospel. On Jesus' subsequent synagogue itinerary, it is reported only that he preaches and casts out demons, i.e., resists temptation; there is no general healing of disease. By the logic of that distinction, Jesus decided during the night of prayer to be a preacher rather than a physician. Had the story ended here, one would conclude that Jesus had found a successful way to be an Elijah/Elisha preacher of repentance without being tempted.

Compassion for a Leper Leading to More Miracles: Mk. 1.40-45

Just when it appears that Jesus has conquered the tempting spirits, he finds a new higher "good" temptation to lure him to a lesser one. Mark created a unique situation in which Jesus could seek to maintain his commitment to being a preacher of repentance and also heal a leper. Jesus is alone in the countryside. The news of his Capernaum mass healings must have spread throughout Galilee, but when Jesus had come to each local synagogue and had refused to heal, people must have lost interest in him. They wanted a magical medical doctor, not a preacher-prophet demanding that they change their lives. His miracles at Capernaum had created an expectation which he was unwilling to fulfill, a reputation he was unwilling to perpetuate. Hence he was alone.

A leper comes to Jesus with a request which asks for healing in the imagery of purification. He comes close enough to Jesus to kneel before him and challenge him: "*If you will, you can make me clean*" (Mk. 1.40). The leper's action was moderately daring because lepers, according to Mosaic law, were supposed to stay away from non-leprous people. Jesus' action was more daring because he was intentionally violating a law about separating oneself from those with noxious skin diseases. Mark logically must have used Num. 5.2-3 as a midrashic source because he wrote stories dealing with all three of its clauses:

> Command the people of Israel that they put out of the camp every leper, and every one having a discharge, and every one that is unclean through contact with the dead; you shall put them out both male and female, putting them outside the camp, that they may not defile their camp, in the midst of which I dwell.

Mark was later to combine the "discharge" and "contact with the dead" particulars in the intercalated story of Jesus going into the presence of Jairus' dead daughter and healing the woman with a discharge who had dared to touch him in the midst of a crowd.

In order to understand the leper story, one must recognize that in ancient Judaism, leprosy was a disease of "uncleanness"; cured lepers were made clean. The leper is interested only in being cured of his leprosy; Jesus is interested only in preaching repentance and in people becoming truly, inwardly clean. If the leper had asked outright for a healing, Jesus probably would have refused. Jesus may have hoped that a true cleansing would occur, with the leper repenting and changing his life. The leper virtually accuses Jesus of having power to heal a social outcast but being unwilling to do so. His accusation has the ring of a minority-group person going to a majority-group physician and being refused treatment because of minority status. The leper's condition creates a new conflict within Jesus. He has decided not to cure diseases. Yet he pities the man, genuinely desiring to remove the uncleanness which has made it impossible for him to return to ordinary society. The same motivation for a healing is offered in Jer. 30.17: "Your wounds I will heal, says the Lord, because they have called you an outcast: 'It is Zion, for whom no one cares!'"

The leprosy *immediately* leaves the man, alerting the reader that Jesus has succumbed once more to temptation. Jesus then "sternly [angrily[23]] charged" the healed leper to tell no one. Jesus may have been angry at the leper for enticing him into curing a skin condition only, with no corresponding inner purification. Furthermore, the external healing brought on the inevitable deluge of healing requests when the man disobeyed Jesus' injunction. Part of Jesus' temptation lies in the fact that the "tell no one" order is not given until after the cure is completed; it is not as if the cleansed man had violated a promise when he "began to talk freely about it." Nevertheless, "Jesus could no longer openly enter a town" because crowds were coming "to him from every quarter" (Mk. 1.45). This implies that they came for miraculous healings and that Jesus was unable to resist, once the ex-leper had announced that the physician was performing healings again.

The healing of the leper fits into the Elijah/Elisha motif by virtue of Elisha's healing of Naaman in 2 Kgs. 5. There, as in Mark, the healing is described in terms of being "clean," a euphemism for a healed skin disease. In Mark's context, healing a leper has broader significance. John the Baptizer contrasted baptizing only with water with baptizing with spirit. Water washes the skin, the external person; spirit washes the heart and changes inner behavior. Now Jesus cleanses skin without making any demand for internal, spiritual cleansing. No one repents; everyone seeks to divert Jesus to bodily healing only. Thus the Elijah model fails. John's failure as the new Elijah was acknowledged in his own distinction between inner and outer cleansing. Jesus' recognition of its failure is implicit in the parallel with John and in the fact that he never again plays the Elijah role of expecting crowds to repent.

The Elijah-Elisha unit comes to an end with a mass miracle situation after Jesus gives in to the leper's plea. Each of Mark's first four units climax with crowd healings. In each, the miracles are the author's most powerful indication of the failure of the particular spiritual ideal of the unit. Only in this unit does more than one mass healing occur. One presents Jesus with the physician/preacher choice; the second shows the failure of both options. Elijah-like authoritative preaching inevitably results only in mass miracle and exposes the inadequacy of the Elijah model. The remainder of the leper pericope deals with sending the leper to the priests for ritual cleansing, based on Lev. 14.19-20. That opens up a new set of midrashic source materials for Mark and becomes the bridge to the next unit.

ENDNOTES FOR CHAPTER THREE

[1]Acts, written later, describes a John movement still alive in the churches, but Acts is midrashic on the gospels at this point and not independent evidence. Acts 18.24--19.5 refers to Apollos, who knew only the baptism of John. Paul, in Acts, reacted by characterizing that as a baptism of repentance without the Holy Spirit.

[2]N. Turner, "The Hasmoneans,"*IDB*. Many other connections between Mark and themes in 1-2 Maccabees will be noted later in the book.

[3]Perrin and Duling, II, 32, for example, assume that the Qumran community practiced baptism from its beginning during the Maccabean period on.

[4]Barnabas Lindars has recognized a marvellous midrash in the phrase "double portion." Deut. 21.17 orders a double portion given to the elder son according to the law of inheritance. Jacob the supplanter got Esau's double portion, the inheritance and the blessing. Thus Elisha, supplanting Elijah, asks for and receives his appropriate double portion. Lindars, "Elijah, Elisha, and the Gospel Miracles," in C. F. D. Moule, *Miracles* (London: A.R. Mowbray, 1965) 73.

[5]H. F. D. Sparks, *The Apocryphal Old Testament* (Oxford: Clarendon Press, 1984) 508-9, cites Kee and Charles as favoring the early date for The Testament of the Twelve Patriarchs, and de Jonge as insisting on a 200 CE date. Sparks quotes Kee as concluding that "they were produced in a Jewish environment that thought and spoke in Greek, possibly Egypt, about 100 B.C."

[6]Sanders, *Canon and Community*, 62-63

[7]Willi Marxsen, *Mark the Evangelist* (Nashville: Abingdon, 1969) II, 60.

[8]Vincent Taylor, Mark 52. Taylor recognized that there are grammatical deficiencies in Mark, but resisted the tendency to "overstress the 'barbarous' character of Mark's Greek."

[9]Richard Longnecker, *Biblical Exegesis in the Apostolic Period*, 45-146.

[10]E. Schweizer, "*Er wird Nazoraer heissen*," as translated by Richard Longnecker, *Biblical Exegesis in the Apostolic Period*, 146.

[11]Kee, *Community of New Age*, 120, 204.

[12]E. A. Speiser, *Genesis* (Garden City, N.Y.: Doubleday, 1964) 38.

[13]Norman H. Snaith, exegesis of 1 Kings, *The Interpreter's Bible* (Nashville: Abingdon, 1954).

[14]William Wrede, English translation, *The Messianic Secret* (Cambridge, 1971).

[15]Robert Bratcher and Eugene Nida, *A Translator's Handbook on the Gospel of Mark* (Leiden: E.J. Brill, 1970) 36-38.

[16]Kee, *Community of New Age*, 42

[17]Type-scene is a "basic situation which occurs several times during a narrative," each with variations on similar characteristics. Robert C. Tannehill, *The Narrative Unity of Luke-Acts* (Fortress Press, 1986), 170. Tannehill in turn credits Robert Alter, *The Art of Biblical Narrative*, 47-62, for the term.

[18]Pericope is a technical term used in biblical study to denote a passage of scripture which could be cut out of its context but would stand by itself.

[19]Andrew is the equivalent of the Old Testament name Adam (Manly). The word "adam" is used about 500 times in the Old Testament to mean mankind and only rarely as a proper name. The Adam stories may well have been midrashic on the word. See Speiser, *Genesis*, p. 18, for a discussion of the difference between man *ha'adam* and the proper name *'adam*. Speiser's recommended translation replaces references to Adam with "man" or "the man." He does, however, note that the LXX, apparently Mark's preferred Bible, favors Adam. Paul (1 Cor 15.45) used the name "Adam" in the sense that "'the first man Adam became a living being' [Gen 2.7]; the last Adam [Jesus] became a life-giving spirit."

[20]Discussion of the etymology of "Simon" is deferred to the exegesis of Mk 3.14 because of its close relationship to "Peter" as "Rock."

[21]Sanders' metaphor for narratives for which three or more interpretations are possible.

[22]The combination of charisma and power is the defining characteristic of the modern cult leader, although the power of the cult leaders is usually stage magic deception of audiences who beg to be deceived.

[23]Bratcher and Nida note many translators who prefer "angrily," but also cite excellent authority for "sternly."

CHAPTER FOUR

MIDRASH ON LEVI-MOSES AND THE CROWDS OF OLD ISRAEL

After abandoning the Elijah model, Mark turned his attention to the example of Levi in Malachi. Levi was the son of Jacob for whom the tribe of priests was named. The name Levi is virtually synonymous with Jewish priesthood and Leviticus, the book named for Levi, in which the priestly rules are enshrined. Mark's dual purpose in this unit was to show that Levitical priesthood is inadequate as a model for Jesus as messiah and son of God, and that there are guidelines for behavior higher than Mosaic laws. Mark made little distinction between Levi and Moses, the main character and supposed author of Leviticus, as the midrashic model for Jesus as priest.

Mk. 2.1—3.12 contains six basic pericopes plus an extended bridge to the next unit. Five of the six deal with contradictions between forgiveness and legalism in a tradition which combines Mosaic laws with Levitical priestly functions. The other pericope centers on the inappropriateness of fasting while Jesus is present. The bridge material at the end climaxes Jesus' experience in both the Elijah and Levi-Moses units to conclude the period of his career in which he seeks positive responses from the masses.

Mark turned his attention to the adequacy of the Moses-Levi priestly model for several reasons. The first was to portray Jesus as adopting the second of John the Baptizer's two unfinished tasks of preaching repentance and proclaiming forgiveness. The former task was inherited by Jesus in his Elijah role, the latter in his Levi role. Forgiveness is generally viewed in the Old Testament as uniquely the task of priests, on the theory that priests are needed to mediate between God and sinners. John had proclaimed forgiveness, but there is no record of anyone accepting it. Jesus' Jacob-like task was to rectify this failure, in the midrashic tradition that one named "God Saves" would complete the agenda of his predecessor.

Mark's second reason for centering on the Levi-Moses model was that in Mal. 1.6—2.17 Levitical priests were supposed to be reconciled to the Father God by following the example of Levi, their patronymic namesake. Their assumed estrangement from God and thus their need for being reconciled is supported by criticisms of the priesthood in The Testament of Levi.[1] Malachi's two routes to Father-children reconciliation (repentance for the masses; purification for the priests) are linked by the fact that part of Elijah's task (3.3) was to "purify the sons of Levi." Mark correctly centered the Levi midrash on Moses who was both a member of the tribe of Levi and a priest as well as the premier lawgiver of Israel. Mark saw advocacy of Mosaic laws and priestliness going hand in hand.

Two supplementary but important midrashic details are the facts that the original successor to Moses was named Jesus ("Joshua" in Hebrew), and that Zechariah had envisioned a priest-messiah named Jesus ("Joshua" in Hebrew). Mark thus had a long list of midrashic reasons for attending to Moses-Levi priestly themes.

References to priests in the leper story (Mk. 1.44) provide the bridge from the Elijah section. Jesus instructed the now-cleansed leper to go to a priest for rituals prescribed in Leviticus, thus introducing the Levi-priest motif. This opens dimensions of meaning which go beyond ritual. Lev. 14 describes "the law of the leper for the day of his cleansing." Part of the cleansing is a "sin offering," on the assumption that leprosy is both a sin and a disease, probably a disease caused by sin. Part of the cleansing is an anointing akin to that received by priests at ordination, thus providing another link to a Levi motif. Lev. 14 is part of a longer section about differences between clean and unclean. Lev. 11.24 rules that anyone who touches the carcass of unclean animals shall be unclean until evening, a theme repeated with variations. Women are temporarily unclean as a result of giving birth, menstruating, or having other "flows of blood." A man with a superficial skin disease is unclean; if he has a deeper disease, including leprosy, "he shall dwell alone in a habitation outside the camp" (Lev. 13.46). In Lev. 15, anyone with a discharge of semen, urine, or blood is unclean; anyone who touches a man or woman in these conditions of impurity, or who touches that which a bleeding person sits upon, becomes unclean.

Mark showed Jesus as firmly opposed to these clean-unclean distinctions. By touching the leper, Jesus knowingly violates the Mosaic prohibitions and thus becomes technically unclean. Mark might have appreciated a later midrash on Lk. 6.4 (paralleling Mk. 2.25) as an interpretation of Jesus' intention: "When on the same day he saw a man doing work on the sabbath, he said to him: 'Man! if thou knowest what thou doest, blessed art thou! But if thou knowest not, thou art cursed and a transgressor of the law.'"[2] Throughout this unit, Jesus shows conscious knowledge of and disdain for priestly rules. By permitting the leper to violate the rule about maintaining a proper distance from a non-leprous person, Jesus has already rendered the leper "clean" in a religious sense prior to healing him or sending him to ask for cleansing rituals. This was more important for Jesus than the superficial cure of skin disease, however sensational the latter seemed to the crowds who heard about it afterward.

Mark's distinction between unclean spirit and holy spirit probably derived from the Levitical differentiation between clean and unclean. Lev. 10:10 generalizes that "you are to distinguish between the holy and the common, and between the unclean and the clean." The parallels, holy with clean and common with unclean, are consistent with Mark's general position that the opposite of unclean spirit is holy spirit. "Unclean spirit" in that sense contains a potential pun which Mark implied but never made explicit: those who condemn others as "unclean" because of superficial physical conditions are themselves people of "unclean spirit" in a far deeper sense.

The Paralytic Who Refused to Be Forgiven: Mk. 2.1-12

The leper incident ended with Jesus trapped into becoming a mass healer once more. He no longer had reason to stay out of Capernaum, the city from which he had departed because its residents wanted medical miracles instead of preaching. Upon returning to Capernaum, Jesus is inside a house offering forgiveness to a crowd so dense that no one can enter. Jesus' appearance at this symbolic site of the beginning of the gospel leads the reader to expect something new to commence. From this basic situation, Mark midrashically developed a compelling story from a rich complex of source material.

Four men, aware that Jesus' message now includes forgiveness, carry a man with a paralyzed leg to the house where Jesus is preaching and cut a hole in the roof[3] in order to lower the man into Jesus' presence, thus at least implicitly asking that the paralysis be healed. Their request is to be seen in the context of a tradition that people with sin-hardened hearts are stiff-necked; i.e., they are paralytics. Old Testament passages such as the following are in the background: "I have seen this people, and behold, it is a stiff-necked people; now therefore let me alone, that my wrath may burn hot against them" (Exod. 32.9-10); "O Lord, let the Lord, I pray thee, go in the midst of us, though it is a stiff-necked people; and pardon our iniquity and our sin, and take us for thy inheritance" (Exod. 34.9); "Zedekiah stiffened his neck and hardened his heart against turning to the Lord" (2 Chron. 36.13); "O Lord, why does thou make us err from thy ways, and harden our heart, so that we fear thee not?" (Isa. 63.17); "They did not listen to me, or incline their ear, but stiffened their neck" (Jer. 7.25). Spiritual paralysis, by implication, causes physical paralysis. Thus the cure for physical paralysis is forgiveness of sins. This is in accord with the broad connection between forgiveness and healing of disease (as in Isa. 33.24; 58.7-8), with the logic of Levitical cleansing of lepers, in which a sin offering is part of the cure, and with Deut. 7.12-15 which argues that God will take away "all sickness" and inflict "none of the evil diseases of Egypt" upon those who "hearken to these ordinances."

The plea for physical cure of paralysis trivializes Jesus' offer of forgiveness by substituting the restoration of a crippled leg for the healing of hardened hearts. The text indicates that Jesus says "You are forgiven" to the paralytic because Jesus sees the faith of the four friends who had brought him. By believing that Jesus could make the paralyzed leg well, they must also have believed that the man was forgivable. Jesus assumes, rightly or wrongly, that they believe the man to be forgivable, therefore that he is, in fact, forgivable. Jesus does not offer forgiveness because he sees the man's faith or because he believes that he himself can forgive sins. This midrashically develops Paul's significant insight in 2 Cor. 2.10-11 that "any one whom you forgive, I also forgive. What I have forgiven, if I have forgiven anything, has been for your sake in the presence of Christ, to keep Satan from gaining the advantage over us; for we are not ignorant of his designs." The author of the Gospel of John midrashically converted Paul's statement to one addressed to the disciples alone: "If you forgive the sins of any, they are forgiven; if you retain the sins of any, they are retained" (Jn. 20.23). John's interpretation suggests the possibility that Mark's "four men" who believed the paralytic could be forgiven were intended by Mark to symbolize the four disciples whom Jesus had called prior to that time. Their subsequent failure to understand Jesus is consistent with an act which devalues forgiveness as if it were no more than the cure of paralyzed limbs. Furthermore, the books associated with the names of Peter, James/Jacob, and John accepted the authority of the Torah from which Mark midrashically developed the story.

Scribes in the audience, "professional exponents and teachers of the law in post-exilic Judaism,"[4] are said to criticize Jesus silently in their hearts. This continues the motif of hardened hearts in a new way, like counterpoint in a symphony. Jesus, in his own spirit, hears their unvoiced accusation. His doing so is not dependent upon magical mind reading; instead, he understands correctly that from their vantage point he is guilty of blasphemy, a death penalty offense, by claiming to have forgiven a man's sins. Their position is that God alone can forgive sins, usually in response to an offering and priestly intermediation. No particular Mosaic law says that only God can forgive sins and that forgiveness proffered by a human being is blasphemous, but the story relies upon scribal acceptance of such a view.[5]

The death penalty for blasphemy in general is based on a law of Moses which states that "he who blasphemes the name of the Lord shall be put to death; all the congregation shall stone him; the sojourner as well as the native, when he blasphemes the Name, shall be put to death" (Lev. 24.13-16). The fact that this Mosaic law is from the Levi's book provides Mark an additional midrashic reason for combining Moses and Levi material.

The relationship between faith, healing, and forgiveness in the story also closely parallels the admonition in Jas./Jac. 5.14-15: "Is any among you sick? Let him call for the *elders* of the church[6], and let them pray *over him*, anointing him with oil in the name of the Lord; and the *prayer of faith will save the sick man,* and the Lord will *raise him up*; and if he has committed sins, *he will be forgiven*." It is not clear whether Mark intended that the elders of James/Jacob be the four whose faith caused the man to be forgiven or the scribes who should have prayed for healing but object because of their legalism. In two of Jesus' later passion predictions (Mk. 8.31 and 10.33), elders, priests, and scribes are linked together as his opponents.

Jesus' reply to the unspoken criticism extends both Moses and Elijah midrashic motifs. He perceives in his spirit that it is an unwritten law of Moses, not just contemporary interpreters of such a law, which accuses him of blasphemy, a crime which could lead to his execution. The death penalty prescribed in the laws of Moses is midrashically resignified for Jesus as the second half of Elijah's temptation: "I, even I only, am left; and *they seek my life to take it away*" (1 Kgs. 19.14). By combining Elijah with Moses, Mark's Jesus sees that believers in the law of Moses are the agents seeking his death. Blasphemy is the "religious crime" later alleged by the scribes and others who condemn Jesus to die. Here is a Markan paradox which speaks to the depth of the author's insights: blasphemy will be the accusation which will lead to Jesus' voluntary death, but in Mk. 2, when Jesus voluntarily substantiates the accusation by "proving" that he has forgiven sin, this is a temptation. The temptation dimension is highlighted by Jesus *immediately* replying to the scribes: "Which is easier, to say to the paralytic, 'Your sins are forgiven,' or to say, 'Rise, take up your pallet and walk'? But that you may know that the Son of man has authority on earth to forgive sins"—he said to the paralytic—'I say to you, rise, take up your pallet, and go home'" (Mk. 2.9-11). Healing the leg is tantamount to forgiving the paralytic and is thus a capital crime. It is a conscious death-inviting act on Jesus' part. In the process, however, he is prevailed upon to be satisfied with the lesser good of healing a paralyzed leg without healing a paralyzed heart. The lame man becomes almost a side issue as the focus shifts to the hardened hearts of the scribes and Jesus' temptation to respond to them on their level.

The assertion that Jesus perceives in his spirit the death penalty consequences of human forgiveness in the context of religious legalism reveals an additional layer of interpretation for the story. The sequence of the accounts of the leper and the paralytic, with the Torah position in each that healing sin is tantamount to healing physical ailments, leads to probability that the root issue in both is Jesus' inner confrontation with the scriptural tradition rather than with particular religious leaders involved. Mark intended the surface stories to do no more than point to a radical discontinuity between religion based on a legal code[7] which declares certain people to be inherently "unclean" and which rejects forgiveness by human beings as blasphemous, and Mark's religion which, though not yet defined, would center around voluntary death. Jesus is "tempted" by the previously almost unthinkable heresy of setting his own human authority against laws of the sacred Torah. Paul interpreted Christ as "the end of the law, that every one who has faith may be justified" (Rom. 10.4). The death penalty consequence of disobeying all the laws is consistent with the generalization in Gal. 3.13: "He took upon himself the curse of the law." Paul also held that "love does no wrong to a neighbor; therefore love is the fulfilling of the law" (Rom. 13.10), and asks rhetorically, "Having begun with the Spirit, are you now ending with the flesh?" "Does he who supplies the Spirit to you and works miracles among you do so by works of the law or by hearing with faith" (Gal. 3.3-5)? The meaning of the latter passage is so similar to that of Mark's man-through-the-roof story that it may have been the original source from which Mark was doing midrash. Jesus' temptation is that faith which ought to have climaxed in spiritual forgiveness is perverted into fleshly healing, in the face of accusations about violating the law.

By shifting the source of the temptation to Jesus' own spirit, Mark demythologized[8] his own previous accounts of unclean spirits. Myth generally is "the narrative embodiment of an idea."[9] The term "myth," as it relates to Mark, refers to a miracle story involving the supernatural and containing a kernel of truth. Demythologizing saves the essential meaning from the original story and discards the supernatural framework. Remythologizing expresses the truth in the form of a new story appropriate to a new time. Twentieth century myths without supernatural characters or miracles in their story lines can equally be de- and re-mythologized. In Mark's myth, temptation comes from Satan or unclean spirits. Mark's demythologization makes it plain that Jesus was tempted in his own spirit, not by supernatural spirits external to himself. Mark took the idea of temptation from the mythic form of stories about unclean spirits, and retold it in a new story form, the story of Jesus being tempted in his own spirit to assess the lethal quality of the scribal devotion to religious legalism and to resist it with a show of authority.

Jesus' struggle is characterized by the confusion about the title "son of man," which he uses for the first time in his response to the scribes and was to use many times later. The title is interpreted variously to mean either a divine figure, as in Dan. 7, or a human being, as in Ezekiel. The importance of "son of man" for contemporary New Testament scholarship is epitomized by the fact that when Perrin, in his *Modern Pilgrimage*, collected his seven best essays for republication, three of them dealt with "son of man" issues. In a note to one, he listed Fuller, Higgins, Hahn, Todt, Vielhauer, and Schweizer as authors on the subject with whom he disagreed.[10] In the postscript to that essay he wrote:

> This remains the most comprehensive statement of my views on the Son of Man sayings in the synoptic tradition.... What is significant about the essay to me in retrospect is the fact that even though I set out to discuss the Son of Man sayings in the synoptic tradition I found myself inevitably discussing the Son of Man in ...the Gospel of Mark. I say "inevitably discussing" because it is my conclusion that the evangelist Mark is so overwhelming a figure in the development of the Christology associated with Son of Man in the New Testament that wherever one begins it is not long before one is talking about him. There is to me an aura of inevitability about the fact that I began by investigating the Son of Man in the synoptic tradition and ended by attempting an interpretation of the Gospel of Mark.[11]

Perrin consistently uses "Son of Man" to indicate that Mark's title corresponded midrashically to the supernatural figure in Dan. 7.13. Perrin is convinced that Mark always meant the same thing each time he referred to Jesus as a son of man. Since Son of Man in Mk. 13 is clearly a supernatural figure on the clouds of heaven, therefore, Perrin argues, any son of man passage always refers to a supernatural figure. That conclusion is wrong on three grounds. The first is that Mark was capable of demythologizing, having already done so by shifting temptation from unclean spirits to Jesus' own spirit. The second is that there is no reason why any author cannot use a variety of meanings when repeating an important literary motif. A reference *may* always mean the same thing, but that is to be determined from the context of the writing and not arbitrarily by some external standard. The third and most important reason that "son of man" does not always refer to a supernatural figure is that this story demands that "son of man" is the opposite of "God."

The issue in Mark's story is whether only God can forgive sins, or whether human beings also can. From a Mosaic point of view, a claim by any human being that he or she is divine would be blasphemous but that is not the issue here. Early in Mark's story, Jesus forgives the man on the basis of the faith of the four stretcher-bearers. Later he holds it to be important that "you may know that the son of man has authority on earth to forgive sins" (Mk. 2.10). Jesus does not imply that "I have authority to forgive sin," but that any human being has such authority. "Son of man" in that reading should be read as an idiomatic way of referring to human beings, as it often is in the Old Testament. In Ezekiel, the prophet is addressed as "son of man" ninety-one times. In other Old Testament passages "son of man" is a euphemism for a person. Mark was not obviously relying on any particular passage, but the key point is that he was not limited to Daniel as his midrashic source.

Mark's advocacy of the possibility of direct human forgiveness, implicit here, is to be made fully explicit in Mk. 11.24-25. The idea threatens the entire cultic temple apparatus, the burnt offerings, the gifts to the temple, the priestly mediation, etc., upon which the priests make their living. The possibility of direct human forgiveness challenges the need for a temple altogether. Priests and their more legalistic supporters have good reason to seek Jesus' death. Mark is likely to have found the germs of his idea in Jas./Jac. 5.15-16, 1 Jn. 5.15-17, and 2 Cor. 2.10. Detailed commentary on these passages will accompany Mk. 11.24-25, where the idea is fully developed.

Mark's treatment of the healing of paralysis brings again to attention his consistent practice of relating types of miracles to types of spiritual ideals. In the Elijah unit about the authoritative demand for repentance, the miracle type was authoritative healing of diseases in general and leprosy in particular. In the Moses-Levi unit about forgiveness, the miraculous counterpart is the healing of paralysis. This type of miracle will occur a second time in the Moses-Levi unit and then never again in Mark. The point is that Jesus was not miraculous in a miscellaneous way, as all of the Old Testament miracle-workers had been. His miracles were not intended in Mark as positive evidences of supernatural power. Instead, in Mark but not in the other Gospels, each is a trivialized version of a spiritual ideal, a lesser potentiality inherent in the nature of a greater value. Each miracle account is a measure of the inadequacy of a spiritual motif which Mark uses the medium of Jesus' career to explore.

The similarities to and differences from Mark's Elijah unit are intriguing. In both, a spiritual ideal is rejected by the masses and is misunderstood as a related type of physical healing. The crowds earlier had praised Jesus for his authoritativeness; now Jesus himself claims authority. Temptation earlier had come from unclean spirits; now it comes in Jesus' own spirit. The crowds earlier had praised Jesus when he acted authoritatively; now, however, they praise God when Jesus claims authority. When "immediately" was earlier used twice in a story, the first one was the equivalent of "as soon as," and the second indicated temptation; now that order is reversed: Jesus first temptatively (immediately) perceives in his heart; then the healed man takes up his pallet as soon as (immediately) he is healed. The shifts of meaning indicated in this paragraph can be read as development of a literary motif. It is equally appropriate to see it as Mark doing midrash on his own earlier Elijah section in the same way that he does on sacred literature written by already accepted authors. This style characteristic continues throughout the Gospel of Mark.

The Calling of Levi, the Son of Alphaeus: Mk. 2.13-14

Jesus calls a fifth follower, Levi, on the shore of the Sea of Galilee. The shoreline was for Mark the dividing line between identification with "Jews" and "Gentiles." Levi, by virtue of his name is a member of the tribe of Levi and hence a Jewish priest. The narrative, however, depicts him as "sitting at the tax office," presumably as a tax collector for the Gentile Romans. The ignobility of the occupation is assumed in Mark's subsequent identification of tax collectors with sinners.

In Num. 3, the tribe of Levi is set aside to be priests. Malachi ignored the tradition that Levites were servant-class priests subordinate to the Aaronic priesthood. Malachi's priests could achieve reconciliation to God by following the example of the original Levi, a wise and righteous man who offered proper sacrifices. By calling any man named Levi, Jesus midrashically enlists that entire tradition, but by calling a particular Levi who had given up priestly functions to collect Roman taxes, Jesus violates that tradition in a significant way. To emphasize the point, this Levi's father, Alphaeus, had been Hellenized at least to the point of having a Greek name. J. M. Morris identifies the name as "purely Greek."[12] J. C. Swaim says that Alphaeus is the Greek transliteration of the Hebrew "Chalphi," a name used in 1 Macc. 11.70. Chalphi means "The Designation Given to a Child Thought of As a Substitute for One Lost."[13] That etymology is so relevant to Mark's only other reference to Alphaeus, in the list of names of the twelve, that it must have been intended by Mark. In the present context the midrash seems to imply that Levi is like a lost child in the world of the Hellenized Levites, and that Jesus accepts him in spite of his lapse. Mark's context hints that calling a Levite who had become a tax collector is in itself an act of forgiveness. Thus were the roles reversed. A Levite, who should have facilitated forgiveness for others, is himself the one forgiven.

The calling of Levi shows Mark's subtle genius in doing midrash. The narratives preceding and following the call both involve Jesus' violation of capital punishment laws, one for blasphemy, the next for sabbath violation. The clearest statement of the penalty of execution for each comes from Leviticus, the book of Levi. Jesus does not merely call a fifth disciple who happens to be a controversial priest; he voluntarily acts so as to be criticized by the legalistic tradition associated with the name Levi which will lead to a death penalty being imposed upon him. All other pericopes in the Levi-Moses unit midrashically involve Jesus' rejection of legalistic interpretations of the Torah. Had that been Mark's only concern, he could have created an incident in which Jesus criticized or separated himself from someone named Levi. By calling a Levi, Jesus sets in motion for himself the very traditional religious way in which one who was to be reconciled to the Father by voluntarily yielding his life would do so. He would be executed because he stood for a good different from that of Levitical scripture.

Levi lives on the Jewish-Gentile borderline, first by virtue of his father with a Hellenized name in contrast to his Levitical ancestry, and second by virtue of his occupation as a Roman tax collector although he is by birth a priest. It is thus appropriate that he is called to be a disciple on the theological-geography dividing line between Judaism and the Gentiles. By calling Levi, Jesus moves again to that borderline, but has not yet crossed it to the Gentile side.

Eating With Tax Collectors and Sinners: Mk. 2.15-17

Mark indicated that "scribes of the Pharisees" criticize Jesus for eating with tax collectors and sinners. No Old Testament law forbids eating with sinners, although Paul strongly recommended against the practice:

> I wrote to you in my letter not to associate with immoral men; not at all meaning the immoral of this world,

> or the greedy and robbers, or idolaters, since then you would need to go out of the world. But rather I wrote to you not to associate with anyone who bears the name of brother if he is guilty of immorality or greed, or is an idolater, reviler, drunkard, or robber—*not even to eat with such a one* (1 Cor. 5.9-11).

Mark's attribution to the Pharisees of an even more sweeping rule against eating with sinners may indicate that he knew that some Pharisees of his time actually had such a rule, or he may have midrashically created the Pharisaic legalism out of the passage from Paul. Another possibility is that the ban against eating with sinners and Gentile tax collectors applied because Jews assumed that they would not serve kosher food or would serve food that had been offered in prayer to idols. In Dan. 1.8, Daniel would not defile himself with the king's food and wine; in Joseph and Aseneth 7.1 and 8.5, Joseph ate at a separate table; in Jubilees 12.16, Abraham instructs Jacob, "Keep yourself separate from the nations, and do not eat with them." Mark's story of eating with sinners and tax collectors combines the legalism attributed to the scribes in the account of the paralytic with the calling of a tax collector Levi.

Jesus' reply to the accusation that he eats with sinners corroborates his earlier decision to preach rather than to be a physician, although he now uses the language of being a physician to souls rather than to bodies. He announces that sinners, not the physically ill, need a physician because true healing is healing of sin. That imagery is found in the prophets. Jeremiah promises that God will heal the faithlessness of "faithless sons" (Jer. 3.22) but questions why there is "no physician" in Gilead to restore "the health of the daughter of my people" (Jer. 8.22). Hosea equates healing "their faithlessness" and loving "them freely" (Hos. 14.4). Isaiah says that God has seen Israel backsliding but will heal him (Isa. 57.17-18). The Isaiah source is particularly relevant because the topic of fasting follows in both Isaiah and Mark. Isaiah distinguished between fasting as abstinence from eating and fasting as changing one's behavior:

> Is not this the fast that I [God] choose: to loose the bonds of wickedness, to undo the thongs of the yoke, to let the oppressed go free, and to break every yoke? Is it not to share your bread with the hungry, and bring the homeless poor into your house; when you see the naked, to cover him, and not to hide yourself from your own flesh?" Then "your healing shall spring up speedily (Isa. 58.5-8).

Mark's preference for Jesus as a physician to sinners rather than to bodies midrashically follows the pattern of Isaiah's healing for persons who fast in the profound ways preferred by God. In Jer. 7-8, people need a physician because they oppress the alien, the fatherless, and the widow; steal; commit murder and adultery; lie; shed innocent blood; and worship false gods.

Why Not Fast? Mk. 2.18-22

Jesus does not require his disciples to fast, as did John the Baptizer and the Pharisees. The implied presumption is that the reference is to abstinence-fasting only. This is the first of several incidents in which Mark showed Jesus as being opposed to Judaism's external rituals in contrast to the more spiritual version of Judaism available in the great prophets. The strongest midrashic source for this is Zech. 7, in which fasting is contrasted with the tradition of the prophets to "render true judgment, show kindness and mercy each to his brother, do not oppress the widow, the fatherless, the sojourner, or the poor." In Mark's story, Jesus gives two detailed reasons why his disciples should not be expected to fast. First, Jesus portrays himself as a bridegroom still present and argues that fasting is inappropriate in the presence of the bridegroom; therefore his disciples ought not to fast. Mark may have adopted the "bridegroom" imagery from Exod. 4.25, in which Zipporah circumcises Moses' son and calls Moses "a bridegroom of blood,"[14] but he developed it from two passages in Jeremiah which refer to the killing or capturing of bridegrooms. Both Jer. 7.34 and 25.10 speak of banishing "the voice of mirth and the voice of gladness, the voice of the bridegroom and the voice of the bride." A contextual argument can be made for Mark's use of Jer. 7.34 because Mark found in Jer. 7-8 many midrashic sources: the temple as "a den of robbers" (7.11), "the false pen of the scribes" (8.8), sinners who have "stiffened their neck" (7.26), no "figs on the fig tree" (8.13), the lack of a physician to restore the health of the people (8.22) "the valley of the son of Hinnom [Gehenna]" (7.31,), and defiling "abominations in the house which is called by my name" (7.30). Each detail from Jeremiah 7-8 has a fairly precise parallel in Mark, four of them in the Moses-Levi section.

The tone of the passage in Mk. 2.19-20 which analogizes Jesus to a bridegroom is at least potentially blasphemous. In Jer. 31.32, God is a husband; in Jer. 2.1, Israel is God's bride; and in Jer. 3.1, Israel has played harlot to her husband God. Assuming that Mark was aware of all of Jeremiah, it is difficult to escape the conclusion that Mark was here midrashically portraying Jesus as analogous to God, the bridegroom whose presence should be celebrated with feasting rather than fasting. This would fit the tone of some late Jewish texts in which the Messiah or awaited one is referred to as God. The Testament of Abraham refers to God's "great and glorious coming" (13.6); the Testament of Simeon predicts that the Lord will "appear on earth as man," taking a body, eating, and saving men (6.5, 7). For Mark's Jesus to perceive himself as God would be another version of the temptation of Elijah's "I, only I" and the unclean spirits' "You are the Holy One of God." Mark does not develop this as a theme elsewhere.

The second reason why Jesus' followers ought not to fast is suggested by Jesus' use of the analogies of new patches on old cloth and new wine in old wineskins to argue that something new has come, making fasting inappropriate altogether. Read out of context, Mark was simply arguing that Jesus brings a new spiritual reality which can no longer fit into the hardened mold of old Mosaic regulations, in this instance the rules about fasting. In context, the analogies may also be a commentary on the bridegroom blasphemy. The law defining blasphemy may be for Mark another example of weakened cloth or brittle skins, unfit for use in the new time. A possible source for one analogy is Josh. 9.4-5, in which Hivites use "wineskins, worn-out and torn and mended, with worn-out, patched sandals on their feet, and worn-out clothes" to deceive Joshua. Jesus in Mark may also have adapted the meaning of Lev. 19.19 to support his analogy of new patches on old cloth: "Nor shall there come upon you a garment of cloth made of two kinds of stuff." These texts seem to provide no help in the interpretation.

Violation of the Sabbath By the Disciples: Mk. 2.23-27

Mark next presented two consecutive stories about violations of the sabbath, the first by the disciples, the second by Jesus himself. Mark's sequence continues to parallel that of Isa. 57-58, in which a section on sabbath observance follows sections on healing of sin and the two types of fasting. After defining an acceptable fast as more than abstinence, the prophet suggested that sabbath observance was also more than abstaining from work. "Going your own ways, or seeking your own pleasure, or talking idly" were held to violate calling "the sabbath a delight and the holy day of the Lord honorable" (Isa. 58.13). Isaiah did not specify what he wanted people to do on the sabbath, but it is clear that he was dissatisfied both with pleasure-seeking and merely not working. Mark put content into Isaiah's principle in two stories of sabbath violation.

In the first, the disciples pluck kernels of grain and chew them as they walk through a field. Four Mosaic law passages establish the rule which is at issue: "When you go into your neighbor's vineyard, you may eat your fill of the grapes, as many as you wish, but you shall not put any into your vessel. When you go into your neighbor's standing grain, you may pluck the ears with your hand, but you shall not put a sickle to your neighbor's standing grain" (Deut. 23.24-25); "Six days shall you gather food; but on the seventh day, which is a sabbath, there will be none" (Exod. 16.26 and elsewhere); "Six days you shall do your work, but on the seventh day you shall rest; that your ox and your ass may rest, and the son of your bondmaid, and the alien, may be refreshed" (Exod. 23.12); "The seventh day is a sabbath to the Lord your God; in it you shall not do any work, you, or your son, or your daughter, or your manservant, or your maidservant, or your ox, or your ass, or any of your cattle, or the sojourner who is within your gates, that your manservant and your maidservant may rest as well as the rest of you" (Deut. 5.14).

Deuteronomy, however, goes well beyond the interpretation of "sabbath" in 5.14. Persons are commanded to keep the sabbath in order to remember that "you were a servant in the land of Egypt, and the Lord your God brought you out thence" (5.15). The same remembrance justifies releasing slaves in the seventh year, celebrating Passover with unleavened bread ("the bread of affliction") for seven days, and celebrating the Feast of Booths for seven days at the end of seven weeks (Deut. 15-16). At the end of the description of the three festivals is the telling line: "Justice, and only justice, you shall follow" (Deut. 16.20). The issue between Jesus and the scribes and Pharisees continues a debate which is integral to the Old Testament Torah and prophets. As is true in all of Mark, the issue is not "Christian" vs. "Jewish," but the differences within Judaism.

The disciples by gathering a handful of food (Mk. 2.23) are "working" on the sabbath; the Pharisees challenge Jesus to justify it. Jesus rationalizes that David and his soldiers once ate what is lawful for priests alone to eat. Therefore Jesus' disciples also can break a law. If the sense of the story is limited to the implied assertion by Jesus that only he and David are superior to the law of God, this would be a counterpoint on the "I, only I" temptation. Jesus, however, argues that David had a spiritually valid reason for sabbath violation: he "was in need and was hungry, he and those who were with him" (2.25). Mark midrashically generalized from that example that "the sabbath was made for man, not man for the sabbath. So the son of man is lord even of the sabbath." Translated that way, Jesus clearly abrogates sabbath observance in the name of that which is human and humane, and declares people in general to be lords of the sabbath. RSV considerably blunts the point by capitalizing "Son of man" to denote a supernatural Jesus. At issue is the apparent difference between the first and second sentences of Jesus' statement. The first says that the needs of human beings are more important than sabbath observance. The second, in the RSV translation, is made to say the opposite, that Jesus himself is Lord of the sabbath by virtue of his supernatural identity. Here is the "I, only I" temptation in a new form. Both translations would infuriate Mark's Pharisees and priests. This was now the second time Jesus had waved a red flag at them, this time by insisting that people are lords of the sabbath or that Jesus, the supernatural Son of man, is lord of the sabbath. In the man-through-the-roof pericope, Jesus had asserted that human beings have the power to forgive which had traditionally been reserved for God alone. In the grainfield episode he argues that the purpose of sabbath observance is to serve human beings, not to shackle them.

Mark's midrashic substitution of Abiathar for Ahimelech as priest in the story (1 Sam. 21) is consistent with the variety of ways

Ahimelech is treated in scripture. In 1 Sam. 21 he is son of Ahitub and father of Abiathar. In 2 Sam. 8.17, 1 Chr. 18.16, and 1 Chr. 24.6, he is Abiathar's son. In 1 Sam. 14.3, 18, 1 Kgs. 4.3, and 1 Chron. 8.7, his name is replaced by Ahijah ("Brother of Yahweh"[15]), son of Ahitub. Given the range of traditions, Mark may have chosen Abiathar ("Father God Gives Abundantly"[16]) because the name would point to God's provision for people's needs. Ahimelech ("The Brother God Rules," "My Brother Is King,"[17] or "Brother of Melek"[18], a Canaanitic deity) would not add to the themes developed in Mark's text. Another possible reason for the name change is Mark's concern that Ahimelech's act of helping David by giving him bread (and a sword) resulted in his own death. Ahimelech's son Abiathar escapes the slaughter of innocent priests and their families and becomes David's loyal priest, stepping into his father's shoes.

In Mark's Levi section Jesus engages in actions which could result in his execution and which do result in the Pharisees and Herodians plotting to kill him. The story of Ahimelech helping David models violation of a law by a righteous person with good intentions, with the result being martyrdom. Ahimelech transforms and expands the traditional meaning of "holy" in order to provide "holy bread" to David on a special journey; he does so innocently, thinking that David is loyal to King Saul. David's hunger and what Ahimelech believes to be the special nature of David's journey justify the expanded use of holy bread. Ahimelech's actions violate Exod. 29.31-34 and Lev. 8.31-32, in which the bread of the Presence is reserved for priests alone, with the remainder to be burned. Lev. 22.10 is specifically violated: "An outsider shall not eat of a holy thing. A sojourner of the priest's or a hired servant shall not eat of a holy thing." In asking David whether he and his men have kept themselves away from women, Ahimelech observes part of the law, according to which any Levite who approaches holy things while unclean shall be cut off from God's presence. In a sense, Ahimelech also observes the commandment in Deut. 26.12-14, according to which "the tithe of your produce," "the sacred portion," is to be "given to the Levite, *the sojourner*, the fatherless, and the widow." In all those respects, it seems that Mark should have used the name Ahimelech as model.

Violation of the Sabbath By Jesus Himself: Mk. 3.1-6

The Pharisees know that Jesus' disciples had committed a death penalty offense by working on the sabbath, but they are eager to enforce the law against Jesus rather than the disciples. They know that "whoever does any work on the sabbath shall be put to death" (Lev. 35.2) and that "everyone who profanes the sabbath shall be put to death; whoever does any work on it, that soul shall be cut off from among his people" (Exod. 31.14-15). They could not secure a conviction of Jesus for the grainfield violation because it had been in private. They need for Jesus to violate the sabbath publicly. They get their chance when a man with a withered hand is in the synagogue with Jesus. If Jesus were to heal him, he would be working on the sabbath in a death-penalty-qualified manner; if he passes up the opportunity he would have to back down from the principle he has announced. Lk. 14.5 assumes that there is a provision in the laws of Moses for handling sabbath emergencies, symbolized by rescuing an ox from a well (Deut. 22.1-4 perhaps), but this is clearly no emergency. A man with a withered hand would be glad to make an appointment to come back tomorrow for miraculous restoration of his limb.

Jesus' dilemma is that he is still the new Moses, interested in forgiveness, not a medical healer. His task to is heal hardened hearts through forgiveness, not to restore bodies to health. The Pharisees, however, do not permit him the privilege of considering the issue on that theoretical level. They want to know whether Jesus was serious on the preceding sabbath when in private he declared people to be the lords of the sabbath. Would he intentionally work on the sabbath? Note that the expectation that hardened hearts are sinfully unnecessary is significantly different from Mk. 4.12 in which it is assumed that the hearts of the crowds are permanently hardened and that only Jesus' disciples can bear proper fruit.

Mark is vague as to whether a "withered" hand is paralyzed or merely useless, as the texts quoted below imply. In some scriptural passages, limbs are withered because of sin. "Worthless shepherds who desert the flock" are punished by the withering of an arm (Zech. 11.17). The exiles in Babylon lament: "How shall we sing the Lord's song in a foreign land? If I forget you, O Jerusalem, let my right hand wither" (Ps. 137.4-5)! Simeon says that his "right hand was half withered for seven days" as punishment for trying to kill Joseph (Test. of Simeon 2.12-13). The rationale which applies to paralysis would thus apply to withered limbs: the cure is forgiveness. Jesus "does good" (Mk. 3.4) on the sabbath, while violating a rigid interpretation of the law. This good is less than forgiveness which might have led to reconciliation with the Father. The sequence of events indicates that the healed man is the lucky pawn in the game set up by the Pharisees, with the issue being whether Jesus' move would support a more or less rigid interpretation of Mosaic laws. Jesus' anger is understandable. He cures the ailment while grieving for the Pharisees' hardness of heart.

Jesus' statement "Is it lawful on the sabbath to do good or to do harm, to save life or to kill?" concerns not only the sabbath observance issue, but alludes to the Pharisees' real agenda. In the name of technical lawfulness, they can hardly wait to plot "to kill" him, apparently also on the sabbath. The Pharisees go immediately to Herodian government officials to take counsel with them about how capital punishment laws might be invoked against Jesus. Mark's midrashic source in scripture was Ps. 2.1-2: "Why do the nations conspire and the peoples plot in vain? The kings of the earth set themselves, and the rulers take counsel together, against the Lord and his anointed [messiah]." In history, the Pharisees collaborated with Herod the Great to secure his victory over the last of the Hasmoneans, who had sided with the Sadducees.

Lest the Crowds Should Crush Him: Mk. 3.7-12

Mk. 3.7-12 is the conclusion of the Elijah and Levi-Moses units in Mk. 1.9—3.12, in which Jesus has sought popular support and has found none. Following the public miracle in the synagogue the floodgates of miracle are opened once more, with people coming to Jesus now not only from Galilee, but also from Judea, Transjordan, Idumea, Tyre, and Sidon. Even borderline Jewish-Gentile crowds want physical healing rather than repentance or forgiveness. The unclean spirits are back in force, openly asking Jesus to make himself known as the one and only Son of God, and Jesus resists their temptation by "strictly ordering" them not to make him known.

The nucleus of the concluding pericope is a metaphorical decision made by Jesus on the seashore: "He told his disciples to have a boat ready for him because of the crowd, lest they should crush him; for he had healed many" (Mk. 3.9.10). The crowds could not inflict upon Jesus any physical damage if he chose to use his miracle powers to protect himself, so there must be a meaning deeper than that. The clue to the exegesis is in the strange ending of "lest they should crush him *for he had healed many.*" In both the Elijah and Levi-Moses sub-sections, Jesus has had a reconciliation agenda; the crowds have had a physical agenda, aimed at medical and "psychiatric" healing. If he gives in to what they want he can never achieve his goal. What the public desires can be achieved only if he yields to the self-definition which the unclean spirits dangle before him: to announce himself as the divine Son of man, only Holy One of God, Son of God. If he does their will, no

Father-child reconciliations will occur. Mark's midrashic source was the rhetorical question of 1 Pet. 4.4: "Do you not know that friendship with the world is enmity with God?" Getting into the boat, implied but not actually stated, is a symbolic act through which Jesus can separate himself from the crowds. Being even a few feet offshore is a symbol of leaving Israel, giving up on the Jews altogether, betting that there is nothing which he could subsequently do which would persuade them to behave so as to merit reconciliation with the Father.

The aftermath of this decision is that Jesus never again preaches to the crowds with the expectation of a positive response as a measure of his own success. He has learned that when he preaches repentance with all the authoritativeness of a new Elijah, no one repents. He has learned that when he offers forgiveness without the need for the mediating priestly rituals, no one accepts. The ideals associated with repentance and forgiveness continue to be relevant to Mark's Jesus, but the strategies for achieving reconciliation by appealing to the public as a new Elijah or a new Levi-Moses are now set aside in Mark. The midrash moves on to other models.

ENDNOTES FOR CHAPTER FOUR

[1]The Testament of Levi agrees with Malachi in praising the purity of the original Levi and criticizing the behavior of the priests in the latter days. Assuming that Kee is correct in dating this document as about 100 BCE, this would probably reflect disillusion with the corruption of the Hasmonean priesthood at that time. In The Testament, the Levites are described as "priests, high priests, scribes, and judges," much like the combination of titles used in Mark's passion predictions. The Testament follows in the tradition of 2 Isaiah in being somewhat pro-Gentile. Some of this could be Christian interpolation and must be used with caution in thinking of Mark's midrashic sources.

[2]As cited from Codex Bezae by Wilhelm Schneemelcher, *New Testament Apocrypha* (Westminster Press: Philadelphia, 1963) 89.

[3]The "hole in the roof" detail illustrates the limited range of issues with which the narrative is concerned. Mark does not address such problems as who repaired the roof or if the owner objected.

[4]Matthew Black, "Scribes," *IDB*.

[5]Two ways of reading the account of Joseph's forgiveness of his brothers in Gen. 50.15-21 relate to the possibility that human forgiveness of sin is blasphemy. The brothers beg him to forgive them and not punish them for the evil they had done. Joseph answers, "Fear not, for am I in the place of God?" (Gen. 50.19). Joseph's answer might mean, "I cannot forgive, for I am not God." Walter Bowie interprets Joseph's answer as, "Fear not, for am I in the place of God, to judge and punish at my pleasure" (*The Interpreter's Bible, Genesis*)? Gen. 45.1-8, The Test. of Simeon 4.4, The Test. of Joseph 17.2-8, and The Test. of Zebulon 8.4-5 support Bowie's interpretation.

[6]If the book of James/Jacob is early first century, the word "church" here is probably a poor translation. The Greek word "*ecclesias*" meant "gathering" or "congregation" prior to the time when it came to be used specifically for a Christian "church."

[7]The reader is asked to remember that statements such as this one by Mark are intended as a condemnation of a particular type of Judaism, not as a characterization of Judaism as a whole. Mark was writing as a Jew. Paul, Peter, James/Jacob, and John had written as Jews. The issue was within Judaism itself, among Jews, with the author specifying what were to him the worst aspects of the opposing view. Unfortunately, statements by New Testament authors which are critical of Jews, Judaism, or a party of Jews are seen by some Christians as grounds for anti-Semitism.

[8]Perrin and Duling summarize Bultmann's program of demythologizing as "the most creative and serious contemporary attempt to understand and interpret myth in the New Testament," II, 49.

[9]Perrin and Duling, II, 49.

[10]Perrin, *Modern Pilgrimage* , 57.

[11]Perrin, *Modern Pilgrimage* , 83.

[12]J. M. Morris, "Alphaeus," *IDB*..

[13]J. C. Swaim, "Chalphi," *IDB*.

[14]The LXX version of Exod. 4.25 does not use the expression "bridegroom of blood." If Mark was using Exod. 4.25 as a source, it is evidence that he could quote either from the LXX or the Masoretic text, either making his own translation or following that of someone else.

[15]F. T. Schumacher, "Ahijah," *IDB*.

[16]R. W. Corney, "Abiathar," *IDB*.

[17]R. W. Corney, "Ahimelech," *IDB*.

[18]F. T. Schumacher, "Ahijah," *IDB*.

CHAPTER FIVE

INTRODUCTION TO MIDRASH ON THE TWELVE AS THE MESSIAH

After demonstrating that Jewish crowds would neither repent nor accept forgiveness from a messiah figure modelled after Elijah and Levi-Moses, Mark turned to the possibility that a group messiah might be able to achieve what Jesus as an individual messiah had not. Toward that end, Mark portrayed Jesus as calling twelve men to work to achieve reconciliation, first as a New Israel and then as the Suffering Servant messiah. Mark did not use either of the terms "New Israel" or "Suffering Servant," but both concepts are implicit in Mark's logic. Mk. 3.13-34 serves as an introduction for both possibilities, but focuses more on the new Israel than on Suffering Servant. Mark used several midrashic sources, centered around Moses naming twelve tribes as the original Israel. The idea of a New Israel comes from the major prophets. Mark overtly combined Elijah and Moses models for the first time, using details not previously reformulated in the separate Elijah and Levi-Moses units. The books of James/Jacob, 1 Peter, and 1 John become increasingly significant as sources for developing a picture of the three leading disciples in particular and the Twelve in general.

The entire unit about the Twelve, 3.13—7.30, is divided into three chapters because of its length. The first includes the calling of the Twelve and sets the problem which Jesus faced in relating to them. The second and third explore, respectively, the possible solutions based on "New Israel" and "Suffering Servant" midrash.

Calling the Twelve to be the New Israel: Mk. 3.13-19

The success or failure of Jesus' previous career had been subject to the vagaries of the Jewish masses in Galilee. Now he calls to himself "those whom he desired!" He names twelve men and assigns them three initial tasks: "to be with him," "to be sent out to preach," and to "have authority to cast out demons," i.e., to resist temptation (Mk 3.14-15). It is strange to think of "being with him" as a job to do, but in Mark's grammar the clause is coordinate to preaching and having authority over demons. Jesus will on several subsequent occasions in Mark call the Twelve or the crowds to be with him. Ultimately the Twelve will be expected to "be with" Jesus in the time of his agony in Gethsemane and at his voluntary death, and they will betray him, deny him, and abandon him. Their long term failure suggests that they are likely to fail in their short term work of preaching and resisting temptation. Those two tasks are midrashically identified with Elijah and Elisha, partly because preaching is the Elijah strategy, partly because a tempting spirit first confronted Jesus in the synagogue in an Elijah context, but mostly because of the already established motif of Elisha succeeding Elijah when he failed. The Elijah motif is heightened by the fact that Jesus "went up into the hills" to name the Twelve. Elijah's original calling of Elisha, in 1 Kgs. 19, had followed Elijah's trip to Mt. Horeb. The Twelve are, in effect, asked to complete Jesus' unsuccessful preaching career. They are expected to be able to do so without authoritative preaching being temptative for them, even though it had been for Jesus. Jesus assumes that listeners will respond positively to the Twelve. The Twelve would then be redefined fishers of men, recruiters now rather than a posse seeking sinners for punishment.

Technically, the Twelve are called to be "apostles," those sent to deliver a message, not "disciples," students. Mark and the later evangelists were usually careful in distinguishing between the two terms. As long as Jesus expects the Twelve to succeed they are "apostles"; only when their failure is accepted by Jesus does he revert to calling them disciples, those who have more to learn before they can become apostles. The implicit reason for expecting assistants to succeed is that the crowds would respond to the message of those who are not identified in the public mind as the miraculous Elijah. Mark's logic divided Elijah as midrashic model into the preacher (from Malachi) and the miracle-working prophet tempted to think of himself as the only Holy One (from I Kings). This separation by Mark was brilliant because it set up a test as to whether the failure of the Elijah model was internal to Jesus or whether it was in the nature of the model.

Moses, on Mt. Horeb, had faced a comparable problem in needing assistants to help him. He had complained to the multitudes, "How can I bear alone the weight and burden of you and your strife? Choose wise, understanding, and experienced men, according to your tribes ['twelve men, one for each tribe'], and I will appoint them as your heads" (Deut. 1.12-13, 23). He gave the twelve authority as commanders of hundreds and fifties, somewhat as the disciples were to be at the feeding of the 5,000 (Deut. 1.15).

In order to create a midrashic New Israel, Jesus had to call exactly twelve followers according to the Mosaic pattern for identifying the original twelve tribes of Israel (Num. 1). The number is important because Israel is defined as "twelve tribes." The tribes were named generally for the sons of Jacob, with the exceptions of Levi and Joseph who were not appointed as namesakes for a tribe in the twelve. Levi's descendants, priests, were to be part of Israel but not one of the twelve tribes. Joseph was doubly represented through two sons, Manasseh and Ephraim, each of whom headed a tribe, bringing the total back to twelve and rewarding Joseph for having saved Jacob's family from famine. Israel was twelve minus one plus one, twelve minus Levi plus the second son of Joseph.[1] All of the tribes were named for sons or grandsons of Jacob, justifying their identification with the names "Jacob" and "Israel."

Mark placed special emphasis on the "minus Levi" part of the model. Prior to calling the Twelve, Jesus had five disciples, one of them Levi son of Alphaeus. Levi, the only one of the five omitted from the Twelve,[2] was replaced by James/Jacob, another son of Alphaeus. J. M. Morris states that Alphaeus is "a purely Greek name, one of many such names used by first-century Jews in Palestine."[3] J. C. Swaim disagrees, identifying Alphaeus with Chalphi and the etymology "the designation given to a child thought of as a substitute for one lost."[4] The Hebrew for Alphaeus and for Chalphi differs slightly, but Mark's context suggests that he equated them as sound-alikes. Thus "Jacob son of Alphaeus" can be read to mean "he who supplants his brother," son of "a child thought of as a substitute for one lost." That is too much of a coincidence to have been merely accidental. Mark must have intended the double emphasis on supplanting, buttressed as it was by the biblical fact that Levi was replaced in the naming of the twelve tribes and the Markan fact that Levi son of Alphaeus was replaced by his brother James/Jacob in the naming of the twelve disciples. Swaim's identification of Alphaeus with Chalphi calls attention to 1 Macc. 11.70 as Mark's midrashic source for Levi, son of Alphaeus. It reads: "All they that were of *Jonathan*'s side fled; not one of them was left, except *Mattathias* the son of Absalom, and *Judas* the son of *Chalphi*, captains of the forces." The three other names are also relevant to Mark's list, as will be seen below in examining the etymologies of names of the Twelve. That may be merely coincidence, but as the number of such parallels grows, so does the probability of Mark's intentionality in relating the twelve to the Maccabean tradition. The Maccabees were for many the embodiment of a "New Israel."

Additional midrashic sources for the Twelve substantiate the probability that Mark viewed them as a New Israel in this portion of his Gospel. The Book of James/Jacob is addressed to "the twelve tribes in the dispersion." In this unit, Mark based his parable of the soils almost entirely on details from James/Jacob, strong evidence that Mark was relying on that book. Paul, in 1 Cor. 15.3-5, refers to Peter, to "the twelve," and to James/Jacob as early witnesses to the resurrection. The James/Jacob reference may merely personify Israel, but the Paul passage sounds as if Paul knew of a historic group of twelve men quite apart from the twelve tribes of Israel, but not necessarily twelve disciples of Jesus. One possibility is that Paul interpreted the introductions to 1 Peter and James/ Jacob midrashically. 1 Pet. 1.3 says that the exiles in the Dispersion (James/ Jacob's "twelve tribes in the dispersion") "have been born anew...through the resurrection of Jesus Christ from the dead." For a midrashically-minded author such as Paul that could have been sufficient ground for reporting an appearance to twelve. Mark almost certainly knew the book called The Testaments of the Twelve Patriarchs, in which there are many parallels to details in the gospels. Calling twelve to preach as a New Israel is midrashic on twelve patriarchs giving testimony.

There is considerable difference between the Twelve as representing the twelve original tribes of Israel and as a New Israel. In the passages which follow their calling, Mark's Jesus explores the possibility that they can be a new, remnant-like Israel bearing fruit in a manner impossible to the masses, thereby paving the way to Father-child reconciliation. The idea of a New Israel is implicit in the books of the prophets Isaiah, Jeremiah, and Ezekiel: "Behold, the former things have come to pass, and *new* things I now declare" (Isa. 42.9); "The nations shall see your vindication, and all the kings your glory; and *you shall be called by a new name* which the mouth of the Lord will give" (Isa. 62.2); "And I will give them one heart, and put a *new spirit* within them; I will take the stony heart out of their flesh and give them a heart of flesh, that they may walk in my statutes and keep my ordinances and obey them; and they shall be my people, and I will be their God" (Ezek. 11.19-20, similar to Ezek. 36.26-28); "But this is the covenant which I will make with the house of Israel after those days, says the Lord: I will put my law within them, and I will write it on their hearts; and I will be their God, and they shall be my people" (Jer. 31.33). Those same prophets also wrestled with the question as to whether all of Israel is to be redeemed or only a remnant. In this section, Mark explores the alternative of a smaller New Israel, disciplined by suffering, as predicted by the prophets in their focus on the idea of a remnant: "In that day the remnant of Israel and the survivors of the house of Jacob will no more lean upon him that smote them, but will lean upon the Lord, the Holy One of Israel, in truth. A remnant will return, the remnant of Jacob, to the mighty God. For though your people be as the sand of the sea, only a remnant of them will return" (Isa. 10.20-22); "And the surviving remnant of the house of Judah shall again take root downward, and bear fruit upward; for out of Jerusalem shall go forth a remnant, and out of Mt. Zion a band of survivors" (Isa. 37.31-32); "In those days and in that time, says the Lord, iniquity shall be sought in Israel, and there shall be none; and sin in Judah, and none shall be found; for I will pardon those I leave as a remnant" (Jer. 50.20); "Then I fell down upon my face, and cried with a loud voice, and said, 'Ah Lord God! wilt thou make a full end of the remnant of Israel?' And the word of the Lord came to me: 'I will gather you from the peoples, and assemble you out of the countries where you have been scattered, and I will give you the land of Israel'" (Ezek. 11.13-17).

Mark's midrashic concept of "New Israel" was adapted more specifically from Paul's vision of a "new creation" in which "the Israel of God" would live by a "rule" according to which neither circumcision nor uncircumcision "counts for anything" (Gal. 6.15-16). That New Israel, for Paul, would be "a remnant, chosen by grace," separated from the masses because "the elect obtained it, but the rest were hardened, as it is written [Isa. 29.10 and Deut. 29.4], 'God gave them a spirit of stupor, eyes that should not see and ears that should not hear, down to this very day'" (Rom. 11.5-8). Paul clearly combined the idea of being a new person in Christ with responsibility for carrying on a reconciling ministry. First Christ did this ministry, which was "entrusted to us" as "ambassadors" because "if any one is in Christ, he is a new creation; the old has passed away, behold, the new has come. All this is from God, who through Christ reconciled us to himself and gave us the ministry of reconciliation; that is, God was in Christ reconciling the world to himself, not counting their trespasses against them, and entrusting to us the message of reconciliation" (2 Cor. 5.17-20). Paul contended that because God "through Christ reconciled us to himself," the believer, midrashically, is also to be a reconciler. This use of midrash conforms to Le Deaut's broadening of the term to include the resignification of historical events as well as the more usual reinterpretation of a text.[5] Mark sensed the contradiction between Paul's affirmation that God has already effected reconciliation and his extrapolation that God has, therefore, entrusted "to us the message of reconciliation." Mark's midrash would ultimately opt for the human obligation in contrast to the divine accomplishment. The four original disciples who are retained as part of the twelve are probably thought of by Mark as fitting into Paul's imagery of being new men in Christ Jesus, especially for the purpose of achieving reconciliation which is Jesus' primary Markan goal. An analysis of their names as evidence of the "new person" hypothesis is presented later.

Detailed attention to the meanings of the names of the Twelve demonstrates that the names are more than incidental. For purposes of that analysis, they should be divided into two groups, the four disciples from Mk. 1.16-19 and eight new ones. The eight added names relate only to the New Israel theme, whereas the names of the four retainees should be viewed both in their relation both to the New Israel as a whole and to the new personhood of each individual, the latter because the reader has known each of them in an old way. The three chief figures among those who remain, Simon, James/Jacob, and John, are each given a surname as a way of defining each man's newness. Mark midrashically adapted surnaming from the Old Testament, in which persons are given additional names whose meaning reflects whatever significant event has occurred. For instance, after having wrestled with God, Jacob is named Israel (meaning "he who strives with God") "for you have *striven with God* and with men and have prevailed" (Gen. 32.27-28). In 2 Sam. 12.24-25, David calls his son Solomon "and *the Lord loved him* and sent a message by Nathan the prophet; so he called his name Jedidiah" (meaning "beloved of the Lord"). The Book of Isaiah is unique in using the term "surname" twice, in 45.1-4 and 44.5, with messianic implications both times: "Thus says the Lord to his anointed [messiah], to Cyrus.... 'For the sake of my servant Jacob, and Israel my chosen, I call you by your name, *I surname you*, though you do not know me'" (Isa. 45.1-4); "This one will say, 'I am the Lord's,' another will call himself by the name of Jacob, and another will write on his hand, 'The Lord's,' and *surname* himself by the name of Israel" (Isa. 44.5). Isaiah also is explicit about another Old Testament pattern of using names which express theological meanings integral to the text. "Behold, I and the children whom the Lord has given me are signs and portents in Israel from the Lord" (8.18). The name Isaiah means "God saves" or "the salvation of God." The names of the sons mean "A remnant shall return" (7.3), "God is with us" (7.14), "The spoil speeds, the prey hastes" (8.1), and "Wonderful counselor, mighty

God, everlasting father, prince of peace" (9.6). These names express the major ideas in I Isaiah.

James/Jacob and John are surnamed Boanerges. Mark's text translates Boanerges from an unknown language as "Sons of Thunder". Bratcher and Nida speculate that "the Semitic idiom [sons of thunder] means that the men thus named are characterized by a wrathful disposition, and so are like thunder."[6] Another possibility comes from J. Rendel Harris: "'Sons of thunder' is closely connected with a cult of twins."[7] Harris' suggestion fits a general twin theme in Mark. Dalman suggests a sound-alike for Boanerges meaning "sons of constant noise" or "*disturbance*." This would fit Jas./Jac. 3.16 as a model for the pericope involving John and James/Jacob in which they selfishly ask for reserved seats in glory (Mk. 10.35-45): "For where jealousy and selfish ambition exist, there will be *disorder* and every vile practice" (Jas./Jac. 3.16).[8]

Thomas, the Aramaic word for "Twin,"[9] is referred to in the Gospel of John as "Thomas called the Twin." He is followed in Mark's list by James/Jacob the son of Alphaeus. Jacob in Genesis was a twin who supplanted his brother Esau. Mark's Jacob (the second Jacob in the list) replaces Levi the son of Alphaeus ("A Child Thought of as a Substitute for One Lost"). Boanerges, if it means "Cult of Twins," would further emphasize the Jacob motif of a twin taking the place of his brother. Mark intended his frequent references to Jacob twins and supplantation of brothers to remind readers of the message in Mal. 1.2-3, that God loves his children, as proven by Jacob's supplantation of Esau.

Matthew means "Gift of God" in both Hebrew and Aramaic. Taylor says that Thaddeus is the equivalent of Theudas, a shortened form of Theodosios, Theodotos, or Theodoros ("Gift of God").[10] Along with Zebedee[11] and Matthew, Thaddeus is a third "Gift of God" in the list. Three "Gifts of God" and one "God is gracious" (John) in a list of thirteen people goes so far beyond mere coincidence that it supports the conclusion that the list is a theological statement by the author. These "Gifts of God" strengthen the possibility that Mark referred to Abiathar ("Father God Gives Abundantly") rather than Ahimelech in Mk. 2.26 in order to emphasize the significance of that name for the text.

Simon's surname Peter raises different interpretive problems. A fundamental question for understanding Mark is why the author chose the name "Simon" for the character derived from I Peter and Paul's epistles. Paul called him only Peter or Cephas, the Aramaic version of Peter. Simon is the Hellenized transliteration of Simeon, the second son of Jacob. The name (Gen. 29.3) has the meaning of Leah's lament that "because the *Lord has heard* that I am hated, he has given me this son also." In Biblical language, in general, for God "to hear" is to grant one's prayer or to function as a rescuer. Given Peter's roles in Mark, it is likely that the author intended the surname as having both positive and negative connotations. The most likely positive meaning of Peter as "Rock" would be its use in Moses' song in Deut. 32 and in an Isaiah midrash on that passage cited in 1 Pet. 2.8: "You were unmindful of the *Rock* that begot you, and you forgot the God who gave you birth" (Deut. 32.18); "How should one chase a thousand, and two put ten thousand to flight, unless their *Rock* had sold them, and the Lord had given them up?[12] For their *rock* is not as our *Rock*, even our enemies themselves being judges" (Deut. 32.30-31); "To you therefore who believe, he is precious, but for those who do not believe, 'The very stone which the builders rejected has become the head of the corner' [Ps. 118.22] , and 'a stone that will make men stumble, a *rock* that will make them fall'" (Isa. 8.14-15; 1 Pet. 2.7-8).

The etymology "God Has Heard," on its negative side, may have led Mark to depict Peter as inherently deaf-blind. A dimension of failure in the surname Peter is easy to understand because of Mark's pun on "Rock" in the "rocky soil" of the parable in Mk.

4.16-17, a prediction that Peter would fall away in the face of persecution. Mark's reason for renaming Peter as Simon could be based on The Testament of Simeon About Envy in The Testaments of the Twelve Patriarchs. In one passage, Simeon says of himself that "I became a *hardened* warrior; no venture deterred me; and I was afraid of nothing. For my *heart was hard*, my will inflexible, and my feelings without compassion" (Test. of Sim. 2.2-4). In another, he expresses anger that his brother Judah permitted Joseph to remain alive. He implies that he tried to kill Joseph, "but God restrained me and withheld from me the use of my hands; for my right *hand was half withered for seven days*; and I *repented and wept*" (Test. of Sim. 2.10-13). Joseph, by contrast, bore him no grudge and led Simeon to learn that "each of you, my beloved children, must love his brother with a good heart" (Test. of Sim. 4.4-7). The latter quotation[13] parallels 1 Pet. 1.22, "Love one another earnestly from the heart" and I John's repeated emphasis that "we should love one another" (3.11). The Testament of Simeon already connects the name Simeon with hardness, that is, with Peter the Rock, and makes Simeon worse than Judah in seeking Joseph's death, just as Simon Peter denied Jesus while Judas betrayed him by seeking to save him. Despite that, Jesus bore him no grudge. The Simeon of the Testament, whose hand was half withered for seven days, could also have been a midrashic model for hardened hearts and for the withered hand healed by Jesus on a sabbath in Mk. 3.1-5, as well as for Peter "repenting and weeping" after denying Jesus. The negative qualities of the name are heightened by an "impious Simon" in 2 Macc. 3.4-12 who betrayed the legitimate high priest to the Greek emperor. Another Simon, a high priest, was the last survivor of the five Maccabee brothers.

In addition to the biblical name "Simeon" as a midrashic base for Mark's delineation of Simon Peter, Mark also had available eighteen references to persons named "Shimei," a slightly different version of "Simeon" with identical etymology. Several Shimeis were Levites. Four were from the tribe of Benjamin. One of the latter (2 Sam. 16.6-13) threw stones (not rocks) at King David and cursed him for having caused the death of Saul. A "Simon" throwing stones may have contributed midrashically to the picture of Peter as a "rocky soil" person.

The presence of a second Simon in the list, designated as "the Cananaean," affects the whole list in several ways. Bratcher and Nida insist that the term "Cananaean" is Aramaic for "enthusiast," hence a member of the party of Zealots who were militantly rebellious against Roman rule.[14] Luke understood "Cananaean" in that way and replaced it with the appropriate Greek word for "Zealot" (6.15). W. R. Farmer translates "Cananaean" as "Zealot" or "Jealous One."[15] 1 Pet. 3.13 alludes to those "who are zealous for the right," i.e., zealots in a general sense of the term which would connect Peter and hence Simon with the title "zealot." If Mark understood "Cananaean" as "Jealous," the name would be appropriate for the pericope about James/Jacob and John when the other ten were jealously indignant at them for seeking guaranteed seats in glory above their fellow disciples. Mark could have midrashically adopted the militancy of Simon from Gen. 49.5-7, in which Jacob says of Simeon and Levi that "weapons of violence are their swords" and pronounces a curse on their anger. The Zealots were the first century version of the Maccabee brothers, one of whom was named Simon, who had earlier led a successful revolution against Greek rule. By having a second Simon who was a Zealot, Mark could have interpreted Zealot militancy as thunderous; hence part of a new Israel (Jacob) who was one of the sons of thunder. The possibilities in such an interpretation of "Cananaean" leads to the hypothesis that the entire list of names and surnames of the Twelve may be variations on messianic themes in the first century or variations on themes which Mark associated with Jesus. Quite apart from that, a built-in dilemma for Mark, because of his predilection toward spirituality, was that any proposal for a messianic New Israel in the first century had to confront the issue of Jewish military/political liberation from foreign domination. In Mark's historical context, any proposal for a New Israel had to wrestle with the Zealot-type of Israel.

A complementary possibility is that Mark was at least partially influenced by names in 1 and 2 Maccabees. Father Mattathias (Matthew) began the revolt against the Greeks which resulted in the Maccabean (Hasmonean) dynasty. His priest sons were named and surnamed as John (Gaddis: "Fortunate"), Simon (Thassis: "Burning"), Judas (Maccabaeus: "Hammer-headed," or "The Hammerer," or "Designated by Yahweh"), Eleazar (Auaran: "Awake"), and Jonathan (Aphphus: "Favorite").[16] All preferred to die rather than be unfaithful to Israel (Jacob). Jonathan's only two faithful followers (1 Macc. 11.70) were Judas son of Chalphi (Alphaeus) and Mattathias (Matthew) son of Absalom. An Absalom in 2 Sam. 3.3 was a "son of David" and a grandson of Talmai. Theodotus, from which Thaddeus seems to have been derived, was a man in 2 Macc. 14.19 whose name and mission both involved the gift of God. The Maccabee family was the prototype for the Zealot party; Mattathias used the root word for Zealot five times in 1 Macc. 2.23-68.[17] Cananean is most likely to have meant Zealot. Mark at other points in his Gospel does midrash from 1 Maccabees. Use of the Maccabee names as a pattern for a New Israel would set in stark contrast a military New Israel and a priestly or spiritual New Israel. The Maccabees were both priests and soldiers. Philip is the name of a Greek general specified in 2 Macc. 9.29 as a "bosom friend" of Antiochus Epiphanes, the emperor against whom the Maccabean revolution was fought.

An additional midrashic explanation for having a Simon referred to as a Cananaean is the sound-alike relationship between

"Cananaean" and "Canaanean," the people of the land of Canaan. The LXX vacillates between "a" and "aa" but RSV uses "aa" consistently, "Canaan." For example, in Gen. 46.10, one of Simeon's sons is born to a "Canaanitish" woman. In the LXX, the word is sometimes *cananitidos*, perhaps justifying Mark's "cananaean" rather than "canaanite." Thus, by sound-alike, a "Simon" could be both a Cananaean Zealot and son of a Canaanean woman. Simon would also be related to Canaanite in that a "Judah went with Simeon his brother, and they defeated the Canaanites who inhabited Zephath, and utterly destroyed it" (Judg. 1.17). This victory occurs in the context of a number of military battles in which the other tribes failed to drive out other Canaanites.

Two names in the list of the Twelve, Andrew and Philip, are entirely Greek. Andrew, no longer specified as Simon's brother, may not have been surnamed because the "Manly" etymology of his name could already be interpreted as "new man." Philip ("Lover of Horses") was the name of several foreign rulers in Macedonia and Israel. His name represents in the New Israel the opposite pole from Simon the Zealot; to include Greeks in general and Philip in particular in the New Israel is to symbolize willing cooperation with foreign domination rather than freedom from it. To include both a Zealot and a Greek in the Twelve is to require reconciliation among the men of the New Israel.

Bartholomew is an Aramaic name ("Son of Talmai"). In Num. 13.22, Josh. 15.14, and Judg. 1.10, Talmai is a Canaanite giant, one of Anak's sons who were driven out after Joshua's entrance into the Promised Land. Judg. 1.10 is a midrashic source not only for Talmai, but perhaps also for Judas Iscariot (of Kerioth) and Simon the Cananaean: "*Judah* went against the *Canaanites* who dwelt in Hebron (now the name of Hebron was formerly *Kiriath-arba*); and they defeated Sheshai and Ahiman and*Talmai.*" Mark's list of the twelve would thus reflect the enmity between Simeon and Judah against the Canaanites and Talmai. In 2 Sam. 3.3, 13.37 and 1 Chr. 3.2, Talmai is King of Geshur, one of David's father-in-laws. If one ignores the distinction between son and son-in-law, Bartholomew could be a euphemism for David. Mark may have associated David, slayer of the giant Goliath, with David, son-in-law of a man named for a giant of yore. That would fit into a messianic context in which many expected that a New Israel would be ruled by David. Talmai and the other sons of the giants frightened ten of the twelve spies when they returned from their assigned task of spying in Canaan. In Num. 13, ten of the twelve spies reported giants who could not be conquered; hence they recommended against an invasion. Only Caleb and Joshua ("God Saves") had faith that the land could be taken. Caleb said in effect that we can do it on our own; Joshua (Jesus), true to his name, said that God will do it for us, i.e., "God Saves." By using Son of Talmai in light of that story, Mark would have been calling attention to Jesus or God saving people from foes others thought to be unconquerable.

Mark's list concludes with Judas Iscariot "who betrayed him" or "who handed him over." "Iscariot" is most often translated as "from Kerioth," a city in Judah. In Josh. 15, the word *kiriath* or *kerioth* is used generically as a prefix meaning "city." Confirmation that Mark may have intended "from Kerioth" is found in Judg. 1.10 (cited in the preceding paragraph).[18] A more meaningful translation for Mark is that "Iscariot" means "Red Dyer."[19] Given the two James/Jacobs plus the references to twins in Mark's list, a strong possibility is that the color red was intended by Mark to identify Judas with Esau, Jacob's twin. Gen. 25.25-30 describes Esau at his birth as having come "forth *red*, all his body like a hairy mantle; so they called his name Esau" (Gen. 25.25). In adulthood, "Esau said to Jacob, 'Let me eat some of that *red* pottage, for I am famished!' (Therefore his name was called Edom [meaning 'Red'])"

(Gen. 25.30). Cohen gives the etymology of Edom as "the red region."[20] Mal. 1.1-6 identifies Esau as the patronymic namesake for Edom in the same way that Jacob is related to Israel. Thus it is highly probable that betrayal by Iscariot was intended by Mark as a midrash on Esau, representing rejection of the love of God which was a gift to Jacob the younger twin and by analogy the gift of God to all Israel. In Gen. 27.41-42, Esau made plans to kill Jacob.[21] The conflict between Esau and Jacob continued to be the source of midrashic treatments in both patristic and rabbinic literature for several centuries after the New Testament was completed.[22]

Judas is the Greek transliteration of the Hebrew Judah ("To Praise") and the namesake for the tribe for whom Judea was named. Judah was also the "betrayer" of Joseph. He persuaded his brothers to sell Joseph into slavery as a way of saving his life, saying "What profit is it if we slay our brother?" (Gen. 37.26). The prediction that Judas will be the "betrayer" appears superficially to involve magical foreknowledge on Jesus' part. At a deeper level the prediction hints that the conflict between higher goods and lesser goods already introduced in the Jesus-crowd unit of Old Israel will continue to operate in the Jesus-Twelve unit about New Israel. Just as Peter, "Rock," becomes rocky soil, Judas, called to "Praise," already represents a betrayal which is inherent in that calling. By the midrashic model of Judah in Genesis, any effort to save Jesus' life, done with however high motives, will result in betrayal. None of the eight other new disciples play any role other than to complete the number twelve. Taken as a whole, the list of names associated with the Twelve divides into three configurations.

Spiritual New Israel

James/Jacob: Israel; He Who Supplants His Brother
Zebedee: his father, Gift of God
John: his brother, God Is Gracious

Iscariot: his twin, Esau
Thomas: Twin
Boanerges: Cult of Twins
Matthew: Gift of God
Thaddeus: Gift of God
James/Jacob: He Who Supplanted His Brother Levi
Alphaeus: A Child Thought of as a Substitute for One Lost
Two Simons: God has heard

Military New Israel

Simon the Cananaean: a Zealot and a Maccabean
Bartholomew: David by being son-in-law of Talmai
Judas: who betrayed Jesus and who symbolizes Judea and Judaism
Simon Peter: who denied Jesus in face of potential persecution

Symbols of a Universal Religion or Empire

Philip: Greek emperor, conqueror
Andrew: Manly
Simon as a Canaanite
Son of Talmai as a Canaanite giant

In Gen. 32-33, Jacob and Esau are reconciled to each other after Jacob sees God face to face and then claims to see God in the face of Esau. The spiritual group, based on Jacob-Esau themes, is thus potentially a reconciliation group, intimately connected with Jesus' overall goal of effecting reconciliation between children and the Father God. Mark does not develop this midrash explicitly, but a perceptive first century Jewish reader would have known its relevance to passages revealing antagonisms among the Twelve.

A feature of Mark's New Israel motif essential to its universality is that it was more than Jewish. Midrashically this follows the trend in Isaiah to have a foreign messiah named Cyrus (Isa. 45.1) and to convert the Jerusalem temple into a "house of prayer for all peoples" (Isa. 56.7). The Twelve have names of mixed Hebraic-Aramaic-Hellenized-Greek origins, plus those of no known language. Just as Jesus earlier had separated himself from Israel by crossing the shoreline of the Sea of Galilee, so the Jesus who calls the Twelve separates himself from Old Israel by calling a New Israel which is broader than Hebrew. The place in the hills where he called the Twelve might have been outside of Israel, thus heightening the dimension of newness for the New Israel.

Jesus Trusts the Crowds: Mk. 3.20-21

After calling the New Israel, Jesus returns "home," a location not specified in Mark. Crowds there are so dense that he and the Twelve cannot even eat. Jesus apparently ventures out into the mass of people by himself. "When his friends [brothers] heard it, they went out to seize [rescue] him" (Mk. 3.21), remembering that he had only recently told them that the crowds might crush him. They fear that he is beside himself for risking himself in a multitude. The story is the first instance of Mark's use of the literary technique known as intercalation: interrupting a story by inserting another in its middle. An intercalation is a literary sandwich, with a new tale filling the two halves of a split bun. The last half of each of Mark's divided stories has a different meaning because of what is intercalated.

Jesus in the first half of this story asks the disciples to put a boat out for him "lest the crowds should crush him." In the intercalation he calls the Twelve to preach for him, after which he ventures out into a crowd, apparently without fear of being crushed. Earlier he was preaching forgiveness to the crowds. The crowds could then distort authoritative preaching as miraculous healing of disease. Calling the Twelve to preach for him frees him from such temptation. The story depends upon the Twelve being unaware that their call to discipleship has changed Jesus' situation. They, remembering only Jesus' words about his vulnerability to crowds, interpret his inconsistent behavior to mean that he is out of his mind; they set out to rescue him. They still perceive their relationship to Jesus as it had been previously when he was subject to temptation from the crowds, whereas he now needs them to become those who obey the will of God.

RSV's designation of Jesus' intended rescuers as "friends" presents an interpretative problem because the Greek word clearly is "brothers." Mark's flow of thought demands that the ones who seek to rescue him from the crowds be those whom he had asked to put the boat out from shore. The word "brothers," if defined in terms of family of origin, makes no sense in that context. "Brothers" would be appropriate if the story were to be interpreted according to Mk. 3.31-35, a pericope in which Jesus distinguishes between biological brothers and new brothers who truly do the will of God. The stories of the "brothers" rescuing Jesus and the "true brothers" would be two halves of an interrupted pericope, with the long saying about Be-el'zebul and unforgivable sin as the intercalation. Based on the word "brothers" alone, that interpretation has much to support it. Nevertheless, the context demands that the rescuers are Jesus' new, true brothers, not his old biological ones. A translator's choice of "friends" or "brothers" in 3.21 will ultimately depend upon the interpretation of 3.31-35.

Scribes from Jerusalem Come to Confront Jesus: Mk. 3.22-27

An implied pun connects the judgment of Jesus' followers that "he is beside himself" and the scribes' accusation that Jesus "has an unclean spirit", that he is "possessed by Be-el'zebul, and [that] by the prince of demons he casts out the demons" (Mk. 3.22, 30). One way to say that a person is beside himself is to say that he is demon-possessed. The scribes are trying to explain Jesus' ability to exorcise unclean spirits, not his changed relationship to the crowds. Be-el'zebul means "lord of the habitation" and is a sound-alike for Ba'al-ze'bub, the god of Ekron, in 2 Kgs. 1.3-6. Matthew clearly recognized the meaning of Be-el'zebul as "the master of the house" (10.25). Mark used the Be-el'zebul imagery to depict Satan's house "divided against itself" (3.23-25) and the impossibility of plundering a house before the strong man is bound. The strong man is no longer Satan or Be-el'zebul.[23] He is Jesus or any human being who is tempted. A strong person's house is one in which a person is able to win in the struggle against a tempter who is trying to enter. The house imagery extends the Cain and Abel concept that "*sin is couching at the door*" for all who do not do well (Gen. 4.7). In stressing human responsibility to resist sin, Mark could have written midrashically on Jas./Jac. 1.13: "God cannot be tempted with evil and he himself tempts no one."

Jesus is in fact tempted to be "a house divided against itself" (Mk. 3.25) and to exorcise demons by the power of Satan. Whenever he accepts the crowd's definition of him as an exorcist instead of as a man resisting his own temptations, he is guilty of what the scribes actually say, although he is not guilty of what they mean. At this deeper level, the scribes from Jerusalem verbalize what the Twelve were thinking when they went out to rescue Jesus. The Twelve saw the crowd threatening him with physical force; they sought to protect him by acting as bodyguards; they saw his power over unclean spirits as physical exorcism. All of that from Jesus' point of view is in fact Satanic. To the extent that Jesus acts in terms of their perception, he would be casting out demons by the power of Satan. He would also be putting himself back into the crunch of the crowds with the ability to crush him.

Mark's continuity here is subtle and easy to miss. Jesus has authorized the Twelve "to cast out demons." Now he has been accused of casting out demons by the power of the prince of demons. His reply applies to the Twelve as much as to himself and hints strongly that they, by going out to rescue him from "being beside himself," were trying for the first time to use their "authority to cast out" the demons which they perceived as inhabiting him, just as the scribes interpreted Jesus' behavior in terms of demon possession. The Twelve, by their misperception, were seeking to exorcise unclean spirits by a method which was in itself temptative. The Twelve, in that regard, may well have been a house divided against itself. A messianic midrash for that phenomenon could have been the historic fact that David's house was divided. What had been one kingdom became two, Israel and Judah.

The house divided against itself calls attention to a line of continuity about brothers, houses, and families. Jesus calls the Twelve, some of whose names emphasize their brotherly relationship (3.13-19). "Then he went home" (3.19). His "brothers" go "out to seize him, for they said 'he is beside himself"(3.21). Jesus talks about "a house divided" (3.25) and plundering a house (3.27). The scribes' charges against him are forgivable only if they are not sins against the holy spirit. His biological "mother and his brothers" seek to speak to him and Jesus redefines family (3.31). This continuity helps to cement the sequence of stories together and define a New Israel as a new family.

Mark described Jesus as replying to the scribes in parables, his first reference to that literary form. Based on the way the term "parable" is used elsewhere in the New Testament, a reader would not guess that what Jesus said here is a parable if Mark had not explicitly labelled it as such. Jesus' reply merely calls attention to the illogic of the scribes' criticism. While Mark leaves the concept "parables" undefined here, what Jesus says is parabolic in the only sense of the term used by Mark: no one really understands what he is saying. Mark's specific use of the concept "parable" warns the modern reader against uncritical acceptance of the definition which is implied in most of the literature about Jesus' parables.

Forgivable and Unforgivable Sins: Mk. 3.28-30

Jesus announces at the climax of his confrontation with the Jerusalem scribes that all sins and blasphemies will be forgiven the "sons of men" except for blasphemy against the holy spirit. This statement appears to be aimed at the scribes because they had accused Jesus of having an unclean spirit. No content is specified for the unforgivable sin, but the tenor of the passage is that anything held to be unforgivable by the scribes or Mosaic laws is in fact forgivable. This would render forgivable the offenses of which Jesus has been accused, namely, people forgiving sins and violation of sabbath laws. If that was Mark's intent, then an unforgivable sin would be one for which a death penalty is justifiable, and there is one such offense. This conclusion has several unmistakable midrashic sources. 1 Jn. 5.16-17 promises that "if any one sees his brother committing what is not a mortal sin, he will ask, and God will give him life for those whose sin is not mortal. There is sin which is mortal; I do not say that one is to pray for that." Isa. 47.10-11 alludes to Babylon acting as God, saying, "I am, and there is no one besides me," resulting in evil "for which you cannot atone" and disaster "which you will not be able to expiate." The most explicit midrashic source for "blasphemy against the holy spirit" is an account in 1 Samuel. Eli asks rhetorically that "if a man sins against a man, God will mediate for him; but if a man sins against the Lord, who can intercede for him?" (2.25). God informs Samuel that "the iniquity of Eli's house shall not be expiated by sacrifice or offering forever" because of blasphemy (3.13-14). Eli's house will fall, be poverty-stricken, and weak, for God will cut off "the strength of your father's house" (3.31). It may be only incidental that the word "house" which figures so prominently in Jesus' argument leading up to the saying about blasphemy against the holy spirit is found in the 1 Samuel source about blaspheming God. Wisd. 1.6 states that "wisdom is a spirit, a friend to man, though she will not pardon the words of a blasphemer since God sees into the innermost parts of him." The original source for the idea that blasphemy is the sole unforgivable sin is probably "You shall not take the name of the Lord your God in vain; for the Lord will not hold him guiltless who takes his name in vain" (Exod. 20.7). It is the only one of the ten commandments which carries with it a punishment in its original statement.

An unforgivable sin in Mark is a sin against the holy spirit. Mark has previously referred to holy spirit only in the baptism and temptation narratives. Based on them, the sin against the spirit of holiness would either have to be rejecting the love of God when it is offered, or distorting the offer of the Father's love by insisting that it is meant for me only, not for other children of God. The flow of thought in Mark leans heavily toward the latter because unclean spirits persistently confront Jesus with the "I only" option, and Jesus is accused of casting out unclean spirits by the power of the prince of unclean spirits.

State-enforced execution would be a strange penalty for either interpretation, but a spiritualized "death sentence" would be appropriate for both. To reject the proffered love of the Father or to distort it in the "I only" sense is to kill the possibility of Father-child reconciliation. Offered forgiveness would of necessity be rejected; such rejection is unforgivable, not because God arbitrarily punishes those who do it, but because the rejection makes forgiveness impossible to be received. Mark could well have derived his interpretation from Paul's powerful statement in Rom. 1.16-17: "For I am not ashamed of the gospel: it is the power of God for salvation to every one who has trust, to the Jew first and also to the Greek. For in it the rightwising of God is revealed through trust for trust; as it is written, 'He who through trust is made right shall live.'" That translation by Kendrick Grobel[24] recognizes righteousness as an activity rather than a state of being and perceives faith as an act of trust in forgiveness which is offered. Not to trust forgiveness would be unforgivable; it would make reconciliation impossible. It would likewise be, as Paul said in Rom. 12.3, "to think of oneself more highly than one ought to think." Mark saw thinking of oneself too highly and rejection of forgiveness as twin attitudes, leading to the only "death penalty" he accepted, the self-imposed one of spiritual death of relationship, suffered by the ego-centered one refusing to be forgiven. The context would lead one to assume that no one who heard Jesus understood what he meant.

Jesus' True Family: Mk. 3.31-35

Mark next portrayed Jesus in another capital punishment midrashic context. Jesus disobeys an apparently direct command by his biological mother, and is likely in turn to have disobeyed a death penalty law of Moses:

> If a man has a stubborn and rebellious son, who will not obey the voice of his father or the voice of his mother, and, though they chastise him, will not give heed to them, then his father and his mother shall take hold of him and bring him out to the elders of his city at the gate of the place where he lives, and they shall say to the elders of his city, 'This our son is stubborn and rebellious, he will not obey our voice; he is a glutton and a drunkard.' Then all the men of the city shall stone him to death with stones; so you shall purge the evil from your midst (Deut. 21.18-21).

The core offense is to be disobedient to one's parents. Presumably the execution would still be ordered if the son was stubborn and rebellious but neither a glutton nor a drunkard. Jesus' mother and brothers are on the fringe of a crowd surrounding him. They pass a message through the crowd asking him to come out, to which he responds by denying in effect that they are his family: "Here are my mother and my brothers! Whoever does the will of God is my brother, and sister, and mother." He seems to be pointing to the Twelve when he says it, calling them to be his New Family as well as to be the New Israel. In doing so, he explicitly disobeys his biological mother, thus becoming eligible for the death penalty sentence. The story may also be related to the example of Moses in a crowd. He was told, "'Lo, your father-in-law is coming to you with your wife and her two sons with her,' Moses went out to meet his father-in-law, and did obeisance and kissed him;" they asked about each other's welfare but Moses presumably ignored his wife and sons whom he had previously sent away (Exod. 18.6-14).

An inclusive synonym for believers throughout 1 Peter, 1 John, James/Jacob, and Paul's epistles is "brothers" or "brethren." Mark's basic midrash for the new family combines that term with the thesis that "the twelve tribes in the dispersion" to whom one epistle is addressed should be "doers of the word" (Jas./Jac. 1.1, 22). Thus the Twelve, the new brothers, are expected to be doers of the word. That fits the tone of their original calling by Jesus to be with him, preach the gospel, and resist temptation. Because it does so, it heightens the probability that Mark intended the word "brothers" rather than "friends" in the pericope about those who sought to rescue him from demon possession because he ventured into the crowd. Jesus' redefinition of those who do the will of God as his brothers and sisters connotes a relationship of equality quite unlike teacher/disciples or master/follower. It follows the logic of 1 Jn. 2.21, 27 that those who are anointed already "know the truth" and "have no need that anyone should teach you." It conforms to his trust that the Twelve are now the ones to carry on the messianic ministry of the quest for reconciliation between parents and children. His very act of redefining familial relationships ironically alienates him from his own parent and thus points to the potential failure of this strategy for achieving reconciliation.

Introducing and Defining Parables: Mk. 4.1-20

Mark continued to introduce the New Israel theme by portraying a large crowd gathered to hear Jesus beside the sea. Jesus distances himself from them by sitting in a boat, symbolizing a new kind of separation which the event itself is to make explicit. Jesus teaches them many things in parables, but only the parable of different kinds of soil is reported. The story and its subsequent interpretation by Jesus are so interlinked that they must be treated as a single pericope. After telling about the soils, Jesus says, "He who has ears to hear, let him hear." Alone later with the Twelve he explains that he had not intended the crowd to comprehend.

Jesus' explanation midrashically paraphrases Isa. 6.9-10: "'Hear and hear, but do not understand; see and see, but do not perceive.' Make the heart of this people fat, and their ears heavy, and shut their eyes; lest they see with their eyes, and hear with their ears, and understand with their hearts, and turn and be healed." Isaiah was to preach in the expectation of not being understood until the nation was largely destroyed, leaving only a remnant from which a messianic seed would emerge. Jesus midrashically adapts that model for the Twelve and himself. He intends to preach to crowds which will be deaf and blind as in Isaiah, but he thinks that the Twelve will be the fruit-bearing seed, able to see and hear with understanding. The Twelve have "been given the secret of the kingdom of God" but the crowd, Old Israel, is to be given only parables "so that they may indeed see but not perceive, and may indeed hear but not understand; lest they should turn again, and be forgiven" (Mk. 4.11-12).

The key line in the Isaiah 6 passage is midrashic in turn on the Moses-Pharaoh story in Exodus. Isaiah 6.10 portrays God ordering Isaiah to "make the heart of this people fat...." In Exodus, God persistently hardened the heart of Pharaoh lest he should too easily do what God commanded. When Moses tried to beg off because of his lack of eloquence, God replied, "Who makes him dumb, or deaf, or seeing, or blind? Is it not I, the Lord" (Ex. 4.11)?

The idea of hiding the truth from outsiders is suggested also by Paul: "And even if our gospel is veiled, it is veiled only to those who are perishing. In their case the god of this world has blinded the minds of the unbelievers, to keep them from seeing the light of the gospel of the glory of Christ, who is the likeness of God" (2 Cor. 4.3-4). The point of Jesus' superficially harsh statement is demonstrated in context to be that those who do not "do the word" are unable to understand the word; thus they function in relation to its truth as if they were deaf and blind. Jesus presumes at first that the Twelve understand the parable of the soils because they are his new family and thus supposedly do the will of God. Jesus is mistaken about them: the Twelve do not comprehend; they also are deaf and blind. Jesus then explains to them the meaning which they ought to have been able to decipher if they were different from the blind-deaf crowds and were doing the will of God.

Jesus' statement provides an implied definition of "parable"[25] as enigma or riddle, clearly based on the citation from Isaiah and the Hebrew word *mashal*.[26] Prov. 1.5-6 (LXX) uses the term that way in referring to "a parable, and a dark speech; the sayings of the wise also, and riddles."[27] Matthew changed Mark's definition to make it conform to a sermon illustration. John T. Greene notes that there are so many different ways to interpret an Old Testament *mashal* that *caveat emptor* is an appropriate warning.[28]

The key terms in the explanation of the soils parable in Mark are "bear fruit," and "word,"[29] which is depicted as "seed." "Word" refers to a preached message and more generally to the Word of God. Each kind of soil is analogous to a way people respond to the word. Good soil bears fruit, thirtyfold, sixtyfold, or a hundredfold. Three bad types of soil are first identified. They are separated below for emphasis.

> Mk. 4.3-4: A sower went forth to sow. And as he sowed, some seed fell *along the path*, and the birds came and devoured it.
>
> Mk. 4.15 [explanation]: And these are the ones along the path, where the word is sown; when they hear, Satan *immediately* comes and takes away the word which is sown in them.
>
> Mk. 4.5-6: Other seed fell on *rocky ground*, where it had not much soil, and immediately it sprang up, since it had no depth of soil; and when the sun rose it was scorched, and since it had no root it withered away.
>
> Mk. 4.16-17 [explanation]: And these in like manner are the ones sown upon rocky ground, who, when they hear the word, *immediately* receive it with joy; and they have no root in themselves, but endure for a while; then, when tribulation or persecution arises on account of the word, *immediately* they fall away.
>
> Mk. 4.7: Other seed fell *among thorns* and the thorns grew up and choked it, and it yielded no grain.
>
> Mk 4.18-19 [explanation]: And others are the ones sown among thorns; they are those who hear the word, but the cares of the world, and the delight in riches, and the desire for other things, enter in and choke the word, and it proves unfruitful.

The word "immediately" points to the temptative nature of the rocky soil and soil along the path. In context, seeds sown on hard ground are the crowds, controlled by Satan to the extent that they can never grow. Seeds sown on rocky ground are the Twelve, symbolized by Peter. The congruence between the description of rocky soil and the career of Simon Peter, "Rock," as portrayed in the Gospel, is too extensive to be merely coincidental; the explanation epitomizes Peter's betrayal and denial when faced with persecution. The seeds growing among thorns are like the rich man of Mk. 10.17-22 who was willing to obey all the commandments but unwilling to part with his property or the religious leaders at the crucifixion who were to prefer a Barabbas freedom fighter Messiah to Jesus. Mark did not develop a path or thorny soil motif. However, he might have expected informed Jewish readers of his time to understand thorns in the light of Jer. 4.3; Mic. 7.4; 2 Sam. 23.6; and Prov. 24.30-31, in which thorns are a symbol for sin. Seeds planted in thorns would of course be choked by sinful greed for wealth or imperial domination of others.

The parable of the soils develops the basic imagery in James/Jacob, which focuses throughout, as does the parable, on doing the word and not just hearing it, for example: "I by my works will show you my faith" (2.18); the faithful are to "be doers of the word, and not hearers only" (1.22); "faith by itself, if it has no works, is dead" (2.14-17); "a doer that acts" (1.25); and "a man is jus tified by works and not by faith alone" (2.24). Fruit-bearing is comparable to James/Jacob's emphasis on the consequences of good works: "Blessed is the man who endures trial, for when he has stood the test he will receive the crown of life" (1.12); God "brought us forth by the *word of truth* that we should be a kind of *first fruits* of his creatures" (1.18). In Mk. 10.36-40, James/Jacob and John demonstrated "jealousy and selfish ambition" (Jas./Jac. 3.14) in contrast to "*good fruits*" (Jas./Jac. 3.17) and "the *harvest of righteousness*" (Jas./Jac. 3.18). The James/Jacob emphasis on works differs sharply from Rom. 11.5-8, in which Paul defined the

New Israel as stemming only from the grace of God because Israel had failed to produce adequate works. Up through Mk. 7.23, Mark organized his New Israel materials around the James/Jacob position, in which a follower is a member of the New Israel by merit. From 7:23 through 8.30, he explored the Pauline possibility that one is made acceptable by the gift of God. Mark illustrated the contrast by Jesus' high expectations for the behavior of the disciples even though most of their names symbolized Israel as the recipient of God's graciousness: two James/Jacobs symbolizing God's preference for Jews; three "Gifts of God" (Matthew, Thaddeus, and Zebedee); Thomas, a twin like Jacob; John ("God Is Gracious"); and two Simons ("God Has Heard"). Mark's parable may have been suggested by the simile of the vineyard in Isa. 5.1-7, in which seeds planted by God in good ground nevertheless produce "thorns" (Isa. 5.4 LXX).

The soils parable concludes that those who hear the word and accept it will "bear fruit, thirtyfold and sixtyfold and a hundredfold" (Mk. 4.20). Isaiah often used the image of prolific bearing of fruit in a messianic time to describe the Jewish remnant, purified by suffering: Jews sent into exile are "a people of no understanding" (27.11 LXX); the "*full fruit*" of the remnant will be "the removal of his sin" (27.9); in days to come "*Israel shall blossom and put forth shoots, and fill the whole world with fruit*" (Isa. 27.6); in that day "the *fruit* of the land shall be the pride and glory of the survivors of Israel" (4.2); the righteous [remnant] "shall eat the *fruit of their deeds*" (3.10). The conclusion of the "hear and hear but do not understand" passage in Isa. 6.9-10 which is paraphrased in Mk. 4.12 is that fruit will grow again from the messianic seed after prolonged suffering: "The holy seed is its stump" (6.13). By analogy in Mark's soils parable, the Twelve ought to be the remnant purified from sin and expected to bear fruit.

Citations from James/Jacob and 1 Peter are persuasive in support of the proposition that Mark midrashically created both the parable of the soils and details of the life of Peter from the books associated with the names of the three key disciples. This is quite apart from the question as to whether or not there was a Peter, a James/Jacob, or a John in history. The "seed as word" imagery of the parable comes from both James/Jacob and I Peter. From Jas./Jac. 1.21 comes the "implanted word" and the "rank growth of wickedness." From 1 Pet. 1.22-25, Mark could have developed the idea of the Twelve as people who are born anew and should grow from the implanted seed of the word of God which had been preached to them, as well as the imagery of the crop which withers:

> Having purified your souls by your obedience to the truth for a sincere love of the brethren, love one another earnestly from the heart. You have been *born anew*, not of *perishable seed* but of imperishable, through the living and abiding *word* of God; for 'all flesh is like grass and all its glory like the flower of grass. The grass *withers*, and the flower *falls*, but the *word of God* abides for ever.' That *word* is the good news [gospel] which was preached to you (1 Pet. 1.22-25).

By the logic of the 1 Peter passage, it should have been impossible for Peter's faith to have withered under conditions of persecution because he had been implanted with the imperishable "word of God which abides forever." Jas./Jac. 1.11 provides an even clearer source for the crop which withers because it was scorched by the sun (Mk. 4.6): "For the sun rises with its *scorching heat* and *withers the grass;* its flower falls, and its beauty perishes." The imagery of the barren soil may have been derived from Isa. 53.2 in which the Suffering Servant is described as growing "like a young plant, and like a root out of *dry ground,*" especially because Isa. 53.10-11 provides the contrast of crops which bear fruit. When the Servant becomes an offering for sin, "he shall see the *fruit* of the travail of his soul and be satisfied." The description of rocky soil in Mk. 4.16-17 is relevant to Peter violating the relevant advice of 1 Pet. 1.6-8: "In this you *rejoice*, though now *for a little while you may have to suffer various trials*, so that the genuineness of your faith, more precious than gold which though perishable is tested by fire, may redound to praise and glory and honor at the revelation of Jesus Christ." The "various trials" in I Peter are only for "a little while," whereas for James/Jacob "trials" are an ever-present part of life (Jas./Jac. 1.2-3, 12-15). This contrast apparently justified Mark in developing the negative picture of Peter from the two earlier books.

The soils parable which Mark created from the early epistles provides specific content for his message of repentance. It establishes that God is giving people an opportunity to hear the word and obey it; to be faithful during tribulation and persecution; and to resist the temptations of riches, worldly concerns, selfish ambition, the desire for things, malice, and sin in general. Furthermore, the parable and its associated explanation provide a reason why proclaiming "forgiveness" is not included in the set of tasks Jesus passed on to the Twelve. Only the chosen few will hear and see with understanding, and they can be forgiven, but for the masses there is only deafness, blindness, and the loss of opportunity for forgiveness.

Jesus' Dilemma: Mk. 4.21-34

The disciples still do not understand even after the soils parable has been explained to them. Jesus should have sensed that their continued failure seemed more likely than success. The Twelve, unlike the crowds, were expected to understand; truth was not supposed to be hidden from them. Mark intended the reader to question whether the Twelve are redeemable: ought Jesus give up on them now or gamble that in the future they can succeed in a way which is now impossible? Jesus' answer to that complex question is presented in three additional "parables" in Mk. 4.21-32. The three, two similes and one metaphor, are parables in the sense that they are incomprehensible to anyone who does not live the truth as Mark perceived it. The metaphor of a hidden lamp is used to argue that "there is nothing hid, except to be made manifest; nor is anything secret, except to come to light" (Mk. 4.22) and that the deafness of the Twelve is temporary: "If any man has ears, let him hear" (Mk. 4.23). The parable assumes that the lamp's light is hidden until needed at night rather than at noon. The light of the disciples' "lamp" is hidden or secret now in order to be made manifest later. The sequence from a parable about the word to one about a lamp may have been suggested by Ps. 119.105: "Thy *word is a lamp* to my feet and a *light* to my path." The lamp imagery may be based also on a messianic servant passage in Isa. 42.1-3: "*A dimly burning wick he will not quench.*" Jesus will not give up on the Twelve although at that time the wick of their lamp is barely flickering.

Mark's explanation of the parable of the lamp continues with the advice to the Twelve to heed what they hear because they will be rewarded according to how much they give. Giving seems to imply that they hear and understand the no longer hidden word and live according to its discipline. They can succeed later if they can learn to do this, even though they are not doing so now. The amount of light they radiate will be equated to any reward they are to receive; if they give out none at all, even the possibility of any reward will be taken from them. This follows the logic of Jas./Jac. 1.8: "A double-minded man, unstable in all his ways, will [not] receive anything from the Lord," and of Jer. 17.10 in which God gives to each person "*according to the fruit of his doings.*"

The next parable portrays the secret growth of grain. No one ever sees it growing, but harvest time always comes. The growth of the Twelve will be analogous to that. Jesus assumes that their current growing in good soil is in secret but that their growth will continue until harvest. The last parable points to the mustard as the smallest of all seeds and the largest of all shrubs. Mark's error does not invalidate the point. Jesus envisions the Twelve as being currently the smallest of all seeds but this does not lessen his confidence that they will grow into the largest of all fruit-bearing shrubs. The three parables symbolize Jesus' decision to continue to distinguish between what he sees as the permanent inability of the crowds to do God's word and the temporary incapacity of the Twelve. That decision justifies him in speaking in parables so that the crowds cannot comprehend but explaining the parables to the Twelve when they do not understand (Mk. 4.33-34). The last two seed parables prepare the way for the next units of Mark. Despite Jesus' confidence in his disciples, it is obvious to the reader that they probably will not comprehend. Jesus appears to argue against the author and reader that there is a secret growth which he alone can see; the Twelve will grow from a tiny, currently invisible faith to a great one. The reader is thus led to expect that they will be provided occasions for such a transformation.

The mustard seed parable is midrashically rooted in Ezek. 31 and Dan. 4. Portions of the same sources are used by Mark in the incident of the blasted fig tree in Mk. 11.

> Behold, I will liken you [Pharaoh king of Egypt] to a cedar of Lebanon.... So it towered high above all the trees of the forest.... All the birds of the air made their nests in its boughs... (Ezek. 31.3-6).

In Daniel, King Nebuchadnezzar relates a dream in which a tree grew to such a height that "it was visible to the end of the whole earth" and "the birds of the air dwelt in its branches" (4.11-12). Mark's use of midrashic sources referring to great monarchs suggests that he intended to contrast the rule of earthly kings with the rule of God in parables which begin with "with what can we compare the kingdom of God." The disciples are expected to be as great or greater than Pharaoh and Nebuchadnezzar.

ENDNOTES FOR CHAPTER FIVE

[1]This insight is to be credited to Edward C. Hobbs' B.D. dissertation on Moses themes in Mark at the University of Chicago Divinity School.

[2]Speculation that he was the same as "Matthew" is irrelevant to Mark, however appropriate it may be in the exegesis of other gospels.

[3]J. M. Morris, "Alphaeus," *IDB.*

[4]J. C. Swaim, "Chalphi," *IDB.*

[5]Le Deaut, "Apropos Midrash," 273.

[6]Bratcher and Nida, 114.

[7]V. Taylor, *St. Mark* , 232.

[8]Frederick C. Grant, *The Interpreter's Bible*, VII, 688.

[9]"Thomas," *The Westminster Dictionary of the Bible*, 603. In some versions, the Greek word for twin "didymus" is also used in the Gospel of John in connection with Thomas.

[10]V. Taylor, *St. Mark* , 233.

[11]See pp. 70-71 above for an extended discussion of the meanings of Zebedee in Mark's text, especially as related to the sound-alike Zebulon.

[12]The phrase "had given them up" reads in the LXX: *paradidomi*: handed them over. This is the verb which Mark used for the arrest of John the Baptizer, the betrayal of Jesus, and in seventeen other contexts. Here it is used in connection with Deuteronomy's distinction between our "rock" and theirs. The verb is too important to be ignored in a passage which Mark may have used midrashically, but it does not appear that Mark was conscious of its meaning at this point in his Gospel.

[13]Test. of Sim. 4.4 and 1 Pet. 1.22 are so much alike that there can be little doubt but that one of them midrashically influenced the other.

[14]Bratcher and Nida, 115.

[15]W. R. Farmer, *IDB* .

[16]Spelling of the Maccabee names varies from one translator to another.

[17]H. Paul Kingdon, "The Origins of the Zealots," *New Testament Studies*, XIX, 74-81, documents many usages of "zealous" and "jealous," both from the root for Zealot, in both the Old Testament and 1-2 Maccabees.

[18]See p. 63 above for a discussion of the probability that Iscariot was also a sound-alike reference to Issachar, "Man of Hire."

[19]Albert Ehrman, "Judas Iscariot and Abba Saqqara," *Journal of Biblical Literature*, IV, 1978, 572-73. Yoel Arbeitman, "The Suffix of Iscariot," *Ibid.*, I, 1980, 122-24.

[20]S. Cohen, "Edom," *IDB*.

[21]It is highly likely that John read Mark as having identified Iscariot with Esau and Edom. John added to the Markan motif the affinities between Peter and Petra, the capitol city of Idumea (Edom), and between Peter and Judas Iscariot as the son of Simon.

[22]A paper by Asher Finkel, "The Conflict of Esau and Jacob in Rabbinic and Patristic Literature" was presented in 1989 to an SBL consultation dealing only with the second through fifth centuries of the Common Era.

[23]Grant, *The Interpreter's Bible*, VII, 692, suggests that the strong man is Satan, who is bound by the Christ, with The Test. of Levi 18.12, Rev. 20.2, and 1 Enoch 10.15 as representative source texts for the predicted binding of tempters in the messianic age. Mk. 3.27 would then be an optimistic statement regarding Jesus already having entered Satan's divided house, tied him up, and plundered his goods, or having made major progress in doing so. This interpretation does not fit the flow of thought in Mark.

[24]Grobel insisted that there is no proper English word to translate *dikaiosune* and coined the term "rightwising" for that purpose.

[25]Perrin and Duling succinctly summarize "modern research" about parables, distinguishing parables from allegories, the parable making "its point as a totality," and the allegory having several parts with "one-to-one relationship" to what each represents. When the analogy of the soils is labeled a parable by Mark, Perrin and Duling blame revision by the evangelists, as if they did not understand the term, 415-416.

[26]Kee, *Community of the New Age*, 190, credits J. Jeremias, *The Parables of Jesus*, 13-15, with discovering that Mark's word for "parable" comes from the Hebrew "mashal" which means enigma. So also Bratcher and Nida, 134.

[27]C.L. Brenton, *The Septuagint with Apocrypha: Greek and English* (Peabody, MA: Hendrickson Publishers, 1987).

[28]John T. Greene, "Balaam: Prophet, Diviner, and Priest...," *SBL Seminar Papers* (1989), 62.

[29]In Greek, the original is *logos* but there is no hint of Logos Philosophy in the passage. Logos Philosophy was a distinctively Greek derivation from Plato. The fact that the New Testament often uses the word "word" (*logos* in Greek) leads to much confusion as to whether the New Testament authors were thinking in terms of Logos Philosophy or in terms of the Old Testament concept of the word of God. The latter option should be chosen unless there is specific reason to think in terms of Greek philosophy, as there is in the Gospel of John.

CHAPTER SIX

MIDRASH ON THE TWELVE AS THE NEW ISRAEL

Mk. 4.35—6.6 focuses on Jesus' effort to leave Old Israel and all that it represents by asking the new Twelve to row him to the Gentile New Israel side of the lake, and the consequences of their failure to be able to do so. The unit introduces new midrashic source material from the Psalms and 2 Maccabees, but is otherwise largely a development of already established motifs. The criterion for the success or failure of the Twelve is their faith or lack thereof.

Rescuing the Twelve from the Storm at Sea: Mk. 4.35-41

What Jesus needs in order for the Twelve to be established as the New Israel is any mustard-seed-sized task at which they can succeed. Mark developed that opportunity out of the previously established circumstance that at least four of the Twelve had been fishermen, presumably at home on the Sea of Galilee. Jesus asks the Twelve, symbolized by these experienced boatmen, to row him to an unspecified destination on the Gentile side of the lake while he sleeps. His nap is his vote of confidence that they can do the task without help from him. While he slumbers, a storm arises. The Twelve, fearful for their lives, waken him to ask implicitly for the miracle of "saving" for which his name stands. He recognizes that they have no "faith," i.e., no confidence in their own ability to control the boat in such a storm. The issue is not lack of faith in him or in God, but in their own capacity to ride out a tempest. He obliges their request by doing for them what he had expected them to do for themselves. His miracle calms the lake and excites them to marvel at the nature of this man who can calm a storm, apparently a miracle greater by far than those which preceded it.

Jesus faces the dilemma of every parent who wants a child to learn to do things on the child's own initiative before the child is ready to do so. The child says "I can't do it, Mommy; do it for me!" To provide what the child is not ready to do is parental compassion; to provide what the child could do without help is paternalism which deters the child's learning. This is Jesus' dilemma. In order for the Twelve to succeed as apostles Jesus would have to restrain himself from rescuing them from difficulties which they might overcome on their own. In that respect, Jesus faces the contradiction between his intention and his name "God Saves." His dilemma is deeply rooted in the Jewish tradition. In Gen. 17.5, the name of the father of the Jews is changed from Abram ("Father Is Exalted") to Abraham ("Father of Multitudes"). In order for Abraham to be father of any Jewish descendants, God miraculously saved Abraham and Sarah from their inability to have children, and later rescued Isaac when Abraham had sufficient faith in God's promise of descendants that he was willing to sacrifice the child of that earlier miracle. Had God not performed both acts of rescue there would have been no Jews. By making "God Saves" into a temptation in the crossing-of-the-lake pericope, Mark was striking at the very roots of religion as understood from the "God-Saves" point of view. In the case of Abraham, there was both faith and rescue. Mark depicted the rescue of the Twelve as occurring in the absence of their faith.

The specific imagery of the episode combines the motifs of lack of faith, a storm at sea, and the possibility of rescue. Mark used as his basic midrashic source Jas./Jac. 1.6 and its roots in the Psalms. James/Jacob urges a person to "ask in faith, with no doubting, for he who doubts is like a wave of the sea that is driven and tossed by the wind" (1.6). Ps. 107 concerns not only people crying to God in fear while on storm-tossed ships, but contains imagery used in the Gerasene demoniac story which follows in Mark.

> Some went down to the sea in ships, doing business on the great waters; they saw the deeds of the Lord, his wondrous works in the deep. For he commanded and raised the stormy wind, which lifted up the waves of the sea. ... Then they cried to the Lord in their trouble, and he delivered them from their distress; he made the storm be still, and the waves of the sea were hushed. Then they were glad because they had quiet, and he brought them to their desired haven" (Ps. 107.25-30).

Psalm 44 is a prayer for rescue from suffering. Mark made midrashic use of its plea to the Lord to "rouse thyself! Why sleepest thou, O Lord? Awake! Do not cast us off forever" (Ps. 44.23)! Ps. 65.5-8 praises God "who dost still the roaring of the seas, the roaring of their waves, the tumult of the peoples." Ps. 89.8-9 exults that "thou dost rule the raging of the sea; when its waves rise, thou stillest them."

One other probable midrashic source is the combination of two passages in 2 Maccabees referring to the miraculous claims and incipient death of the Greek emperor, Antiochus Epiphanes. He is said to have "carried away eighteen hundred talents from the temple, and hurried off to Antioch, thinking in his arrogance that he would make the land navigable and the *sea traversable on foot*, he was so intoxicated in mind" (2 Macc. 5.21). Later, near death, he is castigated as "the man who just now *presumed to command the waves of the sea*, in his superhuman boastfulness, and thought he could weigh the mountain heights in his scales, was flat on the ground and had to be carried off in a litter" (2 Macc. 9.8). The probability that Mark was conscious of these passages is increased by the fact that he twice has Jesus face a temptation related to controlling a storm at sea, once has him walk on top of the water, and uses the metaphor of casting a mountain into the sea to describe the power of faith. The contrast is striking. Antiochus was "arrogant" for believing that he was a divinity who could subdue the waves; Jesus was tempted to master the waves and had to resist the belief that he was divine. His disciples would have preferred him to be more like what Antiochus claimed to be. Mark probably envisioned the scene in terms of the concluding words of Deuteronomy that "there has not risen a prophet since in Israel like Moses, whom the Lord knew face to face, none like him for all the signs and the wonders which the Lord sent him to do in the land of Egypt...and for all the mighty power and all the great and terrible deeds which Moses wrought in the sight of all Israel" (Deut. 34.10-12). The Twelve could rightly ask about Jesus, "Who then is this, that even wind and sea obey him?"

Why would Mark turn to the Psalms and 2 Maccabees as midrashic source material to provide an opportunity for the disciples to become the New Israel? What they have in common is the Davidic messiah imagery. The Psalms were attributed to David, regardless of who wrote them. 2 Maccabees chronicles the Hasmonean (Maccabean) efforts to fulfill the Jewish dream of having a messiah like David by ousting the forces of Antiochus Epiphanes from Israel. They succeeded, off and on, for the better part of a century. In Mark's century, Jews who yearned for freedom from the Roman Empire sought for a new David, a new set of Maccabees to lead the fight for independence. Their "New Israel" would be one of military and political liberty.

The Demoniac Named Legion: Mk. 5.1-20

The consequences of the rescue at sea underscore the temptative nature of the incident. When Jesus steps ashore at Gerasa,[1] he is confronted *immediately* (Mark's word indicating temptation) by a man inhabited by a legion of demons (agents of temptation). The unclean spirits in the man worship Jesus as "Son of the Most

High God," a stronger title than "Holy One of God" and "Son of God" previously used by demons when addressing Jesus. The more elevated title and the multiplicity of the demons (legion) parallel the extraordinary powers of the demon.

> There met him out of the tombs a man with an unclean spirit, who lived among the tombs; and no one could bind him...for he had often been bound with chains and fetters, but the chains he wrenched apart, and the fetters he broke in pieces; and no one had the strength to subdue him. Night and day among the tombs and on the mountains he was always crying out, and bruising himself with stones (Mk. 5.2-5).

Assuming that here, as previously in Mark, a confrontation with the demonic is primarily intended to depict Jesus' own inner condition, his temptation seems to be raging out of control. Mark apparently wanted his readers to recognize the intensification of Jesus' temptation to be worshiped, precisely what was implied in the disciples' question about what kind of person can calm storms. The superficial source of Jesus' temptation is the failure of the Twelve to bear the expected fruit in a mustard-seed-sized task. This corresponds to Mark's earlier Elijah and Moses units in which Jesus' surface temptations originated in the crowds because he was expecting a positive popular response as his indicator of success. Jesus' temptation at a deeper level was the opportunity to display his miraculous power in a sensational manner and thus to lead many to worship the Son of the most High God.

The story culminates with Jesus sending the spirits, at their request, into a herd of swine, which subsequently drown. Mic. 7.19 equates God's salvation with casting "our sins into the depth of the sea." Superficially, the death of livestock threatens the livelihood of their owners, who ask Jesus to leave the country. They are not appeased by the fact that the wild man, having been healed, is "clothed and in his right mind." At greater depth, the drowning of the pigs is incidental because they symbolize the distinction between Old and New Israel. The prohibition against pork was the most widely accepted feature of the kosher food laws, which in turn were indicative of the legalism of what Mark perceived as Old Israel. When demons ask Jesus not to destroy them, but rather to cause the death of the Moses-taboo pigs, they are clearly tempting him to return to the Old Israel which he had sought to escape by having the New Israel Twelve transport him to the Gentile side of the lake. Jesus is led to this result because of his misplaced confidence in the Twelve. In the midrashic imagery of this unit, if the Twelve cannot perform their tiny task then Jesus is powerless to replace the Old Israel with a new one. Jesus is thrown back to Elijah-Moses themes and thus returns to Galilee, the traditional Jewish side of the sea.

Because Ps. 107.26-30 has already been cited as a source for Jesus' calming of the storm, that psalm is the likely source of some of the imagery in the demoniac story, for instance "prisoners in irons" (107.10), "wandered in desert wastes" (107.4), "cried to the Lord in their trouble" (107.6), and "broke their bonds asunder" (107.14). Luke (8.26-39) rewrites Mark's demoniac story so that it fits more closely with the imagery of desert and city in Ps. 107. Jesus' sending the unclean spirits into the bodies of pigs could reflect sending a scapegoat into a wilderness to bear the sins of the people (Lev. 16.16-22). In both stories, the sins leave the people and enter into an animal with the result that humans are cleansed from sin.

The principle that every miracle in Mark is intimately related to the spiritual ideal of the unit in which the miracle occurs is severely tested by the relationship between the calming of the storm on the lake and the calling of the Twelve to be a messianic New Israel. Furthermore, there are to be two more crossings of the lake, in one of which the Twelve are to be "distressed in rowing," and in the other of which they "do not yet perceive or understand." Each of the three is in a different unit in Mark, hence related to a different spiritual ideal. The first story provided Mark a core on which he could ring doublet-type changes in the other two. Superficially, the storm in the first story is an act of nature upon which Jesus focuses his power. At a second, deeper level, the storm is in the Twelve's lack of faith, for they do not believe in their ability to do the truth and hence comprehend the parabolic secrets made available to those who bear fruit thirty-, sixty-, and a hundredfold. At the most complex level, the storm is in Jesus, growing out of his potentiality for being treated as someone super-special because of his power to control nature miraculously. Miracle in that sense contrasts to the earlier miracles in Old Israel which had derived from the traditional religious themes of repentance and forgiveness. This particular miracle, relating to the control of natural forces, occurs appropriately on the Gentile side of the seashore which separated old Judaism and the new Judaism which for Mark included foreigners, thus emphasizing the more-than-Palestinian dimension of the New Israel which Mark had in mind. The response of the demon-possessed man resembles that of the leper earlier: instead of doing what Jesus asks him to do, to tell people what God has done for him, he sets out to advertise what Jesus has done, with the result that Jesus' reputation as a miracle worker continues to grow. Untold in Mark's narrative, the word of Jesus's sensational miracle of healing apparently preceded his return to Old Israel, with the result that a crowd was waiting for his expected homecoming.

Two deeper levels of interpretation are supported by an obscure midrash on 2 Sam. 16.5. A man named Shime-i, from the family of Saul, is designated as "son of Gera ["Sojourner"[2] and is hence a foreigner]." "Gera" could be a sound-alike intended root of "Gerasa," thus referring primarily to a person or to the "place of foreigners" rather than a historical geographical place. Shime-i is a different form of the name Simeon, and hence Simon. This particular "Simon" cursed King David because of his actions as king and thus could be a midrashic model for Simon Peter's rebuking

Jesus for his definition of messiah. If Mark intended "son of Gera" as the source of his "Gerasene" demoniac, Jesus' temptation would be coming from Simon Peter in particular. The author of the Gospel of John understood Simon Peter as the composite disciple who incorporated all the failings of all the others. To the extent that John found clues in Mark upon which to base that characterization, Peter is more likely to have been represented by the Gerasene demoniac.

Intercalated Traditional Miracles in Galilee: Mk. 5.21-43

When Jesus returns to the Galilee shoreline, he is met by Jairus, the ruler of the synagogue, a symbol of Old Israel. The story reads more smoothly if the reader is aware at the onset that Jairus' daughter symbolizes the Twelve as the New Israel, "for she was twelve years old" (5.42). The Old is the parent of the New. Jairus informs Jesus that his daughter is at the point of death and asks Jesus to heal her, a request to which he instantly agrees. The setting is extraordinary apart from the subsequent details. Jesus had previously made three attempts to cross the shoreline to separate himself from Israel. Jairus and the crowd can have had no certain way of knowing that Jesus would be tempted during the storm and would return to them. Yet there they are on the beach, waiting for his return. They represent the pull within Jesus to go back to traditional Israel, almost as if he had manufactured the synagogue crowd to correspond to his inner condition. The synagogue was an institution with which Jesus had had primarily negative experiences. Furthermore, Jesus had earlier sought to avoid being a physician to bodies. Despite all that, the synagogue official is waiting with a request for a miraculous healing for his daughter. Sandmel cites the meaning of the name "Jairus" as either "He Will Enlighten" or "He Will Awaken."[3] The second meaning is appropriate later in the story and may suggest at the beginning that Jesus' return to Galilee involves the awakening of the Old Israel which

Jesus had abandoned.[4] In RSV, the name is written in Num. 32.41; Deut. 3.14; and Josh. 13.30 as Ja'ir, but in the LXX as Jairus. In 1 Chron. 25 a son of Ja'ir is the slayer of the brother of Goliath.

The rest of the story is even more amazing. Using a midrashic intercalation, Mark wrote that on Jesus' way to heal Jairus' daughter, a "great crowd" pressed around him, apparently wanting to touch him, hear his voice, etc., ancient versions of getting a celebrity's autograph. Suddenly Jesus stops to ask in a somewhat accusing manner, "Who touched me?" The text implies that he feels that someone had touched him in a manner which extracted power from his body without his consent. The Twelve, as earlier, misunderstand, knowing that everyone had been touching him. How could he conceivably ask which one person had done so? This continues Mark's development of the crowd motif: in Mk. 3.9 the crowd could crush him; in Mk. 3.20 he ventured into a crowd without fear; now a jostling crowd extracts power from him. A woman who had been bleeding for twelve years confesses that she is the one. She is convinced that if she touches Jesus she will be made well, and this happens according to her belief. Jesus' response to her acknowledges a new type of miracle in Mark: "...your faith has made you well; go in peace, and be healed of your disease." Just as Jesus had relied on others, the Twelve, as his agents to achieve reconciliation by having faith in themselves, the new miracle caricatures that agenda by enabling others, symbolized by the woman, to control Jesus' miracles by their faith in Jesus' inherent power. This type of miracle is found in Mark only in the units dealing with Jesus' reliance upon the Twelve, and only when he is at home in Old Israel. The woman's belief parallels that of the Twelve. They had no faith in their ability to survive the stormy sea and hence could not succeed, but they, like she, were convinced of the miracle power of Jesus. Such trust in their case led to the calming of the storm, in hers to the healing of her twelve-year-old malady. Paul, in Gal. 3.5, suggests that God has performed miracles as a result of "hearing with faith." The Twelve, without faith during the storm, have been deaf when they should have been able to hear.

Part of the drama of the event lies in Mark's midrash on the rules about ritual uncleanness as the result of bodily discharges (Lev. 15; Num. 5.2-3). For men, the rules suggest hemorrhages and emissions of semen. For women, a distinction is made between normal menstrual flow and any discharge of blood beyond seven days. In all cases the person is rendered ritually unclean and is forbidden a wide variety of contacts with other people. None of this is directly alluded to in the instance of the woman with the twelve-year-flow of blood, but it is applicable. For twelve years she would have been somewhat in the position of a social leper, forbidden by Mosaic law to associate closely with ritually clean people. She must have been desperate both to venture into a crowd and to touch someone, two acts forbidden by religious law. Jesus, in turn, ignores her uncleanness as defined by that law and affirms her faith. Demons in the anti-kosher pigs have tempted him to return to Old Israel, but having arrived there he almost instantly finds yet another occasion for objecting to ritualistic rules which separate people from each other.

The intercalation of the healing of the twelve-year-old hemorrhage transforms the Jairus' story. Messengers arrive from his house to inform him that his daughter can no longer be healed; she has died. The superficial assumption is that Jesus is no longer needed. Jesus ignores that despair, having learned from the example of the woman that strong belief has great power to heal. Arriving at Jairus' house, Jesus informs the gathered weepers and wailers that "the child is not dead but sleeping," and takes with him Peter, James/Jacob, John, and the parents into the child's presence. Mark's midrashic reason for taking only the three apostles is the Jas./Jac. 5.14-16 stress on the "great power" of the "prayer of faith [which] will save the sick man and the Lord will raise him up," and the fact that 1 Peter was the first witness to the resurrection. Then, "taking the child by the hand he said to her, '*Talitha cumi*,' which means, 'Little girl, I say to you, arise.' And *immediately* the girl got up and walked; for she was *twelve* years old. And *immediately* they were overcome with astonishment" (Mk. 5.41-42). Now-familiar motifs include two references to "immediately" and one to the number "twelve." To accentuate the latter, Mark inserted it at a place in the sentence where it makes no ordinary sense: of course a twelve-year-old could walk. In addition, the maiden is awakened from sleep according to the etymology of Jairus' name, "He Will Awaken." Jairus believes that Jesus can heal his sick daughter. Jesus, having been taught the power of faith by the hemorrhaging woman, now believes that he can resuscitate the daughter when she is apparently dead and tells Jairus that all that is necessary is for him to believe. At first glance it would appear that Jesus has restored a child to a father and hence has at least symbolically achieved his goal of reconciling Father and children. The apparent success is flawed by the indications of temptation pointing to the likelihood that the apparent healing of the Twelve is no more than a mirage.

Every reader of Mark knows by now that the Twelve are dead to the possibility of ever succeeding as the new Twelve Tribes of Israel. Jesus, however, has internalized what has happened to him in the intercalation. Just as the twelve-year-old hemorrhage was healed by the faith of the afflicted person, so the flow of the story argues that the new Twelve could be healed from their apparent death by their faith in his miraculousness during the storm. Immediately upon seeing that the woman's faith could extract a miracle from Jesus without his prior consent, he wants to believe that the Twelve are only sleeping and that by their own act of faith they too, like Jairus' daughter, can be awakened from that sleep. Thus he metaphorically awakens them from the death-sleep of their inability to bear fruit. The "sleep" imagery is reversed. On the boat, Jesus slept to put the accent on the faith of the Twelve. They awakened him to be rescued. Now the Twelve are asleep in the death of their own failure and have to be awakened in the person of the twelve-year-old daughter of "He Who Is Awakened."

For Jesus to act on the assumption that the Twelve can be roused from their death-sleep is a temptation. He evidences this by forbidding anyone to tell about it, just as he has with each of the unclean spirit temptations. He does not want anyone to know that if the Twelve succeed it was his miraculous healing of them, not their fruit-bearing, which generated the success. The resuscitation of Jairus' daughter and the healing of the woman both distort the meaning of Jesus entrusting to the Twelve the success or failure of his career. The bleeding woman is like the Twelve in her faith in Jesus' miraculousness, in contrast to having faith in oneself. The daughter is like the Twelve in her need to be rescued from a death which Jesus is tempted to believe is only a temporary sleep. If the Twelve subsequently preach in such a way that people repent and thus are reconciled to the Father, Jesus succeeds; if they do not, he fails. For the miracle distortion, it is not important that he entrusts this power to twelve men in particular, but that he depends upon others.

Mark's flow of thought has made it possible to interpret this narrative without much attention to midrashic sources. Midrash, however, provides greater depth to the exegesis. Num. 5.2 accounts for the intercalation. "Every leper, and every one having a discharge, and everyone that is unclean through contact with the dead" is to "be put out of the camp" (Num. 5.2-4). The combination of "having a discharge" and "contact with the dead" accounts for the inclusion of the woman-with-discharge interlude within the dead-daughter story. Jesus, having tried to create in Gentile territory a New Israel which would bypass issues of legalism, has suffered the failure of the New Twelve and as a result has been forced to return to Old Israel to confront Mosaic laws directly. Both Jesus and the ruler of the synagogue know that it would be wrong for either of them to go into the presence of a corpse, just as it was wrong for the woman to be in the crowd which pressed on Jesus. Two laws of Moses make that crystal clear. A person is "unclean" and "guilty" for touching "an unclean thing, whether the carcass of an unclean beast or a carcass of unclean cattle or a carcass of unclean swarming things" or for touching "human uncleanness, of whatever sort" (Lev. 5.2-3). Furthermore, in Num. 6.6, it is forbidden for Nazirites to go near dead bodies, even the bodies of their parents or siblings. The unclean spirits have tempted Jesus to be a Nazirite holy one.

Jesus, by his example, flouts the ritual cleanliness laws in both of Mark's stories, as he had earlier in the healing of the leper. In touching the corpse of Jairus' daughter, Jesus has the positive midrashic examples of Elijah and Elisha, each of whom also violated Mosaic law by lying on a corpse in order to resuscitate it (1 Kgs. 17.21; 2 Kgs. 4.34). In each account, the prophet restored to life the son of a woman with whom he had been associated. The references to "twelve" in the stories of Jairus' daughter and the bleeding women clarify that they are not just stories about the healing of individuals, but about the healing and resurrection of Israel. A number of passages in Jewish scripture deal with these themes. "Come, let us return to the Lord...that he may heal us." "On the third day he will raise us up" (Hos. 6.1-2, 7.1). In Jer. 8.22 and 9.1, the author says "Is there no balm in Gilead? Is there no physician there? Why then has the health of the daughter of my people not been restored?" O "that I might weep day and night for the slain of the daughter of my people!" In 1 Cor. 15.6, 17-20 and Rom. 13.11, Paul refers to death as sleep. All of these may be midrashic sources for Mark's narrative.

No Father in the Fatherland: Mk. 6.1-6

In the concluding pericope in the unit, Jesus comes to a place which Mark designates as Jesus' "fatherland."[5] The word must be translated literally as "fatherland," not "Nazareth," as in Lk. 4.16, or "home town" in order to understand the central point of the story. In Jesus' fatherland, the audience is amazed both at his teachings and his miracles. They know him as "the carpenter, the son of Mary and brother of Jacob and Joses and Judas and Simon," and know that he has sisters living there. They know him as the home town boy who cannot possibly have achieved the kind of greatness they see in him and thus do not believe in him. They know him as a person who has a family in which there is no father. Jesus was for Mark, above all else, the child of the Father God. Hence the irony. His former neighbors see the magnificence of his teachings and miracles, but do not recognize the source of such power in Jesus' relationship to the father God. In an extended sense they are the Galilean Jews of Old Israel, all of whom, according to Mark, reject Jesus, reject their relationship to the Father, and hence limit the power of God in their midst.

The absence of a "father" in Jesus' family in 3.34-35 and 6.3 has nothing whatsoever to do with virgin birth, with Joseph as Jesus' non-biological father, or with the earlier death of Joseph. The account in Mark neither favors virgin birth nor opposes it; Luke creatively reinterpreted Mark's story, eliminating it in its present form from his revision of Mark and transforming it midrashically into the virgin birth narrative. Matthew both copied Mark's story and revised Luke's account of the virgin birth without indicating a clear understanding of either. Jesus was Mark's prototypic example of what it means to be an adult child of God the Father.

The result of the crowd viewing Jesus as a person with no father is that when Jesus seeks to perform mass miracles in his fatherland he is unable to effect the usual floodgate miracle to conclude the unit. Just as the hemorrhaging woman had extracted a miracle from him without his permission, through the power of her faith, so those who reject the fatherhood of God can and do prevent Jesus from performing many miracles, again without his permission, by virtue of the power of their lack of faith. Matthews' revision of Mark's story highlights this point: "And he *did not* do many mighty works there, because of their unbelief" (Mt. 13.58). The "did not" in Matthew differs from Mark's emphasis: "And he *could do no* mighty work there, except that he laid his hands upon a few sick people and healed them. And he marvelled because of their unbelief" (Mk. 6.5). The difference between "did not" and "could not" points to Mark's characteristic treatment of miracle. In this unit, Jesus has entrusted the success of his reconciliation strategy to others. In the account of the bleeding woman who personified the Twelve, that strategy was distorted by her faith-control over his miracle power. Now, in the conclusion, the crowd has a similar faith-control; they do not believe, and his miracle power is thus limited: he "could not" function as miraculously as he had previously.

The midrashic structure for Mk. 6.1-6 was adapted by Mark from 1 Sam. 10.1-27, the account of Samuel's anointing of Saul to be king, i.e., messiah. In the story, Samuel gives as the reason for having a king that the people have rejected "God who saves you" (10.19). The Lord's spirit comes upon Saul; he "is turned into another man" and receives "a new heart," with the result that he prophesies ecstatically (10.6, 9). "All who knew him before" say, "What has come over the son of Kish? Is Saul also among the prophets?" One responds, "And who is their father" (10.11-12)? This source for Jesus' saying that "a prophet is not without honor, except in his own country, and among his own kin, and in his own house" is generally ignored by New Testament scholars in favor of finding a "familiar proverb" in non-Jewish literature.[6]

The fatherland motif holds the unit together. In the first pericope, Jesus sought to leave his home country to go to the foreign side of the sea. Unclean spirits, emerging from the failure of the Twelve, induced him to return. When he did so, the Twelve could be raised from a death-sleep only symbolically as the twelve-year-old child of the ruler of the synagogue and as the hemorrhaging "twelve." Now the people of the fatherland do not recognize the Father. They lack faith. The key names in Jesus' fatherland are Mary, James/Jacob, Joses, Judas, and Simon. The two names new to Mark's Gospel are Mary and Joses. "Mary" is the New Testament counterpart to Miriam, the sister of Moses, spelled "Mariam" in the LXX. The etymology of the name is controversial, with the early rabbis preferring "Bitterness"; Davis and Gehman assume that it means "Obstinancy" or "Rebellion."[7] "Joses" is the Hellenistic transliteration of "Joseph" ("May God Add Posterity").[8] Mark names the five people as members of Jesus' family, but never refers to them again as a family.

Listing the names of Jesus' family is so unnecessary that it calls attention to the probability that the names themselves function as part of a Markan motif. The most likely one is the use of other characters in the career of Jesus to represent dimensions of his own internal struggle with the higher and lower values in each of the strategies under investigation for achieving reconciliation. Judas (Iscariot) and Simon (Peter) will figure in Jesus' life as symbols of two types of messianic expectation, one related to the supernatural aura of the Mount of Transfiguration, and the other to military-political liberation and the triumphal entry. Mary, James/Jacob, and Joses will occupy unique roles in Mark's interpretation of Jesus' burial and resurrection. All five of the names are important in the Old Testament and thus belong to Jesus' fatherland at a superficial level, thus midrashically grounding Mark's use of them in his various accounts.

It was similarly unnecessary to note that Jesus had sisters. They never function as characters in the Gospel. One possibility, creatively enlarged by Luke, is that Mark intended Mary to be modelled midrashically after Hannah in 1 Sam. 2.21. She had three sons and two daughters, all of them born as a result of old-age pregnancies. Mark used incidental details from 1-2 Samuel to supplement his central midrashic motifs throughout the Gospel. Luke promoted the 1-2 Samuel material to the status of primary motifs, especially in the infancy narratives and the Saul-Paul sequence in Acts.

An interesting midrashic motif shows up almost incidentally in the story. Mark refers to Jesus as "the carpenter" and cites the adulation of the crowd as, "What mighty works are wrought by his hands!" (6.2). Since carpenters work with their hands, the combination functions as a pun. "Hands" have been involved in a long string of Markan stories: Jesus "came and took her by the *hand* and lifted her up, and the fever left her; and she served them" (1.31); Jesus "stretched out his *hand* and touched him, and said to him, 'I will; be clean.'" (1.41); Jesus, seeing a man with a withered hand, was "grieved at their hardness of heart, and said to the man, 'Stretch out your *hand.*' He stretched it out, and his *hand* was restored" (3.1-5); "'Come and lay your *hands* on her, so that she may be made well, and live'" (5.23); "Taking her by the *hand* he said to her, 'Talitha cumi'; which means, 'Little girl, I say to you, arise.'" (5.41); "'*What mighty works are wrought by his hands?* Is not this the carpenter?'" (6.2); "And he could do no mighty works there, except that he laid his *hands* upon a few sick people and healed them" (6.5); they "saw that some of his disciples ate with *hands* defiled" (7.2); "And they brought to him a man who was deaf and had an impediment in his speech; and they besought him to lay his *hand* upon him." (7.32); When Jesus "laid his hands upon" the blind man, "he asked him, 'Do you see anything?'" (8.23-25); "But Jesus took him by the *hand* and lifted him up, and he arose"

(9.27); "'The Son of man will be delivered into the *hands* of men, and they will kill him; and when he is killed, after three days he will rise.'" (9.31); "And if your *hand* causes you to sin, cut it off; it is better for you to enter life maimed than with two *hands* to go to hell" (9.43); "And he took them in his arms and blessed them, laying his *hands* upon them" (10.16); "It is enough; the hour has come; the Son of man is betrayed into the *hands* of sinners. Rise, let us be going; see, my betrayer is at *hand*" (14.41); "And they laid *hands* on him and seized him" (14.46); "We heard him say, 'I will destroy this temple that is made with *hands*, and in three days I will build another, not made with *hands*'" (14.58). The connections between the miraculous and the power of hands, and between evil and distortions of hands (withered hand, misconstruing Jesus as a carpenter, Jesus being delivered into the hands of those who would kill him, etc.) are sufficiently consistent in Mark to be read as an intentional motif. In the list of Mark citations above, the first five present Jesus, superficially at least, as a successful miracle worker. The sixth limits that success because of the lack of faith in his fatherland. Most of the rest involve failure, sin, death, misunderstanding, etc. The list culminates finally in the false witness "carpenter" charge that Jesus claims that he will be able to build a temple not made with hands.

The basic imagery of miracles wrought by outstretched hands comes from the Torah, in which hands are viewed as instruments of power: "And the Lord said to Moses, "Say to Aaron, 'Stretch out your *hand* with your rod over the rivers, over the canals, and over the land of Egypt'" (Exod. 8.5); "He shall lay his *hand* upon the head of the burnt offering, and it shall be accepted for him to make atonement for him" (Lev. 1.3-4); "Or has any god ever attempted to go and take a nation for himself from the midst of another nation, by trials, by signs, by wonders, and by war, *by a mighty hand* and an outstretched arm, and by great terrors, according to all that the Lord your God did for you in Egypt before your eyes?" (Deut. 4.34); "You shall remember that you were a servant in the land of Egypt, and the Lord your God brought you out thence *with a mighty hand* and an outstretched arm; therefore the Lord your God commanded you to keep the sabbath day" (Deut. 5.15).

The "fatherland" narrative concludes Jesus' attempt to enable the Twelve to become the New Israel. They have shown themselves to be without faith in themselves during the storm at sea. Jesus has been tempted to achieve their success for them by symbolic miracles of healing people associated with the number "twelve," even to the point of restoring a child to a father. When he comes to his own fatherland, however, no one recognizes him as having a father. The model has been demonstrated to be inadequate, and Jesus is ready to move on to another strategy for enabling the Twelve to achieve the success he has predicted for them.

ENDNOTES FOR CHAPTER SIX

[1]It has long been noted that Mark was in error in naming Gerasa as the place where the boat came to shore, inasmuch as Gerasa was some distance from the sea. This has been correctly interpreted as one more in the long list of indicators that the author was not familiar with the geography of Palestine. K.W. Clark, "Gerasa," *IDB*, defends Mark against error by a broad interpretation of "the country of the Gerasenes."

[2]Davis and Gehman, *Westminster Dictionary of the Bible.*

[3]S. Sandmel, "Jairus," *IDB*

[4] The name "Jairus" is closely related to "Avaran," ("Awake") the surname of Eleazar, one of the five Hasmonean brothers, in 1 Macc. 2.5. The author of the Gospel of John is certain to have used this Eleazar Avaran midrashically in his account of the awakening of Lazarus from sleep. "Lazarus" ("God Has Helped"), in Hebrew, is the slightly shorter form of "Eleazar" ("God Has Helped"). So J.N. Sanders, "Lazarus of Bethany," *IDB*, and T.M. Mauch, "Eleazar," *IDB*.

[5]Bratcher and Nida, 182, contend that the term should refer "'to his own native place': rather than the generalized sense of 'fatherland', 'country' (RSV), the word *patris* (6.4) has here the more specialized meaning of 'home town.' The town of Nazareth is meant."

[6]Schweizer, *Mark*, 124; and Taylor, *Mark*, 301. Taylor notes that Wetstein has collected parallels and that Bultmann holds that *Oxyrhynchus Papyri* 1.11 is the original. As printed in M.R. James, *The Apocryphal New Testament* (Oxford: Clarendon Press, 1924) 27, the passage reads: "Jesus says, A prophet is not accepted in his own home town, nor does a physician work cures upon those who know him."

[7]J.F. Ross, "Miriam," *IDB*; Davis-Gehman, *WDB*.

[8]B.T. Dahlberg, "Joseph," *IDB*. The etymology of Joseph already suggests why Luke would turn Joseph into a non-father for the Christ child who was conceived according to the will of God. It is God, not a human father, who adds that posterity.

CHAPTER SEVEN

MIDRASH ON THE TWELVE AS THE SUFFERING SERVANT REMNANT

Jesus, unsuccessful in establishing the Twelve as the New Israel, was portrayed by Mark as exploring one more possibility of creating a viable role for them. He had previously assigned them only the symbolic task of crossing a lake and had called them to preach but had afforded them no opportunity to do so. His test of their faith had been so unrelated to ministry that it may have been irrelevant to their ultimate success or failure. The Twelve had failed as the New Israel not because they did not preach but because they had no faith in themselves. Jesus now assigns them a ministerial task requiring faith, to preach in an Exodus-type wilderness of personal hardship such as would be appropriate for the Suffering Servant of Isaiah.

The Twelve in a Suffering Servant Wilderness: Mk. 6.7-13

This pericope combines Suffering Servant poems from Isaiah, wilderness living in Exodus and the Jacob story, and insights from the early New Testament epistles.

The latter half of Isaiah (often referred to as 2 Isaiah) is written as if the author was predicting the Jewish return from exile in Babylon (598 or 587 BCE to 538 BCE). It includes the sentence which Mark quoted to justify his assertion that the gospel began in Isaiah and that John was the voice crying, "In the wilderness prepare the way of the Lord, make straight in the desert a highway for our God" (Isa. 40.3). Mk. 6.7-13, by returning to the original meaning of Isa. 40.3, makes obsolete the John-as-wilderness-voice interpretation of Mk. 1, and thus sets the stage for the next pericope in which the death of John is chronicled. John's "wilderness voice" has been supplanted by a model in which the Twelve are midrashically portrayed as a remnant returning from captivity and disciplining their lives en route in a different kind of wilderness.

Some of the poems in 2 Isaiah name the remnant of Jewish exiles as "the Servant." By popular Christian usage, the Servant has become "the Suffering Servant." Isa. 52-53, the major Servant poem, describes the predicted suffering of the remnant in the imagery of a slaughtered lamb. Isa. 53.2 specifies that the Servant grew in the presence of God "like a young plant, and like a root out of dry ground." Had the Twelve been able to do that, there would have been no "barren ground" failure in the parable of the different kinds of soil.

Mark had his choice of a variety of midrashic interpretations about the Suffering Servant lamb. Isaiah asserts that "he was oppressed, and he was afflicted, yet he opened not his mouth; like a lamb that is led to the slaughter, and like a sheep that before its shearers is dumb, so he opened not his mouth" (Isa. 53.7); and concludes, "therefore I will divide him a portion with the great, and he shall divide the spoil with the strong; because he poured out his soul to death, and was numbered with the transgressors; yet he bore the sin of many, and made intercession for the transgressors" (Isa. 53.12). Ps. 44.11 interprets the suffering differently: "Thou hast made us like sheep for the slaughter, and hast scattered us among the nations." The clause, "scattered us among the nations," is the equivalent of the "dispersion" to which both Jas./Jac. 1.1 and 1 Pet. 1.1 are addressed. For the psalmist, the description of suffering was only a prelude to a cry for help.

Paul quoted Ps. 44 and extended it to say that no one "shall separate us from the love of Christ."

> Shall tribulation, or distress, or persecution, or famine, or nakedness, or peril, or sword? As it is written, 'For thy sake we are being killed all the day long; we are regarded as sheep to be slaughtered.' No, in all these things we are more than conquerors through him who loved us (Rom. 8.35-37).

Implicit in the variations in these midrashic sources for Mark is a growing list of ideal types of suffering, including unwanted suffering with the expectation of rescue, voluntary suffering in the expectation of being glorified, and voluntary suffering which rescues others.

Mark enriched the imagery of the remnant Twelve preparing the way of the Lord in a wilderness by midrashic use of specifics from the original Exodus description of disciplined living in the Sinai desert. Jesus sends the Twelve out to live somewhat as if they were those depending upon God for their bread one day at a time (as in Exod. 16 and Num. 11) and relying on the cooperation of the peoples through whose lands they passed (as in Deut. 2). Deuteronomy provides the key for understanding Mark's midrash:

> And he humbled you and let you hunger and fed you with manna, which you did not know, nor did your fathers know; that he might make you know that man does not live by bread alone, but that man lives by everything that proceeds out of the mouth of the Lord. Your clothing did not wear out upon you, and your foot did not swell... (Deut. 8.3-5).

Mark interpreted this to mean that the Twelve should take with them no bread or money, no bag in which to carry bread or money, and no extra clothing or sandals. The prohibition against taking "money nor two cloaks" may derive from 2 Kgs. 5.22, where Elisha's servant requested "silver and two cloaks."[1] Jesus admonishes the Twelve to stay in a house as long as people there are hospitable, but when hospitality is not offered, they are to leave. The instruction about responding to an inhospitable reception is midrashic on Deut. 2.26-37, in which Moses asks permission to pass through Heshbon in peace. When the request is denied, Moses' army utterly destroys both the cities and the people. Sending out twelve in pairs is likely to have come from Num. 13-14, in which Moses sent out twelve spies, with only two, Joshua (Jesus) and Caleb, returning with a positive report.

A deeper underlying version of Jesus' instructions to the Twelve results from studying the midrashic parallels with Gen. 28, 32. Jacob, after his night vision of angels ascending and descending, vowed:

> If God will be with me, and will keep me in this way that I go, and will give me bread to eat and clothing to wear, so that I come again to my father's house in peace, then the Lord shall be my God, and this stone [upon which he had pillowed his head], which I have set up for a pillar, shall be God's house [Bethel]; and of all that thou givest me I will give the tenth to thee (Gen. 28.20-22).

After Jacob's great success, he prayed: "I am not worthy of the least of all the steadfast love and all the faithfulness which thou hast shown to thy servant, for with *only my staff* I crossed this Jordan; and now I have become two companies" (Gen. 32.10). Between Gen. 28 and 32, Jacob was renamed Israel. The Twelve were expected to be a New Israel in the Jacob tradition, taking "nothing for their journey except a staff" and to trust that food and clothing would be provided for them. At the end of their mission they were able to report great successes.

Evaluation of the performance of the Twelve requires careful comparison of their assignment with their deeds. In Mk. 6.7-10, Jesus "began to send them out two by two, and gave them authority over the unclean spirits. He charged them to take nothing for their journey except a staff; no bread, no bag, no money in their belts, but to wear sandals and not put on two tunics. And he said to them, 'Where you enter a house, stay there until you leave the place.'" What they actually did (Mk. 6.12-13) was to preach "that men should repent. And they cast out many demons, and anointed with oil many that were sick and healed them." When they were the New Israel, they had the tasks of being with Jesus, preaching, and exorcising demons, but now they are sent away from Jesus and are not expected to preach. They are to resist temptation (have authority over the unclean spirits) while living sacrificially, but do not do so. Upon their return they have five loaves and two fishes although Jesus had instructed them to take no food for their journey. They have imitated the Jesus-Elijah example, preaching repentance and experiencing new versions of his temptations. They have become authoritative miracle-workers, thereby trivializing the messiah as the *Anointed One* by their acts of anointing with oil to cure the sick.

Their sensational cures are modelled after the admonition in Jas./Jac. 5.14-15 for elders to pray over the sick, "*anointing him with oil* in the name of the Lord; and the prayer of *faith* will *save the sick man*, and the Lord will *raise him up*; and if he has committed sins, he will be forgiven." Mark may have used this Jacob passage as an organizing principle for the pericopes preceding the mission of the twelve: the disciples' lack of faith, the raising of Jairus' daughter, and the disciples' distortion of their instructions, healing instead of resisting temptation. This would fit the assumption that Mark had also developed from Jacob the motifs of bearing fruit in the parable of the soils, and the wave-tossed sea of doubt.

The Intercalated Death of John the Baptizer: Mk. 6.14-29

If Mk. 6.13, the statement that the apostles were anointing with oil and healing, were immediately followed by their return to report their successes in 6.30, that would be a smooth transition. Between the two sentences, however, is the apparently intrusive narrative about the death of John the Baptizer at the hands of "King" Herod. The Herod who ruled in Galilee in the time of Pontius Pilate was Herod Antipas, a puppet Roman governor. His grandfather, Herod the Great, was the only Herod to bear the title of king. It seems incontestable that Mark midrashically blended the figures of King Herod the Great and Herod Antipas to create the new "King Herod." Mark may also have promoted Herod Antipas to "king" in order to accentuate midrashic parallels with Esther and Daniel. Another midrashic possibility is that Mark referred to Herod as "king" because he had used Ps. 2.2 as the basis for the Pharisees going to the Herodians to plot Jesus' death; Ps. 2.2 uses the terms "kings" and "rulers." The story is a Markan intercalation, leading one to ask how the meaning from 6.30 on is changed by virtue of the John account.

The narrative itself is in two parts. In the first, Herod believes that Jesus is John resurrected, whereas others think that Jesus is Elijah or some other prophet resurrected. Herod specifically thinks that the miracles of Jesus are possible because Jesus is the reincarnated John. The story flashes back to the time when Herod had ordered John to be arrested because John had criticized Herod's marriage to his sister-in-law. Herod Antipas had in fact married the wife of his brother Herod Philip, a fact which provided a midrashic source from history rather than from sacred text for this part of the story. John had apparently applied to Herod the law of Lev. 18.16: "You shall not uncover the nakedness of your brother's wife; she is your brother's nakedness." That prohibition in Leviticus is toward the end of a long list of violations which would result in the sinner being "cut off" from his or her people. Thus, Herod and his wife Herodias were threatened by the Mosaic law which John applied to them. Both had reason to be angry at him. Mark blamed Herodias more than Herod, who was said to fear John, knowing him to be a righteous and holy man, and consequently "kept him safe." Herod is like Jacob's demons who believe in God but are afraid. His religiosity is overwhelmed when Herodias' daughter arouses him with a dance and leads him "immediately" to order John beheaded.[2]

One major midrashic source for the pericope is Dan. 6.6-15. Darius was persuaded to issue an edict which resulted in his having to order the death of Daniel, one of the king's favorites. Royal edicts could not be revoked (Dan. 6.12; also Esth. 1.19; 8.8). King Herod, "because of his oaths...did not want to break his word..." (Mk. 6.26) and hence ordered the death of John whom he previously had known to be "a righteous and holy man."

The role of the queen in the beheading has several attractive midrashic models. One is Jezebel's effort (1 Kgs. 19, 21) to seek to kill Elijah and actually have Naboth killed. King Ahab treats Elijah as a prophet, although he always opposes him; Queen Jezebel openly seeks his life. Another midrashic source for the narrative is the book of Esther, in which the king holds a banquet at which he says to Queen Esther "What is your request? It shall be given to you, even half of my kingdom" (5.3; 7.2). Esther's response, although she does not specifically ask for Haman's death, sets in motion the events which result in his hanging (7.6,10). As in Mark, the one killed is the queen's enemy, not the king's, and the queen's request results in his death. Both "King" Herod and King Ahasuerus offer to give "even half of my kingdom." All of this can be argued either from the LXX or the Masoretic text, but Mark's attention to the LXX version of Esther is made likely by one of the many LXX additions to the book. LXX Esther begins with Mordecai the son of Jairus ("He Who Awakes") awaking from a dream, just as the daughter of Jairus was awakened from death in Mark.

One more midrashic source possibility is the apocryphal book of Judith, in which the heroine attends a banquet given by an enemy general, dressed so as to entice him (10.1-4), with the result that he "took great delight in her" (12.20). When he became drunk, she cut off his head, gave it to her maid, and the two of them carried it to display before the men of the city (13.8-15).

The deaths of John and Jesus have strong parallels. A Roman ruler is reluctant to execute each man, but is persuaded to do so. Both have disciples; their bodies are each laid in a tomb. Herod seeks to keep John safe, as does Judas in the betrayal narrative. None of those details matter much for John's death, but they are important in the Jesus story. John's death prepares the reader for the Jesus story. Herod is ironically right: Jesus does relive part of the life of John, not his miraculousness as Herod thought but the very death which Herod reluctantly perpetrated. A further parallel is that John is identified with a wilderness, and Jesus' Twelve are sent into a wilderness. John dies because of his desert message; the Twelve are supposed to be the Suffering Servant. The quintessential reason for intercalating the death of John thus emerges: being servants in the wilderness involves not just short rations of food and clothing, but the certainty of voluntary death.

How Many Loaves Have You? Mk. 6.30-43

The shift of motifs from miracle to death in the John story explains the conclusion of the Twelve's mission. Before the intercalation, the Twelve had reported that they had healed the sick by anointing with oil. They saw miraculousness as messianic; they were physician-anointers. The crowds were so excited that "many were coming and going," and Jesus and the Twelve "had no leisure even to eat." That situation serves as a midrashic doublet for Mk. 3.20, in which the miracle-loving crowds had pressed upon Jesus so tightly that he was not able to eat. The crowds now had the miracle-workers they wanted, a dozen of them, all implicitly willing, by their use of a messianic symbol, to act corporately as the miraculous messiah. The Twelve's acceptance of the crowd's messianic agenda metaphorically causes the death of John the Baptizer. Mark's John emphasizes crowd repentance and forgiveness, but the Twelve's interest in repentance and forgiveness are dead. The physical death of John could have occurred anytime, but his agenda is not dead until the Twelve replace it with messianic miraculousness. The Twelve thus disappoint Jesus' expectation that they could preach without succumbing to the temptation to be the Elijah-type miracle-worker. By Mark's implied definition, miraculousness in the Twelve has been generated by authoritative preaching, not by public belief that Elijah had returned from the dead.

Jesus knows that popular adoration of the Twelve makes the crowds as dangerous to his mission of achieving Father-child reconciliation as they had been when he feared "lest the crowds should crush him." In a doublet on that earlier occasion, he now tells the Twelve to "come away by yourselves to a lonely place." In Mk. 1.35 Jesus had gone to a "lonely place" when he had been besieged by miracle-seeking crowds. Alone, he had decided to focus upon preaching only. If Mark was suggesting that Jesus was taking the twelve to a lonely place where they could make a similar decision, the crowds deprive them of that opportunity.

Mark's story of the feeding of the 5,000 is best read in the contexts of Mk. 6.52 and 8.14-21, in which Jesus states that the disciples do not understand the mass feedings and that the significance of the bread and its leftovers is more than that which could apply to bakery bread. The story affirms Deut. 8.3 that "man does not live by bread alone, but that man lives by everything that proceeds out of the mouth of the Lord." It builds upon the Jewish biblical tradition that persons may eat the word of God, as expressed, for example, through Jeremiah's promise that God will provide shepherds "who will feed you with knowledge and understanding" (Jer. 3.15).

Jesus had instructed the Twelve to go on a Suffering Servant mission, taking no bread, bag, or money. On their return, Mark appropriately called them "apostles" (ones sent out) because they had been sent out to perform a task, but almost immediately demoted them to the status of students (disciples). Jesus is portrayed as a teacher, speaking compassionately to crowds whom he views as sheep without a shepherd. When the "students" call to Jesus' attention the people's need for food, he asks them to feed the crowd. The disciples' response, that it would cost too much for them to feed so many, does not clarify whether they have a lot of money (two hundred denarii) in their possession and object to spending it, or whether they are protesting that it would cost far more than they have to secure enough food. If the Twelve had obeyed their instructions they would have had neither money nor food upon their return. By raising the issue of monetary cost, Mark may be midrashically paralleling Isa. 55.1-3, in which people are invited to eat the bread of God's word, to buy an everlasting covenant of "wine and milk without money and without price." Had the disciples obeyed Jesus' instructions, they would probably also have had the spiritual food of the word of God to give to the people. The disciples, however, have the midrashic precedent of Deut. 2.6 in which the Hebrews in the wilderness are instructed to buy bread for money. Jesus apparently recognizes at that moment that the only food they have to bestow is bakery bread; he asks them how many loaves they have with them. By their orders they should have had none, which is in keeping with the midrashic model of the Exodus wilderness instructions about not saving any manna for the next day. They answer that they have five loaves of bread and two fish. Jesus divides the crowd into fifties and hundreds, apparently multiplies the fish and loaves, and feeds the crowd. The parallel message from the Torah is that those who had been satisfied with manna in the wilderness will subsequently "eat bread without scarcity" (Deut. 8.9). Mark's account does not specify that a miracle occurred, but that probability is heightened by midrash on two passages from 1 and 2 Kings: "Obadiah revered the Lord greatly; and when Jezebel cut off the prophets of the Lord, Obadiah took a *hundred* prophets and hid them by fifties in a cave, and *fed them with bread* and water" (1 Kgs. 18.4); "A man came from Ba'alshal'ishah, bringing the man of God bread of the first fruits.... And Elisha said, '*Give to the men, that they may eat.*' But his servant said, 'How am I to set this before a *hundred* men?' So he repeated, 'Give them to the men, that they may eat, for thus says the Lord, *They shall eat and have some left.*' So he set it before them. *And they ate, and had some left*, according to the word of the Lord" (2 Kgs. 4.42-44). "Fifty" and "hundred" are typical numbers in Elijah-Elisha stories. Elijah killed people by fifties in 2 Kgs. 1 and fifty strong men were sent by the sons of the prophets to find Elijah after his ascension into heaven in 2 Kgs. 2.

Mark's peculiar language "he divided the two fish among them all" suggests a separate midrashic source for the fish. The Testament of Zebulon about Compassion and Mercy reads: "Out of compassion I gave some of my catch to...all men, as each had need...and so the Lord gave me a rich catch of fish; for he who shares what he has with his neighbor is repaid many times over by the Lord" (6.3-6). Zebulon always shared "and there was still enough for [his] household" (6.7). Mark could also have been attracted by the statement that "in the last days" "the Lord himself," "God in human form," shall "arise for you, and healing and compassion shall be in his wings" (9.5, 8).

The disciples have solid midrashic foundation for concern about meeting the physical needs of people: "If a brother or sister is ill-clad and in lack of daily food, and one of you says to them, 'Go in peace, be warmed and filled,' without giving them the things needed for the body, what does it profit?" (Jas./Jac. 2.15); "But if anyone has the world's goods and sees his brother in need, yet closes his heart against him, how does God's love abide in him?" (1 Jn. 3.17). Yet the disciples trivialize Jesus' subtle request that they feed the multitude with the word of God, showing concern only for the people's physical hunger. They answer in terms of money and the groceries which would be needed for 5,000 people. In defense of the disciples, Jesus has changed their Suffering Servant instructions. Originally they had not been called to preach or teach; now they are expected to do so. The crowd is fed bakery bread, a lesser good in contrast with the bread of the word of God. In this sense the feeding of the 5,000 is a temptation.

The imagery of sheep and their shepherd is a rich one in the Old Testament, with many messianic overtones. Mark could have midrashically adapted it from many Old Testament references to shepherds and sheep. Each of the following has the advantage of being relevant not only here but also to some other specific context in Mark. Moses asked God to "appoint a man" in order "that the congregation of the Lord may not be as sheep which have no shepherd" (Num. 27.16-17). God responded by appointing Joshua (Jesus). Isaiah, predicting that the remnant would prepare God's way in a wilderness, promised that God "will feed his flock like a shepherd, he will gather the lambs in his arms" (Isa. 40.3-11). Zechariah saw people wandering like sheep, "afflicted for want of a shepherd," and expressed "hot anger" against the leaders (Zech. 10.2-3).

Three facts are relevant to Mark's use of these texts. Moses was himself a shepherd according to Exod. 3. The word translated as "lonely place" in Mk. 6.31 is the same word which is translated as "wilderness" in Isa. 40.3 and Mk. 1.3. Zech. 13.7 will later be cited by Mark as a midrashic model for the crucifixion, when the shepherd is struck down and the sheep scattered. This indicates a shift from Elijah to themes associated with Moses and the other prophets, and may also be preparing Jesus to make the first prediction of his passion.

The crowd scene provides the Twelve a third chance to succeed. They had failed on the boat and on their Suffering Servant mission. Now, by their inability to feed the crowd, they fail again. Jesus, by feeding the crowd, rescues them by doing what he had asked them to do, as he had earlier during the storm at sea. He does so now by converting compassionate teaching into compassionate feeding, a devaluation implicit in the disciples' failure to comprehend, but which Jesus creates out of the situation and biblical models. Jesus feeds the crowd with bread and fish belonging to the disciples, not his own.

Making Sure That the Disciples Fail: Mk. 6.45-52

The temptative quality of the feeding incident is reinforced when, "immediately" after twelve baskets full of leftovers are gathered, Jesus sends his disciples to Bethsaida (Aramaic for "House of the Fisher" or "House of the Hunter"[3]). Mark portrayed Bethsaida as being on Jewish side of the Sea of Galilee and the feeding as occurring on the Gentile side. Jesus probably intends to dismiss the Twelve from his service altogether by sending them home, i.e., to the House of the Fisher. Bethsaida is the etymological home for fishers (or hunters) of men according to Mark's original midrash on Jer. 16.16: "Behold, I am sending for many fishers, says the Lord, and afterwards I will send for many hunters." The fishermen-followers were at first called from their nets in the Capernaum area. Mark relabeled their origin as the House of the Fishers for the purpose of Jesus dismissing them. One historic village on the Sea of Galilee named Bethsaida had been renamed "Julias" by Herod Phillip, probably before 2 CE.[4] Jews might have called it Bethsaida as a way of resisting Romanization despite its official designation.

Mark developed the narrative along two lines, one related to dismissing the disciples, the other to his praying alone. The latter is a doublet for Mk. 1.35, in which Jesus spent a night praying alone, with the result that he changed directions in his career. In 6.31, Jesus had instructed the Twelve to "come away by yourselves to a lonely place." The crowd's excitement about the miracles performed by the Twelve frustrated that plan. After Jesus had dismissed both the disciples and the crowd, he again went to pray alone. When the boat was on the sea, Jesus "was alone on the land." Mark's otherwise unnecessary emphasis on Jesus' "aloneness" calls attention to it as part of a motif beginning with his temptation to think of himself as "the Holy One, I, only I," and ending with the crucifixion in which Jesus dies alone, having been abandoned by all significant others in his life. At this juncture, Jesus is torn between giving up on the Twelve and rebinding them to himself by rescuing them from another storm at sea.

Exegesis of the account is rendered difficult by the confusion in times. The hour was "now late" (6.35) when the Twelve called to Jesus' attention the crowd's need for food. Jesus sent the disciples away after the meal, dismissed the crowds, went into the hills to pray, and was then alone. "When evening came, the boat was out on the sea, and he was alone on the land" (6.47). He approached them "about the fourth watch of the night," shortly before dawn (6.48). Between evening and then, he saw that they were distressed in rowing. If he saw their distress in early evening but waited till morning to come to them, the story has one meaning; if he did not see them until morning and went immediately to them, a different meaning would apply. Without the reference to "evening," the story would encompass only the events of a single night. With it, the story may run all through the next day and into a second evening.[5] In the shorter version, Jesus would undoubtedly have dismissed the crowd not later than about 10:00 p.m., prayed, and then walked on water during the last hours before daybreak.[6] The Twelve would have been rowing for five hours against a head wind (twenty-nine in the longer version). Whether out of faith or desperation, they had not given up. They were about to succeed in their original mustard-seed-sized task, rowing across the lake during a storm, except that they were doing it for themselves in Jesus' absence. In that setting, "he meant to pass by them, but when they saw him walking on the sea they thought it was a ghost, and cried out; for they all saw him, and were terrified" (6.48-50). When they suddenly saw what they believed to be an apparition of Jesus walking on the water, doing easily what they were doing the hard way, their perseverance collapsed. The inner faith which had kept them rowing just as suddenly deserted them now as it had when they had wakened Jesus from sleep to save them from drowning. Left alone they might have succeeded. In the presence of the possibility of being rescued, they could not.

The details about Antiochus Epiphanes midrashically relevant to the first storm story are even more relevant now: "the man who just now presumed to command the waves of the sea, in his superhuman boastfulness" (2 Macc. 9.8); and the arrogance of Antiochus thinking that he could make "the sea traversable on foot" (2 Macc. 5.21). The likelihood that Mark intended to contrast the emperor Antiochus, who claimed to be divine and to have superhuman powers, with Jesus for whom the possibility of claiming divinity was an ever present temptation is increased by the circumstance that Acts 12.20-23 is midrashically based on 2 Macc. 9.8-10. Herod, in Acts, was acclaimed as God and was consequently eaten by worms and died, like Antiochus. Luke's attention could have been called to the remainder of the midrashic source by his understanding that Mark had already used part of it. The evangelists' attention to Antiochus as a well-known and scandalous false god whose memory lingered on among the Jews would explain why certain kinds of miracles had to be reported for Jesus in order to show that he was what Antiochus only claimed to be. At the same time, that model would establish for Mark a sound justification for his contention that miracles of the sort desired by Antiochus were temptative regardless of whether or not one had the actual power to perform them.

In Mark's narrative, the clause "he meant to pass by them" is open to several interpretations: he meant to come close to them; he meant to go on past them without stopping; or he meant to come close to them with the result as reported in Mark. The lexicons of classical and koine Greek permit all these options. Abbott and Smith, in the *Manual Greek Lexicon of the New Testament*, include such variant possibilities as "to pass by, to neglect, to disregard." Liddell and Scott in their lexicon for classical Greek include "to pass without heeding, to pass without notice, and disregard." The context suggests strongly that Jesus intends to go by them without stopping so as to leave them to the task of rowing on their own, without his assistance. Bratcher and Nida note that Jesus forces or compels the Twelve to go ahead of him to Bethsaida. "The word implies unwillingness on the part of the disciples."[7] The drama of the story is rooted in the fact that if Jesus had genuinely dismissed them from his service, he would not have come close to them at all. If he was tempted to rescue them from their failure in the mass feeding, he could just as well be tempted here to rescue them once more. If he was not tempted, why was he walking on the water in the first place?

Whatever the interpretation above, those who were bravely confronting the storm were terrified when they believed they were seeing a ghost. Jesus "immediately" lets them know who he is, calms the sea once more *without their asking him to do so*, and brings them to shore. This is the second "immediately," and certainly tips the scales toward interpreting the continuous feeding-sea event as a temptation. In Jesus' internal struggle, he both wants the Twelve to succeed in their assigned Suffering Servant messiah tasks and wants them not to succeed. He has fed the crowd for them and has gone through the motions of dismissing them from his service. But when their hours-long courageous struggle against a head wind is on the verge of demonstrating their faith in themselves and their ability to suffer, Jesus reappears in their lives. They give up.

Mark's conclusion is surprising. The wind ceases when Jesus enters the boat and the Twelve are "utterly astounded," not because of Jesus' mastery over nature, which they had seen before, but because "they did not understand about the loaves, but their hearts were hardened" (Mk. 6.52). Mark used the imagery of hardened hearts in the same way he used blindness and deafness, as a symbol of the inner failure of people to be able to live the kinds of lives prerequisite to reconciliation between Father and children. The failure of the Twelve appropriately labeled them as hard-hearted people. The question is what do they not understand about the loaves. The question is highlighted by the fact that in the feeding-the-four-thousand doublet in Mk. 8.1-21 the disciples do not understand either about the loaves or the leftovers. The only available clue at this point is that the disciples do not understand what was wrong about them having more loaves in their possession than they needed for any one day. In that basic violation of the original manna-in-the-wilderness midrashic imagery, they were indeed hard-hearted followers.

In structuring the incident as he did, Mark extended the midrashic imagery of Deut. 8, in which it is said that "man does not live by bread alone." Moses warned people "when you have eaten and are full" and all that they have "is multiplied," that they are in danger of saying in their hearts that "my power and the might of my hand have gotten me this wealth" (Deut 8.11-17). Midrash on

Deut. 8 shifts the onus to Jesus, not the disciples. It was he who relied on his own "power and the might of his hand," both in relationship to stilling the storm at sea and "multiplying" the loaves. The tone of Deut 8. is that people cannot achieve on their own, without God. It was Jesus who undercut the disciples' stouthearted effort to succeed on their own.

Mark, not troubled by such apparent criticism of Jesus, was concerned about the consequences of too much power on the psyche of a power-wielder. The observation, often attributed to Lord Acton, that power tends to corrupt and that absolute power tends to corrupt absolutely, is close to Mark's intention. Careful analysis of Mark's interpretation of Jesus helps Christians understand the manipulation of extraordinarily unchecked power by those who have abused public trust. By presenting miraculous power as a temptation, Mark showed what happens even in the life of the one who is finally reconciled to God. It will come as no surprise to the perceptive reader of Mark that Jesus, in order to be the crucified child of God reconciled to the Father, finally has to reject both his own use of power to do miracles and any kind of miraculous intervention by God.

Beginning Again at Gennesaret: Mk. 6.53-56

Instead of arriving at Bethsaida, the destination symbolizing Jesus' dismissal of the Twelve from his service, they all come to shore at Gennesaret. A plain called Gennesaret was located on the northwest shore of the Sea of Galilee. 1 Macc. 11.67 refers to the Sea of Galilee as "the water of Gennesaret." The name sounds like the Greek word for beginning *genesis* but is of unknown etymology. Mark adopted the sound-alike meaning to represent the idea of beginning again, just as Capernaum had earlier served that same purpose. Jesus had intended to dismiss the disciples, but rescuing them and arriving at the "shore of beginning" restores them to his service.

Attempting to begin again by the miracle which renewed Jesus' reliance on the Twelve as his New Israel and remnant Suffering Servant turns out to be both a massive temptation and failure for Jesus. Mark noted:

> ...immediately the people recognized him, and ran about the whole neighborhood and began to bring sick people on their pallets to any place where they heard he was. And wherever he came, in villages, cities, or country, they laid the sick in the market places, and besought him that they might touch even the fringe of his garment; and as many as touched it were made well (6.54-56).

The brief summary gathers together themes from several miracle events Jesus had previously performed in the presence of the disciples or as symbolic means of remedying their failure. Mass healing by touching his clothing amounts to almost total loss of Jesus' control over his own miracle power. The crowd miracle is an appropriate conclusion for a segment in which Jesus sought to achieve the success of his career through those other than himself. He has expected the Twelve to live according to the models of the New Israel and Suffering Servant, with their Elijah and Moses variations. Just as he has expected others to achieve his own success, so, in the trivialization of that hope, his miracle power has been lodged in others. This is the last mass miracle scene reported in Jesus' career.

The Final Failure of the Twelve: Mk. 7.1-23

A conversation between Jesus and the Pharisees establishes a context for a private exchange between Jesus and his disciples. The two should be dealt with as a continuous story. Jesus' confrontation with the Pharisees (Mk. 7.1-16) begins with the issue of ritual washing before meals. Jesus ignores the accusation that his disciples eat with unwashed hands. He accuses the Pharisees, by quoting Isa. 29.13 against them, of teaching as truth that which is in fact only the opinions of people. This charge probably reflects an ongoing debate between rabbinic Pharisees and other Jews and implies that the handwashing regulations were, from some Jewish perspective, not in scripture.

The Pharisees believed, in opposition to their more conservative opponents, that oral interpretations of scripture, which they called midrash, are as sacred as the written text of scripture itself. Mark seems to side with the conservatives, although his own use of midrash aligns him methodologically with the Pharisees. Thus it is strange that Mark seems to have Jesus accuse the Pharisees of teaching human opinions which vary from the exact text of scripture. Mark's midrashic source may have been Paul's claim that "we impart this in words not taught by human wisdom but taught by the Spirit, interpreting spiritual truths to those who possess the Spirit" (1 Cor. 2.13).

Jesus continues his rebuttal by accusing the Pharisees of justifying not taking care of one's parents by citing the authority of Corban ("Offering" or "Oblation" but translated by Mark himself as "Given to God").[8] In Mark's broader context, he is accusing them of making Father-child reconciliation impossible by their legalistic rationalization for failing to recognize the relationship between what ought to be given to the Father God and to one's own parents: one cannot serve God as Father and yet mistreat one's parents. Malachi's vision of ultimate reconciliation between the Father God and his children assumes that one must be reconciled both to God and to one's parents (Mal. 4.6). Corban, to the contrary, supports the midrashic Elisha imagery involved in the original calling of the first four disciples when reconciliation was implicitly impossible because the new fishers of men abandoned their parents in order to serve God. Now, the Pharisees are overtly condemned for theoretically justifying the abandonment of certain parents.

Midrashically, Mark could have related caring for parents to 1 John's insistence on taking care of one's brothers: "He who does not love his brother whom he has seen, cannot love God whom he has not seen" (1 Jn. 4.20). John, the son of Zebedee, by being identified with the author of 1 John, should have clearly understood Jesus' criticism of the Pharisaic practice of corban, but did not, as the continuing story shows.

Pursuant to his condemnation of Pharisaic legalism about parents, Jesus answers the original charge about unclean hands by announcing the abolition of all kosher food laws for his followers: "Hear me, all of you, and understand: there is nothing outside a man which by going into him can defile him; but the things which come out of a man are what defile him" (Mk. 7.14-15). Jesus is distinguishing between the Pharisees' externalized notion of what is "given to God" and a more internalized version, the gift to God of living a pure life. That ends the conversation with the Pharisees.

The spiritually obtuse disciples later decide that the kosher announcement was a parable and ask Jesus to explain it. His reply acknowledges their final failure: "Then are you also without understanding" (Mk. 7.18)? The "also" puts the disciples into the same class as the crowds, the Pharisees, and the scribes from Jerusalem. It brings to an end Jesus' parabolic hope that the Twelve would find within themselves an invisibly growing, mustard-seed-sized basis for maturing into a great tree of faith. Jesus' explanation brings to a climax the inner-outer motif which has been building in Mark from the beginning:

> What comes out of a man is what defiles a man. For from within, out of the heart of man, come evil thoughts, fornication, theft, murder, adultery, coveting, wickedness, deceit, licentiousness, envy, slander,

> pride, foolishness. All these evil things come from within, and they defile a man (Mk. 7.20-23).

Mark had strong midrashic undergirding for that conclusion: "Circumcise yourselves to the Lord, remove the foreskin of your hearts"; "wash your heart from wickedness; how long shall your evil thoughts lodge within you?" (Jer. 4.4; 4.14). "Wash yourselves; make yourselves clean; remove the evil of your doings from before my eyes; cease to do evil, learn to do good; seek justice..." (Isa. 1.16-17); "Do not look on his appearance or on the height of his stature, because I have rejected him; for the Lord sees not as man sees; man looks on the outward appearance, but the Lord looks on the heart" (1 Sam. 16.7); "I know and am persuaded in the Lord Jesus that nothing is unclean in itself; but it is unclean for any one who thinks it unclean" (Rom. 14.14); "'All things are lawful for me,' but I will not be enslaved by anything" (1 Cor. 6.12; cf. 1 Cor. 10.23-26).

Jesus Abandons Israel Altogether: Mk. 7.24-30

Mark's narrative has led unswervingly toward a decision Jesus would have to make when he finally realized that neither the crowds of Old Israel nor the twelve as a New Israel could do what is necessary to achieve Father-child reconciliation. He must abandon any notion of depending upon others and find some way of doing by himself what must be done. Mark builds a literary bridge to this now necessary choice by portraying Jesus as leaving Israel, going "to the region of Tyre and Sidon," and trying to keep his presence there a secret. Modern Tyre and Sidon are in Lebanon, north of Galilee; biblical Tyre and Sidon were Gentile cities, famous as Phoenician seaports. By going specifically to those places, Jesus not only abandons Israel but also goes to a city associated with the career of Elijah, as reported in 1 Kgs. 17.9, and to a seacoast, as stressed in Isaiah. The latter contains a dozen references to "coastlands," each implying that they are Gentile, typified by "I will send survivors to the nations...to the *coastlands* afar off, that have not heard my fame or seen my glory" (Isa. 66.18-19; cf. Isa. 51.4-5).

The tone of the "coastland" midrashic sources in Isaiah argues that Jesus' departure from Israel is more than an abandonment. It is a possibility built into the structure of the gospel which had begun in Isaiah and which was first exemplified by the model of Elijah. Mark's narrative follows the midrashic pattern of Num. 11 and 1 Kgs. 19. In the former, Moses hears the complaints of people regarding the miraculous manna which sustained them for forty years in the wilderness. He feels so alone and overburdened that he wants to die. In 1 Kings, Elijah has miraculously called down fire from heaven to win a contest against the prophets of the false gods, whom he subsequently kills. Jezebel threatens to kill him. He also responds by asking to die, and is tempted in an "I, I alone" manner. Jesus has recently fed the five thousand and also goes off to be by himself, discouraged and willing to give up on his previous objectives of getting either the crowds or the Twelve to hear the word, change their lives, and bear fruit.

Jesus intends to be hidden in Tyre and Sidon. His fame as a miracle worker precedes him. A foreign woman seeks him out with a request to exorcise a demon from her daughter. The story of the daughter's unclean spirit is multivalent. Jesus has already made it clear that unclean spirits are inner temptations, not external powers. Thus it is likely that the spirit will be in Jesus and in the mother who makes the request rather than in the daughter. At a superficial level, it is assumed that Jesus knows that, but that the mother does not. The text reads:

> She begged him to cast the demon out of her daughter. And he said to her, 'Let the children [implying Jews] first be fed, for it is not right to take the children's bread and throw it to the dogs [implying Gentiles].' But

> she answered him, 'Yes, Lord; yet even the dogs under the table eat the children's crumbs.' And he said to her, 'For this saying you may go your way; the demon has left your daughter'" (Mk. 7.26-29).

When the mother went home she found her daughter healed. The essence of the conversation is that the woman seeks Jesus out to ask for an exorcism despite the fact that she is not Jewish, and he grants her request because of her cleverness.

At a deeper level of the story, the woman, before there is any exorcism, agrees to be content with crumbs. As soon as she is thus satisfied, the demon leaves her daughter. There needs be no exorcism. Jesus simply states the accomplished fact. It is as if the story was told as follows:

> Woman: "Lord, please do something about my wretched daughter."
>
> Jesus: "Why should I do for foreigners what I have quit doing for Jews?"
>
> Woman: "I would be satisfied with table scraps if you would change her behavior."
>
> Jesus: "If you are satisfied with table crumbs, you can be at ease with your daughter in her present behavior. You will see that she is no longer unsatisfactory. Go home and discover that your daughter now pleases you."

At either of these first two levels of interpretation, a parent and a child are reconciled to each other for the first time in Mark. Hence there is a built-in bias that whatever follows this event will set Jesus on the right track toward reconciliation with the Father God. Furthermore, the woman is satisfied with small bits of bread from the table, and Jesus will soon ask his disciples, to no avail, to understand about the scraps left over from the feeding of the 5,000 and 4,000. The words for the leftovers at the feeding and the bits of bread at table are not the same in the Greek text, but they represent a continuous theme for Mark.

The midrashic source for the story is 1 Kgs. 17.9-16. Elijah goes to Sidon and begs a starving widow to bring him a morsel of bread, instructing her to "first make me a little cake of it and bring it to me, and afterward make one for yourself and your son" (17.13). Although she has only a handful of meal, she generously feeds Elijah first, with the result that there is plenty left over, as in Mark's mass feeding stories. In Mark, a woman has a daughter; in 1 Kings, the widow has a son. Both stories occur in or around Sidon. The reversal of details regarding who begs for bread and whether the children are to be fed first or last is consistent with the flexibility of midrash. Tannehill notes that Luke uses details from 1 Kgs. 17.9-16 in his accounts of the widow of Jain, Jairus' daughter, and the convulsed child at the foot of the Mount of Transfiguration, thus strengthening the probability that Mark had previously used the 1 Kings source.[9]

The story is really about Jesus; the woman and her daughter function as manifestations of his inner dilemma. Jesus has been dissatisfied with the unsatisfactory response from both the crowds and the Twelve. They have refused to accept his strategies for reconciliation, each of which has come with its own inherent lesser alternative. They have chosen the lower and temptative dimension of every high ideal he has set before them, symbolized in part by unclean spirits speaking to him from within his own struggle between the greater and lesser good. The woman's example now inadvertently teaches him that he can be satisfied with less than he has previously demanded. The result is that in the next pericope he will be back in Israel and never again make demands on anyone other than himself as the primary condition for his own success in achieving reconciliation with the Father.

Tannehill's concept of "type scene" is midrashically relevant here. Twice in 2 Samuel, King David is confronted with a supplicant. In 2 Sam. 12, it is Nathan the prophet with a report about a wealthy man who had stolen his poor neighbor's lamb. In 2 Sam. 14, it is a woman seeking protection against the death of her son and heir. In both cases, after David had offered the asked-for solution, the supplicant said in effect, "You are the man" (2 Sam. 12.7). True to that type scene, Mark has the woman tell her story, but leaves it to the reader to supply the implication that the incident is really about Jesus and his disciples, not about the woman and her daughter.

Jesus ("God Saves") has used the models of Elijah, Moses, the New Israel and the Suffering Servant for the purpose of having the Old Israel crowds or the New Israel twelve save him from his portion of the general human failure to be reconciled to the Father. When he recognizes that the disciples are "also without understanding," he knows that both Old nor New Israel have failed. Reconciliation with the Father cannot come from outside himself. The foreign woman showed him an example of how to achieve reconciliation by himself. He could be satisfied with scraps.

ENDNOTES FOR CHAPTER SEVEN

[1]Suggested by Roth, *Hebrew Mark*, 50.

[2]A remote possibility is that this story is somehow a midrash on the cruelty of Alexander Janneus, king of Judea from 103-76 BCE, who on one occasion crucified 800 pious opponents and killed their wives and children before their eyes while he enjoyed his concubines, and who on another occasion executed 6,000 Pharisees at the Feast of Booths. Alexander Janneus married the widow of a dead brother. Mark may have connected the names of Janneus and John.

[3]M. Avi-Yonah, "Bethsaida, *IDB*.

[4]M. Avi-Yonah, "Bethsaida."

[5]One source of the difficulty is Mark's poor grammar. Four sentences in a row, as punctuated in RSV, begin with "And." All punctuation in the New Testament is according to the translator's best judgment. In this instance, the text provides no clue as to which clauses to join together with an "and."

[6]It is not known for sure how Mark calculated a watch. In Palestinian custom, the fourth watch of the night was probably the last third or quarter of the night before daybreak, not a designated clock period. But "according to the Greco-Roman system the night...was divided into four watches of three hours each. The fourth watch, the last one, would be from 3:00 to 6:00 A.M." Bratcher and Nida, 213.

[7]Bratcher and Nida, 211.

[8]A comparable Jewish teaching from the oral law is reported in TB Megillah, 16B: "To study the Torah is more important than to honor parents." H. H. Guthrie, Jr., "Corban," *IDB*, indicates that "in later Judaism, anything set apart by the use of the term, even rashly, could not thereafter be used for any other purpose (Ned. III.6; IX)."

[9]Tannehill, 88, f.n. 25.

CHAPTER EIGHT

MIDRASH ON PERSONAL EFFORT TO ACHIEVE RECONCILIATION BY MIRACLE

Mark has previously portrayed Jesus as being totally dependent upon the responses of the crowds and then the Twelve to determine his success in seeking reconciliation between the Father and his children. All of that is now behind him. The general question for Mk. 7.24—10.45 is whether Jesus can accomplish Father-child reconciliation on his own without positive responses from anyone other than himself. In Mk. 7.24—8.30 he uses the intentional miracle strategies of Moses, Joshua, Elijah and Elisha and fulfills Isaiah's vision of God's miraculous saving. From 8.31—10.45 he shifts to the model of an individual Suffering Servant with particular focus on the guaranteed reward dimension of Isa. 52-53 and its reflections in James/Jacob, 1 Peter, and 1 John. The Suffering Servant imagery is intermixed with Elijah and Moses material. This chapter is limited to the intentional miracle strategies.

Miraculously Heal the Blind, Deaf, and Mute: Mk. 7.31-37

Jesus had previously used muteness as a metaphor for his own inability to communicate truth, and blindness and deafness as metaphors for the non-comprehension of the crowds and the Twelve. His problem now is how to overcome the disciples' blindness and deafness and thereby his own inability to speak plainly. Mark had abundant midrashic source material. Moses had complained about himself that he was unable to speak eloquently, but God had promised that this defect would be overcome (Exod. 4). Isaiah had predicted that "the deaf shall hear" and "the blind shall see" (29.18) and that the messiah servant will be "a light to the nations, to *open the eyes that are blind*" (42.1-7). The LXX version of Isa. 35.5-6 addresses all the themes:

> Then shall the *eyes of the blind be opened*, and the *ears of the deaf shall hear.* Then shall the lame man leap like a hart, and the tongue of the *stammerers shall speak plainly* [Masoretic reads "shall sing for joy"].

Mark's words for dumb and speaking plainly are, however, not the same as those in LXX Isaiah 35. In one version in Isaiah, the messiah will be blind and deaf himself: "Who is blind but my servant, or deaf as my messenger whom I send?" (Isa. 42.19). The latter passage gave Mark midrashic justification for recognizing that blindness and deafness at the depth level of the narrative are partially in Jesus as well as in others.

Mark's interpretative framework for the miracles of this unit involve Jesus returning by a circuitous and unlikely route from Tyre (north to Sidon, then southeast to Transjordan) to get to the Gentile side of the Sea of Galilee,[1] to be confronted by a deaf-mute. Jesus puts his fingers in the deaf-mute's ears to unplug his deafness; he spits and touches the man's tongue to enable him to speak. Later he heals a blind man in the same general way. Jesus' use of such "imitative magic" is similar to the style of miracles in 2 Kgs. 13.14-19 and Exod. 17.8-13. According to Mark's unique psychology, the miracle designed to cure the deaf-muteness of another has the effect of healing the muteness of the healer. In Mk. 4, when all who heard Jesus were deaf, he had to speak in parables, i.e., without clarity. Now the deaf-mute is said to "speak plainly." A few pericopes later, Mark will report of Jesus that he says something plainly, with the implication that healing the deafness of others has freed Jesus from his peculiar muteness. In this sense, the story uses imitative magic at two levels: Jesus opens the man's ears in order to cure the disciples' deafness, and the man's clear speech is restored in order that Jesus be freed from his own inability to communicate plainly.

The healing is only superficially successful. Mark followed it with a stereotypic warning signal about temptation, having Jesus order those present not to tell. The admonition falls on still-deaf ears; the man and all others who see the wondrous event tell everyone. The nature of Jesus' temptation is not yet obvious, but it is clear that even though he speaks plainly at the surface level, his hearers are still deaf to what he asks of them. The temptation is likely to be connected to the new fact that Jesus in this narrative is intentionally miraculous. Neither people nor events have inveigled him into a healing of physical deafness-muteness which trivializes his cure of their lack of understanding. Jesus has done this on his own; he is exploring intentional miracle as a way for him alone to do what is necessary to achieve Father-child reconciliation. Consciously intended miracle puts him in the tradition of Moses, Joshua, Elijah, and Elisha, the four great miracle-workers of the Old Testament.

Feeding the Four Thousand: Mk. 8.1-10

With virtually no transitional statement, Mark creates a doublet for the feeding of the 5,000. Jesus is compassionate because a crowd has been with him in a wilderness[2] for three days, ready to faint, and is without food for the stomach. He takes seven loaves plus a few fish from the disciples, multiplies the food, serves 4,000 people without requesting the disciples to feed them, and has seven full baskets left. In the earlier event, Jesus had been a compassionate teacher intending to feed the bread of the word of God to those who were like sheep without a shepherd. He had fed them bakery bread only after the disciples demonstrated that they could not manage that task on their own. The focus of the new story is entirely food for the stomach; Jesus is not even referred to as teaching. The disciples ask, "How can one feed these men with bread here in the desert?" (8.4). Any Jew hearing this question should automatically have thought of the classic answer, that God fed the people a plentiful supply of manna in a wilderness. Ps. 78 asks, "Can God spread a table in the wilderness? ... Can he also give bread or provide meat for his people?" and answers by noting that "He [being "compassionate"] sent them food in abundance...and they ate and were well filled" (78.19-29). Mark's feeding stories may have both fish and bread as a midrash on the Torah story of God providing both manna and quail to the Jews in the wilderness (Num. 11.31, Exod. 16.14). The disciples, as fishermen, would provide fish rather than other meat.

It may be no more than an accident that Mark's expression about Jesus and the loaves, "having given thanks he broke" them, is identical in Greek to 1 Cor. 11.24. This is the first known expression of the ritual which has come to be associated with the Lord's Supper.[3] If Mark intended a midrash on those words, the temptative quality of the event appears immediately. Paul portrays Jesus as breaking his own body, symbolized by bread. In Mark, Jesus, without self-sacrifice, breaks only the the disciples' bread left over from eating when 4,000 others around them are hungry. All Elijah-Elisha details in the first feeding story are omitted from the second one: the crowd is not fed by fifties and hundreds; there are "about 4,000," not 5,000.

Mark had three reasons for creating the feeding-of-the-4,000 doublet. Jesus' intentional miracle of feeding bread alone functions as a caricature of the 5,000 theme that people do "not live by bread alone" but by the Word of God, just as healing deaf ears is a distortion of healing incomprehension. More important is the midrashic resignification of the baskets full of leftovers. In the 5,000 account, there were twelve basketfuls of scraps, but scraps had no significance in the story. Now, with the 4,000, there are seven baskets of leftovers, but the context has provided enormous importance for scraps because they symbolize Jesus' satisfaction with a method of reconciliation involving no necessity of positive responses from anyone other than himself. Finally, at the 5,000 feeding, the number twelve symbolized the New Israel. Jesus was asking the Twelve to feed the crowds with the bread of the Word of God; thus the New Israel was analogized by the twelve baskets full of leftovers. If twelve represents the New Israel, seven must point to the old one. Seven is the ultimately sacred number for Judaism, representing ritual sabbath observance. Just as Jesus' temptation at the end of the feeding of the 5,000 frustrated his first effort to send the Twelve back to their homes, his temptation in the 4,000 incident sends him back to Old Israel, to Dalmanutha where he disembarks long enough to be confronted by Pharisees, the ultimate advocates of sabbatarianism according to Mark.

After feeding the 5,000, Jesus sent the disciples away in a boat and then dismissed the crowds. At the second feeding, he first sends the crowds away and then *immediately* embarks with the disciples to go by boat to Dalmanutha. The name is of unknown etymology; no plausible sound-alike has been proposed; the location is equally unknown. V. Taylor mentions several proposals which have been made to explain Dalmanutha. All of them have been oriented toward correcting an error by Mark or a copyist to make the name conform to some other historical place, rather than making sense out of why Mark used the unusual name in this context.[4] The fact that Jesus went there *immediately* lends even more urgency to the quest for an explanation based on meaning rather than historical geography. A Markan intercalation in this context is fruitful in providing possibilities for an answer which makes sense in Mark's narrative.

The Demand For Sensational Miracle: Mk. 8.11-13

Pharisees seek from Jesus "a sign from heaven, to test him." The request implies that his previous miracles, however sensational, have not sufficed as "a sign from heaven" and that something more is required. Jesus responds by stating that "no sign shall be given to this generation." This story must be considered with Jesus' subsequent warning: "Take heed, beware of the leaven of the Pharisees and the leaven of Herod" (8.15). The disciples obtusely think he is referring to bakery loaves such as they had twice provided for him and protest that they have none. Jesus is thinking about leaven as a metaphor. The Pharisees and Herodians have held counsel together regarding Jesus' execution (Mk. 3.6). Herod had ordered John's death. Mark's language about Jesus' opponents in 3.2-6, 10.2, and 12.13 suggests that the Pharisees in Mk. 8.11 are "testing" Jesus with hostile intent. Jesus has criticized the Pharisees and scribes for their hypocrisy (7.6), for "rejecting the commandments" (7.9), and for internal uncleanness (7.6-23).

The Pharisees' request for a sign as proof that Jesus is from God follows the logic of Exod. 4, in which Moses has protested that people will not believe his claim to represent God. The Lord gives Moses three signs to perform as proofs: turning a shepherd's staff into a serpent, making his own skin alternately leprous and clean, and turning water on the ground into blood. Deut. 34.10-11 summarizes Moses' life in terms of such miraculous powers: "And there has not arisen a prophet since in Israel like Moses, whom the Lord knew face to face, none like him for all the signs and the wonders which the Lord sent him to do in the land of Egypt."

Whether Jesus could or could not do a Moses-like sign would not matter to the Pharisees. If he could, he would be their kind of leader and they would follow him; if not, their bias against him would be confirmed. Jesus recognizes their request as the temptative side of his strategy: no miracle is so big that some will not demand an even more sensational one. This has to be seen in the context of Jesus' two previous successful miracles. In the first, he symbolically healed the lack of understanding of the deaf disciples and hence enabled himself to speak plainly. In the second, he fed the crowds with enough left over to feed all of Old Israel. Now, back in Old Israel with the Pharisees, he recognizes that his strategy has failed for at least one segment of Old Israel. He promises that no sign of the exciting kind they have demanded will be given to the Pharisees' entire generation.

At a deeper level in Mark, the allegation that the Pharisees made their request in order "to test him" suggests that Mark's midrashic source may have been Wisd. 2.6-20. The passage is so powerfully important for the rest of Mark that we quote it in its entirety here and often allude to it hereafter as "the death trial of the virtuous son of God."[5]

> Come then, let us enjoy what good things there are, use this creation with the zest of youth; take our fill of the dearest wines and perfumes, let not one flower of springtime pass us by, before they wither crown ourselves with roses. Let none of us forgo his part in our orgy; let us leave the songs of our revelry everywhere, this is our portion, this the lot assigned us.
>
> As for the virtuous poor, let us oppress him; let us not spare the widow, nor respect old age, white-haired with many years. Let our strength be the yardstick of virtue, since weakness argues its own futility. Let us lie in wait for the virtuous man, since he annoys us and opposes our way of life, reproaches us for our breaches of the law and accuses us of playing false to our upbringing. He claims to have knowledge of God, and calls himself a son of the Lord. Before us he stands, a reproof to our way of thinking, the very sight of him weighs our spirits down; his way of life is not like other men's; the paths he treads are unfamiliar. In his opinion we are counterfeit; he holds aloof from our doings as though from filth; he proclaims the final end of the virtuous as happy and boasts of having God for his father.

> Let us see if what he says is true, let us observe what kind of end he himself will have. If the virtuous man is God's son, God will take his part and rescue him from the clutches of his enemies. Let us test him with cruelty and with torture, and thus explore this gentleness of his and put his endurance to the proof. Let us condemn him to a shameful death since he will be looked after—we have his word for it.

By the logic of Wisdom, the sign demanded by the Pharisees would ultimately be Jesus' rescue from the cross in the face of an otherwise certain death. The "leaven of the Pharisees" would in the long term be their efforts to kill Jesus and hypocritical willingness to follow him only if he could avoid that death. Luke recognized Wisd. 2-4 as Mark's major source text for his stories about the Pharisees, as evidenced by his two references to Solomon, the supposed author of Wisdom, in his section on "no sign for this generation" and the "leaven of the Pharisees" (Lk. 11.31; 12.27). The "leaven of Herod" in Mark might be Herod's role as executioner and hypocrite, for he had killed John even while believing him to be a holy man.

Signs in the Bible are not always miraculous and are not always presented positively. In Exod. 3.12, it a sign that Moses would bring the Hebrews to a particular mountain. Moses warns against any prophet who "gives you a sign or wonder" and invites you to "go after other gods" (Deut. 13.1-3). God tells Ezekiel that he is "a sign for the house of Israel" (Ezek. 12.6-11). Paul also is aware that signs can be used in a variety of ways. He speaks of winning "obedience from the Gentiles, by word and deed, by the power of signs and wonders, by the power of the Holy Spirit" (Rom. 15.18-19). He notes, however, that "Jews demand signs and Greeks seek wisdom, but we preach Christ crucified, a stumbling block to Jews and folly to Gentiles, but to those who are called, both Jews and Greeks, Christ the power of God and the wisdom of God" (1 Cor. 1.22-24). He suggests that "the signs of a true apostle" are his "weaknesses, insults, hardships, persecutions, and calamities," that when he is weak he is strong, and that he is foolish when forced by others to perform "signs and wonders and mighty works" (2 Cor. 12.9-12). Finally, he chastises those who "desire proof that Christ is speaking in me" (2 Cor. 13.2-4). Mark apparently sought midrashically to label the Pharisees with Paul's denigration of "Jews [who] seek signs" and those who "desire proof."

The Boat Trip to Bethsaida: Mk. 8.14-21

Jesus' conversation with the Pharisees functioned as an intercalation between two boat stories. Jesus and the Twelve, now in a boat headed for Dalmanutha, arrive instead at Bethsaida ("House of the Fisher"), their originally intended destination after the feeding of the 5,000. This signals that the dismissal of the disciples to their figurative home, aborted earlier when Jesus miraculously rescued them from their fright, may be in the process of being completed. Jesus expects that the disciples will understand about the leaven and the bread because their deafness-to-meaning has been healed. His voice must have been filled with despair when he said to them: "Why do you discuss the fact that you have no bread? Do you not yet perceive or understand? Are your hearts hardened? Having eyes do you not see, and having ears do you not hear" (Mk. 8.17-18)? He then asks the disciples if they do not remember the twelve and seven baskets of leftovers after the two feeding incidents. They do, but still do not understand. Mark did not explain why Jesus asked about the different number of baskets of excess food. One possibility is that the discussion of the quantity of leftovers points the disciples toward the plentifulness of bread/the Word of God, as if Jesus had said, "What do you mean, 'You have no bakery bread?! Remember all those leftovers of both types of bread!'" Enough leftovers for their twelveness and for old Judaism should be a tangible message to them that they should stop sinning and start bearing fruit. The model could have been Lev. 26.3-26, in which those who live according to the commandments will have leftovers after abundant harvest: "you shall eat old store long kept, and you shall clear out the old to make way for the new;" "you shall eat your bread to the full." Those who don't obey the commandments "shall eat and not be satisfied." A more probable reason for Jesus not explaining the significance of seven and twelve is that the deeper drama in the narrative is that it is still Jesus who is blind and deaf, who does not yet understand that intended miracle has not and cannot achieve what this midrashic model promises. Jesus does not yet know that the stopover at Dalmanutha to argue with Pharisees is only a way station en route to Bethsaida where the Twelve will forever cease to be the New Israel. The disciples will continue to be associated with him, but never again will they function as the Twelve symbolizing either the New Israel or the remnant Suffering Servant. The reason is that Jesus cannot by his own private miraculousness heal their blindness and deafness. Whatever the etymology of Dalmanutha, it functions as a non-place, a non-destination.

The Twice-Healed Blind Man: Mk. 8.22-31

The two apparently separate pericopes of the twice-healed blind man and Peter's confession that Jesus is the messiah have to be dealt with as one unit. Together they function as Mark's bridge from the intentional miracle unit to the Isaiah Suffering Servant passages in the next unit.

At or near Bethsaida ("House of the Fisher") Jesus uses imitative magic to heal a blind man. Jesus spits on a man's eyes, lays hands on him, and asks uncertainly, "Do you see anything?" The man does see, but distortedly so that people look like trees. Without the spittle, Jesus tries again, touching the man's eyes with the result that he sees everything clearly. Jesus sends him to his home, with instructions to "not even enter the village," perhaps a sterner version of "tell no one!" If the event occurred in Bethsaida the man's home must have been in the countryside near some other village. The significant part of the story is that Jesus is not immediately successful in performing a healing miracle. His experience with the deaf-mute casts doubt on Jesus' ability to restore the disciples' spiritual sight and hearing by intentional miracle. Despite Jesus' own "muteness" being healed, the Twelve still do not understand his meanings.

A remote possibility is that Mark intended the entire unit from the healing of the deaf-mute to the healing of the blind man as a midrashic recreation of the vision of Isa. 29-30, in which God will do "*marvelous things with this people, wonderful and marvelous*," "the deaf shall hear," "the blind shall see," "and those who err in spirit will come to understanding" (29.14-24). The Pharisees who question Jesus about signs may be those "[who] draw near with their mouth and honor me with their lips, while their hearts are far from me" (29.13). The famished crowds may be Isaiah's "hungry man [who] dreams he is eating and awakes with his hunger not satisfied" (29.8). Isaiah'smetaphoric "bread of adversity" (30.20) could have been Mark's midrashic source for the warning against the leaven of Jesus' adversaries, the Pharisees and Herod.

Jesus left Israel twice, once to the Tyre-Sidon area where he confronted the Syrophoenician woman, and once to Caesarea Philippi, a city at the north end of the Jordan Valley[6] with a symbolically foreign name. He midrashically traced the journeys of Elijah and Elisha, each of whom left Israel once, Elijah to go to Sidon and Elisha to go to Damascus. En route to Caesarea Philippi, Jesus asks the disciples about whom they and others think him to be. They say that the public identifies him as Elijah, John the Baptizer, or a prophet; Peter, seeming to speak for all of them, says that Jesus is the Messiah, the Christ. Jesus was called "Jesus Christ" (Jesus the Messiah) in James/Jacob twice, in 1 John eight times, and in 1 Peter nine times plus thirteen more as Christ alone.

This numerical preponderance midrashically justified Mark in designating Peter as the first to affirm that Jesus is the Christ.

Jesus replies to the disciples as he had responded to unclean spirits who had used right words with wrong meanings, charging them to tell no one. Jesus sees them as the half-healed blind man, seeing the right thing in the wrong way. He knows without further evidence that Peter's vision of him is temptative. The issue is not a denial of Jesus' messiahship as in 1 Jn. 2.22, in which antichrist-liars deny that "Jesus is the Christ" and deny "the Father and the Son." Peter affirms Jesus' messianic role in a way which is temptative for Jesus. Such praise could not have tempted Jesus if he did not intuit what Peter meant by it and had not already internalized that possible interpretation. In that respect, Jesus also is the half-healed man. The disciples had been half-healed of blindness and its accompanying deafness. Jesus was thus only half-healed of muteness, so that when he assays "plain speaking" in response to Peter his words are still as puzzling as ever. He too, for the moment, says the right words and adopts wrong meanings for them.

The healing of the blind man is followed by the demonstration that Peter's lack of vision has been only half healed: he distortedly recognizes Jesus as the wrong kind of a messiah, comparable to seeing men as trees. Thus the story of the twice-healed blind man is an analogy of Peter's partial sightedness. The strategy of intended miracle fails: deafness, blindness, and muteness remain. After Jesus' return from Tyre, he had intentionally healed the deaf-mute, fed the 4,000, tried to get the twelve to understand, and healed the blind. During Jesus' trip to Tyre and Sidon he had learned to become content with crumbs, with small gains by others, but, to his disappointment, he is unable to transform the Twelve so that they can hear, see, or understand even in small ways. After his patient second effort to heal their blindness, Jesus abandons the intentional miracle strategy for creating a New Israel and begins to apply to himself the suffering servant model.

Endnotes for Chapter Eight

[1]Commentators with otherwise diverse interests such as Kee (*Community of the New Age*, 210) and V. Taylor (*St. Mark*, 361) agree that Jesus was on the Gentile side of the Sea of Galilee in this story and the next, the feeding of the 4,000.

[2]Bratcher and Nida, 3 and 246, suggest that the RSV word "desert" is more likely to mean an "uninhabited territory" than an arid place. "Wilderness" is therefore preferable to "desert."

[3]Schweizer, *Good News* , 157, discusses the possibility that the language of Mark came from a church liturgy.

[4]V. Taylor, *St. Mark*, 361.

[5]At the 1989 national meeting of the Society for Biblical Literature, there was considerable talk about the possibility that Greek philosophers had a well-established ideal of a voluntary suffering poor man. This in turn led to the discussion as to whether it was valid to see Jesus as a "Cynic in rags."

[6]D. C. Pellett, "Caesarea Philippi," *IDB*.

CHAPTER NINE

MIDRASH ON JESUS AS THE INDIVIDUAL SUFFERING SERVANT

Mark performed one of his brightest acts of midrashic genius by combining in this unit the individual Suffering Servant motif with two others. He brought to a decisive close the primacy of the recurring Elijah and Moses models, symbolized by the disappearance of Moses and Elijah from the Mount of Transfiguration, and he gave unique roles to Peter, James/Jacob and John, integrating apparently unrelated passages from the books identified with their names into a smooth narrative flow in his Gospel. The unit is dominated by three predictions, usually referred to as passion (suffering) predictions. To think of them as "passion" predictions is to distort their role. Each concludes with a forecast of resurrection which functions as an automatic reward for the expected suffering. They deal more with reward for suffering than with suffering alone and hence are better referred to as passion-reward predictions.

The First Passion-Reward Prediction: Mk. 8.31—9.1

Jesus, speaking plainly as if the disciples' blindness and deafness had been healed, tells them that he, as a son of man, will be rejected and killed by the religious leaders and that "after three days" he will rise again. A source for Jesus' forecast of his own death is Moses' statement in Deut. 4.22: "For I must die in this land; I must not go over the Jordan." The fact that Jesus can now speak without the "muteness" of parables has an important midrashic source parallel. "And you, *son of man...you* shall speak and *no longer be dumb* [speechless]" (Ezek. 24.25-27). Isa. 30.20-21 refers to a time of adversity and affliction when "*your teacher will not hide himself any more,* but your eyes shall see your teacher. And your ears shall hear...."

Mark's most important midrashic source for this unit is 1 Cor. 15.3-5, in which Paul asserts that "Christ died for our sins in accordance with the scriptures, that he was buried, that he was raised on the third day in accordance with the scriptures" and first appeared to Cephas (Peter). Paul never specified which passage he meant by "according to scripture." Mark is likely to have assumed that Paul was referring to 1 Peter's midrashic paraphrase of Isa. 53 as demonstrated in the parallels below.

1 Pet. 1.11; 2.22: "Predicting the sufferings of Christ...he committed no sin; no guile was found on his lips."	Isa. 53.9: "He had done no violence, and there was no deceit in his mouth."
1 Pet. 2.23: "When he was reviled, he did not revile in return."	Isa. 53.7: "He was oppressed and afflicted, yet he opened not his mouth."
1 Pet. 2.24: "He himself bore our sins."	Isa. 53.12: "He bore the sin of many."
1 Pet. 2.24-25: "By his wounds you have been healed. For you were straying like sheep."	Isa. 53.5-6: "With his stripes we are healed. All we like sheep have gone astray."

The fact that 1 Peter is among the first authors to proclaim Jesus as messiah virtually guarantees that Mark's Peter should affirm Jesus as the Suffering Servant type of messiah according to the midrashic paraphrases of Isa. 53 in Peter's book.

The high drama in Mark's account is that Peter and Jesus rebuke each other after Peter accurately calls Jesus the Messiah and Jesus plainly interprets messiahship in terms of the Suffering Servant model. One explanation for this is found by comparing

Jesus' statement about death and resurrection with the original sources in 1 Peter and Isaiah. In Isa. 53 the Suffering Servant "poured out his soul to death." His reward was division of "a portion with the great" and "the spoil with the strong." The reason for that death was to make "himself an offering for sin," to bear "their iniquities" and "the sin of many," and to make "intercession for transgressors"; "he was wounded for our transgressions, he was bruised for our iniquities...and the Lord has laid on him the iniquity of us all." 1 Peter proclaims that the prophets "inquired what person or time was indicated by the Spirit of Christ within them when predicting the sufferings of Christ and the subsequent glory. It was revealed to them that they were *serving not themselves but you*" (1.11-12). Peter's problem relates to the words "serving you." Peter does not object to Jesus' forecast of suffering or resurrection but to the fact that Jesus does not indicate that his death will benefit anyone other than himself. The author of 1 Peter would not have objected had Jesus gone all the way in interpreting his death in terms of the Suffering Servant who was to die for others. The self-centeredness of a person who is delighted that someone else has suffered *for me* is mirrored in 1 Peter: "By his [God's] great mercy we have been born anew to a living hope through the resurrection of Jesus Christ from the dead" (1.3); "He himself bore our sins in his body on the tree, that we might die to sin and live to righteousness. By his wounds you have been healed" (2.24). The central concern in such statements is what others receive as a result of Jesus' suffering.

By contrast, Jesus' passion predictions in Mk. 8-10 focus on reward for himself only, with no mention of gain for others. It is as if he has ceased seeking reconciliation for other children of God and is seeking only his own. Peter rebukes Jesus for shutting the disciples out of "partaking in the glory that is to be revealed" (1 Pet. 5.1) which will result from the Suffering Servant Messiah's voluntarily accepted death. Jesus responds that the rebuke is Satanic. Superficially, Jesus' reference to Satan may originate in 1 Pet. 5.8, in which "the devil prowls around like a roaring lion, seeking some one to devour." In Mark's context this does not mean that what Peter has said is evil, but that it is a temptation to Jesus. Jesus orders the temptation, both his own and Peter's, to get behind him, out of sight. This is a variation on the "do not tell" order associated with temptation by unclean spirits. Mark is likely to have had in mind Jas./Jac. 4.7, "Resist the devil and he will flee from you," as if Jesus could overcome the temptation merely by ordering it to get behind him. Throughout this unit new versions of this theme appear, indicating that Mark was focusing on the temptativeness of expecting automatic rewards for suffering.

Mark may have been attracted to a passage in 2 Samuel in which a relative of Saul named Shime-i (a variation of Simon) curses David:

> Begone, begone, you man of blood, you worthless fellow! The Lord has avenged upon you all the blood of the house of Saul, in whose place you have reigned; and the Lord has given the kingdom into the hand of your son Absolom. See, your ruin is on you; for you are a man of blood (2 Sam. 16.7-8).

The twofold repetition of "man of blood" reinterpreted in terms of Jesus' willingness to die could well have figured in Mark's picture of Simon Peter rebuking Jesus. The Shime-i in the passage is the son of Gera, a sound-alike with the Gerasene demoniac.

An additional midrashic precedent for the three passion-reward predictions may come from the account of Elijah's death journey and assumption into heaven in 2 Kgs. 2.1-14. Three times Elijah says that he is sent by the Lord, first to go from Galgala (LXX) to Bethel, then to Jericho, and finally to the Jordan River to be "taken away," presumably by death. Elisha acknowledges that he is aware of Elijah's forthcoming departure. At the end of the story, Elijah is taken up into heaven; if he "dies" it is a non-death type of death. Jesus' passion-reward prediction is as if he is imagining his death to be like that: "As the Messiah Elijah, I will permit myself to be killed but three days later I will be resurrected from the dead and go to live in heaven much as I did in 2 Kgs. 2 when I died without really dying and gloriously ascended to heaven." His temptation is to die in order to be the "Son of Man" who "comes in the glory of his Father with the holy angels" (Mk. 8.38).

Mark's phrase "*after three days* rise again" supports the use of Elijah imagery in the narrative. The expression, repeated in all three passion-reward predictions, was changed in Mk. 15-16 to mean "on the third day" because Jesus was dead not more than 39 hours stretching over a period of three days (mid-afternoon Friday to early Sunday). The fact that the passion-reward predictions accurately forecast virtually all details of the crucifixion and resurrection other than "after three days" calls attention to the word *after* connected with *three*. The Elijah-Elisha cycle in 1-2 Kings implicitly designates several events as happening *after* a *three*: resurrections of sons after Elijah or Elisha did something three times to a body (1 Kgs. 17.21; 2 Kgs. 4.29-36), Elijah going to Ahaziah to forecast his death after being sought by three squads of soldiers (2 Kgs. 1.9-16), Elijah's ascension after moving three times from one place to another (2 Kgs. 2.1-6), and Elisha's proof of that ascension after disciples had searched for Elijah for three days (2 Kgs. 2.17-18). Mark used Josh. 10 (Jesus in LXX) as the midrashic source for details of Jesus' burial cave. Josh. 3.2 and 9.16-17 use the expression "at the end of three days," implying that the events alluded to were continued afterward. Mark intended to model the resurrection part of the passion-reward predictions after the Jesus of Joshua and the Elijah of 1-2 Kings, thus buttressing his contention that the eventual failure of this model would be one more way in which Elijah would be exorcised from Jesus' life as a midrashic pattern to be emulated.

Jesus' prediction introduces for the first time in Mark the idea of his own resurrection. The term denotes being fully dead and returning to life as the same person in the same body. In Mark the idea of the revivification of the dead has previously surfaced in the awakening of Jairus' daughter and in Herod's belief that Jesus is John returned to life. If Jairus' daughter was really dead, the term resurrection applies, but if John came back to life as Jesus, reincarnation is the proper term.

Most Christians have associated the concept of resurrection so exclusively with Jesus that it is surprising to discover midrashic sources for it. 1 Peter and Paul's letters had earlier announced the resurrection of Jesus, with 1 Pet. 1.3 having been the first to proclaim it. For Paul, it was possible to "die every day" (1 Cor. 15.31), and therefore presumably to be resurrected daily. One could die in the future and be resurrected: "We shall all be changed, in a moment, in the twinkling of an eye, at the last trumpet" (1 Cor. 15.52). Paul regarded Jesus as having been resurrected.

Mark, although aware of Paul's diverse usage, apparently attended to the Elijah-Elisha texts (1 Kgs. 17; 2 Kgs. 4) and passages from Hosea and Ezekiel for the details of his imagery of resurrection. Hosea said in reference to the nation Israel, "Come, let us return to the Lord; for he has torn, that he may heal us; he has stricken, and he will bind us up. After two days he will revive us; *on the third day he will raise us up*, that we may live before him" (6.1-2). Ezekiel envisioned that he was to prophesy to a valley full of bones:

> "Say to them, O dry bones, hear the word of the Lord. ... Behold I will cause breath to enter you, and you shall live. And I will lay sinews upon you, and will cause flesh to come upon you, and cover you with

> skin, and put breath in you, and you shall live [in a future messianic age]; and you shall know that I am the Lord" (37.1-6).

Ezekiel states that the bones which will be "raised from the graves...are the whole house of Israel" (37.11-12). The Elijah and Elisha stories describe resurrections in which each of the prophets did something three times in order to bring life to individuals. Bodily resurrection of an individual messiah on the third day combines these passages. All of Paul's concepts of resurrection differ from Hosea's resurrection of the nation Israel, Elijah's resuscitation of the dead, and Ezekiel's automatic resurrection for Jews at Judgment Day. Mark was using a midrashic metaphor already rich in meanings, which he continued to expand throughout his gospel.

In the Old Testament, good things often occur in connection with the number three: life for the Gibeonites on the third day (Josh. 9.3-17), the revelation of God at Mt. Sinai on the third day (Exod. 19.11), God's desire to be worshiped after a three day journey into the wilderness (Exod. 3.18), those who keep sabbatical years will have crops which produce fruit for three years (Lev. 25.21), etc. Why "three" was used in that way is unclear, but there can be little doubt that it was. Hosea's resurrection of Israel on the third day and the accomplishment of resurrections by Elijah and Elisha by means of series of three actions were consistent with the Torah/Joshua tradition about three as a good number.

The entire discussion above applies equally to all three passion-reward predictions. The only major detail that changed significantly from one prediction to the next is the identity of those who are to kill the son of man. In Mk. 8.31 they are the elders, chief priests, and scribes, all associated with Jewish leadership in Jerusalem. The Test. of Levi 8.17 refers to elders and scribes as if they were priests, an identification which would link the leadership specifically with the temple. Mark could well have been influenced by that tradition because his narrative of the last week of Jesus' life is sharply focused on Jesus' relationship to the temple as a barometer of changing patterns during the week.

After the first passion-reward prediction, Jesus generalizes that automatic rewards are available to everyone, not just to himself: "If any man would come after me, let him deny himself and take up his cross and follow me. For whoever would save his life will lose it; and whoever loses his life for my sake and the gospel's will save it" (Mk. 8.34-35). The principle claims for others what Jesus had claimed only for himself in the passion-reward prediction. For an ordinary person to die with no guarantee of returning to life in this world is quite different from going into death with a guarantee that death will not last, and that thirty-nine hours later one will be alive. The magnitude of the sacrifice is quite different if one is willing to die permanently (e.g., never again play with the grandchildren), or is willing to die only in such a way that a weekend is lost. The context suggests that "losing one's life" is intended by Mark as a metaphor consistent with his use of "resurrection." Losing one's life in order to save it differs from willingness to lose it with the unexpected result that it is saved. Regardless of whether one seeks to be saved for eternal life or for full human living now, the individual who is concerned only for private salvation loses the chance; the only way to be fully human or to be saved for eternal life is to cease striving for the reward and to be willing to die. Bratcher and Nida conclude that the word "life" is used in such a way as to suggest a tension between physical life and true spiritual life, perhaps even future life, and thus justify such a translation as this: "Whoever seeks not to die will die; and whoever dies for my sake and the gospel's will live at a qualitatively different level."[1] Such a translation introduces still another metaphorical use of resurrection, quite different from superficial emergence from a grave three days after dying and with an automatic reward which one must not covet.

The details of Mk. 8.34-36 have strong parallels in 1 John and 1 Peter. Mark's sentence "If any man would come after me, let him deny himself and take up his cross and follow me" midrashically rephrases 1 John 2.5-6: "He who says he abides in him ought to walk in the same way in which he walked," and 1 Peter 2.21: "Christ also suffered for you, leaving you *an example*, that you should follow in his steps." The 1 Peter idea of Jesus being "an example" comes close to being thematic for the entire Gospel of Mark.[2] Mark's continuation, "For whoever would save his life will lose it; and whoever loses his life for my sake and the gospel's will save it," virtually paraphrases 1 Jn. 3.14-16:

> We know that we have passed out of death into life, because we love the brethren. He who does not love remains in death. Anyone who hates his brother is a murderer, and you know that no murderer has eternal life abiding in him. By this we know love, that he laid down his life for us; and we ought to lay down our lives for the brethren.

Mark rhetorically questions what it profits "a man to gain the whole world and forfeit his life?" thus midrashically using the central insight of 1 Jn. 2.15-17:

> Do not love the world or the things in the world. If any one loves the world, love for the Father is not in him. For all that is in the world, the lust of the flesh and the lust of the eyes and the pride of life, is not of the Father but is of the world. And the world passes away, and the lust of it; but he who does the will of God abides forever.

Mark appropriately presented Peter and John as if they should have been committed to the ideas in the writings in their names. In addition, taking up one's cross to follow Jesus on the way to death is midrashic on Elisha knowingly following Elijah on the way to the death of the latter in 2 Kgs. 2. Elisha ripped his own clothing to don the prophetic mantle of Elijah and thus, by extension, took on the possibility that his career as prophet would lead to his own premature death.

Jesus knows that disciples who yearn for a Messiah to dominate the whole world will not follow in his path:

> "For whoever is ashamed of me and of my words in this adulterous and sinful generation, of him will the son of man also be ashamed when he comes in the glory of his Father with the holy angels." And he said to them, "Truly, I say to you, there are some standing here who will not taste death before they see the kingdom of God come with power" (Mk. 8.38-9.1).

The saying introduces an implied pun on "son of man." It hints that whoever is ashamed of a son of man who is willing to lose his life now will at Judgment Day be condemned by a supernatural Son of man. The son of man's willingness to lose his life was mentioned for the first time in the passion-reward prediction, but had been established by each confrontation in which Jesus had intentionally disobeyed the capital punishment laws associated with Moses. Thus, whoever is ashamed of Jesus in any of his current protests against ritual religion would in turn be condemned at the Day of Judgment.

Jesus' statement has strong midrashic parallels with the early epistles. 1 Pet. 1.11-12 holds that "angels long to look" into "the sufferings of Christ and the subsequent glory." 1 Pet. 1.21 envisions God raising Jesus from the dead and giving him glory. 1 Jn. 2.28 urges having confidence in Jesus so that people will "not shrink from him in shame at his coming." 1 Pet. 4.16 recommends that "if one suffers as a Christian, let him not be ashamed, but under that name let him glorify God." 1 Pet. 2.6 quotes Isa. 28.16 that "he who believes in him will not be put to shame." 1 Jn. 2.18 claims that "it is the last hour; and as you have heard that antichrist is coming, so now many antichrists have come; therefore we know that it is the last hour." 1 Pet. 4.7 affirms that "the end of all things is at hand."

Mark wrote that "there are some standing here" who will "see the kingdom of God" before they die. The notion that some will not taste death before they see the reign of God come with power is probably midrashic on references to suffering followed by reward: "So I exhort the elders among you, as a fellow elder and a witness of the sufferings of Christ as well as a partaker in the glory that is to be revealed" (1 Pet. 5.1); "Blessed is the man who endures trial, for when he has stood the test he will receive the crown of life which God has promised to those who love him" (Jas./Jac. 1.12). Mark's general phraseology is similar to Heb. 2.9: "But we see Jesus, who for a little while was made lower than the *angels, crowned with glory and honor* because of the suffering of death, so that by the grace of God he might *taste death* for every one." Such passages provide the context within which Mark struggled for an appropriate balance among crucifixion, resurrection, and the final times.

One question in Mark's context is whether those who were to see the reign of God in power prior to death would see it accurately or distortedly as the half-healed blind man. Mark may have presumed that the content of Peter's temptation had to have been alluded to in the early epistles. This fits a broader context in Mark. The analogy of the twice-healed blind man, combined with Mark's theme of seeing without understanding, suggests that Jesus is accusing those who "see" the kingdom of God coming with power as "seeing" mistakenly, and that Jesus, on a parallel track, is being tempted by "seeing" himself as the Elijah-like supernatural Son of man coming in the glory of the Father. Jesus' reference to himself as the "son of man" who will "come in the glory of his Father with the holy angels" sets up the disciples in the following story to see him as a transformed, supernatural person in unearthly, glistening white, presumably similar to Elijah and Moses who have come back from the dead. Although Jesus has also referred to himself as the Son of man who will suffer, be killed, and be raised; and although he is talking as a man who plans to deny himself, take up his own cross, give up the whole world, lose his life, and then save it, the disciples are more interested in seeing Jesus as supernatural and transformed. Jesus as an ordinary person would, of course, prefer to be such a "Son of man" rather than to die.

The Transfiguration Model of Glory: Mk. 9.2-13

Mark's midrashic genius is again evident in the account of the Mount of Transfiguration. Peter, James/Jacob and John see Jesus radiantly transformed and see "Elijah with Moses," conversing with Jesus. The text hints that the appearance of Elijah and Moses with the transformed Jesus may have been intended by Mark as a distortion in the "sight" of the disciples, a theme which is continued in the exorcism story which follows. Mt. 17.9 confirms this possibility by referring to the transfiguration as a "vision." The distortion is suggested in part by the fact that Jesus has taken Peter, James/Jacob, and John "away by themselves," in contrast to 6.31 in which Jesus had asked all of the Twelve to "come away by yourselves" in order to isolate them from the crowds. The result is that his transfiguration is "before them" only. A midrashic reason for this is that the transfigured Christ is the counterpart of the lord of glory envisioned in 1 Pet. 1.11 and Jas./Jac. 2.1.

Peter, in fright, offers to build booths, apparently so that Jesus might dwell forever on the mountain or be worshiped there with Elijah and Moses. From an overshadowing cloud, God's voice announces to the disciples that Jesus is "my beloved son," urging them to listen to him, as if they had not been doing so. God's admonition to them to "listen" to the son is ironic because their hearing has at best been only partially healed. Suddenly they see only Jesus. It is not certain that they see Jesus as God's son. No longer, however, do they see Jesus as belonging in the company of Elijah and Moses.

Mark's midrashic base is clear: when God spoke to the exodus Jews, his mountain was "wrapped in darkness, cloud, and gloom.... You heard the sound of words, but saw no form; there was only a voice" (Deut. 4.11-12); the disciples thought of Jesus as Moses' predicted "prophet like me...*him you shall heed*" (Deut. 18.15). The three could have heeded the voice had Jesus been content to be a new Elijah-Moses, but they could not hear a contemporary child of God. After God's voice calls attention to Jesus as his son, Elijah and Moses disappear; the disciples "see" Jesus only. Jesus may have been transfigured in part because he is midrashically like Moses, who when he "came down from Mount Sinai with the two tablets...did not know that *the skin of his face shone because he had been talking with God.* And when Aaron and all the people of Israel saw Moses, behold, the skin of his face shone, and *they were afraid* to come near him" (Exod. 34.29-30). Exod. 34 states that Moses' face shone each time after he talked with God. In Exod. 24.15-16, Moses went up the mountain and "the *glory of the Lord* settled on Mount Sinai, and *the cloud covered it six days;* and *on the seventh day he [God] called to Moses out of the midst of the cloud*" (see also Deut. 4.11-12; Exod. 19.9). In Mark's story, Jesus leads the three up a high mountain "after six days;" God speaks out of a cloud, apparently on the sixth or seventh day. In Deut. 31.14-15, God "*appeared* in the tent *in a pillar of cloud*" when he announced a passion prediction for Moses and a commissioning for Jesus: "'Behold, *the days approach when you must die;* call

Joshua [Jesus] and present yourselves in the tent of meeting, that I may commission him.'"

The unusual dating of the event as occurring *after six days* may be Mark's way of saying that the transfiguration is properly understood as an event of the sixth day of Passion Week. This is supported by Jesus' telling the disciples on the return from the mountain that the son of man has already come, has suffered, and has been treated with contempt. It stands in stark contrast to the reinterpretation in Lk. 9.28-36 in which the dating is "about eight days after." By Mark's dating, Luke's eighth day would be resurrection Sunday rather than crucifixion Friday. Luke eliminates the conversation on the way down the mountain.

The importance of an adequate interpretation of the transfiguration narrative is indicated by Kee's judgment that "the one architectural feature that stands out Mark has placed at the centre of his gospel (Mark 9.2 ff.), the eschatological vision of Jesus' exaltation at God's right hand."[3] Beck refers to those who see the account as "a post-resurrection story...which has been displaced in the gospel records."[4] The disciples' vision on the mountain is better seen as part of the tradition of the half-healed blind man, seeing the right thing in the wrong way. They mistakenly view Jesus as the Messiah characterized by unearthly brightness, a supernatural person whose self-predicted death should be modeled after Elijah's fiery ascent into heaven (2 Kgs. 2.11-12) and perhaps after Moses' ascension/death as presumably once described in the now lost ending of The Assumption of Moses. Seeing Jesus in that way provides additional content for Peter's Satanic rebuke of Jesus and a reason for viewing "Elijah *with* Moses" rather than Elijah and Moses as separate persons.

Afterward, Jesus instructs the three "to tell no one what they had seen [his transfiguration and the resurrections of Elijah and Moses], until the son of man should have risen from the dead."

They respond by questioning among themselves what "rising from the dead" means. They believe in their confusion that they have seen both Elijah and Moses resurrected, but Jesus implies that "the rising from the dead" is something different from their experience on the mountain. They would have been justified, according to their perception, in believing that they had seen the fulfillment of Jesus' prediction about those "who will not taste death before they see the Kingdom of God come with power" (Mk. 9.1). They see Jesus in glory, but do not see their own suffering as prerequisite to participation in that glory.

The three disciples are also confused about the scribal contention "that first Elijah must come," presumably before the predicted coming of the Messiah. Jesus' answer is complex. "Elijah does come first to restore all things" (as in Mal. 3.1, 3; 4.6). The son of man, as "it is written," must suffer many things and be treated contemptuously.

There are two clues to Jesus' meaning. One is that Elijah had "come" midrashically many times already in Jesus' career: as John the Baptizer with Elijah's uniform and message; as Jesus the Elisha recipient of Elijah's spirit; as Jesus the destroyer and healer envisioned by crowds; and as both Elijah and Jesus on the Mount of Transfiguration. The assertion that Elijah had already come refers to all the Elijah roles of John and Jesus thus far. People have done to each of the "Elijahs" as they pleased; the Elijah who was John the Baptizer had been killed.

The other clue lies in identifying the appropriate "as it is written" texts, both for Elijah and for the son of man as either Elijah or Jesus. Jesus' suffering as son of man is based broadly on the assertion that "Christ died for our sins in accordance with the scriptures [Isaiah's suffering servant]" (1 Cor. 15.3) and on the unnamed "virtuous man" of Wisd. 2-5 who is God's suffering and dying beloved son (2.13, 4.10). Elijah's suffering and death are based the prediction of execution for prophets who wear a "hairy mantle" and thus model themselves after Elijah, as John and Jesus have done in various ways. When any such person prophesies, God "will remove from the land the *prophets and the unclean spirit*" (Zech. 13.2-4). The likelihood that Mark intended this text for his midrashic source is increased in the very next pericope by Jesus exorcising the last unclean spirit.

Jesus' charge to "tell no one," as always in Mark, indicates that the transfiguration has been a temptation for Jesus. God had to remind Jesus, as well as the three, that Jesus is God's beloved son, not the miraculous Elijah-Moses type of figure who escapes death by a guaranteed reward resurrection.

Exorcising the Last Unclean Spirit: Mk. 9.14-29

The vanishing of Elijah and Moses from the sight of those on top of the mountain is incidental to their more significant disappearance from Jesus' imagination as paradigms for achieving reconciliation. In modern idiom, Jesus' response to the disciples would be that it is true that the concepts associated with Elijah had first to be explored, but that the only Elijah who will ever come has already been here and is in the process of disappearing. Because neither Elijah nor Moses can achieve the reconciliation of parents and children, Jesus must evict from his life and career the enduring themes connected with them.

Unclean spirits function as part of the Elijah motif. Hence exorcising the last unclean spirit is one way in which Jesus puts Elijah models behind him in his quest for reconciliation with the Father. In the story line, while Jesus and the three were descending the mountain, other disciples (presumably nine) had been trying unsuccessfully to cast a deaf and mute unclean spirit out of a boy. Jesus takes over for them and exorcises the spirit, telling it never to return. Jesus explains to them that a spirit of this kind can be cast out only by prayer, implying that miracle would not suffice as a method.

Beneath the surface of the tale, Jesus has been the primary person in Mark who has been limited in the ability to speak. His speaking-only-in-parables limitation was originally caused by the deafness-blindness of the multitudes. When it became known to Jesus that the disciples were equally deaf and blind, he sought to heal their condition with two miracles, one which linked their deafness to his "muteness" and another in which their blindness was half-cured to the extent that they were able to communicate right words with wrong meanings. Even when he attempted to "speak plainly" in the first passion-reward prediction the disciples still heard and he still spoke temptatively. The mute unclean spirit is, hence, not just incidentally mute. It represents a temptation which has been nagging at Jesus through his career to date. This unclean spirit, furthermore, inhabits a child and causes agony to a father; Jesus has been the son of the Father about whom Mark has been centrally concerned. Inner struggles tear the boy apart (convulsions, crying, and the threat of being drowned or burned to death); the struggles finally lead to an apparent death. So it has been with Jesus; every attempted tactic has fallen short; temptations have emerged from every good.

Jesus and the three, as they arrived, "saw a great crowd," including scribes, arguing with the nine. The details in the story of the deaf-mute spirit which are in common with the transfiguration story suggest that, whatever the specific argument is, it is a continuation of the disciples' discussion with Jesus about the scribes' view that Elijah would return before the Messiah came (Mk. 9.11). The father addresses Jesus as "teacher" in a story in which Jesus does not teach, thus providing another possible link to the discussion on the way down the mountain, in which Jesus taught about scripture. A less likely possibility is that the scribes were arguing in the tradition of scribes in Mk. 3.22 who accused Jesus of casting out demons by the power of Be-el'zebul.

Mark's peculiar language calls attention to itself and to broader contexts in the Gospel. "Immediately" when the crowd "saw him," they were "greatly amazed and ran up to him." Later, an unclean spirit, "when it saw" Jesus, "immediately" convulsed a boy. Mark's mode of expression is justified in part by the midrashic relationships to Moses and the people of Exodus in the stories of Moses returning from Mt. Sinai. When Moses returned from the mountain in Exod. 20.18 the people were "afraid and trembled." In Exod. 32, Moses was not expected to return, and the crowd seduced Aaron to make for them a golden calf god. Three thousand were killed for their role in the blasphemy. In Exod. 34.30, Moses' face shone brightly and the people "were afraid to come near him." In Deuteronomy's version of these events, the people came near to Moses but were afraid that they would die because they had "seen God speak with man" (Deut. 5.24). The crowd may have been tempted to see Jesus as the three disciples had, as a glistening, unearthly supernatural being. They may have been amazed when they saw him because that was how he looked to them, or because they expected him to look supernatural but he looked ordinary instead. They may have been amazed that he came down the mountain at all, instead of staying there forever. Any such reason for amazement at the base of the Mount of Transfiguration would midrashically parallel Moses' crowd at the foot of his mountain.

After Jesus tells the father that "all things are possible to him who believes," the father cries out "immediately" for help for his unbelief. Jesus then, for a second time, "saw that a crowd came running together." This superficially contradictory description parallels Mark's paired use of "immediately" to indicate "at once" in one context and "automatically" in another.[5] Here the crowd runs physically toward Jesus and surrounds him; then it rushes toward him in his psyche, as if to overwhelm him with the agenda of the multitudes. Jesus' inner sense that he is in danger of perceiving himself as the divinely transfigured exorcist desired by the crowd is the catalyst which hastens the event to its climax. Jesus is once again like Moses, for whom the whole journey from Egypt to freedom in the promised land was threatened with failure because of the crowd's temptation to worship a lesser god. Mark assumed that his readers would supply Moses' context for comprehending Mark's event. The nine disciples may roughly have occupied the role of Aaron; the scribes who argued with them may have been spokespersons for the crowd's desire for a cheap miracle. The nine are men of no known convictions. They apparently side with the multitude in desiring an exorcism and are trying to deliver it.

A key point in the unusual language is Jesus' lament: "O faithless generation, how long am I to be with you? How long am I to bear with you?" This could be two separate questions: how long until I die, and how long must I bear with you? The reference to "faithless generation" makes it more likely that the second question predominates and interprets the first. That is precisely the question which was implicit in Jesus earlier relationship to the Twelve when he was unrealistically hoping that they would succeed. Part of his expectation was that they would have "authority over the unclean spirits" (Mk. 6.7). The crowds were ecstatic then that the Twelve became the kind of exorcists which people wanted Jesus to be. In Mk. 9, Jesus regrets that neither the disciples nor the crowds have changed; he now has to decide sharply to renounce their failure by exorcising their spirit from his life. The unclean spirit is not merely in a boy; it is in Jesus as "son" of the "Father." The contrast between his position and the crowds is heightened by the difference between Jesus' observation that "all things are possible to him who believes" and the father's "if you can," followed by "I believe; help my unbelief!" The father wants to believe in an ordinary physical miracle; Jesus is beginning to explore the possibility of a human being adopting for himself as a positive model a life of suffering and being treated with contempt, the passion part of the passion-reward prediction.

Jesus' temptation is intense. In the form of the boy, it has convulsed him and cast him into both fire and water to destroy him. It is a condition which he has brought upon himself by the reward portion of the passion-reward prediction. He has been stirred to show himself in transfigured glory and to announce himself to the crowd as the Son of Man coming "in the glory of his Father with the holy angels." Decisive action by Jesus is necessary. It takes the form of ordering the deaf-mute unclean spirit to come out "and never enter him again," with the result that everyone thinks the boy to be dead rather than merely needing a hand up. Mark has prepared for this moment by less decisive results in Jesus' previous specific confrontations with unclean spirits:

1. "Be silent, and come out of him" (Mk. 1.25).
2. "And whenever the unclean spirits beheld him, they fell down before him and cried out, 'You are the Son of God.' And he strictly ordered them not to make him known" (Mk. 3.11-12).
3. The legion of unclean spirits "begged him, 'Send us to the swine; let us enter them.' So he gave them leave" (Mk. 5.12-13).
4. "And he called to him the twelve, and began to send them out two by two, and gave them authority over the unclean spirits" (Mk. 6.7).

Despite the apparent decisiveness of the exorcism, Jesus is of a divided mind at this moment. On one side, he orders the tempter never to return in the form of an unclean spirit. It never does. On the opposite side, Jesus has done exactly what the crowd asked him to do and thus submits in part to the temptation in the very act of resisting it. Mark handled this contradiction deftly by later introducing a tempter named Son of the Unclean (Bartimaeus) and by quoting Jesus as struggling between the desire of his own spirit and the weakness of his flesh. Thus the point of the exorcism at the foot of the mountain is that the Elijah form of temptation is overcome, but that the substance of the temptation will return in new guises.

Details in the exorcism story point forward to Gethsemane. Jesus (14.36) prays as his reluctant flesh struggles against his willing-to-die spirit. His temptation to "remove this cup [of death] from me" because "all things are possible to thee" (14.36) is comparable to 9.23: "All things are possible to him who believes," and Jesus exorcising the unclean spirit by prayer. The father's temptative words "I believe; help my unbelief!" can be understood as Jesus' inner struggle, perhaps implying that "if I believe hard enough then I won't have to die, and I can be the supernatural type of Christ whom the disciples see in me rather than the son of man and son of God who will suffer, die and be raised." Jesus, who has been looking at his own death since the first passion-reward prediction, would have preferred such a non-death for himself. The Gethsemane parallels confirm that in the passion-reward predictions Jesus is struggling personally with the issues about the suffering, death and resurrection of the son of God or son of man.

The fact that this unclean spirit can ultimately be driven out only by prayer is Mark's first overt statement that there is a difference between exorcising unclean spirits presumed to possess other people and those which symbolize the power of temptation within oneself. The former can be done by miracle, the latter only by the non-miraculous but great power of prayer. Confusing miraculousness with the efficacy of prayer misses this point altogether. Mark gave no clues in this pericope as to what the power of prayer is, but laid a foundation for returning to the theme later.[6] What is important here is that prayer works in the sense that the unclean spirits never return.

Mark has often told stories which harked back to earlier ones. The exorcism account is the first one, however, which appears to be a midrashic montage of previous ones. It contains elements of the synagogue unclean spirit, Legion, Jairus' daughter, being threatened by crowds, "immediate" temptation, lifting up Peter's mother-in-law, and healing by faith. Just as Jesus had seen fruit-bearing possibilities in the Twelve when everyone else thought they were dead, like Jairus' daughter, so now he sees such possibilities in himself. He who was almost dead to the possibility of reconciliation with the Father when he spoke of his own glory and acted it out on the mountain is not yet a corpse. He is lifted up to the continuing possibility of reconciliation. In its composite sense, the story functions to gather the Elijah themes thus far and to prepare Jesus and the reader to move beyond them.

The Second Passion-Reward Prediction: Mk. 9.30-32

The geographical location of the mountain of transfiguration and exorcism is not specified, but Mark begins a second passion-reward prediction with the information that "they went on from there and passed through Galilee." On Jesus' earlier trip to the Gentile region of Tyre and Sidon, Mark reported that Jesus "would not have any one know it" (Mk. 7.24). Now he goes into hiding again. Jesus' new reason for secrecy was that he was teaching his disciples about his death. Earlier he could not be hidden; now he is successful in his strategy of staying out of the public eye. One justification for the return to Galilee might be that Elijah motifs could effectively be eliminated from Jesus' career in Gentile territory, but Moses motifs could not. That does not account for out-of-public-sight teaching of his followers. The content of Jesus' teaching in the second passion-reward prediction seems similar to the first except for the place of the teaching and the identity of the expected killers. It is spoken in Galilee, the one place which, for Mark, is the borderline between Jewish and Gentile identity. The expected killers are to be people in general, "men" in the generic sense of the term. As before, the son of man will be killed and after three days rise. This time they do not rebuke him; they merely admit that they do not understand.

One preliminary question to be answered is why Mark has more than one passion-reward prediction. It appeared to be the case in the exorcism of the boy's unclean spirit that Jesus had overcome the temptation of the first prediction and the Mount of Transfiguration. Why then does he revert immediately to the same theme in a second prediction, with a third one yet to come? It makes no sense for him to be hiding in Galilee from those whom he had identified as his potential killers, first because he is predicting his death, and second because those religious leaders are identified more with Judea and Jerusalem than with Galilee. Another possibility is that he is avoiding the "crowds" of the previous pericope because he has not resolved for himself the temptation which they represent. This possibility is heightened by the fact that the automatic reward of guaranteed resurrection is still part of the teaching. Another explanation is that Jesus has yet to dispose of the Elijah and Moses themes in his life. Some of the pericopes which follow are explicit in dealing with specific laws of Moses.

One important clue to the meaning of the event is that the disciples have no idea what he is talking about and "were afraid" to ask him. The women at the resurrection tomb (Mk. 16) are afraid when they are instructed to tell the disciples to return to Galilee, from whence the son of man began his journey to voluntary death.

Another clue is that the first passion-reward prediction accurately forecasts the trial before the Sanhedrin; the third one, the trial before Pilate. The second one logically parallels Peter's experience in the courtyard where people in general put Peter on trial and he is afraid. By that logic, the son of man who is to be delivered into the hands of men is not Jesus, but Peter (and probably James/Jacob, John and all of the Twelve). Luke, who understood Mark in that way, adapts the second prediction in his Gospel so that the son of man is merely "delivered into the hands of men" but not killed (Lk. 9.44). In Acts, however, Luke midrashically authenticates Mark's original meaning by having James/Jacob executed (Acts 12.2).[7] Mark's meaning, confirmed by Luke, makes sense out of Jesus teaching the disciples in private; he is telling them about the relevance of the crucifixion path for their lives. They do not understand and are frightened.

Jesus' Private Teachings to His Disciples: Mk. 9.33-50

In three consecutive pericopes, Mark set forth the nature of the disciples' misunderstanding of the passion-reward prediction as applied to themselves. All have strong midrashic connections to the epistles in the names of James/Jacob, Peter and John, to Paul's comments about these men, and to Moses motifs which Jesus has rejected for himself but apparently still applies to the disciples. Jesus and the disciples are alone together in Capernaum, which by its name symbolizes the beginning of the gospel. If there is a beginning here, it is the gospel of the crucifixion and resurrection of the followers of Jesus. Luke confirms this interpretation of Mark's intention by beginning a new Deuteronomy (Second Law) at this point in his Gospel, a different kind of starting again.

Jesus intuits that the disciples have been debating which of them is the greatest, with their silence indicating that they recognize their ambition as wrong. Their epistles say so: "Have you not made distinctions among yourselves?" (Jas./Jac. 2.4); "As it is, you boast in your arrogance. All such boasting is evil" (Jas./Jac. 4.16); "God opposes the proud, but gives grace to the humble" (Jas./Jac. 4.6, quoting Prov. 3.34; also quoted in 1 Pet. 5.5); "Humble yourselves before the Lord and he will exalt you" (Jas./Jac. 4.10); "Humble yourselves therefore under the mighty hand of God, that in due time he may exalt you" (1 Pet. 5.6); "If you have bitter jealousy and selfish ambition in your hearts, do not boast" (Jas./ Jac. 3.14). An additional midrashic source for the disciples' discussion about greatness is Paul's references to James/Jacob, Cephas and John as "those who were of repute" (Gal. 2.2), "who were reputed to be something" (Gal. 2.6), and "who were reputed to be pillars" (Gal. 2.9).

The Moses midrashic source at first is Num. 12.1-8. Miriam and Aaron are claiming to be equal to Moses in receiving words of the Lord. God himself intervenes to demonstrate the preeminence of Moses on the ground that he "was very meek, more than all the men that were on the face of the earth." Thus, the last is first.

Jesus responds to the disciples' silence through a powerful generalization and then an example. His generalization that "if any one would be first, he must be last of all and servant of all" is based on the admonitions to humility from the early epistles and hence should already have been known to the disciple-authors. One can be last of all with the incidental result that one is first of all, or be last of all in order to be first of all. The words spoken by Jesus to the disciples on this occasion advocate the first alternative. The passion-reward predictions of this unit demand the second. That is the core distinction between a passion prediction and a passion-reward prediction. One involves the expectation of death, followed by an unexpected resurrection. In the other, one would predict one's death, followed by certain resurrection.

The disciples so understand Jesus and get into the dispute about greatness by applying the prospect of resurrected glory to themselves. Nothing in Mark's context other than the prediction of resurrection should have occasioned an argument about which disciple was the greatest. Peter, James/Jacob and John may have been greater than the others because of their special treatment on the Mount of Transfiguration and at the raising of Jairus' daughter, but it is inconceivable that any of the nine could legitimately claim to be the preeminent disciple. All of them had apparently experienced sensational success in doing miracles for crowds, but none more than another.

Jesus continued his answer to the disciples by setting a child in their midst as an example. He promised them that "whoever receives one such child in my name receives me; and whoever receives me, receives not me but him who sent me" (Mk. 9.37).

Using the example of a child is undoubtedly rooted in 1 John, in which followers of Jesus are alluded to as children of God or children fourteen times, and Jesus himself as Son of God almost that many times. For Mark, that was a powerful combination because it spoke directly to the issue of Jesus' temptation to see himself as the only child of God. Based on 1 John, Jesus was saying, in effect, "Whoever receives any other child of God in my name receives me as a child of God." 1 John said it in the following ways: "Every one who believes that Jesus is the Christ is a child of God, and every one who loves the parent loves the child" (1 Jn. 5.1); "No one who denies the Son has the Father. He who confesses the Son has the Father also" (1 Jn. 2.23); "He who does not love his brother whom he has seen, cannot love God whom he has not seen" (1 Jn. 4.20).

Jesus' choice of a child as a model may have come from the contrast between his own role as a son and Peter's attribution of greatness to Jesus as the Christ, along with the disciples' arguments about which of them was the greatest. By pointing out that all are children, Jesus defines himself as no more a child of God than any other. To accept any child of God completely would be to accept God as Father completely and thus be on the road to reconciliation. Jesus affirmed an even closer identity between himself and God by arguing that anyone who receives him also receives God.

Mark's small section on Jesus and the child is midrashic on 1 John only. One should not overlook the fact that Jesus refers to himself as having been "sent" by God. The only other passage in Mark which may have the same meaning is in the vineyard parable of 12.1-9, in which God "sent" a number of servants, who were beaten, treated shamefully, and/or killed, then "sent" his beloved son, who was also killed (12.6). 1 John also writes of God "sending" his son (4.9, 4.10, 4.14).

The disciple John makes his only solo appearance in the Gospel in the next pericope. He tells Jesus that he and the others had forbidden a stranger to exorcise demons in Jesus' name. Jesus tells John not to forbid anyone who is "not following us," assuming that those not openly "against us" are "for us." This is demonstrated by an example in which anyone who gives a cup of water to a person who bears the name of the Messiah will be rewarded. Mark's midrashic model for the giver of the cup of water was the woman in 1 Kgs. 17.10 who brought Elijah "a little water in a vessel" to drink and was rewarded eventually by Elijah's resurrection of her son. The language of Mark's text does not clarify whether Jesus is the only one who "bears the name of Christ" or whether the phrase applies also to followers of Christ. If the latter, all three of the early epistles provided midrashic parallels for Mark. Jas./Jac. 2.7 says that the rich "blaspheme that *honorable name* by which you are called." 1 Pet. 4.14-16 speaks of being blessed "if you are reproached for *the name of Christ*...if one suffers as a Christian, let him not be ashamed, but under that name let him glorify God." 1 Jn. 3.23 makes it a commandment that "we should believe in *the name of his Son* Jesus Christ and love one another. " In Mark, the guaranteed reward is limited to outsiders. It is not a promise that a disciple will be rewarded for giving someone a cup of water. In the passion-reward predictions, the benefit is only for Jesus; now it is only for outsiders. The disciples are thus shut out of rewards in a second way. The distinction between those who are "with us" and those who are "not against us" may be midrashically based on 1 Jn. 2.19: the antichrists "went out from us, but they were *not of us*; for if they had been *of us*, they would have continued *with us*; but they went out, that it might be plain that they all are *not of us*." John, as the personified author of 1 John, spoke negatively of those "against us" in both 1 John and Mk. 9.38.

Mark's incident in which an outsider was performing exorcisms is midrashic upon Num. 11.24-30. Two men other than the registered elders were prophesying:

> "And Joshua [Jesus] the son of Nun, the minister of Moses, one of his chosen men, said, 'My Lord, Moses, forbid them.' But Moses said to him, *'Are you jealous for my sake?* Would that all the Lord's people were prophets, that the Lord would put his spirit upon them.'"

John has virtually unimpeachable precedent on his side in forbidding an outsider to cast out demons: Jesus, the name which John would have read in the Greek Torah, had himself, in that story, forbidden outsiders to prophesy. In this instance, however, Jesus, rather than arguing against Mosaic religion, implicitly cites Moses as being correct. The Num. 11 source text makes explicit that Mark's account of John forbidding an outsider is, like the disciples arguing about who is the greatest, a story about the sin of jealousy.

Mk. 9.42-50, a section about punishment for causing "little ones" to sin, could well follow immediately after 9.36-37, in which Jesus had talked about receiving "a child." The intervening pericope about forbidding the outsider and giving a cup of water functions as an intercalation. The meaning of the text, given that continuity, is likely to be that anyone who gives water to one who believes in me will be rewarded, but one who causes a child of God to sin, in contrast to receiving the child of God in my name, will be punished. That sequence, from acceptance to condemnation, transforms the whole unit after the second passion-reward prediction into an interpretation of Mosaic legalism. Mark built mostly on the Torah and passages from the early epistles. Jesus admonishes in Mk. 9.43 that a hand which causes sin should be cut off because "it is better for you to enter life maimed than with two hands to go to Gehenna [Jerusalem's city dump, symbol of eternal punishment], to the unquenchable fire." This is rooted in "Blessed is the man...who keeps his hand from doing evil" (Isa. 56.2), and "When men fight with one another, and the wife of the one draws near to rescue her husband from the hand of him who is beating him, and puts out her hand and seizes him by the private parts, then *you shall cut off her hand;* your eye shall have no pity" (Deut. 25.11-12). The law of retaliation advocates that one should purge evil by taking "life for life, eye for eye, tooth for tooth, hand for hand, foot for foot" (Deut. 19.20-21). Peter urged his readers to "abstain from the passions of the flesh that wage war against your soul" (1 Pet. 2.11). James/Jacob saw the tongue as "an unrighteous world among our members, staining the whole body, setting on fire the cycle of nature, and set on fire by hell"[8] (3.6) and observed that the cause of war is "your passions that are at war in your members" (4.1). Mark's line, "whoever causes one of these little ones who believe in me to sin" paraphrases 1 Jn. 2.1: "My little children, I am writing this to you so that you may not sin." "Hell," for Mark, is "where their worm does not die and the fire is not quenched." It approximates Isa. 66.24: "For their worm shall not die, their fire shall not be quenched, and they shall be an abhorrence to all flesh."

A mixed metaphor in Mk. 9.49, "salted with fire," connects the preceding sentence in which fire is clearly eternal punishment with the succeeding sentence in which salt is good. Mark probably achieved this transition by a conscious play on words, with fire suddenly taking on the alternative meanings of purification and trials. Malachi used the term both ways, a fire in which "all the arrogant and evildoers will be [burned as] stubble" (4.1), in contrast to "a refiner's fire...[which] will purify the sons of Levi" (3.3). 1 Peter refers to "the fiery ordeal which comes upon you to prove you" (4.12) and to testing the genuineness of faith "by fire" (1.6-7). Mark would later write about the disciples being tested by the trials of persecution (13.9-13). In Mk. 9.49, being "salted with fire" leads to the imagery of salt as an internal seasoning, probably an inner discipline which serves as a continuing trial. If being "salted with fire" is a euphemism for being purified by trials, then Mark's reference to the impossibility of restoring taste to salt which has lost its saltness may mean that those who do not pass their personal trials will not have a second chance; they should have cut off whatever was causing them to sin, for they must go to Gehenna.

A midrashic possibility is that Mark's "salt" and "fire" imagery is derived from Jas./Jac. 3.6—4.2. There the "tongue is a fire...setting on fire the cycle of nature and set on fire by hell." Individual passions "are at war" in the members of the body. Those who both bless and curse are like "salt water" which cannot "yield fresh" (the reverse of Mark's salt which "has lost its saltness" and cannot be seasoned). Those, however, who live by the wisdom which "comes down from above" will reap "the harvest of righteousness [which] is sown in peace by those who make peace." The number of overall parallels is convincing evidence that Mark may have intended a midrash on the James/Jacob passage.

Mark concludes that salt is flavoring, not punishment; therefore be seasoned within yourselves "and be at peace with one another." Jesus' final answer to the disciples' dispute as to which one was greatest dispute is "be at peace with one another," i.e., accept each other as children of God. Mosaic laws, *as interpreted by Jesus in Mark*, would never permit such peace. In legalism, there is only the unquenchable fire of Gehenna: punishment for wrongdoing. Mark could have learned that from Paul's complex midrash on Ps. 14.1-2; 53.1-2; 5.9; 140.3; 10.7; 36.1; and Isa. 59.7-8, culminating in Paul's judgment that "no human being will be justified in his sight by works of the law" (Rom. 3.20). The sequence which began with no recognizable connection to a Moses midrash thus concludes with a potent distinction between Jesus' way and what Mark presents as Mosaic legalism.

Why Moses Was Wrong About Divorce: Mk. 10.1-12

Jesus and the disciples depart from Galilee, going to Judea and the region east of the Jordan River. When they do so, the anti-Moses spirit is revived. Pharisees ask him about divorce and quote to him the laws of Moses. The context of the pericope is the principle that if people "have salt within themselves," they will live "at peace with one another" and hence not need divorce. Jesus observes that God had permitted divorce (and, by extension, all other laws) in Moses' time only as a temporary arrangement because of the hardness of heart of the people. But now no divorce is permissible. Deut. 24.1-4 forbids the original husband from marrying his divorced wife a second time after she has lost a second husband. Jesus' response is explicit. People who marry become one and are hence inseparable. Their relationship is adulterated when either of them weds another. The answer comes as a surprise because Jesus had earlier abolished Mosaic ritual laws altogether, but now his own moral law is even more strict than that of Moses.

Jesus cites a passage from the Adam and Eve story as his authority for opposing a law of Moses: "Therefore a man leaves his father and his mother and cleaves to his wife, and they become one flesh" (Gen. 2.24). That same passage from Genesis is quoted, even more loosely, by Paul: "Do you not know that he who joins himself to a prostitute becomes one body with her? For, as it is written, 'The two shall become one'" (1 Cor. 6.16). Paul's teaching on the subject is middle ground between Moses and Mark:

> "To the married I give charge, not I but the Lord, that the wife should not separate from her husband (but if she does, let her remain single or else be reconciled to her husband)—and that the husband should not divorce his wife.... But if the unbelieving partner desires to separate, let it be so; in such a case the brother or sister is not bound. For God has called us to peace" (1 Cor. 7.10-16).

Mark's concept that hearts were hardened in the days of Moses is likely to stem from 2 Cor. 3.13-16, in which Paul argues that Moses veiled his face as a symbol of the fading splendor, the veiled truth resulting from the hardened minds of the people whenever the laws of Moses are read. By labeling Mosaic laws as eventuating from hardened hearts, Mark justified the observation that Jesus "grieved at the hardness of heart" of those who were willing to kill to enforce ritual religious laws (Mk. 3.5).

In the Mount of Transfiguration story, Jesus definitively rejects the way of death of both Moses and Elijah. Moses made divorce a prerogative of males only, whereas Mark assumed that either a husband or wife could initiate divorce proceedings. The practice of women doing so may already have been accepted in the Dispersion as an updating of the law by Mark's time.[9] Oral midrash made such adjustments. Apart from that, Jesus' absolute disagreement with the Torah is a valid indicator of the extent to which Mark portrayed Jesus as having put Moses entirely out of his life. The tone of Mark's pericope goes beyond bringing Mosaic laws up to date or objecting to others doing so. It rejects the authority of Moses and, with it, the Torah as the core of Judaism. For Mark, that was prerequisite both for getting the Moses model out of Jesus' life and setting up the crucifixion story as the new narrative which must be told in order for true believers to identify adequately with the story of their faith.

Receive the Sovereignty of God Like a Child: Mk. 10.13-16

Despite Jesus having earlier urged the importance of receiving children as a way of accepting Jesus and God, the disciples rebuke adults who bring children for Jesus to touch. The disciples may have remembered the time when the public had sought miraculous cures merely by touching him. For Jesus the issue has now changed. He forbids the disciples to hinder children from coming to him because "to such belongs the kingdom of God. ... Whoever does not receive the kingdom of God like a child shall not enter it."

The two pericopes about children are virtually continuous in thought. They are interrupted by a complicated intercalation including one pericope about causing "little ones" to sin and another about divorce. In the divorce teaching, Jesus has defined the will of God as being much purer and tougher than laws of Moses which had compensated for hardness of heart, demanding obedience to the sovereignty of God rather than to Mosaic law. Thus, the second half of the interrupted teaching: a major characteristic of children is that they obey their parents, as people should obey God. A child is a proper model for people in accepting the sovereignty of God. Children's entrance into the kingdom is suggested in Deut. 1.39: "Your children, who this day have no knowledge of good or evil, shall go in there, and to them I will give it [the promised land], and they shall possess it." Do not forbid children; they can inherit the kingdom even if their parents do not.

Mark is likely to have adapted this teaching from 1 Jn. 5.1-3: "Every one who believes that Jesus is the Christ is a child of God, and every one who loves the parent loves the child. By this we know that we love the children of God, when we love God and obey his commandments. For this is the love of God, that we keep his commandments." The disciples, personifying the early epistles, should already have known that Jesus would welcome children. Perhaps the reason why they did not was the confusion between obeying "his commandments" (as if 1 John meant only the Mosaic laws) and Jesus' reinterpretation of the commandments of God as contradicting those of the Torah. They did not understand that it is the sovereignty of God which children accept, not that of Moses.

The New, Non-Mosaic Law—Give to the Poor: Mk. 10.17-22

The poor in the Bible are close to the heart of God. Mosaic laws show great concern for the indigent, spelling out related duties in at least eleven different settings. In Exod. 23.10, for example, a field is to be left fallow once every seven years "that the poor of your people may eat." Isaiah expresses that same concern in terms of one's duty to "defend the fatherless, plead for the widow" (1.17) and not to abuse the poor: "It is you who have devoured the vineyard, the spoil of the poor is in your houses. What do you mean by crushing my people, by grinding the face of the poor?" (Isa. 3.14-15). Jas./Jac. 2.15-16 argues that "if a brother or sister is ill-clad and in lack of daily food, and one of you says to them, 'Go in peace, be warmed and filled,' without giving them the things needed for the body, what does it profit?"

The teaching of Jesus in Mk. 10.17-22 goes far beyond all such admonitions by dealing both with the needs of the poor and consequences in the life of potential givers. Jesus is approached by a rich man who is usually referred to as "the rich young ruler" because interpreters have made a composite figure of the accounts in all three synoptic Gospels. In Mark, he is merely a rich man who asks Jesus how he personally can be rewarded: "'Good teacher, what must I do to inherit eternal life?' And Jesus answered him, 'Why do you call me good? No one is good but God alone'" (Mk. 10.17-18). Jesus responds to the honorific much as he had previously responded to unclean spirits when they had called him Holy or Son of God. Since God alone is good, it would be temptative and blasphemous for Jesus to accept the rich man's milder compliment of "good teacher."

Jesus reminds the rich man of six of the ten commandments, changing "do not covet" to "do not defraud."[10] The rich (who will be punished) apparently have too many possessions to need to covet; the "treasuries of wickedness" in their houses have come from their using "wicked scales" and "deceitful weights" (Mic. 6.10-12). Jas./Jac. 5.1-4 is a typical text:

> Come now, *you rich, weep and howl for the miseries that are coming upon you.* Your riches have rotted and your garments are motheaten. Your gold and silver have rusted, and their rust will be evidence against you and will eat your flesh like fire. You have laid up treasure for the last days. Behold, the wages of the laborers who mowed your fields, *which you kept back by fraud,* cry out.

The man insists that he has obeyed all the commandments since youth. Jesus tells him that he must sell all his possessions and give the proceeds to the poor in order to have treasure in heaven; then the rich man can follow Jesus. The price is too great. It is as if the rich man is condemned by the commandment in 1 Jn. 2.15: "Do not love the world or the things in the world. If any one loves the world, love for the Father is not in him."

The fact that Jesus requires of the rich man more than the laws of Moses require is consistent with his teaching on divorce, also more stringent than the laws of Moses. The point is that in getting rid of the Moses motif for his career, Jesus was not merely rejecting the laws of Moses; he was occasionally exceeding them, going beyond them. Matthew was to later develop this point midrashically in the Sermon on the Mount.

If the Rich Cannot Be Saved, Who Can Be? Mk. 10.23-31

Jesus explains to the disciples that it is almost impossible for the wealthy to obey God. The same is true for the poor who seek for riches. Jesus desires voluntary giving up of possessions, regardless of whether one has much or none, and thus does not pit the rich against the poor. Mark emphasizes the disciples' astonishment about rich people not being able to enter the kingdom of God. They should have been familiar with the idea from the widespread negative stereotypes of the wealthy in Jewish sacred literature. "Treasures gained by wickedness do not profit, but righteousness delivers from death" (Prov. 10.2); "He who trusts in his riches will wither, but the righteous will flourish like a green leaf" (Prov. 11.28). The disciples ask, "Then who can be saved?" to which Jesus replies that it is impossible for human beings to save anyone. God, however, can save people. This answer speaks to the meaning of Jesus' name: "God Saves."

Meanwhile, Peter protests that he and the others have left everything to follow Jesus. Jesus at first seems to approve, listing the sacrifices which Peter claims to have made, and repeating them with one major change. Peter's list was: house, brothers, sisters, mother, father, children and lands. Jesus had abandoned his mother, brothers and sisters in Mk. 3.31-35, and had urged the rich man to give away houses and lands in Mk. 10.21, thus providing Peter a substantial basis for his list. Jesus' answer to Peter makes it clear that there is no one who has left all that "for my sake and the gospel, who will not receive a hundredfold now in this time, houses and brothers and sisters and mothers and children and lands, *with persecutions*, and in the age to come eternal life. But many that are first will be last, and the last first" (Mk. 10.28-31). "With persecutions!" Just as Jesus had put his finger on the weak link in the chain of the rich man's obedience, so he points to Peter's weakness, which is the inability to remain faithful to the word in the face of persecution. The phrase "with persecutions" replaces "father" in the list. From Mark's point of view, a person could leave mother, brothers, sisters, children, lands and houses, but not the Father. One could not both leave God and be reconciled to God, i.e., receive eternal life in the age to come. This significantly changes the psychology of the passion-reward predictions. Instead of the reward wiping out the suffering, as in the predictions, the reward is now continuingly accompanied by persecutions. Merely "leaving everything" physically is not sufficient. The two lists could function as a midrash on Job, who lost everything and received more in return (Job 42.10-17). It is more likely that they are a midrashic extension of Gen. 12.1-2, in which Abraham is to be rewarded for voluntarily departing from his land, kindred, and father's house.

The Third Passion-Reward Prediction: Mk. 10.32-34

Jesus leads the disciples toward Jerusalem. Some of them are amazed and others are frightened that they are going to the place where Jesus expects to be killed. He renews the forecast:

> Behold, we are going up to Jerusalem; and the son of man will be delivered to the chief priests and scribes, and they will condemn him to death, and deliver him to the Gentiles; and they will mock him, and spit upon him and scourge him, and kill him; and after three days he will rise (Mk. 10.33-34).

The details are now like the actual crucifixion story: preliminary condemnation by the Jewish religious leaders, a death penalty handed down by Gentiles, mocking, spitting, scourging, and death, except that the automatic, third day resurrection reward is still intact. The flow of thought almost exactly matches that of the previous pericope: sufferings with reward. Spittle, once used for healing of a blind man, is now a token of mockery. The third prediction is not significantly different from insights in James/Jacob and 1 Peter: "Blessed is the man who endures trial, for when he has stood the test he will receive the crown of life" (Jas./Jac. 1.12); "In this you rejoice, though now for a little while you may have to suffer various trials, so that the genuineness of your faith...may redound to praise and glory and honor at the revelation of Jesus Christ" (1 Pet. 1.6-7).

One reason for having a third passion-reward prediction may be that the three passages, as a whole, embody an interesting example of theological geography.[11] Each of them contains a reference to the place where it was spoken and to the people who were predicted to kill the messiah. The site of the first prediction was in Caesarea Philippi, in Gentile territory, and the killers were to be Jewish religious leaders; the second was spoken in Galilee, and the killers were to be people in general; the third, on the road to Jerusalem, in the heart of Jewish territory, labeled the killers as Gentiles. The balancing is obvious: blaming Jews when in Gentile territory, Gentiles when in Jewish territory, and people in general when in the mixed Jewish-Gentile territory of Galilee. Mark, by having three passion-reward predictions, was able to point to Jews and Gentiles alike as killers of the son of man.[12] In earlier pericopes, Mark had vividly identified the legalistic death penalty laws as setting up the inevitable death of any son of man who opposed ritualistic religion. Antipathy is evident between priestly legalists and a son of man who holds that human values are superior to food taboos, sabbatarianism, and the need for sacrifices to pave the way for ritual forgiveness. Such antipathy is less obvious between Jesus as a son of man and Gentile themes. Why did Mark shift from rule-oriented Jews to people in general and then foreigners in particular as the designated killers of the son of man? In terms of the dichotomy between Jew and foreigner, the Moses' model has been most explicitly Jewish in contrast to Elijah and Elisha both having strong foreign connections and Isaiah at one point naming Cyrus as a Gentile messiah. Shifting blame to the Gentiles may have been for Mark a minor way to demonstrate the inadequacy of the Elijah and Isaiah motifs.

Suffering Without Guaranteed Glory: Mk. 10.35-45

James/Jacob and John come to Jesus asking for a guaranteed-in-advance reward: reservations to sit at Jesus' side when he comes in his glory. Mark may have had Sir. 7.4 in mind: "Do not ask the Lord for the highest place, or the king for a seat of honor." Wisd. 5.5 asks of the suffering servant/son of God, "How does he come to be assigned a place among the saints?" The two passages are consistent with the attention given to glory throughout the three early epistles. Mark emphasized the form of their question by having Jesus parrot it back to them, "What do you want me to do for you?" The interchange is midrashic on 2 Kgs. 2.9, in which Elijah says to Elisha, "Ask what I can do for you, before I am taken from you." Jesus has just enunciated his third death prediction and thus is soon to "be taken from" them. Their reply is to repeat the error which has characterized the entire passion-reward unit from the disciples' point of view: they want a reward with no suffering on their part, even though the Suffering Servant Messiah has to do it for them. Mark made it appear that this is the first time that Jesus realized how little the disciples have understood the passion aspect of his predictions. He had announced both reward and suffering but by selective hearing, they had heard only his predictions of the former. Hence the transfiguration vision and this present request for seats of honor. Elijah's response to Elisha in 2 Kgs. 2.10 was that he had "asked a hard thing." Jesus tells the two disciples, "You do not know what you are asking. Are you able to drink the cup that I drink, or to be baptized with the baptism with which I am baptized?" They assure him that they are able. Jesus at that point could have cited Paul: "When we cry 'Abba! Father!' it is the Spirit himself bearing witness with our spirit that we are children of God, and if children, then heirs, heirs of God and fellow heirs with Christ, provided we suffer with him in order that we may also be glorified with him" (Rom 8.15-17). Instead, Jesus' reply rejects the reward motif: "The cup that I drink you will drink; and with the baptism with which I am baptized, you will be baptized; but to sit at my right hand or at my left is not mine to grant, but it is for those for whom it has been prepared" (Mk. 10.39-40). Suffering is symbolized both by baptism and by a cup. The latter imagery is likely to have been based partially on 1 Cor. 11.23-26:

> For I received from the Lord what I also delivered to you, that the Lord Jesus on the night when he was handed over took bread, and when he had given thanks, he broke it, and said, 'This is my body which is for you. Do this in remembrance of me.' In the same way also the cup, after supper, saying, 'This cup is the new covenant in my blood. Do this, as often as you drink it, in remembrance of me.' For as often as you eat this break and drink this cup, you proclaim the Lord's death until he comes.

The Old Testament background of the imagery is Jer. 49.12, which Mark would have read as a contrast between Jesus and the two disciples: "If those who did not deserve to drink the cup must drink it, will you go unpunished? You shall not go unpunished, but you must drink." Apocryphal books may have been influenced by Mark in referring to a "cup of death."[13] Baptism as a symbol of suffering is midrashically rooted in a passage in Paul in which both crucifixion and resurrection are treated as metaphors:

> How can we who died to sin still live in it? Do you not know that all of us who have been baptized into Christ Jesus were baptized into his death? We were buried therefore with him by baptism into death, so that as Christ was raised from the dead by the glory of the

Father, we too might walk in newness of life" (Rom. 6.2-4).

The other ten disciples are indignant at James/Jacob and John for trying to get ahead of them, but only after Jesus has denied their request. Their displeasure was midrashically modelled by Esau's indignation at the original Jacob (Gen. 27.41) and expressed in Jam./Jac. 5.9: "Do not grumble, brethren, against one another, that you may not be judged." Jesus treated the reaction of the ten as if it were a continuation of the earlier argument among the twelve as to which of them was the greater. His answer, addressed to all twelve, appears at first glance to do no more than rephrase his earlier answer that "if any one would be first, he must be last of all and servant of all" (Mk. 9.35). Here, however, that principle is introduced by the assumption that it is Gentiles who "lord it over" others and "exercise authority over them" (Mk. 10.42). In light of the immediately preceding third passion-reward prediction, in which it was to be Gentiles who would execute the son of man, the potential crucifiers become anyone who seeks to "lord it over" or "exercise authority over" others. Mark's midrashic source was 1 Cor. 2.7-10 in which Paul claimed to "impart a hidden and secret wisdom of God." He continued: "None of the rulers of this age understood this; for if they had, they would not have crucified the Lord of glory. But as it is written, 'What no eye has seen, nor ear heard, nor the heart of man conceived, what God has prepared for those who love him,' God has revealed to us through the Spirit." Mark differed from Paul in that Jesus thought that God had not revealed his secret to anyone, but Paul claimed to know it. By Paul's understanding, Jesus was crucified by all the rulers of the age, an insight which Mark used midrashically to describe the Gentile use of authority.

Jesus concluded his answer by declaring that "the son of man also came not to be served but to serve, and to give his life as a ransom for many" (Mk. 10.45). The clause "give his life as a ransom for many" is as close as Mark gets to quoting the Suffering Servant poem of Isa. 52-53. Isaiah wrote that

> All we like sheep have gone astray; we have turned every one to his own way; and the Lord has laid on him the iniquity of us all.... Yet it was the will of the Lord to bruise him; he has put him to grief; when he makes himself an offering for sin, he shall see his offspring, he shall prolong his days.... Therefore I will divide him a portion with the great, and he shall divide the spoil with the strong; because he poured out his soul [life] to death, and was numbered with the transgressors; yet he bore the sin of many, and made intercession for the transgressors (Isa. 53.6-12).

The quotation contains the full passion-reward motif which has characterized Jesus' exploration of the individual Suffering Servant model. The Servant will share with the great and divide the spoil with the strong because he is willing to die. Jesus' statement that the son of man comes only to serve and to give his life omits any reference to reward. Mark knew that Peter, personifying 1 Peter, would of course object to such a sacrifice and therefore derived from 1 Peter the midrashic source for Jesus' death as a ransom: "You know that you were ransomed from the futile ways inherited from your fathers, not with perishable things such as silver or gold, but with the precious blood of Christ, like that of a lamb without blemish or spot" (1 Pet. 1.18). 1 Pet. 2.21-24 had in turn paraphrased the Suffering Servant poem from Isa. 52-53. The statement that the son of man came to "give his life as a ransom for many" confirms the "God-Saves" meaning of Jesus' name. It turns out not to be Mark's ultimate position on the subject, but it is the conclusion for Jesus' career prior to Passion Week. Its function is to serve as a bridge to the last portion of Jesus' career in which

Jesus' death is portrayed much more like the suffering of Jeremiah than like that of the Suffering Servant. The gospel which, in Mk. 1.1, began in Isaiah will at the cross be patterned much more after Jeremiah.

Endnotes for Chapter Nine

[1]Bratcher and Nida, 266-67.

[2]Bishop Papias of Hierapolis (about 140 CE) is quoted by Eusebius, *Church History* (III, 39.15), as having referred to Mark as "the interpreter of Peter." Bishop Irenaeus of Lyons, *Against Heresies* (III, 1.1), in about 180 CE, wrote that Mark "handed down to us in writing the things which Peter had proclaimed." Scholars have long discussed reasons from the history of the times which would have occasioned the hypothesis of a close connection between Peter and Mark; the "Jesus as an example" passage supports it textually despite Mark's vigorous criticisms of Peter himself.

[3]Kee, *Community of the New Age*, 75.

[4]D. M. Beck, "Transfiguration," *Interpreter's Dictionary of the Bible*. V. Taylor, *Mark*, 386 ff., summarizes scholarly debate about four interpretations of the story: actual history, a vision, "a Resurrection-story which has been read back into the earthly life of Jesus," and a legend based on Hellenistic mystery religion. Most of the great biblical scholars have opted for the misplaced resurrection narrative idea. Taylor, ignoring the temptative qualities of Peter's confession that Jesus is the Christ, concludes that the transfiguration had the effect of deepening and confirming the confession "in an incommunicable experience of prayer and religious insight." All of the options identified by Taylor ignore the flow of thought in Mark.

[5]The Gospel of John uses this same device in describing Mary Magdalene turning twice toward Jesus in John 20. One time was probably physical, the other psychological or emotional. Was this a standard literary convention of the time?

[6]One could conclude that prayer is essentially decision-making for Mark, inasmuch as Jesus made important decisions in times of prayer (1.35-39; 6.45-52; and 14.32-42), but one could not draw that definition from the story in Mk. 9 alone.

[7]The arguments to support this interpretation of Luke are much too technical and lengthy to be conducted here, but will be spelled out in detail in our forthcoming book on Luke-Acts.

[8]The word which RSV translates as "hell" is Gehenna, the valley of Hinnom, a reference to Ezek. 37 and its Jerusalem city dump, the place of eternal fires. In 2 Kgs. 23.10 it is mentioned as a place which had become a shrine for pagan worship. King Josiah converted it to a dump which, because of its fires, has become a symbol for punishment and hence hell.

[9]Taylor, *St. Mark* , 415-421, has a long discussion of this point.

[10]In the midrashic tradition, there was apparently great freedom to change either the content or the order of the ten commandments.

[11]Norman Perrin developed this point in his presidential address for the American Society of Biblical Literature.

[12]Luke was so impressed with this insight of Mark's that he midrashically organized the Central Section of his gospel around it. It is the blending of this midrash and the one on Jesus' "second law" from Deuteronomy, not Q, which explains Luke's Central Section.

[13]A book variously known as The Ascension of Isaiah or The Testament of Isaiah describes the martyrdom of the prophet. He died by being sawed in two, with his enemies gloating and promising to stop the execution if he would do what they wanted. He neither cried nor wept, but instructed other prophets to flee to Tyre and Sidon because "God has mixed this cup for me alone" (5.13). The parallels with Mark are so strong that it is probable that the author of one book was doing midrash on the other. Evidence appears to point toward the primacy of the Markan text. H. F. D. Sparks, *The Apocryphal Old Testament*, distinguishes two original "Isaiah" books, one Jewish, one Christian, the latter including the passage cited in the text. He says of it, "In any case, vi-xi show clear signs of Christian authorship (e.g., ix.12-17 and xi 1-22), whether we are prepared to leave it at that or prefer to particularize further and attribute their origin to 'Christian-Gnostic circles' (so Hembold)" (779). The earliest hard evidence for its existence cited by Sparks is a reference by Origen, who died in 251 CE. There are also references to the "cup of death" in Joseph and Asenath, an apocryphal book dated variously from 100 BCE—450 CE, but it is not evident that it was a source for Mark (Sparks, 468-70).

CHAPTER TEN

MIDRASH ON SOLOMON

Mark claimed in his first sentence that the gospel began as midrash on Isaiah's "God Saves" theme. He shifted increasingly after Mk. 10.46 to a midrash on Jeremiah as a model for a crucified Messiah who neither saves others nor is saved by God. Nowhere in Jeremiah is there a single passage as compellingly poignant as the poem of Isa. 52-53 in which the Suffering Servant redeems others by his death, but from Mark's point of view, Jeremiah is spiritually superior in that it presents suffering without any guaranteed reward. Mark wove the Jeremiah material into four units, featuring Jesus as a messiah-king in the imagery of David and Solomon, and God Himself as the messiah-savior in apocalyptic, Passover, and psalmic models. The Jeremiah section as a whole has two additional organizing principles. One is a "passion week," organized so that on each of six days there is, with slight variations, a patterned repetition of references to Bethany (or figs), the Mount of Olives (or olive oil), an entry into Jerusalem, a temple-related event, and a departure from Jerusalem. Overlapping that theme are unpatterned references to messianic fruits: figs, olives (or oil), and grapes (or vines). Mark may have derived the idea of a passion "week" from references to weeks in Dan 9.24-27: the anointed prince who was cut off "shall make a strong covenant with many for one week; and for half of the week he shall cause sacrifice and offering to cease." In Mark, Jesus disrupts sacrifices at the temple and refers to the covenant "poured out for many;" the pattern of repetitious events is stronger for the first half of the week than the second.

Jeremiah was the major prophet who believed that Israel needed a land of its own and thus had to have a messiah-king to bring that about. On the occasion of the Babylonian exile, Jeremiah predicted that God would bring back a remnant and "raise up for David a righteous Branch, and he shall reign as king and deal wisely, and shall execute justice and righteousness in the land ... and this is the name by which he shall be called: 'The Lord Is Our Righteousness' ['Josedec among the Prophets'—LXX]" (Jer. 23.3-6; Jer. 33.15-16). In LXX Zech. 6.11, Jesus the messiah is "son of Josedec." Mk. 11-13 interprets Jesus as the king who shall "deal wisely," first as midrashic on Solomon, the Son of David messiah and wise man, and then on the apocalyptic imagery centered generally around Daniel as the second great wise man of the Old Testament. Solomon and Daniel are implicitly linked in Mark in more ways than their wisdom. Both were loved by God, as was Jesus: Gabriel told Daniel that "You are greatly beloved" (Dan. 9.23) and God said of Solomon as his son: "I will not take my steadfast love from him" (2 Sam. 7.14-15). Solomon built the temple; Daniel's strongest concern was the desolation of that sanctuary; Jesus' passion week included the temple in his daily routine. The result, for Mark, was the intertwining of Solomon, Daniel and Jeremiah motifs .

Healing the Blindness of Son of the Unclean: Mk. 10.46-52

Mk. 10.46-52 is another of Mark's extraordinary achievements in writing a midrashic bridge story. It makes sense both as a reformulation of motifs which had already come to their culmination in the previous unit and as an interpretation of Davidic materials from the Bible being introduced for the first time. Looking backward in Mark, the account is filled with parallels to the Elijah-Moses details which had already been eliminated from the core of

Jesus' agenda for achieving Father-child reconciliation. In the narrative, Jesus has moved from Galilee to Jericho, and is leaving there bound for Jerusalem, escorted by an enthusiastic crowd which is unaware that he is headed toward his predicted death. En route he is confronted by a blind beggar, Bartimaeus ("Son of the Unclean"), who by his name is a midrashic counterpart of the tempting unclean spirits. He shouts a messianic title to Jesus: "Son of David, have mercy on me!" He does not call Jesus "Son of David" until he has heard that it is "Jesus of Nazareth" who is passing by. The "of Nazareth" nomenclature has been used in Mark to point to Jesus' temptation to think of himself as "the only holy one" in the tradition of Nazarite holy men. The crowd tells the blind beggar to keep quiet, probably because they consider him unworthy of the messiah's attention, but are unaware that they are voicing the order which Jesus has characteristically directed to unclean spirits. Bartimaeus persists because he wants his sight restored, not because he supports Jesus as the messiah. Jesus accommodates him despite the trivialization of the messianic title, rationalizing that the beggar's faith has made him well, as he had said on an earlier occasion when he was in the presence of a crowd representing Old Israel (Mk. 5.34). So many links with the earlier units of Mark suggest that the ouster of Elijah and Moses from the center of Jesus' concern was a "palace revolution" in which new figures would be introduced to replay old roles in superficially different garb.

The Bartimaeus and triumphal entry episodes should also be seen as a continuous midrash on Isa. 35, in which the exiles returning from Babylon are saved by God, "who will come with vengeance" and will perform miracles. Note the parallels between the Isaiah material and the Bartimaeus and triumphal entry stories in Mark 10-11.

Isaiah 35: Say to those who are of a fearful heart.	Mark 10-11: Take heart; rise, he is calling you.
Our God... will come and save *us* [LXX].	Son of David, have mercy on me.
Then the eyes of the blind shall be opened.	Master, let me receive my sight.
...the lame man leap like a hart.	...he sprang up and came to Jesus.
And a highway shall be there...the Holy Way.	[He] followed him on the way.
The unclean shall not pass over it....	Bartimaeus [Son of the Unclean]
The ransomed of the Lord...shall come to Zion with singing.	"Hosanna! Blessed be he who comes in the name of the Lord."

The Isaiah 35 midrash makes clear that the blind man/unclean spirit represents the crowd at the triumphal entry; they want Jesus to be a military rescuer who "comes with vengeance," not one who goes to Jerusalem to die. Jesus' healing of their blindness is superficial only. He may also have healed the blind man due to the implicit challenge to him as "son of David" to reverse David's legendary hatred of the blind and lame, who were supposed to prevent David from entering Jerusalem (2 Sam. 5.6-8).

Much biblical messianic imagery centers on David, Israel's greatest king. "The root of Jesse" [Jesse was David's father] was to "stand as an ensign to the peoples" (Isa. 11.10). Paul refers to the messiah as "the root of Jesse" (Rom. 15.12). God promised to "cause a righteous Branch to spring forth for David; and he shall execute justice and righteousness in the land"(Jer. 33.14-15); God also promised to "set up over them one shepherd, my servant David, and he shall feed them" (Ezek. 34.23). God predicted that those who died in exile would be resurrected and return to Israel, where "my servant David shall be king over them; and they shall all have one shepherd" (Ezek. 37.12, 24). Since the psalms have at least a legendary connection to David, Psalmic messianic references are appropriately considered as Davidic. The second psalm implies that the Lord's messiah is King David whom God will set on God's own holy hill and will designate as God's son in some special sense. Mark generally adopted all the Davidic imagery from the Psalms and elsewhere, but modified it to refer to "the son of David." Mark's new midrashic construction looks to both the David and Solomon traditions. Just as Mark had earlier portrayed Elisha-Jesus as including all of the Elijah tradition, and Joshua-Jesus all of the Moses legacy, so now he presents Jesus-Solomon incorporating the entire legacy of David. This may be a unique Markan contribution inasmuch as anticipation about a Davidic messiah-king had previously centered on David himself, a more obscure figure named Zerubbabel (in Zech. 4.14 and Hag. 2.23) and possibly King Cyrus (in Isa. 45.1). David had many sons. Solomon succeeded David as king even though he was not the eldest and therefore the legal heir, thus, Jacob-like, supplanting his elder brothers. Solomon maintained the empire which David had created; he built the temple which David had wanted to build, and he had a reputation for being wise. Mark used all those dimensions of Solomon's life in this sub-section. Mark midrashically presented Jesus as son of David rather than as David to fit his theme of Father-child reconciliation. Just as Jesus had been son of man, so he must be son of David here to highlight what it means to be son of God.

First Day—The Messiah's Entry Into Jerusalem: Mk. 11.1-11

One of the commonly recognized midrashic sources of Davidic messianic imagery is Zech. 9.9, reproduced here in the form of Hebrew poetry to call attention to each of the second lines which mirror or explain the first ones but do not add extra content to them.

Rejoice greatly, O daughter of Zion!
    Shout aloud, O daughter of Jerusalem!
Lo, your king comes to you;
    Triumphant and victorious is he [LXX "just and a savior],
Humble and riding on an ass,
    On a colt the foal of an ass.

In Hebrew poetry, a second line of a poem modifies or gives details for the previous line, but does not add to it. N. K. Gottwald identifies this passage as an instance of synonymous parallelism in which "lines 2, 4, and 6 introduce no new thought but rather repeat or echo the immediately preceding lines."[1] The messiah is to ride into Jerusalem on one animal, the foal, not the adult animal. The prediction follows a precedent set by King David in his very old age. He voluntarily yielded his throne to Solomon to put a halt to his sons' murderous competition to be his successor. The story is told in 1 Kgs. 1.38-40:

> So Zadok the priest, Nathan the prophet, and Benaiah the son of Jehoiada...went down and caused *Solomon to ride on David's mule,* and brought him to Gihon. There Zadok the priest took the horn of oil from the tent [the original "temple"], and anointed Solomon. Then they blew the trumpet; and all the people said, "Long live King Solomon!" And all the people went up after him, playing on pipes, and *rejoicing with great joy,* so that the earth was split by their noise.

So it was that Jesus was pictured by Mark as entering into Jerusalem, coming as the new Solomon to occupy the throne of David. Ps. 118, referring apparently to David's entrance as a military hero, contributes details to Mark's celebration: "*Blessed* [LXX reads *Hosanna*] *be he who enters in the name of the Lord!* We bless you from the house of the Lord. The Lord is God, and he has given us the light. *Bind the festal procession with branches,* up to the horns of the altar" (118.26-27). The strewn branches in Mark are not palm; that detail is added in John 12.13, probably as a midrash on the Markan detail that Jesus had traveled to Jerusalem from Jericho ("City of Palms"). The word translated as "blessed" in RSV's Ps. 118.26 would be "hosanna" if one were translating from the Greek LXX version, thus making it even more likely that this psalm was Mark's midrashic source for the hero's welcome. The welcoming parade idea may also have stemmed from 1 Sam. 29.5, in which the multitudes shout: "Is not this David, of whom they sing to one another in dances: 'Saul has slain his thousands, and David his ten thousands'?" The garments thrown on the colt and on the road are reminiscent of the blind beggar "throwing off his mantle" to come to the Son of David messiah and serve as an initial indicator that the Jerusalem crowd is also "blind" in its adoration. A midrashic reason for having a Son of David political messiahship proclaimed first at Jericho may have been the fact, reported in 1 Macc. 9.50, that Jericho was a fortress associated with the Maccabees. It was, in addition (Josh. 6), the site of the armed conquest by Joshua (Jesus) when the walls tumbled miraculously after a seven-day-long triumphal march around the city.

Actually the welcome was not for Jesus. It was primarily a cry of exultation that the miracle-man from Galilee had finally agreed to do what Homeland Jews[2] wanted most: drive the Romans out of the country and reestablish the empire of David. In the LXX[3] the permanence of David's kingdom predominates over the messiahship of David himself. So it is in the entry celebration. The jubilation is for the prospect of the kingdom which is sure to come because the miraculous Jesus will be leading the revolution. One midrashic model for the now-expected-event reads: "And he [Simon the great high priest, captain, and leader of the Jews] entered into [the Jerusalem citadel] with praise, and *palm-branches*, and with harps and with cymbals, and with viols, and with hymns, and with *songs; because a great enemy had been destroyed out of Israel*" (1 Macc. 13.51).

Mark's "Triumphal Entry" on Palm Sunday is not presented as a spiritually positive event; its overall significance is temptative. What is at issue is the investment of the messiah's resources in a military-political revolution against Rome or any other imperial aggressor. The messiah of the triumphal entry is celebrated as a military freedom fighter who is expected to win battles. Such a messiah could not possibly be voluntarily crucified. Looking forward to the rest of Passion Week, the irony is that those who celebrated Jesus' arrival on Sunday were the same ones who shouted "crucify him" on Friday. Joe Grubbs[4] captured this idea well in a sermon entitled "When the Cheering Stopped." It dealt with the reality of Jesus consciously turning his back on the aspirations heightened by his messianic entry: he refused to lead the expected military rebellion. Disillusioned patriots supported his execution because he had disappointed them.

Mark used the entry into Jerusalem to establish the messianic pattern of the days of the week and its messianic fruits. On the first day of Passion Week, Jesus and the disciples pass through Bethphage and Bethany, towns with names meaning "House of Unripe Figs," a reference to a species of figs which remain always green.[5] Mark implied that the towns were located on or near the Mount of Olives, the first hill east of the temple mount, and that a person coming from Bethany to Jerusalem would either cross the mount or skirt its foot. Both figs and olives have messianic significance. When King Solomon was established in office, there followed a time of unusual prosperity, characterized by Judah and Israel dwelling in safety, "every man under his own vine and under his fig tree, all the days of Solomon" (1 Kgs. 4.25). Mic. 4.3-4 uses the same imagery as a messianic expectation regarding the latter days:

> He shall judge between many peoples, and shall decide for strong nations afar off; and they shall beat their swords into plowshares, and their spears into pruning hooks; nation shall not lift up sword against nation, neither shall they learn war any more; but they shall sit *every man under his vine and under his fig tree,* and none shall make them afraid.

In Zech. 3.9-10, when the guilt of the land is removed in a single day, "every one of you will invite his neighbor under his vine and under his fig tree." Isa. 36.13-20 notes that a foreign king was falsely using the vine-fig tree promise. The messianic significance of olives is that their oil is used to anoint a messiah. Every king of Israel was a messiah, i.e., one anointed with olive oil. By extension, the Mount of Olives is messianic. A Jewish legend says that when the dead come back to life they will appear first on the Mount of Olives. That legend may be related to Zechariah's vision of the Day of Judgment that the Lord will come to "stand on the Mount of Olives which lies before Jerusalem on the east; and the Mount of Olives shall be split in two from east to west by a very wide valley" (Zech. 14.4). The context in Zechariah is explicitly Davidic and may have helped create in the mind of Mark an association between Jesus and the Mount of Olives.

The sequence of events on this first day follows a pattern which will persist through the week. Jesus goes 1) from Bethany, 2) by way of the Mount of Olives, 3) to Jerusalem, 4) specifically to the temple, and 5) out of Jerusalem, this time back to Bethany. In the temple he does nothing but look around, as if it were important for him just to be there even though there is nothing for him to do. In that sense Jesus is Solomon going to his place, the temple. The original building constructed by Solomon had long since been demolished and had been twice rebuilt, but midrashically this was still Solomon's temple, the one place in Jerusalem uniquely associated with his name.

In addition to the midrashic sources treated above, Mark used 1 Sam. 9, Saul's invitation to kingship, as a basis for the triumphal entry account. 1 Sam. 9 and Mk. 11 in turn become the midrashic source for the story of the Last Supper and Gethsemane. The entire parallelism will be treated in relationship to the Mk. 14 material.

Second Day—The Fig Tree And the Temple: Mk. 11.12-19:

On Monday, the second day of the week on a Jewish calendar, Jesus comes from Bethany ("House of Figs") to a particular fig tree which is not bearing fruit because it is not the season, not the right time for figs.[6] This is the first half of an intercalation sequence; the intervening story concerns Jesus' attention to objectionable practices in the temple. Jer. 7-8 provides the organizing structure for Mark's fig tree incident, disruption of temple activities, and dialogue with scribes and wise men on the following day. Jeremiah condemns the "*abominations in the house* which is called by my [God's] name" (7.30). He quotes God as saying, "When I would gather them [any righteous people]...there are *no* grapes on the vine, nor *figs on the fig tree*; *even the leaves are withered*, and what I gave them has passed away from them" (8.13). He excoriates the wise men and scribes who have made the Mosaic law a lie, putting them to shame (8.8-9) as Jesus does in Mk. 12.38-40. Jesus looks for figs to gather. Finding none, he condemns the tree, cursing it so that it will never bear fruit again, thus fulfilling the threat of Mk. 4.25 that "from him who has not, even what he has will be taken away."

Psalm 1 and Jeremiah provide midrashic images for fruitful trees, each of which is relevant by way of providing a counter-image for Mark's unproductive fig tree.

> Blessed is the man who walks not in the counsel of the wicked.... He is like a tree planted by streams of water, that yields its fruit in its season, and its leaf does not wither. In all that he does he prospers (Ps. 1.1).
>
> Blessed in the man who trusts in the Lord, whose trust is in the Lord. He is like a tree planted by water, that sends out its roots by the stream, and does not fear when heat comes, for its leaves remain green, and is not anxious in the year of drought, for it does not cease to bear fruit (Jer. 17.5-8).

Jesus had earlier expected the twelve disciples to be seeds which bear fruit one hundred fold (Mk. 4.20), and, when that turned out to be too much to expect of them, to be a tiny seed which would grow into the greatest of all trees. By the time of his first passion-reward prediction, he had realized that they were not bearing fruit and could never be counted on to do so. The change of imagery from a great tree to a fruitless one does not reflect Jesus' reevaluation of the disciples. The intercalation of the temple cleansing establishes a clear analogy between a non-fruitful tree and a non-fruitful temple. Hearing the curse sets the stage for the disciples' later question as to when the temple will be destroyed.

Jesus, arriving in Jerusalem, goes straight to the temple and ousts the merchants whose activities were necessary for conduct of the temple's ritual business.[7] People could make only two kinds of offerings there, special temple coins and animals or birds guaranteed to be free from impurities. For those coming from afar, it was easier to buy an animal or bird in Jerusalem than to bring one along. Since Roman coins rather than temple coins were the medium of ordinary monetary transactions, people had to have money-changers in or near the temple precincts in order for the worshiper to make the correct offering. The merchants in the temple were a supportive adjunct for those who accepted priestly rituals as religiously positive acts.

Nevertheless, the practice had long generated controversies among Jews. Some of the prophets of Israel had condemned priestly religion altogether. Zechariah envisioned a time when "there shall no longer be a trader in the house of the Lord of hosts on that day" (Zech. 14.21). Jeremiah criticized the temple for having "become a den of robbers in your eyes" (Jer. 7.11).

Controversies about the cleansing of the temple are still alive today among Christian interpreters. Craig A. Evans paraphrases E. P. Sanders as saying "that he knows of no evidence of corruption in the first-century Temple. Therefore, the traditional understanding that Jesus 'cleansed' the Temple is unfounded and ought to be dropped."[8] Sanders interpreted the event as anti-temple rather than as purification of the temple. Midrashic interpretation makes it possible for both Sanders and Evans to be correct. Evans documents the enormous wealth and concomitant corruption of the high priesthood and thus corrects Sanders' factual error. Taken out of context, the known fact of immoral priestly behavior would justify Jesus' action as a protest against the "den of robbers." Put back into context, Mark was concerned about two much more powerful criticisms of the temple operation. If there was to be a temple, it should be opened to Gentiles, but, in fact, the temple was no longer necessary because direct human forgiveness is possible without the intermediation of priests. Jesus was thus in the tradition of the prophets who opposed priestly religion rather than among those who would be satisfied if it were tidied up.

The passages from Zech. 14.21 and Jer. 7.11 were obviously midrashic for Mark when he had Jesus refer to the temple traders as a "den of robbers." Jesus makes an even more incendiary accusation, quoting Isaiah: "My house shall be called a house of prayer for all the nations" (Isa. 56.7). Jesus, like Isaiah, thus advocates that the temple should no longer be an exclusively Jewish place; it ought to be opened to Gentiles as a place of prayer.

Temple-oriented Jews had for many generations fought vigorously against both Greek and Roman rulers to maintain the ritual purity of the temple. The Seleucid emperor Antiochus Epiphanes had sought to enforce Greek cultural practices in Israel and had made observance of Jewish religious rituals a death penalty offense. When he finally installed a statue of Zeus in the Jerusalem temple on top of the altar of burnt sacrifices in 167 BCE, open revolt broke out and was eventually successful. The crowning glory of the revolt was the day when Judas Maccabeus restored the temple to its ritual purity. Later, in 40 CE, the Roman emperor Caligula had sought to have his own statue erected in the Jerusalem temple. Again there was a great Jewish protest, this time successful short of a military revolt. Granted that this date is later than the presumed time of Jesus, it certainly is earlier than when the Gospel of Mark was written. For Mark's Jesus, advocacy of the presence of Gentiles in the temple was an explosive issue which helped to guarantee his execution.

In Mk. 11.15 ff., Jesus may be objecting only to trading in the temple. The Jer. 7-8 midrashic source suggests, however, that there are no righteous people, no "figs on the fig tree, even the leaves are withered" (8.13) because (as in Mark) the proper rituals are being performed at the same time that people are living in sin. "Will you steal, murder, commit adultery, swear falsely, burn incense to Ba'al...and then come and stand before me in this house...and say 'We are delivered!'—only to go on doing all these abominations? Has this house...*become a den of robbers* in your eyes?" (7.9-11). The contrast to this type of temple abominations is the widow who gives all she has, her living, in Mk. 12.42-44, at the end of the dialogue section which is based upon Jer. 8.9. At any rate, Jesus takes on the task of halting the temple trading temporarily; he has given up on getting people to bear fruit by changing their lives.

Public opinion would have considered that the most outrageous part of Jesus' actions was that the statements antithetical to the well-established traditions of the temple were being made by Jesus-Solomon. David generated the idea of a beautiful temple (1 Chron. 28-29), and Solomon erected it (2 Chron. 2-7). To have the messianic son of David disrupt the temple sacrifices and demand that the building be opened to Gentiles must have seemed to the priests to be the ultimate insult to their traditions. However much anyone shared the prophetic vision that Gentiles and Jews ought ultimately to worship together, that wolves and lambs should lie down safely with each other, and that spears should be turned into pruning hooks, it certainly was not yet time for such a culmination. Jesus does in the temple exactly what he had done to the fruitless fig tree: he expects it to bear fruit out of season and condemns it when it does not. When evening comes, Jesus and the disciples leave the city. His only agenda for that day had been to oppose the temple rituals. On this day there was no reference to the Mount of Olives, except as it is assumed that the fig tree may have been located there. The observation in Mk. 11.18 that the priests and scribes "sought a way to destroy" Jesus is directly parallel to Jer. 26.8 after Jeremiah had spoken against the temple: "Then the priests and the prophets and all the people laid hold of him, saying, 'You shall die!'" Jer. 26 develops the pattern of religious officials handing Jeremiah over to a civil court, which in turn found the prophet innocent, just as Mark had religious officials hand Jesus over to Pilate, who found him to be innocent.

Third Day—The Withered Fig Tree: Mk. 11.20-26

On the next day Jesus and the disciples "passed by" and "saw the fig tree withered away to its roots." The language may be based on Ps. 37.35-36, in which a wicked man is a "cedar of Lebanon. Again I passed by, and, lo, he was no more...." Mark implies that they start from Bethany or come by way of the Mount of Olives. The fig tree is somewhat like the word scattered on rocky ground in the parable of the soils: "And since it had no root it withered away" (Mk. 4.6). Even worse, this tree drooped despite the fact that it had roots.

Jesus' explanation about the desiccated fig tree shifts attention from the inadequacies of practices at the Jewish shrine to the nature of forgiveness which was supposedly the sole purpose of the rituals there. It is also to be understood as his commentary on the possibility of the temple rites being so destroyed. Jesus says: "Have faith in God. Truly, I say to you, whoever says to this mountain, 'Be taken up and cast into the sea,' and does not doubt in his heart, but believes that what he says will come to pass, it will be done for him. Therefore, I tell you, whatever you ask in prayer, believe that you receive it, and you will" (Mk. 11.22-24). Mark may have used a passage from 1 Corinthians as the midrashic inspiration for the imagery about casting a mountain into the sea: "And if I have prophetic powers, and understand all mysteries and all knowledge, and *if I have all faith, so as to remove mountains*, but have not love, I am nothing" (1 Cor. 13.2). This was the second time that Jesus had attributed an extraordinary result to prayer, distinct from miracle. Based on this pericope, prayer is not asking God to do something for me, but, rather, is believing that what I pray for does in fact come to pass, and thus it will. The power of prayer is not in somehow persuading an intervening deity to be on a supplicant's side, but in committing oneself so totally to a goal perceived to be godly that one can work with undivided effort toward its achievement.

To believe that prayer will result in mountains being cast into the sea and other such apparent impossibilities requires one of two things. A person could be quite demented and genuinely believe that impossible things will miraculously come to pass,[9] or, conversely, the person would have to be sufficiently competent to be able to see all the means by which the envisioned result is to be attained and to believe the result to be attainable. Isaiah describes God as having that latter kind of power:

> I will lay waste mountains and hills, and dry up all their herbage; I will turn the rivers into islands, and dry up the pools. And I will lead the blind in a way that they know not, in paths that they have not known I will guide them. I will turn the darkness before them into light, the rough places into level ground (Isa. 42.15-16).

In applying that vision of possibilities to the temple, Jesus is saying that it really is possible for the temple to be a universal place of prayer and to exist without the mercantile underpinning, whether corrupt of not, which he, along with Jeremiah, thought to be thievery. If Mark was writing sometime after the temple had been demolished by the Romans and when synagogues or perhaps even churches had of necessity replaced it, religion without a temple would be much less impossible than it would have seemed to a Jerusalem Jew when the temple building and practices were still intact.

Jesus' concluding comment about the temple and the fig tree is, "Therefore I tell you, whatever you ask in prayer, believe that you receive it and you will. And whenever you stand praying, forgive, if you have anything against anyone; so that your Father who is in heaven may forgive you your trespasses" (Mk. 11.24-26). This is similar to Sir. 28.2: "Forgive your neighbor the hurt he does you, and when you pray, your sins will be forgiven." Although Jesus' statement contains no direct reference to the temple, he has not changed the subject. The essential business of temple priests is to mediate between the people and God in order that they may be forgiven by God. Jesus advocates the replacement of the temple ritual procedure with the imaginative possibility that human beings can forgive each other, a theme which Mark had found in James/Jacob and Paul: "And the prayer of faith will save the sick man, and the Lord will raise him up; and if he has committed sins, he will be forgiven. Therefore confess your sins to one another, and pray for one another, that you may be healed. The prayer of a righteous man has great power in its effects" (Jas./Jac. 5.15-16); "Any one whom you forgive, I also forgive. What I have forgiven, if I have forgiven anything, has been for your sake in the presence of Christ" (2 Cor. 2.10). Whenever human beings forgive each other directly and believe that what they pray for will in fact occur, temples are innately abolished. Buildings may stand; there may still be priests; but the institution is rendered useless, antiquated, unneeded; temple apparatuses collapse by default. So also do the lines which ritually divide people from each other, Jew from Gentile, male from female, etc. Mark thus makes midrashic sense out of Paul's statement about the discontinuance of such distinctions now that an era of trust has come: "There is no longer Jew nor Greek, there is neither slave nor free, there is neither male nor female, for you are all one in Christ Jesus" (Gal. 3.21-28). Forgiveness mediated by temple rituals is part of what is demolished when legalism and ritual are replaced by the trust which human beings have in each other when they forgive and accept forgiveness. The midrashic sources for the pericopes about the fig tree, the temple, and prayers of forgiveness do not include any from the Torah. Yet the laws of Moses and the Levitical priesthood are the targets of this unit, midrashically developed by Mark from the perspective of the major prophets of Israel.

A supplementary interpretation of the withering of the fig tree is suggested by the Ezekiel and Daniel midrashic sources for the mustard seed parable in Mk. 4. In each, a great tree was a great king, Pharaoh in one, Nebuchadnezzar in the other. Of one it was said, "Hew down the tree and cut off its branches, strip off its leaves and scatter its fruit..." (Dan. 4.14). Of the other: "Foreigners, the most terrible of the nations, will cut it down and leave it" (Ezek. 31.12). The tree is no longer a parable for the kingdom of God, as in Mk. 4, but now is analogous to the temple. Once great, it will be withered away even as the mightiest of the monarchs. The Ezekiel passage lends a touch of irony. Isaiah wanted a temple in which Gentiles could worship. Because the Jews resisted that, it would be Gentiles who would cut the temple tree down and leave it. Historically, that is what happened in the Roman destruction of the temple.

Jesus as Solomon the Wise man: Mk. 11.27—12.34

Mark portrayed Jesus in Jerusalem, later in the day after the discovery of the blasted fig tree, arguing with three groups of religious opponents. Jesus' cleverness in each episode clearly marks him as the new wise man Solomon, as in 1 Kgs. 3.16-28 in which Solomon correctly adjudicated the conflicting claims of two women to be the mother of a child, and as in 2 Chron. 9.1 in which his answers satisfied the Queen of Sheba who had intentionally tested him with difficult questions. After Jesus disposes of the questions designed to entrap him, a sympathetic scribe asks a more general question about the greatest commandment in the law. Only when Jesus' opponents hear his answers to all four questions do they recognize their defeat and cease to question him.

The cleansing of the temple moves the scribes and chief priests to actively begin to seek a way to destroy Jesus. They intend to put him in an embarrassing position in which he would either have to confess guilt to a death penalty crime or lose his popularity. Their model is Deut. 17.8-13, in which God gives the priests absolute authority to render decisions in difficult cases and to impose the death penalty on anyone who does not obey. The priests thus legitimately ask him by what authority he has been opposing them by disrupting the temple and promising that anything asked for in prayer will be granted if the one praying believes strongly enough. The question is also midrashic on Jeremiah's situation when he predicted in the "name of the Lord" that the temple of his time would be destroyed, and his answer was used as the rationale for a death penalty trial (Jer. 26.6-11).

Jesus sees through their plot and responds first by asking them whether the baptism performed by John the Baptizer was "from heaven or from men." They know that if they answer that it was heavenly, Jesus can rightly accuse them of not having followed the divine guidance which John has given them. But if they answer that it was merely human, they too will lose their popular support. They dodge the issue, and so does Jesus, citing their refusal as his precedent.

Jesus then draws an analogy which the temple officials perceive as targeted at them. God is analogized as the owner of a vineyard, Jesus is his son, and the religious leaders are renters who at first merely abuse God's representatives but who at the climax of the story kill his son. The story is primarily based on a tradition about David, Bathsheba and Solomon from 2 Samuel and its midrashic expression in the account of Naboth's vineyard in 1 Kings. Many of the parallels are precise, as indicated in the following comparison.

2 Samuel	**1 Kings**	**Mark**
11.2: David wanted Uriah's wife who was bathing on a nearby roof.	21.1: Ahab wanted Naboth's vineyard near the palace.	12.1: The tenants wanted the vineyard for themselves.

2 Samuel	1 Kings	Mark
11.11: Uriah refused to go home to go to his wife to lie with her.	21.3-4: Naboth refused to yield "the inheritance of my fathers."	12.6-7: The owner sent his beloved son, his heir.
11.5: Uriah's wife told David she was pregnant.	21.7: Queen Jezebel promised Ahab the "inheritance."	12.7: "Let us kill him and the inheritance will be ours."
12.16: After Bathsheba's son died, David fasted and "lay...upon the ground."	21.4: Ahab "lay down on his bed" and "would eat no food."	No parallel
11.13: David falsely pretended that Uriah was being honored.	21.10: False witnesses were set up against Naboth.	14.57: False witnesses testified against Jesus at his trial.
No parallel	21.10: The charges: cursing God and king. [Exod. 22.28: do "not revile God, nor curse a ruler of your people."]	14.64—15.2: The charges at Jesus' two trials: blasphemy against God, treason against Rome.
12.25: Second son of David and Bathsheba was Solomon [known as Jedidiah, "Beloved of the Lord"].[10]	No parallel.	12.6: Confidence that they would treat a beloved son with respect. 14.61: "Are you the Son of the Blessed?"

2 Samuel	1 Kings	Mark
11.14: Uriah was killed outside a city wall.	21.13: They took Naboth outside the city to kill him.	15.20: "And they led him out to crucify him."
11.14: Man was killed with a millstone dropped on him from the wall.	20.13: Naboth was stoned with stones.	12.10: "The very stone which the builders rejected has become the head."
11.14: The millstone was dropped on his head.	No parallel.	12.4: A servant was wounded in the head. 15.19: "They struck his head with a reed."
12.1: God sent the prophet Nathan to confront David with his guilt.	20.17: God sent the prophet Elijah to confront Ahab with his guilt.	12.12: The accusers saw "that he told this parable against them."

The Greek words for vineyard, hedge and tower are taken directly from the Isaiah 5 vineyard song; the term for wine vat is similar to that in Isaiah 5.[11] Additional sources include the Song of Solomon: "Solomon had a vineyard at Baal-hamon. He entrusted it to overseers, and each one was to pay him the value of its produce, a thousand shekels of silver" (8.11). The tenants are like those to whom Jeremiah addressed the word of God: "I have persistently sent all my servants the prophets to them, day after day; yet they did not listen to me, or incline their ear, but stiffened their neck" (Jer. 7.25-26). The predicted result is that God will come and kill the tenants. Jesus quotes the messianic Psalm 118 to establish that the son who was rejected will be made "the head of the corner." The temple leaders are unable to oppose Jesus openly after this. Mark designated the analogy as a parable, thus raising the question as to whether he intended all parables specified as such to be midrashic.

What had appeared at first to be an intercalation between the first two trap questions now emerges as the interpretative key to both of them. Jesus is not merely parrying the thrusts of his opponents; he is aware that he is living out in advance his death penalty trials. The query "by whose authority do you act?" is a different form of the accusation that Jesus claims to be the Son of God. That is, it is a question about blasphemy. According to the Davidic model he is Jedidiah "the beloved son" who is to be killed in the vineyard parable for the same two false reasons alleged against Naboth: blasphemy and treason. David got off easy; his potential heir who was not the beloved son died; Solomon lived to reign. Mark's new Solomon would be killed. The complicated pun on the heirs and the vineyard as inheritance attests to the humor of the authors of both 1 Kings and Mark.

Mark's conclusion that the priests "feared the multitude" and "went away" because they perceived that Jesus had told the vineyard parable against them provides an interesting midrashic interpretation of Deut. 18.20-22. God orders that a prophet "who presumes to speak a word in my name which I have not commanded him to speak, or who speaks in the name of other gods, that same prophet shall die." If the consequences demonstrate that the prophet has spoken "presumptuously, you need not be afraid of him." The priests' "fear" is Mark's implicit midrashic proof that Jesus was in fact speaking in the name of God in overruling priestly practices and beliefs. The scenario is also similar to Jer. 26.16, in which the people believe Jeremiah to be innocent and oppose the priests who wish to kill him.

The next challenge comes from Pharisees, linked again with Herodians as in Mk. 3.6, who ask a question related to the Sadducees' reputation for collaborating with the Romans and paying Roman taxes willingly. Thus the question is double-edged, both to embarrass Jesus and the Sadducees. The question is if it is religiously valid to pay taxes to Caesar. If Jesus replies negatively, he will be guilty of a capital crime of treason against Rome; if positively, he will lose his popular support. Jesus was charged with treason in the trial before Pilate (Mk. 15.2-3).

The midrashic genesis of the question lies also in a pair of passages in Romans and 1 Peter. Paul insisted that believers are to pay taxes because authorities, including Roman ones, are appointed by God. "Pay all of them their dues, taxes to whom taxes are due, revenue to whom revenue is due, respect to whom respect is due, honor to whom honor is due" (Rom. 13.6-7). 1 Pet. 2.13-14 makes the same point more broadly: "Be subject for the Lord's sake to every human institution, whether it be to the emperor as supreme, or to governors as sent by him to punish those who do wrong and praise those who do right."

Jesus avoids the question (12.13-17) by pointing out that the coins used for paying Roman taxes have Caesar's picture on them, not God's. Therefore, "render to Caesar the things that are Caesar's, and to God the things that are God's." Any politician would be proud of such an answer: it says nothing but sounds like a complete response to the question asked. It can mean almost anything that anyone wants it to mean and has indeed been interpreted in many ways in subsequent centuries. The answer, however, did not fit the expectations of military revolution against the Romans which Jesus' Solomonic entry into Jerusalem on Sunday had raised.

Just as Pharisees had framed their question to embarrass Sadducees, Sadducees did the same in return. The Pharisees believed in bodily resurrection; the Sadducees did not. So the Sadducees inquired about resurrection, as related to a Torah law:

> If brothers dwell together, and one of them dies and has no son, the wife of the dead shall not be married outside the family to a stranger; her husband's brother shall go into her, and take her as his wife, and perform the duty of a husband's brother to her. And the first son whom she bears shall succeed to the name of the brother who is dead, that his name may not be blotted out of Israel (Deut. 25.5-6).

Based on that law, the Sadducees contrive a midrashic trap in which a woman has been married successively to seven brothers but has borne no child to any of them. All seven brothers, then the woman, die. When the resurrection of all Jews occurs, whose wife will she be? Jesus avoids answering the question directly, but unlike the previous two occasions he does not avoid it altogether. He confronts the Sadducees on the issue of what resurrection means, giving two different implied definitions. One is that those who rise from the dead "neither marry nor are given in marriage, but are like angels in heaven." 1 Enoch 15.6-8 says that God did not provide wives for spiritual angels. Jesus' answer sounds much like a disembodied immortality in which resurrection would be a spiritual condition rather than a physical condition of bodies coming alive again. Such an interpretation would be consistent with the Hellenistic cultural environment in which Dispersion Jews lived.

The second answer is that "as for the dead being raised, have you not read in the book of Moses [Exod. 3], in the passage about the [burning] bush, how God said to him, 'I am the God of Abraham, and the God of Isaac, and the God of Jacob'? He is not the God of the dead, but of the living; you are quite wrong" (Mk. 12.26-27). This answer is more like what is known today as social immortality. It implies that as long as there are Jews in the world, descendants of Abraham, Isaac, and Jacob, those men will still be alive. In a broader sense, the three continue to live in the lives of those who have converted to Judaism and have no Jewish biological ancestry. They nevertheless continue the "life" of the Jewish patriarchs. It is in that same sense that virtually everyone in Western civilization today is a "Greek," i.e., the living embodiment of the thought patterns of Plato and Aristotle, and a "Jew," i.e., the embodiment of the value structures of the Bible. Mark apparently implied a distinction between "rising from the dead" and "being raised from the dead." Angels rise from the dead, perhaps as disembodied spirits in Sheol, the abode of the dead; Abraham's descendants are raised from the dead by virtue of surviving the calamities which by ordinary standards should have put an end to Judaism.

The concluding sentence, that God "is not God of the dead, but of the living" is part of Jesus' "being raised from the dead" statement. Deut. 32.39 says: "There is no God beside me; I kill and I make alive." Deuteronomy maintains a persistent preference for the living over the dead, for example in forbidding cutting oneself or shaving a bald spot on behalf of the dead (14.1), in not eating anything "that dies of itself," and in not boiling "a kid in its mother's milk" (14.21). Paul more explicitly named Jesus as lord of both the living and the dead: "None of us lives to himself, and none of us dies to himself. If we live, we live to the Lord, and if we die, we die to the Lord; so then, whether we live or whether we die, we are the Lord's. For to this end Christ died and lived again, that he might be Lord both of the dead and of the living" (Rom 14.8-9). James A. Sanders contends that God was with Moses in his death and actually buried him, and uses this as an attestation that God is Lord of both the dead and the living.[12] God being with people in their death does not necessitate resurrection. Such an interpretation would accord with Mark's.

The Sadducees' story of the seven childless brothers who die in succession, followed by the wife to each of them, is clearly a midrash on 2 Macc. 7 and 4 Macc. 8, in which seven brothers were gruesomely martyred, one at a time, after the king gave each one an opportunity to remain alive by eating pig's flesh in violation of the law. "Last of all after the sons the mother died" (2 Macc. 7.41). Some of them spoke of their belief in bodily resurrection. 4 Macc. 16.9-10 refers to the mother as a widow and affirms that all of her sons were childless.

After Jesus evades each of the three traps set by his opponents, a sympathetic scribe asks him which commandment is most important. He refers to Jesus as "teacher," but not "good teacher," thus avoiding the temptative quality of the rich man's question to Jesus in Mk. 10.17-18. Jesus answers that two laws are greater than any other: "The first is, 'Hear, O Israel: The Lord our God, the Lord is one; and you shall love the Lord your God with all your mind, and with all your appetites, and with all your power' [Deut. 6.4-5].[13] The second is this, 'You shall love your neighbor as yourself' [Lev. 19.18]" (Mk. 12.29-31). The scribe agrees, repeating Jesus' statement to emphasize that loving God and neighbor is much "more than all whole burnt offerings and sacrifices."

Jesus' answer, distinguishing loving God and loving one's neighbor, functions as a commentary on the three preceding questions as well. Jesus has been asked by what authority he operates, whether he accepts Roman civil authority on paying taxes, and how he interprets the religious authority of scripture on a remarriage issue. His overall answer is that obeying God is superior to all the above, although loving God is one of the commandments of scripture.

Jesus' answer on this occasion contradicts his earlier evaluation of the importance of obeying the commandments of Moses

(Mk. 10.17-22). There is at least a weak midrashaic doublet in the passages in Mk. 10 and 12 and their contexts. Recognizing the relationships contribute to apprciation of Mark's focus on loving God.

Mark 10:2-12: Teaching about divorce and remarriage.	Mark 12:18-23: Question about remarriage and resurrection.
10-12: Jesus opposes the law of Moses about adultery.	18-23: Sadducees assumed truth of law of Moses.
14: Those like children will enter the kingdom of God.	18.23: Going to after life without children. 18.34 You are not far from the kingdom of God.
17: What must I do to inherit eternal life?	24-27: Nature of eternal life.
18-20: Give to the poor in addition to obeying the ten commandments.	29-31: Loving God is more important than loving one's neighbor.
23: It is hard for the rich to enter the Kingdom of God.	41: The rich put large sums into the temple treasury.
23-31: (admonition to the disciples to give all.)	43: (woman's example called to attention of the disciples.)
21: Sell what you have, give, and have treasure in heaven.	44. Out of her poverty she gave all she had.

Several comments are in order. The question and Jesus' answer follow closely upon his assertion that God is Lord in both life and death. Love of God is not to be limited to times when a benefit is received, such as resurrection in the form of highly desired personal immortality. Mark explicitly disagreed with early New Testament writers about the greatest commandment. Jas./Jac. 2.8 reads: "If you really fulfill the royal law, according to the scripture, 'You shall love your neighbor as yourself,' you do well." Rom. 13.8-10 had agreed with James/Jacob:

> Owe no one anything, except to love one another; for *he who loves his neighbor has fulfilled the law.* The

> commandments, 'You shall not commit adultery, you shall not kill, you shall not steal, you shall not covet,' and any other commandment, are summed up in this sentence, 'You shall love your neighbor as yourself.' Love does no wrong to a neighbor; therefore love is the fulfilling of the law.

Gal. 5.14 had made the same point: "For the whole law is fulfilled in one word, 'You shall love your neighbor as yourself.'" In regard to the relative importance of loving God and neighbor, Mark agrees more with 1 Jn. 4.20-21: "If any one says, 'I love God,' and hates his brother, he is a liar; for he who does not love his brother whom he has seen, cannot love God whom he has not seen. And this commandment we have from him, that he who loves God should love his brother also." But even the 1 John passage does not state starkly, as in Mark, that loving God is primary, distinctively greater than loving neighbor.

One reason for Mark's disagreement with the earlier writers on this point was Mark's gradual shift toward focusing on God rather than on Jesus as savior, a consequence of Mark's agenda of exploring many meanings of "God Saves." Another reason is Mark's overall goal of reconciliation with the Father: love of God should have priority. Mark's theology is what the word Jesus suggests; it is God-ology, not Jesus-ology. His Jesus will not accept any temptation to the contrary more than temporarily, and that only to allow for its refutation.

The scribe, in agreeing with Jesus, midrashically paraphrased 1 Sam. 15.22: "Has the Lord as great delight in burnt offerings and sacrifices, as in obeying the voice of the Lord? Behold, to obey is better than sacrifice." By so arguing, the scribe set the two great commandments over against the temple and ritual religion. Jesus' final statement to the scribe makes sense in terms of that same priority: "And when Jesus saw that he had answered wisely, he said to him, 'You are not far from the kingdom of God'" (Mk. 12.34). The wise man Solomon thus appropriately comments on the wisdom of the scribe's response. Jesus implies that verbalizing right answers is not enough; his focus is on doing the truth, not just speaking it; one must obey God. Throughout Mark, the scribes have stereotypically been knowers, not doers. Obedience to God (the kingdom of God) requires doing. After that answer that no one dared ask Jesus any further question. The wise man, Jesus-Solomon, had won.

The flow of thought underlying Mark's text makes sense out of the following story, in which Jesus rejects the model of the son of David as Christ. In the Mk. 10.17 story in which Jesus was asked "Good teacher, what must I do to inherit eternal life?" he answered that one should keep the commandments and give to the poor. Paul had written in Rom. 13.8-10 that all of the commandments are summarized as loving one's neighbor. Jesus' dialogues with his critics end with him being asked what is the greatest commandment; he answers that the greatest is to love God completely, with one's entire self; second is to love one's neighbor. That which had been adequate for Jesus in the first story is no longer adequate in the second.

Each of the confrontations with the scribes and priests had an underlying theme of Jesus' impending voluntary death. The question put to Jesus in 11.29 about the authority behind his actions regards blasphemy, for which Jesus was finally condemned to death by the Sanhedrin. It is also the reason why, at the last minute, the people opposed the priests in deciding not to kill Jeremiah (Jer. 26.16), because he spoke for God. The vineyard parable states that the beloved son of God will be killed. In the dialogue about Caesar's coin, the Herodians and Pharisees attempt to get Jesus to make a treasonous statement; in Mk. 15.2-3, attempts will apparently be made to persuade Pilate that Jesus as "king of the Jews" is treasonable. The Sadducees' story about the seven brothers points to the Jewish martyrs who chose death. Jesus says that the greatest commandment is to love God completely, with all one's being. The widow at the temple in Mk. 12.42-44 who gives "everything she has—her whole living" actualizes the story of the greatest commandment and points Jesus toward that love of God which requires the greatest sacrifice--his whole living. Solomon the son of David can no longer be a model for Jesus, for Solomon never risked death or made any personal sacrifices for God.

The Scribes Who Neither Know Nor Do the Truth: Mk.12.35-40

Apart from the one scribe above, all other scribes are characterized by Jesus as neither knowing nor doing the truth. He points out that they are wrong about the messiah being a son of David. By a legalistic midrash on Ps. 110.1, Jesus reflects that David could not possibly have called his son his lord and imputes a contrary belief to the scribes. The public is delighted to have Jesus put down the scribes. The subtle point of this passage in Mark's overall scheme is that David could not accept his son as his messiah. To call the messiah the *son of David* is automatically to eliminate the possibility of father-son reconciliation.

Jer. 8.8-9 was Mark's primary midrashic source for Jesus' arguments with the opponents, culminating in condemnation of the scribes:

> How can you say, "We are wise, and the law of the Lord is with us"? But, behold the false pen of the scribes has made it into a lie. *The wise men shall be put to shame*, they shall be dismayed and taken.... ...from the least to the greatest every one is greedy for unjust gain.

Jesus denigrates the immorality of the scribes, enumerating in detail their faults, especially hypocrisy and parasitic living on the wealth of widows. The charge that the scribes like the "best seats" may midrashically parallel the distinction in Jas./Jac. 2.1-4 between offering seats only to the rich and not to the poor.

Third Day—Contrast with the Widow's Gift: Mk. 12.41-44

It is not historically likely that there was a way in which spectators could watch other people presenting money gifts to the temple treasury. Mark nevertheless pictured Jesus "seeing" some contributing out of their abundance, some of them giving very large sums. Jesus points out that a poor widow has contributed most: two coins which were all that she had. This pericope brings to an end the wisdom of Jesus as the new Solomon, just as the preceding pericopes had ended the identification of Jesus as the new son of David. A weak midrashic possibility is that the narrative is about a widow, not just any poor person, somewhat as in the original wise man story of Solomon in 1 Kgs. 3. There, two harlots contended that each was mother of a child. Solomon had just previously asked God for "an understanding mind to govern thy people, [to] discern between good and evil." Jesus demonstrated that quality of discernment in distinguishing between the quality of the large gifts of the rich and the extraordinary gift of the poor widow.

Just as Jer. 7-8 has provided much of the basic midrashic imagery throughout the Solomon unit, so it provides the midrashic conclusion. Jer. 7.4-7 was Mark's source for combining in his last two pericopes an attack upon ritualistic religion coupled with the injustice of the scribes and praise for a widow:

> Do not trust in these deceptive words: "This is the temple of the Lord, the temple of the Lord, the temple of the Lord." For if you truly amend your ways and your doings, if you truly execute justice one with another, if you do not oppress the alien, the fatherless, or the widow, or shed innocent blood in this place...then I will let you dwell in this place.

One can well imagine the anger growing in Jesus which will result in the next unit in his prediction that the temple loved by the scribes would be destroyed.

Endnotes for Chapter Ten

[1]N. K. Gottwald, "Hebrew Poetry," *IDB*.

[2]"Homeland Jews" is an expression adapted from James Sanders' distinction between Jews who defined their religion in such a way that Judaism could exist whether or not the Jews had a land of their own, and other Jews who insisted that, in order to be fully Jewish, they had to have a homeland in which they would be politically and militarily independent.

[3]The LXX contains more books than the Masoretic Old Testament, with the effect that the story of Israel's history did not end with the Babylonian exile but with the Maccabean victory over the Greek Empire. Even though Mark did midrash on the LXX as sacred writing, he thought in terms of the parameters of the Masoretic Text, with its emphasis on God being with people in disaster and suffering rather than rescuing them from such occasions.

[4]Rev. Joe Grubbs, minister at the First Christian Church, Des Moines, Iowa.

[5]According to K. W. Clark, "Bethany," *IDB*, there are four meanings of Bethany: "House of Ananiah," "House of the Poor," "House of the Afflicted," and "House of Late-Season Green Figs." Mark makes use of the three latter etymologies; Luke undoubtedly uses the first one as the source for his three different characters named "Ananias" in Acts.

[6]Werner Kelber, *Mark's Story of Jesus* (Philadelphia: Fortress, 1979), 59-60, points out that RSV ought to read "right time" rather than "season," and correctly concludes from this that Mark intended the reader to understand that it was not the right time for the Kingdom of God.

[7]2 Chron. 29 describes a cleansing of the temple during the reign of Hezekiah to rid it of kinds of impurities different from those identified in Mark.

[8]Craig A. Evans, "Jesus' Action in the Temple...," *SBL Seminar Papers* (1989) 522, citing E. P. Sanders, *Jesus and Judaism* (Philadelphia: Fortress, 1985) 61-76.

[9]A modern one-liner which expresses this point is worth passing on: "Your cravings as a human animal do not become prayer just because it is God whom you ask to attend to them" [no author attributed].

[10]Also 1 Chron. 17.13.

[11]The argument that Mark was relying on Isaiah 5 is strengthened by the fact that the word for thorns in Isa. 5.2 is also repeated in Mark's crown of "thorns" in Mk. 15.17.

CHAPTER ELEVEN

MIDRASH ON APOCALYPSES

Mark next set out to refute the idea that the appearance of the messiah on earth should be described in terms of Jewish apocalyptic literature. Mk. 13 is known almost universally as the Little Apocalypse. "Apocalypse" is technically a synonym for "revelation," from the root "to uncover"[1] and does not in itself denote any particular kind of revelation. In popular usage, apocalypse refers to a prediction of extraordinary destruction of this world and visions of a world which will replace it. Mk. 13 is divided into two types of prediction about the future, and perhaps a third. The two distinctive types are clearly apocalyptic in ordinary usage; the third is not. Both Jewish and Christian apocalyptic writings are midrashic, i.e., highly dependent upon their predecessors for their basic imagery.

The changing state of scholarship about apocalyptic was illustrated in a 1989 verbal exchange between John J. Collins, M. Eugene Boring, Bruce Chilton, John Dominic Crossan, and Helmut Koester on the subject: "Jesus and Apocalyptic: End of the World Expectation?" The session at the Society of Biblical Literature at which they spoke was co-sponsored by the Historical Jesus Section and the Jesus Seminar. The five men acknowledged two facts: that earlier scholarship in this century had assumed that Jesus expected some kind of a cataclysmic end of the world in his near future, and that a high percentage of scholars recently polled on the subject voted that Jesus had not expected such a catastrophe. The five not only disagreed with each other on the issue of whether Jesus had such an expectation, but also on the definition of apocalyptic as it applied to Jesus.

The five scholars did generally seem to concur that Mark would have voted affirmatively had he been included in the recent poll. To the contrary, our analysis of the "Little Apocalypse" indicates that Mark was already involved in such a controversy in his day. He described a sudden end of history and then rejected the notion as an adequate interpretation of the messiah's agenda.

Third Day—Faithful Disciples Under Persecution: Mk. 13.1-13

Having just come from the temple, Jesus predicts that the temple buildings and possibly all of Jerusalem will be leveled. Jeremiah provides the connecting link with the previous sections in Mark, in which scribes will be condemned (12.40), Jesus can find no righteous persons or fruit-bearing trees (11.13), and each dialogue story points to Jesus' impending death (11.27—12.34). Jer. 7.9-16 says that because the temple "has become a den of robbers" (as in Mk. 11.17) and because the people have committed a long list of sins, God will destroy the temple. In Jer. 26.4-9, Jeremiah prophesies that "this house shall be like Shiloh and this city shall be desolate, without inhabitants." Everyone responds by "laying hold of him, saying 'You shall die!'" (a model for Jesus' trials in Mk. 14-15). Jer. 4.18-6.8 describes a destruction similar to that depicted in Mark 13, complete with earthquakes, fleeing people, desperate women in labor, darkened sky, and false prophets. Mk. 13.1-2 is ambiguous as to whether the "great buildings" refer to more than one temple building or to the whole city of Jerusalem. Jer. 4.18-31, 6.8, and 9.11 suggest the latter; Luke read Mark that way.[2] However, the context of all of Passion Week in Mark focuses so much on the temple that the author may have intended it only.

Mark suggested positive reasons for disposing of the temple. If loving God and neighbor is more than burnt offerings and sacrifices, as Jesus and the scribe had agreed, a temple would no longer be needed. If the widow's offering was qualitatively better than the offerings of the rich, the temple operation could not be maintained. Thus the temple has been psychologically destroyed in the logic of Jesus' teachings before he predicts its physical demolition. Assuming that Mark was writing after its destruction, the prediction appears to be a classic example of a *vaticinium ex eventu*, a prediction after the event.[3] Mark's interest, however, was less in showing Jesus as an accurate prognosticator than as a prophetic analyst of the growing irrelevance of the temple. John Robinson makes a strong case from Mark for the Gospel having been written when the temple was still standing.[4] Even if the building had been still standing when Mark wrote, it was already non-existent in his religion, as if it had already been levelled.

Having predicted the demolition of the temple, Jesus leaves Jerusalem and goes to the west side of the Mount of Olives. There, he and the original four disciples look at the temple and talk about it. Mark does not seem to have made anything of the fact that this conversation is in secret and could therefore fit the temptation motif, as in the second passion/reward prediction. The four ask him for a sign as to when the temple destruction will occur. In doing so, they fail to "beware of the leaven of the Pharisees" who had earlier elicited from Jesus the lament "Why does this generation seek a sign" (Mk. 8.15, 12)?[5] Jesus responds as if he had been asked not about the temple in particular, but about the date of a general destruction in terms of the kinds of events predicted in Jewish apocalyptic. His answer, extending from Mk. 13.5-36, ranges over a wide variety of midrashic sources from Jewish tradition.

The heart of the unit is a midrash on the book of Daniel ("God Has Judged") and Daniel's probable source in Jeremiah. Identifying that midrash is made easier here than in the rest of Mark because Lars Hartman has written an insightful chapter on Mk. 13 in relationship to the Old Testament, with emphasis on

Daniel.[6] Hartman thought in terms of passages which influenced Mark in five descending degrees: direct or nearly direct quotation, certain influence without quotation, parallel motifs, motifs which resemble each other, and phraseology which resembles each other. Most of his proposals will be included in this chapter, but will be separately noted as his only when they are unique.

Daniel was a wise man like Solomon, a new Solomon for his time; this may have been part of Mark's justification for following the Solomon unit with a Daniel unit. Mark could midrashically associate Daniel's wisdom with a unit on the temple because that wisdom was granted to him by Gabriel "at the time of the evening sacrifice" (Dan. 9.21-22). It is remotely possible, given Mark's midrashic mind, that he pictured Jesus with only four of the disciples rather than all twelve because in Daniel there are four holy young men: Daniel, Hananiah, Mishael, and Azariah (the latter three being usually referred to by their Babylonian names: Shadrach, Meshach, and Abednego).

Daniel was written as if its events occurred during the time of the Babylonian captivity and its predictions were for a distant future. Scholars generally agree that the book was written after the desecration of the temple by the emperor Antiochus Epiphanes in 167 BCE and that most of the events predicted in the book had already occurred.[7] Thus the author could write with confidence, as in 11.27 and 11.35, that the appointed time (the time of the end) had not yet come, knowing that the events predicted had in fact occurred between the fictional time of the writing and the actual time. *Vaticinium ex eventu* predictions intend to deceive the reader and can appropriately be labeled as fictions. Daniel, knowing that the Maccabees had prevailed over Antiochus Epiphanes, predicted that a messiah would restore Jerusalem after evil forces had both desecrated the temple and decimated the male population. It mattered little to Mark that Jesus was a messiah very different from

Daniel's forecast. Every reference to anointing or any anointed one was messianic for Mark.

The vague question asked by the disciples about when "all these things will be accomplished" is a midrashic adaptation of Dan. 12.7-8 paralleling Daniel's inquiry about "the end of these things." Jesus gives three answers; the first is the most puzzling. He predicts that "many will come in my name, saying, 'I am he,'" to lead people astray. The Greek for "I am he" permits a translation, "I am," which would give the sentence a different meaning, but one still relevant to Mark.[8] "I am" was the answer given by God at the burning bush when Moses asked God's name. Anyone who said that would be claiming divinity, and would thus be succumbing to the temptation to declare himself "the holy one" which Jesus had faced and overcome. Consistent with this interpretation, Hartman calls attention to Dan. 8.24-25 and 11.32, but without noting that the destructive and deceptive ruler in those passages was Antiochus Epiphanes ("The Manifest" [God][9]) who did in fact claim to be God, i.e., "I am."[10] Mark would also have been interested in him because Dan. 8.23 says of him that he "understands riddles" (parables) which no one but Jesus could interpret correctly according to Mark.

One of Mark's minor concerns was to show that Jesus could actually do everything that the emperor who claimed to be divine contended he could do, even though in Jesus' case all those powers were to be rejected as temptative. "Many will come in my name" sounds like a warning from Mark that either there were in Mark's time or already had been people claiming to be a resurrected messiah and leading people astray. Mark wanted it to be known that Jesus himself had predicted that all such claimants would be false and that the resurrection. therefore, is not to be defined in terms of the appearance of a man who had previously died in a biological sense. This is consistent with the fact that the Gospel of Mark does not include any resurrection appearance stories. Hartman suggests a parallel motif in Jeremiah: "Do not let your prophets and your diviners who are among you deceive you, and do not listen to the dreams which they dream, for it is a lie which they are prophesying to you in my name; I did not send them, says the Lord" (Jer. 29.8-9; cf. Jer. 14.14-16; 23.21-25).[11] Jer. 5.30-31 is more to Mark's point: "An appalling and horrible thing has happened in the land: the prophets prophesy falsely, and the priests rule at their direction; my people love to have it so, but what will you do when the end comes?" The midrashic root of the Jeremiah passages[12] in turn is Deut. 13.1-3: "If a prophet arises among you, or a dreamer of dreams, and gives you a sign or wonder, and the sign or wonder which he tells you comes to pass, and if he says, 'Let us go after other gods,' which you have not known, 'and let us serve them,' you shall not listen...." Ezekiel alludes to "prophets who see delusive visions and who give lying divinations" and who "have misled my people, saying, 'Peace,' when there is no peace" (Ezek. 13.9-10).

Jesus' second answer to the query about the time of the end is that wars, rumors of wars, earthquakes, and famines must occur; "the end is not yet"; "this is but the beginning of the sufferings." Mark's summary statement about wars and rumors of wars could have been his midrashic interpretation of Daniel, in which wars are predicted. Famines are predicted more often in Jeremiah than in any other biblical book, often in connection with the sword and pestilence. Jer. 14.13-16 attacks the lying prophets who claim that "sword and famine shall not come on this land," whereas their hearers shall be "victims of famine and sword, with none to bury them." Jer. 13.13-14 announces that God will dash one against the other the kings, priests, prophets and all the inhabitants of the land without pity or compassion. Either of these visions of the future would justify Jesus' statement that famines, earthquakes, wars and destruction of buildings would be merely the "beginning of the sufferings." Hartman correctly notes that "nation will rise up against nation" and "kingdom against kingdom" are nearly direct quotations from 2 Chron. 15.6 and Isa. 19.2.[13] The phrases in their original contexts, however, have no other parallels to their context in Mark; therefore they cannot be justified as midrashic for Mark. Several biblical references to earthquakes seem to be no more than incidental allusions in relation to Mark.

Jesus' third answer to the question about when "all these things will be accomplished" is that the disciples themselves will "be delivered up" to be beaten in synagogues, tried before rulers and councils, and experience treacherous treatment by relatives; but through it all, there will be widespread preaching of the gospel. The verb, "to be delivered up" is the same as is used for Judas "betraying" Jesus and John the Baptizer "being arrested," suggesting that Mark intentionally framed Jesus' answer as an invitation to the disciples to participate in the crucifixion. In such a setting, the holy spirit will guide the disciples in what they are to say. "The gospel must first be preached to all nations" (Mk. 13.10) perhaps because in II Isaiah the gospel or good news of salvation is not for Jews alone, for "I will give you as a light to the nations" (Isa. 52.7, 49.6). Mark's anticipation of persecution is likely to have been influenced by Paul's recounting his harassment of the church: "For you have heard of my former life in Judaism, how I persecuted the church of God violently and tried to destroy it; and I advanced in Judaism beyond many of my own age among my people, so extremely zealous was I for the traditions of my fathers" (Gal. 1.13). Whatever Mark knew from history otherwise, he knew from Galatians that there had been "beatings in synagogues, trials before councils," etc., and Mark could thereby have Jesus predict that such events would occur. It appears that Jesus wants the future to support his earlier confidence that the Twelve would, in fact, bear fruit and be the Suffering Servant and New Israel. Mark's view, however, was that Jesus went alone to the cross, reconciling himself alone with God, deserted by all. The Twelve were to fail in the future as they had failed in the past.

Mark may have used midrashic sources in Dan. 7.25, 8.24-25, and 11.30-32, each of which depict persecutions, the latter two by Antiochus Epiphanes. Dan. 7.25 refers to saints who are given into the hand of an anti-godly king. Mark's midrashic inspiration for "you will stand before governors and kings for my sake" may have been the three youths' bravery in disobeying the king's interdict against worshiping God (Dan. 3.12-17) or Ps. 2.2: "The rulers take counsel together against the Lord and his anointed [plural]." Mark's "you will be hated by all for my name's sake" resembles "your brethren who hate you and cast you out for my name's sake" of Isa. 66.5. The instruction to "say whatever is given you" is modeled after God's advice to Moses: "Is it not I, the Lord? Now therefore go, and I will be your mouth and teach you what you shall speak" (Exod. 4.10-12). Mark used three parallels from Mic. 7. Mk. 13.12's "brother will deliver up brother to death" lies opposite "They all lie in wait for blood, and each hunts his brother with a net" (Mic. 7.2) together with Jer. 9.4: "Put no trust in any brother, for every brother is a supplanter." Mark's parent-child animosity is equivalent to "the son treats the father with contempt...; a man's enemies are the men of his own house" (Mic. 7.6). Despite all that, Mic. 7.7 affirms, "I will wait for the God of my salvation," the counterpart of Mk. 13.13's "he who endures to the end will be saved." Dan. 11.32 ("people who know their God shall stand firm and take action") is another midrashic source for Mark's "he who endures to the end will be saved."

The Final Times of tribulation: Mk. 13.14-27

In Mk. 13.5-13, Jesus envisioned that the disciples would be faithful under persecution, bearing testimony, being brought to trial, enduring to the end—all the things that they do not do in Mark. In 13.14-15, Jesus says that when they "see the desolating sacrilege set up where it ought not to be," they *should* flee, for tribulation will intensify so much that the righteous elect will barely survive. Mark begins this section with a midrash on Dan. 9.27: "And he shall make a strong covenant with many for one week; and for half of the week he shall cause sacrifice and offering to cease; and *upon the wing of abomination shall come one who makes desolate, until the decreed end is poured out* on the desolator." Dan. 11.31 and 12.11 make clear that "the abomination that makes desolate" is a desolating sacrilege set up in the temple, profaning it after the proper continual burnt offering had been taken away. In Daniel, the desolating sacrilege is one event in a sequence of sufferings and persecutions, close to the appointed time of the end, when the righteous will be saved and sinners punished. 1 Macc. 1.54 writes of the same desecration, ordered by Antiochus Epiphanes: "And on the fifteenth day of Chislev in the one hundred and forty-fifth year they set up upon the altar an *'abomination of desolation.'*" Antiochus ordered a statue of a Hellenized version of a Canaanitish "God of Heaven" to be set up in the temple under the name of Zeus Olympias. The Hebrew name for that god is closely similar to the verb "to be abominable."[14] Like Mark, 1 Macc. 2.28 warns that people should flee to the mountains in the time of trouble and 1 Macc. 9.24-29 describes distress such as had not been known before, including famine.

In referring to the "desolating sacrilege," Mark comments parenthetically, "let the reader understand." It is usually supposed that this is his way of saying to the reader, "Please understand that I am talking about a desecration of the temple much later than the one by Antiochus Epiphanes." He could have been referring either to Caligula's statue being placed in the temple in 40 CE or the destruction of the temple in 69-70 CE or both. If Mark was referring to a historical occasion, the 69-70 event would be the best guess because Mk. 13 begins with a prediction of the temple's destruction. However, the Danielic details which surround Mark's mention of the "desolating sacrilege" in the final days would suggest that Mark had the desolating sacrilege of Dan. 9-12 primarily in mind. Mark may have been writing midrashically on both the destruction of the temple in 69-70 CE and on the texts above.

Jesus' warning to flee to the mountains, without entering the house, getting possessions, or turning back from the field is similar to Gen. 19.15-17, in which angels sieze Lot and his family, urging them not to linger in Sodom: "Flee for your life. Do not look back or stop anywhere in the valley; flee to the hills, lest you be consumed." Jer. 6.1 also urges people to "flee for safety" when destruction comes to Jerusalem. Both Isa. 13.16 and Mk. 13.17 write about terrible things happening to infants as people flee. A portion of Dan. 12.1-2 is cited by Mark almost verbatim and the remainder revocalized:

> *And there shall be a time of trouble, such as never has been since there was a nation till that time;* but at that time your people shall be delivered, every one whose name shall be found written in the book. And many of those who sleep in the dust of the earth shall awake, some to everlasting life, and some to shame and everlasting contempt.

In Mk. 13.19-20, God allows some humans to be saved by shortening the days of tribulation. Deut. 4.30-31 also writes of a merciful God in a time of unexcelled tribulation: "*When you are in tribulation,* and all these things come upon you *in the latter days,* you will return to the Lord your God and obey his voice, for the Lord your *God is a merciful God; he will not fail you or destroy you.*" Mark in this portion of his Gospel totally reversed his messianic imagery. Prior to the sentence, "If the Lord had not shortened the days, no human being would be saved," Mark has been interested only in Jesus as the messiah. Subsequent to that sentence, all the rest of Mark centers on God as *the savior.* The story of Jesus ("God

Saves") henceforth focuses on God's direct saving activity rather than any saving activity of Jesus.

As in Mk. 13.5-6, Mk. 13.21-22 forecasts false messiahs: "And then if any one says to you, 'Look, here is the Christ!' or 'Look, there he is!' do not believe it. False Christs and false prophets will arise and show signs and wonders, to lead astray, if possible, the elect." Mark's midrashic sources for this warning are identical to those for the earlier caution about those who would say, "I am," except that Deut. 13.1-6 becomes primary because of the focus on "signs and wonders" and Jer. 23.16 secondary. Hartman understands Mark to have relied on the phrase "god whom his fathers did not know" which is found in Deut. 13.6 and Dan. 11.38.[15] The false messiahs and false prophets alluded to in Mk. 13.21-22 may not be people claiming to be Jesus or God, as in the earlier sentence, but people claiming to be the true messiah or prophet as if Jesus had not been a true messiah or prophet. Mark may have been influenced here by the idea of antichrist in 1 John or by any of four passages from Paul: "Children, it is the last hour; and as you have heard that antichrist is coming, so now many antichrists have come; therefore we know it is the last hour" (1 Jn. 2.18); "For such men are false apostles, deceitful workmen, disguising themselves as apostles of Christ. And no wonder, for even Satan disguises himself as an angel of light" (2 Cor. 11.13-14); "The signs of a true apostle were performed among you in all patience, with signs and wonders and mighty works" (2 Cor. 12.12); "Since you desire proof that Christ is speaking in me. He is not weak in dealing with you, but is powerful in you" (2 Cor. 13.3); "Not that there is another gospel, but there are some who trouble you and want to pervert the gospel of Christ. But even if we, or an angel from heaven, should preach to you a gospel contrary to that which we preached to you, let him be accursed" (Gal. 1.7-8). The 1 John allusion to antichrists is to be used by Mark again in his portrayal of Peter's denials. Mark may have been referring to historical figures during the first century who had already claimed to be the Jewish messiah.[16] It is more likely that when Mark was writing in terms of Jesus' messiahship, pretenders would say "I am," but when Mark shifted to God's saving activity they would claim to be messiahs and prophets. This would be an additional instance of the type of balancing Mark used when he had Jewish killers on Gentile territory and foreign killers in Judea. Mark's implied message would be that impostors will find a way to turn any high ideal to their private advantage and lead many astray.

After establishing that God was to be the savior, Mark depicted a sensational season of God's supernatural revelation by a lavish display of the powers in the heavens. Each detail in Mk. 13.24-27 has one or more parallels in the Old Testament. The following passages by no means exhaust the possibilities, let alone other Jewish literature which is here omitted entirely.

> Mk. 13.24-25: But in those days, after that tribulation, the sun will be darkened, and the moon will not give its light, and the stars will be falling from heaven, and the powers in the heavens will be shaken.
>
> > For the day of the Lord is near in the valley of decision. The sun and the moon are darkened, and the stars withdraw their shining (Joel 3.14-15; also 2.10).
> >
> > And I will give portents in the heavens and on the earth, blood and fire and columns of smoke. The sun shall be turned to darkness, and the moon to blood (Joel 2.30-31).
>
> Mk. 13.26: Then they will see the Son of man coming in clouds with great power and glory.
>
> > I saw in the night visions, and behold, with the clouds of heaven there came one like a son of man, and he came to the Ancient of Days and was presented before him, and to him was given dominion and glory and kingdom (Dan. 7.13-14).

I looked to the heavens, and they had no light. I looked on the mountains, and lo, they were quaking (Jer. 4.23-24).

All the host of heaven shall rot away, and the skies roll up like a scroll (Isa. 34.4).

Behold, the day of the Lord comes, cruel, with wrath and fierce anger, to make the earth a desolation and to destroy its sinners from it. For the stars of the heavens and their constellations will not give their light; the sun will be dark at its rising and the moon will not shed its light. (Isa. 13.9-10).

When I blot you out, I will cover the heavens, and make their stars dark; I will cover the sun with a cloud, and the moon shall not give its light (Ezek. 32.7).

Mk. 13.27: And then he will send out the angels, and gather his elect from the four winds, from the ends of earth to the ends of heaven.

In that day the Lord will extend his hand yet a second time to recover the remnant which is left of his people.... He will raise an ensign for the nations, and will assemble the outcasts of Israel and gather the dispersed of Judah from the four corners of the earth (Isa. 11.11-12).

Then I will gather the remnant of my flock out of all the countries where I have driven them (Jer. 23.3).

Fear not, for I am with you; I will bring your offspring from the east, and from the west I will gather you; I will say to the north, Give up, and to the south, Do not withhold; bring my sons from afar and my daughters from the end of the earth (Isa. 43.5-6).

The Lord your God will restore your fortunes, and have compassion upon you, and he will gather you

> again from all the peoples where the Lord your God has scattered you (Deut. 30.3).
>
> I saw in my vision by night, and behold, the four winds of heaven were stirring up the great sea (Dan. 7.2).

Through all that mass of midrashic details, Mark's central point is clear. The time will come (already has come if this is a prediction after the event) when those who ought to be faithful in the face of persecution will not be. It will be a time of great suffering. The only hope in such a day is that God himself will come to the rescue in supernatural ways beyond the control of human beings. In that day, God, not Jesus, will be the savior. In that manner, Mark eliminates the proposition that Jesus saves and introduces the direct meaning of Jesus' name: "God Saves."

Daniel's "one like a Son of man" who appeared "with the clouds of heaven" was a supernatural figure. The common assumption that Jesus, by referring to that "Son of man," was announcing his true supernatural identity is wrong on two counts. It ignores the midrashic character of apocalyptic and it disregards the context of this particular apocalypse in the whole of Mark. The nature of apocalypse is that many details from previous apocalyptic literature are cited, most of them fanciful to the extreme, such as stars falling out of the sky, the powers in the heavens being shaken, the gathering of the elect from the four winds, etc. To think of those images as metaphorical and then to insist on one like a Son of man coming with the clouds of heaven as a literal statement of predicted fact is both illogical and contextually unjustified. In addition, the Little Apocalypse is only one unit of many in Mark. Each previous unit has proposed a spiritual ideal from scripture and has demonstrated its inadequacy for achieving Father-child reconciliation. There is no reason to think, without evidence to the contrary, that this unit is any different. One can expect that the apocalyptic imagery from the Old Testament will also be defined in some manner as inadequate by Mark. To the extent that in most of the other sections of Mark one characteristic of failure has been the attempted elevation of Jesus to supernatural status by the tempters, it certainly can be expected that the elevation of Jesus to the status of the supernatural Son of man would be a temptation and not a personal affirmation of his identity.

Still the Third Day—No One Knows When: Mk. 13.28-37

Breaking Mark 13 into a third unit at verse 28 may be a mistake. The question is whether 13.28-31 is separate and discrete from that which precedes it or whether Mark intended a continuous flow of thought. The latter alternative is hinted at primarily by the word "but" which starts verse 32. Jesus refers first to a fig tree bearing leaves in spring, thus extending the Bethany-fig motif. In this case, spring is a natural sign that summer is on the way. Mark drew a strange conclusion from that simple fact: "When you see *these things* taking place, you know that *he* is near, at the very gates." What "things"? Who is near? Whatever is meant by *these things*, they are to occur during the generation in which Jesus is speaking. Even if heaven and earth were to pass away, Jesus' words, including his assurance that these "things" will happen, would not cease to be.

The fig tree from which the disciples are to learn its lesson is likely to be the withered fig tree of Mk. 11.21-24. That tree was punished by being withered because it did not bear fruit. Even though it was not the proper season for figs, there was no time left to wait; the tree had no second chance, for Jesus said, "May no one ever eat fruit from you again." When the "branch becomes tender and puts forth its leaves" (Mk. 13.28), it was presumably the "summer is near" time for the tree to bear fruit. Mark's flow of thought apparently is that in the final days angels will be sent out to gather the elect, those to be saved. That will be the time for harvesting people, for separating the good fruit from the unfruitful sinners. No one except God knows when harvest day will be. But on that day "he" (apparently the "Son of man coming in clouds with great power and glory") will be "near, at the very gates" (13.26, 29). In Mk. 13.3-4, the four disciples had asked when the great buildings would be destroyed and what would be the sign. Jesus apparently returns to their question in 13.28-38: the sign won't be spectacular like earthquakes or stars falling out of the sky. It will be common sense and ordinary, just as leaves growing on trees indicate that summer is both inevitable and near. Whenever that day will be, it will be soon, so watch!

Jesus says that "this generation will not pass away before *all these things* take place" (13.30). It is not clear which events are to occur within the generation. Mark 13 up to this point has been replete with spectacular signs and events, climaxed by the coming of the Danielic Son of Man. With the possible exception of the darkness at the crucifixion (15.33), none of the events or signs referred to before 13.30 occur later in Mark, literally, symbolically or allegorically! This difficulty may be resolved by applying the saying in 13.30 only to events predicted in 13.31-37. There are strong midrashic parallels between the allegory in 13.32-37 and the sequence in Mk. 14.32-72. After Jesus has generalized that no one other than the Father knows the "hour" when "these things" will occur, a master warns his doorkeeper to keep watch lest he come at cockcrow or some other unexpected time and find him sleeping. Jesus repeatedly tells the disciples to watch (14.34, 14.37-38, 13.33, 13.34, 13.35, 13.37); the master Jesus returns and finds the disciples asleep (14.41, 13.35-36); Peter is surprised when he denies Jesus at cockcrow (14.72, 13.35); and Jesus refers three times to the "hour" which has come when Jesus decided to obey the Father (14.14.35, 14.37, 14.41).

Mark has shifted gears, rejecting or transforming the traditional "final judgment" apocalyptic images. The time which will come is no longer that of earthquakes, falling stars, people fleeing, the earth passing away, and buildings being razed. The hour which will come began at Gethsemane with Jesus' prayer to God that "the hour might pass from him" but then he agrees to die. Jesus instructs the disciples to watch with the vigilance that they were supposed to exhibit at Gethsemane rather than looking for spectacular events or signs. The signs will be routine, like leaves budding or the master coming home unexpectedly. Thus the apocalypse will not be the supernatural shaking of the heavens of traditional apocalyptic, but the result of natural events, such as those in Gethsemane, leading to Jesus' crucifixion. Mark's thesis that there is no Father-child reconciliation in the apocalyptic model is loosely supported by the fact that the Father knows the time but the son does not. Both in the Solomon section and this one, the father-son theme is stated in a way which calls virtually no attention to itself.

The reference to "he is near" is often referred to as a parousia, a term generally interpreted to allude to a future coming of Jesus.[17] James/Jacob, I Peter, I John, and Paul's letters each use the concept in a way which is instructive for reading Mark's allusions to the master of the house who will come suddenly, at some unknown time, or to the Son of man who will send out the angels to gather those who are saved.

> *Be patient, therefore, brethren, until the coming of the Lord.* Behold, the farmer waits for the precious fruit of the earth, being patient over it until it receives the early and the late rain. You also be patient. Establish your hearts, for *the coming of the Lord is at hand* (Jas./Jac. 5.7-8).
>
> In this you rejoice, though now for a little while you may have to suffer various trials, so that the genuineness of your faith...may redound to praise and glory and honor *at the revelation of Jesus Christ*.... Therefore, gird up your minds, be sober, set your hope fully

upon the *grace that is coming to you at the revelation of Jesus Christ* (1 Pet. 1.6-7, 13).

But rejoice insofar as you share Christ's sufferings, that you may also rejoice and be glad *when his glory is revealed.* ... For the time has come for judgment to begin with the household of God; and if it begins with us, what will be the end of those who do not obey the gospel of God (1 Pet. 4.13, 17)?

So I exhort the elders among you, as a fellow elder and witness of the sufferings of Christ as well as a partaker in the *glory that is to be revealed.* ... *When the chief shepherd is manifested* you will obtain the unfading crown of glory.... And after you have suffered for a little while, the God of all grace, who has called you to his eternal glory in Christ, will himself restore, establish, and strengthen you (1 Pet. 5.1, 4, 10).

And now, little children, abide in him, so that when he appears we may have confidence and not shrink from him in shame at his coming.... Beloved, we are God's children now; it does not yet appear what we shall be, but *we know that when he appears we shall be like him, for we shall see him as he is* (1 Jn. 2.28; 3.2).

I give thanks always for you because of the grace of God which was given you in Christ Jesus, that in every way you were enriched in him...so that you are not lacking in any spiritual gift, *as you wait for the revealing of our Lord Jesus Christ; who will sustain you till the end, guiltless in the day of our Lord Jesus Christ* (1 Cor. 1.4-8).

Therefore do not pronounce judgment before the time, *before the Lord comes,* who will bring to light the things now hidden in darkness and will disclose the purposes of the heart. Then every man will receive his commendation from God (1 Cor. 4.5)

For as often as you eat this bread and drink the cup, *you proclaim the Lord's death until he comes* (1 Cor. 11.26).

In each instance, the future coming of Christ is more plausibly interpreted in context as if it would be his first appearance as a human being in history rather than as his second such appearance. For each author, the appearance which had previously occurred was the breaking into history of the significance of voluntary suffering and forgiveness, read as the fulfillment of the messianic idea. The second coming, by contrast, was more likely to be a particular person in history. Mark midrashically combined the two in Jesus' crucifixion and the events leading directly to it, which would be for the disciples the time for which they were to be on watch, the culminating time. It would be as if Jesus had not come until he became the crucified one, his true identity for Mark. Thus in the pre-crucifixion time of Mk. 13, Jesus' parousia was still in the future; from Mark's vantage point as an author it had already occurred. That distinction between the time of the narrative and the time of the author is of great importance in interpreting all of the Gospels. It was true in Paul's letters. Paul's language about the death and coming of Jesus vacillated back and forth as to whether it was an event which belonged in either the past or the future, or whether it was an event of Paul's present experience. Mark accurately reflected the tension which Paul's text evidenced.

Endnotes for Chapter Eleven

[1]C. F. D. Moule, "Revelation," *IDB*.

[2]Indicative of a major distinction between Mark and Luke, Mark's Jesus opposed the temple and its law-based rituals; Luke's Jesus opposed Jerusalem and Judaism in general but not the temple and the law.

[3]Bo Reicke argues that there are no prophecies after the event among Jesus' utterances in the Gospels because each of them which has been alleged by scholars is a midrash. He does not not use the term "midrash," but he cites the passages from Jewish sacred literature upon which each was based. Reicke recognizes the midrashic-type passages only when arguing for a date of authorship for all the synoptic gospels prior to the destruction of the temple in 69-70 CE. All of the sources which he recognizes are included in the argument in this book that all of Mark, not just these few passages, is midrashic in nature.

[4]John A. T. Robinson, *Redating the New Testament* (Philadelphia: Westminster, 1976).

[5]One of the proofs that Luke understood Mark's midrash is the fact that Luke developed this precise point with great power in his presentation of the apostles' request for a sign in Acts 1.

[6]Lars Hartman, *Prophecy Interpreted* (Lund, Sweden: Coniectanea Biblica, 1966), esp. 145-77. In a footnote on p. 150, Hartman acknowledges the relationship between midrash and what he terms five degrees of parallelism by referring to what "an imaginative midrashist" might find in a specific instance.

[7]Arthur Jeffrey's exegesis of Daniel in *The Interpreter's Bible* takes the connection between Daniel and the Maccabean revolt so completely for granted that he begins with a long history of the Hellenization of the Orient and Jewish resistance to it, without even raising the question as to whether some other explanation is feasible.

[8]Bratcher and Nida, 398.

[9]N. Turner, "Antiochus," *IDB*.

[10]Hartman, 150.

[11]Hartman, 147.

[12]Or vice versa. Majority scholar opinion is that Jeremiah and Deuteronomy were written within the same very narrow time period. Thus, theoretically at least, the lines of influence could have gone in either direction. Mark would probably have thought of Deuteronomy as having been written centuries before Jeremiah.

[13]Hartman, 148.

[14]Arthur Jeffery, *Interpreter's Bible*, VI, 499.

[15]Hartman, 173.

[16]Werner Kelber, *The Kingdom in Mark*, 113-116, argues that these historical persons were "parousia [second coming of Christ] pretenders." and that the "false Christs" and those who said "I am he" were the same persons. The latter argument is used by Kelber also in *Mark's Story of Jesus*, 68.

[17]H. K. McArthur, *IDB*. Technically the term means "presence," "arrival," or "coming." It has been transliterated from the Greek term to refer to a future coming of Jesus.

CHAPTER TWELVE

MIDRASH ABOUT PASSOVER GOD AS SAVIOR

Mark concluded his description of Jesus' quest for Father-child reconciliation by exploring possibilities involving God's direct activity as savior. Mark did so with midrashic interpretations of rescue themes from the Psalms and of the Passover, a Jewish holy day celebrating God's act of saving the Hebrew people from Egyptian slavery. Mk 14.1-52 culminates in a new version of the Passover meal. It is a doublet of the original triumphal entry into Jerusalem. Jesus for the first time commits himself to voluntary death with no expectation of reward. The relationship between God and the son is thus transformed; the son no longer thinks of God as his potential savior. Mark's midrashic uses of Jeremiah continue.

Fourth Day—Passover and the Death Plot: Mk 14.1-2

Mark dates this unit as beginning two days before Passover and the Feast of Unleavened Bread. This is either a technical error or Mark is confusing the Jewish definition of a day, beginning at sunset, with the Roman custom in which an evening is part of the preceding day.[1] The latter is likely the case. The chief priests are trying to find some way to get Jesus arrested and killed privately before the multitudes gather in Jerusalem for the Passover. They assume that if he were to be killed during the celebration it would cause more of a tumult. This impression is substantiated by Josephus' descriptions of uprisings during major Jewish gatherings in Jerusalem.[2] The midrashic justification for advance planning to have Jesus killed is the scheme to kill Jeremiah devised by his foes

(Jer. 11.19-21; 18.18) and the death trial of the virtuous son of God (Wisd. of Sol. 2.6-20). Mark used both as a midrashic model for Jesus' trials.

Passover celebrates the end of Hebrew slavery in Egypt under the Pharaohs. Passover comes from the translation of a word used to portray God as passing over the Hebrews, protecting them from the death which was inflicted on each Egyptian dwelling. Passover is a definitive ritualization of the etymology of Jesus' name "God Saves" and is thus an appropriate dimension of the messianic tradition for Mark to explore. With the priests and scribes now added to the list of those actively seeking Jesus' death, the question which Mark implicitly raises is whether the rescuing God of Passover will save from death the Messiah whose name stands for the saving activity of God.

Fourth Day—The Messiah of Burial: Mk. 14.3-9

Two of the meanings of the word "Bethany" are "House of the Poor" and "House of the Afflicted." Mark incorporated both into his midrashic reflection on Isaiah's description of the messiah's mission: "The Spirit of the Lord is upon me, because he has anointed me; he has sent me to preach good news to the poor, to heal the brokenhearted, to proclaim liberty to the captives, and recovery of sight to the blind...." (LXX Isa. 61.1). Having already made Bethany ("House of Figs") thematic because of the messianic significance of figs, Mark went out of his way to intrude the other two meanings of Bethany into his narrative. He portrayed Jesus engaged in conversation about the poor in the home of Simon the Leper, a man who is both physically afflicted and unclean according to the Mosaic law.

Why is the leper named Simon? The most intriguing possibility is that each of the Simons toward the end of Mark is an extension of Simon Peter's identity as "Satan" in Mk. 8.33. The series would include Simon as a leper, Simon of Cyrene, and Peter who denies Jesus. To establish that point it is necessary to demonstrate parallels between the Mk. 8 material and subsequent accounts. We propose the following:

8.31: And he began to teach them that the Son of man must suffer many things, and be rejected by the elders and the chief priests and the scribes, and be killed....	14.1: And the chief priests and the scribes were seeking how to arrest him by stealth, and kill him....
8.32: Get behind me, Satan! [Satan is chief of the unclean spirits.]	14.3 And while he was at Bethany in the house of Simon the leper.... [A leper has "unclean" skin.]
8.32: And he said this plainly. And Peter took him, and began to rebuke him. But turning and seeing his disciples, he rebuked Peter....	14.5-6: And they reproached her. But Jesus said, "Let her alone; why do you trouble her? She has done a beautiful thing to me."
8.36: For what does it profit a man, to gain the whole world and forfeit his life? For what can a man give in return for his life?	14.4-5: Why was the ointment thus wasted? For this ointment might have been sold for more than three hundred denarii, and given to the poor.
8.29: Peter answered him, "You are the Christ [the anointed one]....	14.8: She has done what she could; she has anointed my body beforehand for burying.
8.38: For whoever is ashamed of me and of my words..., of him will the Son of man also be ashamed....	14.9: And truly, I say to you, wherever the gospel is preached in the whole world, what she has done will be told in memory of her.
8.34: If any man would come after me, let him deny himself and take up his cross and follow me.	15.21: And they compelled a passer-by, Simon of Cyrene...to carry his cross.

The doublets are not as precise as some others in Mark, but they seem sufficient to establish the author's intention to incorporate Simon the Leper and Simon of Cyrene into the person Simon Peter. Both John and Luke understood Mark in this manner and considerably developed the ways in which others in their stories were included in Simon Peter. An obvious example is Peter's vision about "unclean" foods on the roof of Simon the tanner, a man with an "unclean" occupation.

The narrative centers around a woman who performs a symbolic messianic act by anointing Jesus' "body beforehand for burial" with an expensive ointment. Jesus had responded in Mk. 8.31

to Peter by affirming that he was indeed the messiah, even though Peter misunderstood what that meant. Now, however, Jesus is literally made a messiah by being anointed. The pattern may have been set by 1 Sam. 10.1, in which Samuel poured oil on Saul's head and pronounced the words of anointing him as "prince over his people Israel," or by 1 Sam. 16.13 and 2 Sam. 2.4, in which Samuel privately and the Judeans publicly anointed David "king over the house of Judah." Jesus interprets the woman's act as making him a messiah who is to die and be buried. The disciples are much more likely to have been envisioning him as a new Saul or David.

The woman contrasts with Peter in another less obvious way. Jesus had told him that he was "not on the side of God, but of men" (Mk. 8.33). The woman exemplified what it meant to be on the side of the God who at Gethsemane would insist that Jesus' duty was to die voluntarily. The disciples, by raising economic issues, stood on the side of men. The incident is midrashically reminiscent of Samuel's comment when David was anointed: "The Lord sees not as man sees; man looks on the outward appearance, but the Lord looks on the heart" (1 Sam. 16.7).

The disciples change the subject by complaining that the ointment might better have been sold for the benefit of the poor. Jesus tells the disciples:

> Let her alone; why do you trouble her? She has done a beautiful thing to me. For you always have the poor with you, and whenever you will, you can do good to them; but you will not always have me. She has done what she could; she has anointed my body beforehand for burying (Mk. 14.6-8).

It was an anointing which seemed directly to contradict that of Isa. 61.1, in which the messiah was to "bring the gospel to the afflicted." The disciples' concern for the poor is rooted in earlier literature connected with their names: "James/Jacob and Cephas and

John...would have us remember the poor, which very thing I was eager to do" (Gal. 2.9-10); "If a brother or sister is ill-clad and in lack of daily food, and one of you says to them, 'Go in peace, be warmed and filled,' without giving them the things needed for the body, what does it profit?" (Jas./Jac. 2.15-16); "But if any one has the world's goods and sees his brother in need, yet closes his heart against him, how does God's love abide in him?" (1 Jn. 3.17). Jesus' reply that "you always have the poor with you" may have seemed to be an inescapable truth in that day. Mark constructed the scene midrashically from an apparent contradiction in Deut. 15.4-11 in which it is stated that "the poor will never cease out of the land," but that "there shall be no poor among you [Jews]," because they will be specially blessed. Because of that promise, the Jews had an obligation to "open wide your hand to your brother, to the needy and to the poor." Because of the power of the Wisdom account of the death trial of the virtuous son of God, Mark may also have been midrashically aware of the irony that those who sought Jesus' life pledged themselves to "oppress the poor man" and take their "fill of the dearest wines and perfumes" (Wisd. 2.6).[3]

The incident established two new relationships between Jesus and the disciples. The first is that Jesus acknowledged a self-affirming messianic right which was midrashically akin to the "I, only I" temptation of his Elijah days (Mk 1), the "do not fast while the bridegroom is still with you," and the "David did it; so can I" of his Moses-Levi days (Mk 2). In addition, Jesus' messiahship was now to be defined by burial only, an extraordinary shift from the disciples' vision of him as a messiah transfigured in glory, his own predictions of guaranteed resurrection, and the public yearning for him to lead a freedom revolt.

The Fourth Day—A Judas-Type Betrayal: Mk. 14.10-11

One of Mark's superb acts of midrashic genius was in combining the Passover motif with the narrative of betrayal by Judas

Iscariot.[4] Judas is the Greek transliteration of Judah, a son of Jacob who had betrayed his brother Joseph, the favorite son, into slavery for twenty pieces of silver.[5] Reuben, the eldest brother, had contrived to leave Joseph in a pit, so that he might later rescue him. Judah agreed that Joseph should not be killed or left to die, but sold him into slavery before Reuben could perform the rescue. Joseph, who providentially became a ruler in Egypt, later saved his entire family when they faced death from famine. Judas hoped that the end of the story would be as it had been in Gen. 50.20 when Joseph told his brothers, "You meant evil against me, but God meant it for good, to bring it about that many people should be kept alive." The betrayal led to the Hebrews being in Egypt; Joseph saved his family from starvation; the Passover was the event which eventually freed the Hebrews from Egypt. Thus the betrayal of Joseph and God's act of saving at Passover are the beginning and end of the same story.

By adding the surname "Iscariot" ("Red Dyer," i.e., Esau), Mark overlaid the Judah-Judas midrash with a Jacob-Esau one.[6] Esau tried to kill his brother Jacob (Gen. 27.41-45), the one loved by God (Mal. 1), but was unsuccessful. As Iscariot, Judas acts in opposition to Jesus, the beloved son of God. One of Jesus' brothers is named Judas (Mk. 6.3). Ironically, when Judas, like Judah, tried to betray Jesus (Joseph) in order to save him, he was Iscariot (Esau) and killed his "brother," as Esau sought to do. Judas wanted to be Judah, but was Iscariot.

In Bethany, the place of the poor and afflicted, the disciples hear Jesus implicitly predict his death and subsequent burial. His earlier death predictions had cushioned the blow with a guarantee of resurrection, making them less threatening than the final defeat associated with burial. Furthermore, they hear his tacit acceptance of a new interpretation of messiahship, symbolized by the woman "anointing" him for burial. Jesus had made quite a different messianic announcement by his "triumphal entry" into Jerusalem on the animal associated with Solomon and his acceptance of the tumultuous welcome of a popular hero. This had heightened expectations that he would lead a successful messianic revolt against the Roman imperial hegemony over Israel. That announcement anticipated neither his own death or burial.

Just as the Judah of Genesis had help from his brothers in betraying Joseph, Judas midrashically functions as spokesperson for all the disciples in betraying Jesus in that many of them had objected to the "burial anointing." Judas could have reasoned that he might as well strike a deal for his own benefit, as long as Jesus was so set on dying. He is more likely to have thought that the only way to force Jesus to quit talking such defeatist language was to put him in a situation where his life would be so threatened that he would fight back. If Jesus' life really hung in the balance, he would use the miraculous powers at his command to save his own life and then strike out against the Romans. Jesus would thus become a Joseph-like rescuer of his people, betrayed into winning by the new Judah. Judas left Bethany on the fourth day, entered Jerusalem, met with the temple priests, and agreed to inform them when Jesus was to be somewhere in private so that they could arrest him out of public view. The detail that Jesus was to be betrayed when he was not publicly visible fits so unobtrusively into the narrative that its midrashic source in the Judas-Joseph story goes almost unnoticed: Joseph was hidden in a pit when he was sold. The priests in turn promise Judas a monetary reward, for which he may not have asked. Judah's motive in Gen. 37.26-27 is ambiguous; it could have been either monetary gain or saving his brother from death. Matthew converted Judas' motive into one of greed.

Jesus himself stays in Bethany for the entire day. Judas performs for him four of the five events which Mark has used to characterize the routine of each day, lacking only the mention of olives or the Mount of Olives. Mark substituted an oil more expensive than olive oil in the anointing by the woman.

Fifth Day—The Anti-Rescue Seder Celebration: Mk. 14.12-25

The first event of day five of Passion Week is a doublet of the triumphal entry pericope from the first day, and hence internally midrashic in Mark. As before, Jesus sends two disciples into a town to make a strange request. The first time, they went to Bethany to ask for an animal so that Jesus might ride it into Jerusalem and then return it. On this second occasion, Jesus instructs them to ask a man carrying a jar of water in Jerusalem for a room in which Jesus and his disciples are to eat the Passover meal. Both of those who were asked immediately accede to the unusual requests. The doublet calls attention to the meanings of the two occasions. The first was a Jewish version of a "ticker tape parade" for a hero expected to rescue the Jews from the Romans. The second, the seder, was the ritual celebration of God's saving the Jews from the Egyptians. Delivery from the Romans was what Judas hoped for as a result of betraying Jesus. Rescue from the Egyptians was what God had accomplished on the original Passover night. During the triumphal entry the crowds quoted Ps. 118.26: "Blessed be he who comes in the name of the Lord." After the last supper, Jesus and the disciples sing a hymn, commonly understood to have been the *Hallel* from Ps. 115-118.[7] In the first half of the doublet Jesus visited the temple, but in the second the temple functions only as background. The Passover celebration in Jerusalem in New Testament times occurred partly in the temple and partly in private homes. Some of the food, probably only the meat, was prepared in the temple. People took it to their homes for the actual meal. Jesus has no association with the temple on this day, except for the obscure connection via the food preparation.

Mark midrashically developed the triumphal entry and the continuous account of the Last Supper and Gethsemane from 1 Sam 9, as the following comparisons demonstrate.

Samuel 9	**Mark 11**	**Mark 14**
9.3: You & a servant go.	11.1: Sent two disciples.	14.13: Sent two disciples.
9.3: Look for asses.	11.2: Find a colt tied.	No parallel
9.10: Girls coming out to draw water.	No parallel	14.13: A man carrying water will meet you.
9.9: They went to the city.	11.2: Go into the village.	14.13: Go into the city.
9.13: You will meet him as soon as you enter the city.	11.2: As soon as you enter you will find a colt tied.	No parallel.
9.6: All that he says comes true.	11.4: They found the colt as he had told them.	14.16: Found it as he had told them.
14.13: 9.18: Where is the seer's house?	No parallel	14.14: Where is my room?
9.20: The lost asses have already been found.	11.6: The master will send the colt back here .	No parallel
9.19: Samuel supervised preparing a feast.	No parallel	14.16: They prepared the passover.
9.24: "Eat!"	No parallel	14.22: He gave them bread to eat.
9.22: Saul ate with 70 [LXX; 30 in Masoretic]	11.9-10 [Celebration of Jesus' kingship]	14.18: Jesus ate with his disciples.
9.25: Saul slept on the roof.	No parallel.	14.15: The upper room.
9.27: Saul and Samuel left the city.	11. 11 : Jesus went to Bethany with the 12.	14.32: After dinner, they went to Gethsemane.
9.27: Tell servant to leave us alone.	No parallel.	14.32: "Sit here while I pray."
9. 27: Saul received the word of God.	No parallel.	14. 36: Jesus talks with God.
[No parallel.]	11.9: [Quoted from Ps. 118]	14.26: [Sang Ps. 115-118]

The Samuel story ends with Saul being anointed a king who will be a military hero; Jesus, in Mk. 11, received a welcome which would ordinarily be accorded a military hero, but in Mk. 14 is anointed in preparation for his death.

Mark apparently depicted Jesus at the supper as instituting a new ritual to replace both the temple and the Passover seder. The primary midrashic source for what happens at the meal is 1 Cor. 11.23-34. The meal Paul describes is an informal dinner, neither the Passover seder nor a ritualized Last Supper. Jeremias characterizes it in terms of "sharing of the meal with poor brethren."[8] Nevertheless, the midrashic seeds of Mark's version of the "seder" are present:

> When you meet together, it is not the Lord's supper that you eat. For in eating, each one goes ahead with his own meal, and one is hungry and another is drunk.... For I *received from* the Lord what I also delivered to you, that the Lord Jesus on the night when he was *handed over* took bread, and when he had given thanks, he broke it, and said, "This is my body which is *for you*. Do this in remembrance of me." In the same way also the cup, after supper, saying, "This cup is the *new covenant* in my blood. Do this, as often as you drink it, in remembrance of me." For as often as you eat this bread and drink the cup, you proclaim the Lord's death until he comes. Whoever, therefore, eats the bread or drinks the cup of the Lord in an unworthy manner will be guilty of profaning the body and blood of the Lord . Let a man *examine himself*, and so eat of the bread and drink of the cup (1 Cor. 11.20-28).

Earlier in the same epistle, Paul consciously created a midrash on the Passover seder unrelated to the event he labeled above as the Lord's Supper. He interpreted Jesus' death as that of a paschal[9] lamb, spiritualizing the Passover custom of removing every crumb of leavened bread from the house: "Cleanse out the old leaven that you may be fresh dough, as you really are unleavened. For *Christ, our paschal lamb,* has been sacrificed. Let us, therefore, celebrate the festival, not with the old leaven, the leaven of malice and evil, but with the unleavened bread of sincerity and truth" (1 Cor. 5.7-8). The imagery is much like that in Jesus' earlier conversation with the disciples when he warned them against the leaven of the Pharisees, which, in context, could well have been "the leaven of malice and evil." In 1 Cor. 5, Jesus was the paschal lamb; those who believed in him were the unleavened bread of sincerity and truth. In 1 Cor. 11, however, it was Jesus who was the bread which is "my body." Mark midrashically combined the two passages so that Jesus was both the lamb and the bread, both of which were to be eaten as "my body" at Mark's new version of the seder. Other seder practices are not paralleled in Mark, calling attention to Mark's implied recommendation that the seder be replaced by the Lord's Supper, but also raising questions about the assertion above that Jesus was the paschal lamb as well as the broken bread which was his body.

Jesus, in Mark's version of the Lord's Supper, asks the disciples to drink of the metaphoric blood of the lamb's self-sacrifice, thus significantly differing from 1 Cor. 11. The imagery of wine as blood is likely to have come from "the blood of the grape" (Deut. 32.14). Jesus' request to the disciples that they should "drink blood" is a clear violation of Mosaic ritual prohibitions, as is indicated by the two following passages from Leviticus: "It shall be a perpetual statute throughout your generations, in all your dwelling places, that you eat neither fat nor blood" (3.17); "Moreover, you shall eat no blood whatever, whether of fowl or of animal, in any of your dwellings. Whoever eats any blood, that person shall be cut off from his people" (7.26-27); "If any man of the house of Israel or of the strangers that sojourn among them eats any blood, I will set my face against that person who eats blood.... For the life of the flesh is in the blood" (Lev. 17.10); "You shall not eat the blood; you shall pour it out upon the earth like water" (Deut. 12.16 and 12.24). Mark's treatment of this detail is consistent with his position throughout the Gospel of having Jesus disagree with or ignore Mosaic law.

Paul's version had no "blood" in the cup: "This cup is the new covenant in my blood. Do this, as often as you drink it, in remembrance of me" (1 Cor. 11.25). Paul's Jesus interpreted the cup in terms of his own death and hence originated a "new covenant in his blood," much in the spirit of Jer. 31.31-33, in which the Lord promises "a new covenant" written "on their hearts." Paul's "cup" could have been derived from the custom described in Jer. 16.7 of sharing bread and "the cup of consolation" with mourners. Paul claims to have learned that "from the Lord," i.e., from scripture; Mark learned it from Paul. Mark portrayed Jesus as using the occasion as a conscious affront to Jewish law by asking the disciples to drink "my blood of the covenant, which is poured out for many" (Mk. 14.24), even if only metaphorically. In the Torah, blood was to be "poured out" on the ground. Intentional violation of the law about eating blood would make Father-son reconciliation impossible. Yet only a few lines later, Mark would have Jesus saying, "*Abba*, Father" in a reconciliatory sense. "Abba" is the affectionate form of the more formal word "father," more like "daddy" or "papa."

Mark had Jesus say, "This is my blood of the covenant, which is poured out for *many*. Truly, I say to you, I shall not drink again of the fruit of the vine until that day when I drink it *new* in the kingdom of God" (Mk. 14.24-25). The blood of the covenant is to be poured out *for many*, instead of *for you*, as in Paul. This may come from a messianic context in Dan. 9.27: "And he shall make a strong covenant *with many* for one week; and for half of the week he shall cause sacrifice and offering to cease; and upon the wing of abominations shall come one who makes desolate, until the decreed end is poured out on the desolator." Daniel's week could have been resignified as Mark's Passion Week, during half of which Jesus, by disrupting the temple, causes sacrifices and offerings to cease. Jesus also refers to abominations which make desolate (Mk. 13.14). Those parallels strengthen the contention that Mark was midrashically reinterpreting Daniel's "covenant with many."

In Paul, the cup was to be the new covenant in my blood. Mark's relocation of Paul's word "new" changes its meaning. The term "kingdom of God" is best interpreted in Mark's context as "God's sovereignty" or "the reign of God." Jesus means that he will not drink wine again until he does so in full obedience to God. Superficially this portends the occasion when Jesus is offered wine on the cross, even though he refuses to drink it. In a deeper sense, the wine is his own blood. Paul did not mention wine in 1 Cor. 11. The reference there is to a "cup." Paul may have assumed that the cup would contain wine, but Mark had to make the "fruit of the vine" more explicit in order to contribute to his midrash on the messianic significance of the vine. Jesus as messiah drinks the wine of his own self-sacrifice in obedience to the Father. In biblical descriptions of the seder (Exod. 12, 34; Deut. 16; Lev. 23; Num. 28), the food details include roast lamb and unleavened bread, but not wine. In the modern seder four glasses of wine are drunk, interspersed with various ritual questions and answers. No one is certain when that practice began, but it probably goes back at least to New Testament times.

Mark's fourth difference from Paul relates to "betrayal." Jesus says that one of the disciples "who is eating with me," specifically, "one who is dipping bread in the same dish with me" would betray him or hand him over (Mk. 14.18-20). The word "betray" in Mark may be misleading. The phrases "received from" and "betrayed" in 1 Cor. 11.23 (RSV) are translated from variants of the verb *paradidomi*, which is rendered as "betray" when applied to Judas Iscariot, but is used twenty times in Mark. It means "hand over," "turn over," "give up a person," or "hand over into the custody of."[10] Forms of the verb *paredoken* or *paredoka* are translated as "delivered to you" in the sense of "passed on what I heard" in 1 Cor. 11.23 and as "arrested" in Mk. 1.14. The rather harsh word "betray" may not have been intended by either Paul or Mark.[11] The rendering into English as "betrayed" is based on the translator's judgment that it is the one of many options which best fits the context. Judas' intention, however, was to "hand Jesus over to the authorities," but not to "betray him." Only after Judas' strategy had resulted in the death which he had sought to avoid could his action be construed as a betrayal. In Mark's account, the verb is used, from the vantage point of the crucifixion, in Jesus' statement that "one of you will betray me" and "woe to that man by whom the son of man is betrayed (Mk. 14.18-21). Mark's midrashic source for "eating with me" is Ps. 41.9: "Even my bosom friend whom I trusted, who ate of my bread, has lifted his heel against me." Jesus' statement could apply equally to all of the disciples, for all were eating with him, and thus presumably dipping bread in the same dish. Paul had argued in 1 Cor. 11.27 that at "the Lord's supper" anyone who "eats the bread or drinks the cup of the Lord in an unworthy manner will be guilty of profaning the body and the blood of the Lord." Paul was thinking primarily of gluttony. In Mark's midrashic reformulation, a particular man who was eating with Jesus was to be the only one to hand him over, but all of those at table with Jesus were in different ways to betray him or already had. Judas alone was to be tagged with the label. The others betrayed Jesus substantively; Judas did so midrashically. What all of them wanted Jesus to do and be would betray the possibility of reconciliation with the Father. In 1 Cor. 11.28, those eating and drinking must "examine" themselves; In Mk. 14.18-19, the Twelve, while eating, question, "Is it I?"

Mark's fifth major change from Paul was to have Jesus refer to himself as son of man, the one who is to die "as it is written of him." Paul, in introducing a long discourse about resurrection, said in 1 Cor. 15.3-4 that "Christ [the Messiah] died for our sins *in accordance with the scriptures*, that he was buried, that he was raised on the third day in accordance with the scriptures."[12] In the seder story, Mark equated the title "son of man" with Paul's title "Messiah." Even though "son of man" is ordinarily in Mark a euphemism for any "human being," here at the seder it is clearly a self-reference. It is Jesus the messiah, the son of man, who is to be betrayed "as it is written of him" by someone close enough to him to eat with him. Mark may imply that all sons of men are betrayed only by near acquaintances. There is no explicit prediction of a betrayal of a messiah in any one passage in the Old Testament. Therefore what Mark meant is that by midrashic combination and interpretation of the many passages discussed above the betrayal of the son of man is as it is written in scripture.

The setting for the Last Supper reintroduces Elijah-Elisha midrash. The two men are provided "upper rooms" (1 Kgs. 17.19 and 2 Kgs. 4.10) in which to live. In each of those rooms an only son is resurrected by the prophet. Elijah first met the widow of Zerephath by asking her for "a little water in a vessel (1 Kgs. 17.10), just as Jesus' emissaries identified the man with an upper room because he was "carrying a jar of water (Mk. 14.13). Jesus sent two disciples to get the room; the woman in 2 Kgs. 4 sends a servant for Elisha. The Mark room was "furnished and ready," as was the room in 2 Kgs. 4.10. The Mark request was for a "guest room, where I am to eat the passover with my disciples (Mk. 14.14); the room in 2 Kgs. 4.9 was set aside for the "holy man of God." The Elijah-Elisha details are no longer a model for emulation, but a setting appropriate to the later expectation of the populace that Elijah will come to rescue Jesus from death on a cross.

Fifth Day—Prediction of Peter's Denials: Mk. 14. 26-31

Mark reported that Jesus and the disciples sang a hymn and then went to the Mount of Olives. The hymn is widely presumed to have been the *Hallel*, sung at the conclusion of the seder, containing the lines: "Out of my distress I called upon the Lord; the Lord answered me and set me free.... I shall not die, but I shall live" (Ps. 118.5, 17). The psalm is ironic in the context of Jesus singing it on his way to Gethsemane to commit himself to voluntary death and Judas leaving the group some time during the evening to set up the betrayal and arrest. Judas is nonetheless included in Jesus' statement to the group on the Mount of Olives that "You will all fall away; for it is written [Zech. 13.7], 'I will strike the shepherd, and the sheep will be scattered.'" Micaiah had envisioned Israel scattered, "as sheep that have no shepherd" (1 Kgs. 22.17; 2 Chron. 18.16). Jesus continues with a prediction that "after I am raised up, I will go before you to Galilee" (Mk. 14.27-28). This suggests that they, the scattered sheep, will be reunited to him in Galilee, an event which does not occur within the parameters of Mark's Gospel but which is relevant to the conclusion of the book.

Peter, rocky Peter, the one who by name would always immediately receive the word with joy, quickly insists that he will not fall away even if all the others do. All of them say the same. 2 Sam. 15-16 is Mark's midrashic model. David's son with the ironic name Absalom ("Father in Peace") rebelled against him, threatening David's life. David fled up the Mount of Olives, leaving behind groups of followers, including one group of three (LXX 2 Sam. 15.27), as Jesus was to leave behind one group of eight and one of three disciples when he went to pray alone on the Mount of Olives. Like David, who "went up the ascent to the Mount of Olives, weeping as he went," Jesus "began to be distressed and troubled," and was "very sorrowful, even to death" (2 Sam. 15.30; Mk 14.33-34). En route, David invited a foreigner, Ittai the Gittite, to return for Ittai's safety. Ittai replied, in words similar to those later used by Peter, "Wherever my Lord the king shall be, whether for death or for life, there also will your servant be" (2 Sam. 15.21). Many others, without saying anything, also went with David. On the mountain, a man named Shimei (an alternative version of Simon) cursed David and threw stones (Peter: "Rock") at him. Jesus responds to Peter's rash promise with a forecast that Peter will deny him three times "before the cock crows twice." This probably refers to a three-hour watch of the night from our 3:00-6:00 a.m., meaning that Peter would deny him three times before the next 6:00 a.m.[13] Peter insists that this will not occur. The parallels are too precise and too numerous to be merely accidental.

Fifth Day—Messiah of Voluntary Death: Mk 14. 32-42

On the Mount of Olives Jesus and the disciples go to Gethsemane ("The Oil Press"),[14] the name of which functions as the symbolic source of the oil of anointing for the Messiah. Jesus divides the disciples into two groups, leaving some further away, and taking Peter, Jacob, and John with him. Mark midrashically singled out the three to be alone with Jesus in his time of great distress because two of the books in their names allude to suffering in connection with the messiah (e.g., 1 Pet. 2.21; 1 Jn 3.16). This fact is responsible for Mark's peculiar phraseology: "And he took with him Peter and James/Jacob and John, and began to be greatly distressed and troubled" (14.33). This "Big Three," the ones reputed by Paul to be the pillars of the church (Gal. 2.9), were, ironically, those to fail him in his time of greatest need. At Gethsemane, Jesus prays privately three times after asking the three to serve as his wide-awake watchers: "Abba, Father, all things are possible to thee; remove this cup from me; yet not what I will, but what thou wilt" (Mk. 14.36). Mark midrashically adapted the affectionate term "abba" from Paul, who insisted:

> All who are led by the Spirit of God are sons of God. For you did not receive the spirit of slavery to fall back into fear, but you have received the spirit of sonship. When we cry, 'Abba! Father!' it is the Spirit himself

> bearing witness with our spirit that *we are children of God,* and if children, then heirs, heirs of God and fellow heirs with Christ, *provided we suffer with him* in order that we may also be glorified with him (Rom. 8.14-17).

Paul had used the word *abba* earlier in his affirmation in Gal. 4.6-7 that "because you are sons, God has sent the Spirit of his Son into our hearts, crying, "Abba! Father!" So through God you are no longer a slave but a son, and if a son then an heir." Mark has adopted the position of Paul in Romans that to say "abba" is to be willing to suffer and to acknowledge oneself as a child of God. The Pauline passages provide positive midrashic support for the position that all can be children of God. Whoever is a child of God must suffer with Christ. The reward of being glorified with him is contingent upon suffering with him.

Apart from the circumlocution in Mk. 8.38, in which Jesus referred to God as Father of the son of man, this is the first time since the baptism that Jesus has openly acknowledged God as Father. Paul's "Abba, Father" references make explicit what was only implicit in the baptism-temptation episode, namely that all people are or can be children of God. The Gethsemane pericope still leaves open the possibility that Jesus is thinking of himself as the only faithful son of God, and hence the only beloved son. The most important source of this part of the Gethsemane story is Abraham's obedience to God in being willing to sacrifice his son Isaac (Gen. 22). The word "abba" is the etymological root of the beginning of Abraham's name; hence he is appropriately "father Abraham." He had only one son of his Jewish wife, the gift of God in their very old age. God demands that Abraham sacrifice Isaac but then intervenes to substitute an animal, thus both saving Isaac and enabling Abraham to become the progenitor of a multitude of descendants, the Jews. Jas./Jac. 2.20-24 understands Abraham's willingness to offer his son upon a sacrificial altar as the act which proved his faith in God. Gen. 22.16 refers to the fact that Abraham has "not withheld your son, your only son." Paul, midrashically adopting that same language, says that God "did not spare his own Son but gave him up for us all; will he not also give us all things with him?" (Rom. 8.32). As the Suffering Servant passage in Isa. 53.10 says, "It was the will of the Lord." Mark midrashically used that tradition in writing the Gethsemane story to insist that voluntarily death is the will of the Father. Jesus has to decide whether or not to adopt that model. He gives the three preeminent disciples the opportunity to share that moment with him, but they are not up to the task. In Gethsemane, Jesus comments both on their failure and his own struggle by observing that "the spirit indeed is willing but the flesh is weak."

Jesus' willingness to be obedient to God's will in death is derived in part from 2 Sam. 15.25-26. David states, "If I find favor in the eyes of the Lord, he will bring me back and let me see both it [the ark] and his habitation; but if he says, 'I have no pleasure in you,' behold, here I am; let him do to me what seems good to him." Sanders translates Deut. 34.5 to read: Moses died "according to the summons of the Lord." The concept is found also in Deut. 8.3, in which people are humbled so that they may know "that man does not live by bread alone, but...by the summons of God."[15] The tone of the Gethsemane experience is that Jesus was summoned to death and accepted the summons as the condition for being reconciled to the Father God. In the story line of Deuteronomy, the death of Moses resulted in the mission to enter the Promised Land being turned over to "God Saves" (Joshua/Jesus).

Jesus prays three times. This continues the Passion Week use of the number three which began with Jesus' prediction that Peter would deny him three times. The three men, by sleeping three times when they were asked to stay awake, have already denied him three times. Jesus' act of praying three times may have had a midrashic origin in Paul's "thorn in the flesh," like Jesus' weakness of the flesh: "Three times I besought the Lord about this, that it should leave me; but he said to me, 'My grace is sufficient for you, for my power is made perfect in weakness'" (2 Cor. 12.8-9). The number "three" is related to the three times Jesus decided to resist the weakness of the flesh in order to accept voluntary death, and to the third day resurrection as the victory associated with voluntary death. The "threes" associated with the failure of the disciples are the opposite sides of that spiritual coin; since they refuse to suffer with Jesus they are doomed to three failures. When Jesus finds them asleep the third time, he says, "Are you still sleeping and taking your rest? It is enough; the *hour has come;* the son of man *is betrayed* into the hands of sinners. Rise, let us be going; see, my betrayer is at hand" (Mk. 14.41-42). When the three are not watchful, the final failure according to Mk. 13.37, the time has already come. The son of man has already been betrayed by the three who sleep the sleep of spiritual death even though the son of man will also be betrayed a few minutes later by Judas. Isa. 56.9—57.2 can be summarized as: "While the righteous man perishes and devout men are taken away, watchmen love to slumber." Mark's expression "the hour has come" probably derived midrashically from 1 John's reference to "the last hour": "many antichrists [those who deny both Father and son] have come; therefore we know that it is the last hour" (1 Jn. 2.18). The antichrists in Mark's context were Judas, Peter, James/Jacob, and John.

Fifth Day—Betrayal by Judas and the twelve: Mk. 14. 43-52

Mk. 14.43 introduces the betrayal scene with the observation that "immediately, while Jesus was still speaking, Judas came." Those words, so innocent and mundane in a non-Markan context, are striking. This "immediately" seems in RSV to be unpaired because the translators chose "at once" instead of "immediately" to describe Judas' going to Jesus. The sequence implies that the betrayal experience is a temptation for Jesus; Judas' behavior tends to confirm that hypothesis. He says, "'The one I shall kiss is the man; seize him and lead him away safely.' And when he came, he went up to him at once [immediately], and said, 'Master!' And he kissed him'" (Mk. 14.44-45). Judas thus indicates his support for Jesus, trying to guarantee in advance that Jesus will not be hurt. Midrashically, he hopes to do for Jesus what Reuben and Judah did for Joseph in the Old Testament model for the betrayal. To the extent that Jesus accepts that version of betrayal, he certainly is tempted. Immediately! Here was a way to go through the motions of being betrayed to death and to be kept safe at the same time. The midrashic model for Judas' "friendly betrayal" may have been 2 Sam. 20.7-10, in which Joab, who is with armed men, greets Amasa as a brother, then kisses him while stabbing him.

Judas and all of the disciples for whom he acted must have been chagrined. They probably had hoped that Jesus would begin his resistance program "immediately" upon being arrested. One of "those who stood by," presumably a disciple since no other follower is reported as having been there, was already armed with a sword, ready to join in such a resistance movement. The armed one cut off the ear of a slave of the high priest. Luke understood Mark's source to be 2 Sam. 16.9-11. David, weeping on the Mount of Olives, is cursed by Shime-i; one of David's followers wants to "take off his head"; David says to "let him alone." The story about the ear may extend the deafness motif in the book, perhaps suggesting that the priests would be permanently deaf, but Mark did not develop the point.[16] The reference to cutting off a slave's ear is so unnecessary for the context that it calls attention to itself and requires midrashic explanation. Two likely sources, both related to priests, describe the ritual of consecrating men to the priesthood: "And you shall kill the ram, and take part of its blood and put it upon the tip of the right ear of Aaron and upon the tips of the right ears of his sons, and upon the thumbs of their right hands, and upon the great toes of their right feet, and throw the rest of the blood against the altar round about" (Exod. 29.20); "Then he presented the other ram, the ram of ordination; and Aaron and his sons laid their hands on the head of the ram. And Moses killed it, and took some of its blood and put it on the tip of Aaron's right ear...and Moses put some of the blood on the tips of their right ears" (Lev. 8.22-24). Lev. 14.17 prescribes virtually the same ritual for cleansing of lepers except that oil is substituted for blood. Thus cutting off the ear of a servant of a priest may be a veiled way of saying that priests, having lost an ear, can no longer properly be ordained, or that their priesthood is invalid. This would fit into the anti-temple mood the of the entire week. Judas may also have been disappointed when Jesus passed up a normal opportunity to perform a compassionate healing miracle. Jesus' own agenda at this moment would not permit a miracle because he was exploring the Passover model, in which God alone does the miracles on behalf of the children of Israel. One "child" does not effect a miracle.

Jesus' disregard of the servant's severed ear is an excellent example of a phenomenon throughout Mark. Jesus does not function as a psychologically predictable character with a personality which persists from one unit to another. He is more like an actor playing radically different roles in several dramas. In the earlier units of Mark, Jesus explored models which required miracles, albeit different kinds of miracles in each. Now he is in a non-miracle role; any miracles will be done by God. Poor Judas understands none of that! He wants so badly to be bolstering Jesus' potential for personal and national glory. But he is in fact making Jesus' death inevitable.

Jesus' reaction to the betrayal is to do nothing and thus to "let the scriptures be fulfilled." As soon as he speaks those defeatist words, all the disciples flee. They are all like Judas, wanting something which is inconsistent with their Messiah being under arrest. Their flight is symbolized by a young man clothed only in a linen cloth who had followed them from the house in which they had eaten the non-seder seder and who ran away naked when the arresting party tried to seize him (Mk. 14.51-52). The only other time Mark mentions linen cloth is in the description of the garment in which Jesus is buried. This makes sense in this pericope. What the twelve were really fleeing from was Jesus' willingness to be buried. The disciples wanted a new Passover. When Jesus accepted arrest, with neither protest nor miracle, they lost interest in being associated with him. With Jesus rejecting the protection of Passover and the disciples insisting upon it, Mark's position is clear. Passover salvation is another inadequate model for portraying the messiah.

The linen cloth may be a midrash from 2 Sam. 6.14: "And David danced before the Lord with all his might; and David was clothed in a linen ephod." This very weak possibility is strengthened by David midrashic parallels from Psalm 31. Ps. 31.11 refers to those who "flee from me" because "I...am an object of dread to my acquaintances." Others "plot to take my life" (Ps. 31.13). The possibility that the young man who fled is midrashic on specific psalms creates a smooth transition to Mark's next model, the rescuing God of Psalms.

Endnotes for Chapter Twelve

[1]Schweizer, *Mark* 287, and Taylor, *St. Mark*, 527, consider a wide variety of ways to deal with the difficulty in dating the event while protecting Mark from the accusation of being in error.

[2]Josephus, *Antiquities*, XVIII, 5, claims a similar motivation for Herod's execution of John.

[3]See full text of this passage on pp. 199-200 above.

[4]See the commentary on the calling of the Twelve for detailed documentation of the midrashic origins of the names Judas and Iscariot, pp. 125-126 above.

[5]In the LXX, "Judah" has already been transliterated as "Judas."

[6]See the commentary on the calling of the twelve disciples for a technical discussion of the meaning of the name "Iscariot" and the reasons why it is to be identified with Esau.

[7]Taylor, 548.

[8]Joachim Jeremias, *The Central Message of the New Testament* (New York: Charles Scribner's Sons, 1965) 65.

[9]The word "paschal" is the Greek transliteration of a Hebrew word from which the name "Passover" is derived. The paschal lamb is the lamb which is slain for the purpose of being ritually eaten on the occasion of the Passover seder. See Exod. 12.

[10]Bratcher and Nida, 35.

[11]Hatch and Redpatch in their *Concordance to the Septuagint* list 16 different Hebrew terms for which *paradidomi* is the Greek translation in the LXX.

[12]Jeremias points out that the term "the scriptures" was already in Judaism a synonym for "the Bible" and thus does not require more than one midrashic source in order to be accurate. Jeremias thinks the source to be the Suffering Servant passage in Is. 53. Jeremias, *Central Message* , 40.

[13]V. Taylor, *St. Mark*, 550. "Either the threefold denial will take place before a cock crows twice, or, more probably, the reference is to the beginning of the fourth watch when the signal known as *gallicinium* ('cock-crowing') was given by a bugle call."

[14]Elizabeth Struthers Malbon, *Narrative Space and Mythic Meaning in Mark* (San Francisco: Harper and Row, Publishers, 1986) 34: "*Gethsemane* is generally taken to mean 'an oil press,' that is, a press for olives, and is thus linked with the Mount of Olives." K.W. Clark, "Gethsemane," *IDB*, just as certainly defines the word as "oil vat," from an indeclinable Aramaic word.

[15]James A. Sanders, Kansas School of Religion Lectureship, 1988, unpublished.

[16]The Gospel of John did develop the ear motif, naming the servant of the priest as Malchus ("King") and thus suggesting a priest-king target.

CHAPTER THIRTEEN

MIDRASH ON THE PSALMIC GOD AS SAVIOR

Without a break in the narrative, Mark shifted away from the Passover rescue model, as discussed in the previous chapter, to the expectation that God would intervene and effect reconciliation as is suggested in several psalms of rescue. At the conclusion of this unit, Mark implicitly defined crucifixion as refusal to accept any form of being saved. Such a definition stands in stark contrast to thinking of crucifixion as a particular mode of execution. It would include Paul's willingness to die daily or the stoning of Steven as "crucifixions."

Intermixed with the psalmic motif is an outline taken from Jer. 26, in which religious leaders determine that Jeremiah should die for having spoken against the temple and hand him over for trial to princes who in turn find him innocent. At the end of the day Jesus is taken out of the city to be executed. Mark did not refer to Bethany, figs or any related theme on the sixth day.

Sixth Day—Fulfilling the First Trial Prediction: Mk. 14. 53-65

The story of the sixth day begins with a complicated intercalation. Jesus is taken into Jerusalem to a place where "all the chief priests and the elders and the scribes were assembled," apparently in the temple area. Just outside that place is "the courtyard of the high priest." Jesus is first led to the priests, after which it is mentioned that Peter had followed Jesus to the courtyard at a distance. Then the story of Jesus' trial is told, after which the scene returns to the narrative of Peter's thrice-repeated denial. The trial before the Sanhedrin council, the Jewish religious ruling body, follows the pattern of the Mk. 8 passion prediction. The council, as Mark described it, was composed of chief priests, scribes, and elders, as in Mk. 8. Mark implied that the meeting was at night. Mark apparently intended to emphasize the illegality of a night meeting or was contrasting with the original Passover, in which, on the first night, Jewish sons were saved from death. Mark emphasized that God's son Jesus was betrayed on the first night of Passover, with the betrayal culminating in the night trial.

Some opponents had arranged for the testimony of false witnesses who claimed that Jesus had said that he would destroy the temple and replace it in three days with a temple not made by hands. The "not with hands" detail stems from Heb. 9.11, 25:

> But when Christ appeared as a high priest of the good things that have come, then through the greater and more perfect tent (not made with hands, that is, not of this creation), he entered once for all into the Holy Place...thus securing an eternal redemption (9.11). For Christ has entered, not into a sanctuary made with hands, a copy of the true one, but into heaven itself, now to appear in the presence of God on our behalf (9.25).

Mark is also likely to have been midrashically influenced by a passage from Paul: "For we know that if the earthly tent we live in is destroyed, we have a building from God, a house not made with hands, eternal in the heavens" (2 Cor. 5.1). The charge of destroying the temple is based on Jer. 26.8-9: "Then the priests and the prophets and all the people laid hold of him, saying, 'You shall die. Why have you prophesied in the name of the Lord, saying, This house shall be [destroyed] like Shiloh...'?"

False witness is explicitly forbidden in the ten commandments and at greater length in Deuteronomy:

> Only on the evidence of two witnesses, or of three witnesses, shall a charge be sustained. If a malicious wit-

> ness arises against any man...the judges shall inquire diligently, and if the witness is a false witness...then you shall do to him as he had meant to do to his brother...life for life, eye for eye, tooth for tooth... (Deut. 19.15-21).

No testimony was presented against Jesus which was sufficient, according to the council, to put Jesus to death.

The most important midrashic source for the whole incident is Jer. 26. The prophet has predicted that the temple of his day would be destroyed as Shiloh had been and that Jerusalem would become a "curse for all the nations. ... Then the priests and the prophets and all the people laid hold of him, saying, 'You shall die.' ... Then the princes and all the people said to the priests and the prophets, 'This man does not deserve the sentence of death...'" (Jer. 26.6-16). Another prophet, Uriah, who had uttered words similiar to those of Jeremiah, was executed for having done so, thus emphasizing Jeremiah's rescue. Jesus, like Jeremiah, was not to be put to death for having spoken against the temple.

Mark's deeper reason for creating the story about the "temple lie" was that it was true. What the people of Jerusalem had wanted since at least the first day of Passion Week was for Jesus to be a powerful, miraculous version of Solomon the temple builder. In that respect, Jesus was the "carpenter" as he had been viewed in Mk. 6.3. On the second day of Passion Week, Jesus had privately predicted that the temple function of mediating forgiveness was to be replaced by any person's total-faith prayer of forgiveness for a neighbor. On the next day he had privately predicted that not one stone of the temple would be left on top of another, but he had not promised to rebuild it. At the Passover seder, Jesus had eliminated the need for the temple ritual of slaughtering paschal lambs, replacing it with the ritual of broken bread and wine. After his death, the temple curtain, which symbolized God's hiddenness, was to be torn asunder, thereby dissociating God's presence from the temple. Thus the destructive aspect of the "temple lie" was true. On the constructive side, the sole function of the temple was to provide for forgiveness. By advocacy of non-ritual forgiveness almost from the beginning of his career Jesus had built a temple "not made with hands." Jesus is silent in response to the true false accusation. His silence is midrashically consistent with his policy of ordering unclean spirits, disciples, and the healed to be still when right words would give a wrong impression about his identity. It is also consistent with Jeremiah's reply to the destroy-the-temple accusation: "I am in your hands. Do with me as seems good and right to you" (Jer. 26.14).

The Sanhedrin refuses to accept the "true lie" and turns its attention instead to a documented truth which would turn out to be a blind distortion. The second charge against Jesus begins in the form of a question: "Are you the Messiah [Christ], the Son of the Blessed [God]?" Jesus' answer is short, but even so consists of two parts, separated here for emphasis: "I am." "And you will see the Son of man sitting at the right hand of Power [God], and coming with the clouds of heaven" (Mk. 14.62). If the two parts of Jesus' answer have the same meaning, he has pled "guilty" to the capital punishment crime of blasphemy, i.e., to claiming to be a supernatural being or otherwise usurping the role of a supernatural being. Both Jesus and the high priest bear witness to the law forbidding blasphemy by the language they use to talk about God. Instead of pronouncing the name of God, "Yahweh," the priest said "the Blessed" and Jesus said "Power." It was considered blasphemous even to say the name "Yahweh," let alone to claim to be Yahweh or the Son of Yahweh. The Sanhedrin is apparently unanimous in interpreting Jesus' twofold answer as an admission of guilt. What they heard him say was that he was the Messiah, the supernatural Son of God, and that they would see him as the supernatural Son of man coming with the clouds of heaven.

The key word in Jesus' answer is "see." From Mk. 4 on, seeing vs. blindness has been used as a metaphor for understanding or lack thereof. No one in the entire book has seen Jesus clearly. All have been either blind or afflicted with the distorted vision of the half-healed blind. It would be strange indeed if, without warning, Mark suddenly abandoned that well-developed metaphor to use "seeing" in an ordinary way. It would be strange if the members of the Sanhedrin, those who had sought and arranged for Jesus' death, would suddenly be gifted with accurate sight. That being improbable, Jesus' reply to the second charge must mean "Yes, I am the Messiah, a child of God. I know that you will misunderstand that, perhaps even intentionally, wanting me to claim to be the supernatural Son of man Messiah coming with the clouds of heaven, and thus to commit blasphemy." The council so badly wanted Jesus to be guilty of some death penalty crime that it did not take much to persuade them that Jesus had pled guilty. Had Jesus actually done so, he would finally have succumbed to the temptation which he had been resisting since his baptism. He would have been announcing that he was the Only Holy One of God, exactly what the unclean spirits and other tempters wanted him to say.

Jesus' reply is distorted in an apocalyptic direction if it is read that he was predicting what the council members would really see. He no more identifies himself with the Danielic supernatural Son of man here than he did in Mk. 13 when that model was exposed as inadequate. F. H. Borsch has called attention to the midrashic roots of Jesus' statement about being the son of man on the clouds of heaven:[1]

> I saw in the night visions, and behold, with *the clouds of heaven* there came one like a *son of man* (Dan. 7.13).
>
> And I will pour out on the house of David and the inhabitants of Jerusalem a spirit of compassion and

> supplication, so that, when they *look upon him* whom they have pierced, they shall mourn for him, as one mourns for an only child (Zech. 12.10).
>
> And they shall be downcast of countenance, and pain shall seize them, when *they see* that *Son of Man sitting on the throne of his glory* (1 Enoch 62.5).
>
> The Lord says to my lord: 'Sit at *my right hand* till I make your enemies your footstool'" (Ps. 110.1).

Borsch argues that the elements as combined in Mark had already been brought together by some source on which Mark depended, and that the 1 Enoch passage, which has those elements in the same order as in Mark, was relying on that same source. A simpler explanation is that Mark wrote midrash on 1 Enoch, the author of which had in turn written a midrash on the three Old Testament passages. The greater simplicity of that analysis does not necessarily make it correct. It does, however, avoid the tendency to downgrade the authors of books which have survived in history by implying that they did not have the ability to create their own combinations of texts, but had to rely on other more accomplished writers whose works have not survived.

Another probable source for Mark was 1 Peter 3.21-22: "Baptism, which corresponds to this [being made alive in the spirit], now saves you, not as a removal of dirt from the body but as an appeal to God for a clear conscience, through the resurrection of Jesus Christ, who has *gone into heaven and is at the right hand of God*, with angels, authorities, and power subject to him." Borsch was probably unable to consider 1 Peter as a midrashic source because he perceived it to have been written later than Mark.

Jesus' statement to the Sanhedrin embodies the irony of much basic truth. At the higher level he is a son of man, and his death will make God more known. His opponents, from a lower level, see him claiming to be a divine Son of Man associated with Power and fulfilling miraculous prophecy. By looking at truth from the perspective of a lesser good, a high truth is automatically distorted, diminished, turned into a lie, or in some other manner rendered false without changing a word of its text. The entire Jesus story illustrates that principle, constantly ringing new versions of it in the changes of Jesus' career.

The parallels between the passion prediction in Mk. 8 and the first trial of Jesus raise an interesting issue about "the Jews" as those responsible for killing Jesus. Mark assumes that under Roman rule the Sanhedrin did not have the power to execute a death penalty sentence against Jesus or any one else. The Gentiles could put Jesus to death, but the "Jews" could not. This is consistent with the situation as suggested by Paul. In Romans, 1 and 2 Corinthians, and Galatians, there is not the remotest hint that "the Jews" or anyone else in particular killed Jesus. Those letters make many critical statements about Jews, including Paul's claim that he had on five different occasions received 39 lashes from Jews, but there is no suggestion of a connection between the "Jews" and crucifixion. By contrast, in 1 Thessalonians, a later letter with a style and content quite different from Paul's writings, the charge is made that the readers "suffered the same things from your own countrymen as they did from the Jews, who killed both the Lord Jesus and the prophets, and drove us out" (1 Thess. 2.14-15).[2] Another contrast is found in Acts 9.1-2 in which the high priest is assumed to have the power to send emissaries to diaspora synagogues for the purpose of arresting followers of Jesus and bringing them to Jerusalem for the purpose of executing them.[3] Mark's interpretation stands halfway between Paul and the developments in Thessalonians and Acts. He puts as much blame as he can on Jesus' religious opponents without actually accusing them of being responsible for Jesus' death.

At the Sanhedrin trial, Jesus is physically and psychologically mistreated. Some spit on him and strike him; guards hit him; his eyes are covered, and he is asked to prophesy. Such mockery mirrors the spiritual blindness of the members of the Sanhedrin who misunderstood what it means to be a child of God. In addition to developing Mark's motif of seeing/blindness, the passage as a whole is midrashically rooted in 1 Kgs. 22.24 in which an accuser "struck Micaiah on the cheek and said, 'Which way did the Spirit of the Lord go from me to speak to you?'" and in Isa. 50.6: "I gave my back to the smiters, and my cheeks to those who pulled out the beard; I hid not my face from shame and spitting."

Sixth Day—Fulfilling a Second Trial Prediction: Mk. 14.66-72

While Jesus was being tried indoors, Peter was undergoing trial in the courtyard. The narrative continues the story interrupted by the Jesus-trial intercalation. Apart from Mark's sequence, the account would carry only the surface meaning that "Peter denied knowing Jesus" and that he was lying to protect himself. With the intercalation and the specific context in Mark, levels of meaning at greater depth appear. The conversation in the courtyard was mostly between Peter and a maid of the high priest. The interchange went as follows:

She: You also were with the Nazarene, Jesus.

He: I neither know nor understand what you mean.

She [to bystanders]: This man is one of them.

[Peter again denied it.]

Bystanders: Certainly you are one of them; for you are a Galilean.

He [after invoking a curse on himself]: I do not know this man of whom you speak.

The cock then crowed twice; Peter remembered that Jesus had predicted that he would do what he had done; and "he broke down and wept."

The cockcrow detail relates Peter's denials to Mk. 13.35-37, in which Jesus had specifically admonished Peter, Andrew, John and James/Jacob to be watchmen, at evening, midnight, and cockcrow "lest [the master] come suddenly and find you asleep." The Big Three had slept at Gethsemane in the evening-midnight period; now Peter, "sitting with the guards," denies Jesus at cockcrow. He is like the watchmen/shepherds of Isa. 56.11 and 53.6 who "have all turned to their own way."

Peter's denials parallel the second of the passion-reward predictions of Mk. 8-10, in which it was to be people in general who would kill the son of man. His denials are representative of all who deny Jesus. In the course of his career, he had neither repented nor become a fisher of men; he had not understood when he was expected to be able to do so; he had spoken satanically when he called Jesus the Messiah; he had seen with distorted vision, as the half-healed blind man, when he saw Jesus transformed in unearthly brightness; he had helped turn away children from Jesus and had argued with the other disciples about which of them was greatest; he had not understood the distinction between inner and outer uncleanness; he had slept through Jesus' decision-making prayer time in Gethsemane and then fled after the arrest. His denials in the courtyard were not something new or out of context. They were the logical consequence of what had been going on from the beginning. Just as the temple lie about Jesus was true, so Peter's "lies" were true. Peter did not know the man Jesus. He did not recognize the man Jesus who at that moment was telling the high priest that he was a child of God in a way which the priest blindly saw as blasphemous. Peter was appropriately telling his lies to a high priest's maid. He did not know Jesus' willingness to die, despite having heard the words. Luke and John, reading Mark accurately, converted Peter's "true lies" to non-recognition in Jesus' resurrection appearances to Peter and the others.

The particulars of the charges against Peter begin with the accusation that he was with the "Nazarene," which in Mark's context means a holy man (a Nazarite). When unclean spirits had called Jesus a holy man, Jesus himself had ordered them to be silent. Therefore Peter had a reason not to know what it meant to say that he had been with the "Nazarene." The second charge was that he was "one of them," presumably one of the disciples of Jesus. In fact, at this moment, Jesus had no disciples, for all of them had deserted him, and he had made no effort to retrieve them. His true answer was in itself a denial of Jesus. The third charge involved Peter being a "Galilean." For Peter to deny that was for him to deny his own identity as well as his connection to Jesus. Furthermore, on the occasion when Jesus had predicted Peter's denials, he had said to them:

> "You will all fall away; for it is written, I will strike the shepherd, and the sheep will be scattered. But after I am raised up, I will go *before you to Galilee.*" Peter said to him, "Even though they all fall away, I will not." And Jesus said to him, "Truly, I say to you, this very night, before the cock crows twice, you will deny me three times" (Mk. 14.27-30).

Intercalated between the statements about falling away and denial is the prediction about going to Galilee after the resurrection. For Peter, the resurrection is not good news, but bad. Women in Mark hear the resurrection message that the disciples are to go to Galilee and they react the same way. They are so filled with fear that they tell no one about it (16.8). When Peter denies being a Galilean, he denies that he should return to Galilee to pursue his own voluntary death with Jesus. Peter did not know the man who would make such a request; it was not his kind of messiah.

It is not Peter alone who does not know the man and is thus responsible for Jesus' death. Had any disciple been able to achieve reconciliation with God the Father by use of any of the models which Jesus had explored, the crucifixion would have been unnecessary. The most important perpetrators of the crucifixion were neither the Jewish religious leaders nor the Roman rulers, but people in general and the disciples in particular. Mark knew that all of them had made reconciliation between the Father and his sons and daughters impossible without a crucifixion. All of them and, from Mark's point of view, all people who cling to life are like Peter: they do not know the man. Ernest Best calls attention to an admonition in 1 Pet. 3.15-16 which highlights Peter's failure and which provided an additional reason for Mark choosing Peter to be the disciple who would voice the denials: "Always be prepared to make a defense to any one who calls you to account for the hope that is in you, yet do it with gentleness and reverence; and keep your conscience clear, so that, when you are abused, those who revile your good behavior in Christ may be put to shame."[4] Peter failed by the standards of his own book.

The fact that Peter's denials occur in the twice-repeated context of Peter "warming himself at the fire" (Mk. 14.54, 67) calls attention to its potential meaningfulness. Jubilees 49.18-21 claims that the rules for celebrating the Passover include eating the flesh of the paschal lamb which has been roasted "on the fire in the court of the house which has been hallowed in the Lord's name." The context specifies that this is either the tabernacle or the "house where his name dwells." In sequence, Jesus has observed and transformed the Passover by denying that God will rescue His son; Peter is now warming himself at a "Passover fire," an act which obeys the regulations by being in the courtyard of the high priest and which implicitly constitutes betrayal because it affirms that the first-born son, Jesus, ought to be rescued or that his death should rescue others. Furthermore, in 1 Pet. 1.7, there is testing by fire, and in 4.12 a "fiery ordeal" of suffering. The statement in 1 Pet. 4.12-14 is paralleled by details in Mark's account: "Beloved, do not be surprised at the fiery ordeal which comes upon you to prove you, as though something strange were happening to you. But rejoice in so far as you share Christ's sufferings, that you may also rejoice and be glad when his glory is revealed. If you are reproached for the name of Christ, you are blessed...." Being tested by fire is also derived from Dan. 11.35 (LXX only): "And some of them that uanderstand shall fall, to try them as with fire, and to test them, and that they may be manifested at the time of the end...." By repeating the reference to the fire, Mark probably intended to focus the reader's attention on the connection between the Petrine teachings about reproach beside the fire and the Passover fire.

An additional midrashic direction points the reader to Ps. 69, which begins, "Save me, O God!" The Gospel of John later quoted Ps. 69.9, "Zeal for thy house will consume me," as a midrashic justification for Jesus' cleansing of the temple. Ps. 69.21 reads, "For my thirst they gave me vinegar to drink." It is the probable midrashic source of Mk. 15.31, in which Jesus on the cross is given vinegar to drink. Ps. 69.23, "Let their eyes be darkened, so that they cannot see," could have served Mark as a commentary on the "blindness" of those who condemned Jesus to death because they "saw" him confessing to a mistaken vision of the Son of man. In light of all that, one sentence from Mark calls attention to itself. Peter, having denied that he was "with the Nazarene, Jesus," "went out into the gateway," where the other accusations against him were made. The psalmist bemoans that he is "the talk of those who sit in the gate" and that "the insults of those who insult thee have fallen on me" (Ps. 69.12, 9). The conclusion of Ps. 69 is that "God will save Zion and rebuild the cities of Judah" (v. 35), a vision somewhat like the accusation that Jesus would rebuild the temple.

A different interpretation of the whole event relates midrashically to the references to antichrist in 1 John. The antichrists in 1 John are ex-members, people who had once joined and then left the movement. Mark reinterprets them as those who had had every opportunity to know the truth, but who denied it at the last hour. 1 John contends that "it is the last hour" because "many antichrists have come." Mark sees them as the disciples in Mark who fled from Jesus' arrest, as those who "went out from us, but they were not of us" (1 Jn. 2.18-19). Peter three times denied any knowledge of Jesus; thus he is the liar "who denies that Jesus is the Christ...who denies the Father and the Son" (1 Jn. 2.22). A problem with that interpretation is that the resurrection message is addressed to the "disciples and Peter." The author of John was aware of this difficulty in Mark and distinguished between the anti-christs who left the movement (Jn. 6) and those like Peter and Judas who denied and betrayed Jesus but nevertheless remained followers of Jesus to the end.

Sixth Day—Fulfilling a Third Trial Prediction: Mk. 15.1-20

The council holds what seems to have been another consultation at daybreak and decides to deliver Jesus to Pontius Pilate for an official Roman trial. Their ostensible purpose in doing so is to have Pilate order a legal execution, just as the priests and prophets brought Jeremiah to the princes for such a purpose in Jer. 26.10-11. The trial conforms midrashically to Ps. 2.2: "The kings of the earth set themselves, and the rulers take counsel together against the Lord and his Messiah." The chief priests accuse Jesus of many things, but Pilate questions him only about whether he claimed to be king of the Jews. Had Jesus made such a claim, he would have been guilty of treason against Rome, a death penalty offense. The treason charge is logical because, in the Sanhedrin trial, Jesus had answered affirmatively to the question as to whether he considered himself to be the messiah. One way to be a messiah is to be an earthly king; hence it could be legalistically attested by witnesses that Jesus had told the priests that he was guilty of claiming to be king of the Jews. In the trial before Pilate, Jesus makes no reply. His "you have said so" reply to Pilate is a way of saying "that's how you see me," implying distorted vision. The Suffering Servant of Isa. 53.7 "opened not his mouth" when being led to the slaughter, just as Jesus "made no further answer" (Mk. 15.5). Mark implies that Pilate, by asking rhetorically "Why, what evil has he done?"

found Jesus innocent, as the princes found that Jeremiah "does not deserve the sentence of death" (Jer. 26.16).

Mark then introduced into his narrative another midrashic masterpiece by alluding to a custom of dubious historicity that Pilate at each Passover feast released one prisoner. Pilate offers the priests and the crowd their choice between Jesus and Barabbas as the prisoner to be released. Barabbas ("Son of the Father") is, according to the text, known to be a murderer and insurrectionist against the Roman government guilty of the charge of treason levied by the priests against Jesus. Jesus had been condemned by the priests for blasphemy for claiming to be the Son of the Father, an identity which in fact characterizes Barabbas by virtue of his name. Mark's Barabbas is both blasphemous and a traitor to Rome. Jesus is not guilty of either charge except by distorting the meanings of messiah and son of the Blessed. The real issue in the trial is the Sanhedrin's anger that Jesus would not excel Barabbas by the latter's standards. They desperately want him to do well what Barabbas had tried but failed to do, that is, to use his power to drive the Romans out of the country and establish a new version of independent Israel in the Maccabean tradition. Jesus' word to them, "You will see the Son of man sitting at the right hand of Power," now appears as more than a casual euphemism for God; "Power" is the definition of God which the priestly vision preferred.[5]

The Barabbas narrative in Mark is a midrash on the meaning of "son of God." Mark intended by the story to incriminate the religious leaders for their hypocrisy in pretending to seek the execution of Jesus for the very crimes of which Barabbas was factually guilty. Barabbas symbolically embodied both the priestly and popular messianic vision. He was the self-proclaimed Son of God who sought to liberate Israel from foreign domination. He was what people in Jerusalem had been led to assume Jesus was claiming as his identity when he had entered Jerusalem in the role of the new

Solomon, riding on the animal associated with the powerful monarch David.

The priests stir up the crowd to ask for Barabbas' release and Jesus' crucifixion. Pilate, not believing what had been told him and noting that the priests were merely envious of Jesus, nevertheless yields to their request. His reluctance in sentencing Jesus to death has much in common with Herod in the death of John the Baptizer. According to the third passion-reward prediction in Mk. 10, the Jews were to deliver Jesus into the hands of the Gentiles, who in turn were to mock Jesus, spit upon him, and scourge him before killing him. In Mk. 15.15-20, they first scourge and then mock him by clothing him with a purple cloak and a crown of thorns.

The name Barabbas suggests that he was the son of an unknown father, i.e., an illegitimate child.[6] His designation as a murderer, the preference for an illegitimate son over a valid one, the general mocking, and the thorns of the crown are all likely to be midrashic upon Judg. 8.29-9.21. Gideon had 70 sons by legal wives and one named Abimelech by a concubine.[7] One of them would succeed Gideon as king. Abimelech persuaded the people to back him and murdered 69 of the brothers, all but the youngest, Jotham. Jotham, in turn, told a parable about the trees of the forest asking the olive tree, the fig tree, and the vine, Mark's three messianic fruit trees, to be their king. Each fruit-bearing tree refuses, letting the office go by default to a bramble tree, Abimelech. Assuming that the crown of thorns originates midrashically from the bramble tree as king, Jotham's parable is analogous to the situation in which the people mock Jesus as their thorn-king and give allegiance to Barabbas.

Sixth Day—The Psalmic Model of Rescue by God: Mk.15.21-36

Mark's reference to mocking introduced a series of connections with a particular type of psalm. In Ps. 22 and 69, the psalmist finds himself in great difficulty because of his enemies and prays to God for rescue, i.e., salvation. Until he is saved he blames God for his misfortunes; afterwards, he praises God for God's saving acts. In both the praising and blaming, the entire responsibility is put on God. Six details from Ps. 22 and 69 are used midrashically to develop the crucifixion narrative after the trial before Pilate is completed. The mocking comes from Ps. 22.7 in which "all who see me mock me; they make mouths at me; they wag their heads." The most important of the six is Jesus' citation of a lament which is usually referred to as a cry of dereliction: "My God, my God, why hast thou forsaken me?" (Ps. 22.1). Ps. 22 continues with the joyous news that God "has not despised or abhorred the affliction of the afflicted...but has heard when he cried to him" (Ps. 22.24). Ps. 18 contains that same rhythm of distress and relief when God intervenes to save.

Jesus was not doubting God when he uttered the cry of dereliction. He was calling attention to the most powerful but mistaken idea in Mark's definition of "Judaism." This was the definition of God as the deity whose major function is to miraculously intervene to save "us" when "we" are in difficulty. It was the definition of God implied in Jesus' name: God Saves. Jesus, by speaking the words a short time before his death, called attention to the fact that his God was of a different nature, not a saving intervener.

Mark wanted the reader to think of Ps. 22 as a whole, not just the opening lament, and therefore used three additional details from it: "They divide my garments among them, and for my raiment they cast lots" (Ps. 22.18); "a company of evildoers encircle me; they have pierced my hands and my feet [implied by crucifixion but not directly alluded to by Mark]" (Ps. 22.16); "he has committed his cause to the Lord; let him deliver him, let him rescue him" (Ps. 22.8). Another detail comes from Ps. 69.21: "For my thirst they gave me vinegar to drink."

Mark could have been additionally influenced by LXX Jer. 20.2, 7, 10. Jeremiah, smitten and imprisoned says, "I am continually mocked." Mark may have had another midrashic reason to portray Jesus as deserving to be rescued. In Num. 13-14, Caleb and Joshua [Jesus] are the only two spies to return from Canaan with a positive report. The others are afraid to invade the land. Jesus (Joshua) and Caleb say in Num. 14.7-9, in effect, "God will take it for us." The people try to stone both of them to death, and God quickly intervenes to save their lives [Num. 14.10-12].

A man named Simon of Cyrene, designated as the father of Alexander ("Man's Defender") and Rufus ("Red-Haired"), carries Jesus' cross (Mk. 15.21). None of these new names or their etymologies appear to have any immediate thematic meaning for Mark's story. This is so unusual in Mark that it calls attention to itself. The name Simon is virtually certain to be a midrashic counterpoint on Peter's original name, with the implication that Simon Peter should have been carrying his own cross because he had said, "Even though they all fall away I will not" (Mk. 14.29). Rufus ("Red-Haired") could be a counterpart to Iscariot ("Red Dyer") and thus another Esau, the unloved ruddy brother who is supplanted by Jacob. Alexander ("Man's Defender" and also the name of the great Macedonian conqueror) could be read as savior. That makes an interesting procession to the execution site, with a new Simon carrying a cross for Jesus' death but not for his own, followed by his sons, the betrayer and the conquering rescuer of man. An "Esau" who at the time of Jesus' crucifixion should have been supplanted by a beloved son was instead the brother of a political-military savior. Such a reading illuminates the opportunity people had to choose between Jesus and Barabbas earlier in the story.

But why then Simon "of Cyrene"? Mellink identifies Cyrene as a major coastal city in North Africa with a large population of Greek-speaking Jews.[8] Mark may have chosen a Cyrenean "coming in from the country" because of a sound-alike city in Isa. 49.12

[Masoretic text only]: "Lo, these come from afar, and lo, these from the north and from the west, and these from the land of Syene." Syene is the modern Assuan in southern Egypt, near the first cataract of the Nile and the site of the modern Aswan (Assuan) Dam.[9] Both Cyrene and Syene were "from afar." The probability of Mark's use of the term from Isa. 49 is increased because the subject of the poem is "my servant" (v. 3) who is "to bring Jacob back to him" (v. 5), who is also to be "a light to the nations" (v. 6), who is "deeply despised" (v. 7), who is to be given as "a covenant to the people" (v. 8). The servant laments, "The Lord has forsaken me; my Lord has forgotten me" (v. 14). The poem asks, "Can the captives of a tyrant be rescued?" (v. 24). It ends with the assurance that "I am the Lord your Savior [rescuer], and your Redeemer" (v. 26). The possible midrashic parallels are not strong enough to constitute proof, but neither are they weak enough to be ignored. If Cyrene is a sound-alike for Syene, chosen because of its prominence in the world of Hellenistic Judaism, a Simon from Cyrene carried with the cross the meanings attached to the names of his sons and those of Isa. 49. Rescue in response to despair over "the Lord having forsaken me" is thus clearly affirmed. Mark's crucifixion story is an intentional midrashic reversal of Isa. 49's emphasis on a servant messiah being saved by God when he is in the hands of a tyrant such as Pilate and despairs at being forsaken. The effect is to heighten the tension in the Mark text.

A supplementary possibility is that Simon of Cyrene is a composite name made up by Mark from 2 Macc. 2.24 and 41-29, in which Jason (a different transliteration of Joshua into Greek, i.e., another Jesus) of Cyrene is identified as the author of the source being summarized in 2 Maccabees. The high priest Onias is supplanted by Jason after a Simon had tried to supplant Onias. Simon's brother, Menelaus, then supplants Jason. "So Jason who had supplanted his brother was in turn supplanted by another" (2 Macc. 4.26). The emphasis on "supplanting" in the 2 Maccabees sequence was probably midrashic on Jer. 9.4 in which everyone is warned not to trust his brother because "every brother is a supplanter." By that logic, Simon of Cyrene would be a different kind of traitor, not picking up his cross to follow Jesus, but carrying Jesus' cross to expedite the execution.

Many of the details of the crucifixion story have midrashic sources which illuminate Mark's reason for using each item. They bring Jesus to Golgotha ("Skull" in Aramaic; in Latin, "Calvary"). The name connotes death; it has no other function in Mark. Assuming that Golgotha was outside the city limits, going there would represent one more element in the daily routine, Jesus leaving Jerusalem on the sixth day. The story is divided into three-hour periods, the last being three hours of darkness from noon till 3:00 p.m., leading up to the moment of Jesus' death. Possible connections between the three-hour periods and a Jewish liturgical calendar do not fit into overall Markan themes. What is more likely to be the case is that the three-hour periods constitute one more way in which Mark called attention to the number three. There have been three passion-reward predictions, three trials, three prayer periods in Gethsemane, three denials by Peter, the charge that Jesus would rebuild the temple in three days, three people being crucified (Jesus and two robbers); and the sequence will be climaxed by resurrection on the third day as predicted. The darkness itself, however, may be midrashic on a psalm of rescue, Ps. 18: "He made darkness his covering around him, his canopy thick clouds dark with water" (Ps. 18.11). For Mark the darkness at the cross may have fulfilled the internal prediction in Mk. 13 about the sun not giving its light and is in that sense midrashic. Another midrashic possibility comes from Joshua in which a king is hanged; "at the going down of the sun," his body is taken "down from the tree" (8.29). A battle against five other kings is won when the sun stays "in the midst of heaven" for a whole day (10.13); when the sun goes down "they took them from the trees, and threw them into the cave" and "set great stones against the mouth of the cave" (10.26). Mark has stones temporarily rolled against the entrance of a burial cave (16.3-4), and a sun which does not give light in midday (15.33). The details may midrashically reflect but reverse the imagery of Josh. 8-10.

Mark developed the rescue motif in the narrative in a variety of midrashic ways. Jesus is mockingly challenged to save himself if he could rebuild the temple in three days or if he could save others: "Let the Christ [Messiah], the King of Israel, come down now from the cross, that we may *see* and believe" (Mk. 15.32). His mockers act as if he could not do it, but they would truly have believed and been excited if he had rebelled against the Roman will by cheating a Roman cross of its victim. Had he elected to get off the cross, all would have seen the supernatural Son of man at the right hand of Power. Had Jesus come down from the cross he would have been more like Barabbas than like himself. The midrashic source for the skepticism of the priests comes from the core of the death trial of the virtuous son of God.

> [He] boasts of having God for his father.... Let us see if what he says is true; let us observe what kind of end he himself will have. If the virtuous man is God's son, God will take his part and rescue him from the clutches of his enemies. Let us test him with cruelty and with torture.... Let us condemn him to a shameful death since he will be looked after—we have his word for it (Wisd. of Sol. 2.16-20).

In response to the mocking, Jesus keeps silent, his stereotypic response to temptation. His silence midrashically follows the pattern of the Suffering Servant in Isaiah who "opened not his mouth; like a lamb that is led to the slaughter, and like a sheep that before its shearers is dumb, so he opened not his mouth" (Isa. 53.7). Mark's midrashic model was further developed in 1 Pet. 2.21-25:

> He [Christ] committed no sin; no guile was found on his lips. When he was reviled, he did not revile in return; when he suffered, he did not threaten; but he trusted to him who judges justly. He himself bore our sins in his body on the tree, that we might die to sin and live to righteousness. By his wounds you have been healed. For you were straying like sheep, but have now returned to the Shepherd and Guardian of your souls.

Both Isa. 53 and 1 Pet. 2 insist that the reason the messiah acts that way is to save others. Mark midrashically disagreed. Jesus refused to be rescued. A second way Mark developed the rescue motif was a pun in the question, "My God, my God, why hast thou forsaken me?" The word for God in "my God, my God" is *elohim*, a generic word for god which sounds like and provides the first syllable for the name Elijah. Some "heard" Jesus calling for Elijah to rescue him, a midrash rooted in the 2 Kgs. 2 story of Elijah going to heaven without really dying.

Another way Mark developed the rescue theme is the direct use of the word "god" in "My God, my God, why hast thou forsaken me?" The "God Saves" etymology of the name Jesus has been waiting in the wings since Mk. 1.1. The reader has known about "God Saves" throughout the book; many passages have been interpreted in light of it. Mark, however, had never previously explicitly asked if God himself would come to save his son. The midrashic original is at the heart of the Jewish tradition. Abraham and Sarah had been given a son by God. Then, as Sanders states:

> God...asks for him back. Abraham had loved Isaac so much he simply forgot his son was God's gift. Loving God's gift is a beautiful and wonderful thing and much to be desired; but lurking within it is the seed of idolatry, the displacement of the giver by love of the gift.... How can a good God ask Abraham to sacrifice his son

> (Gen. 22.2)? ... How can Isaiah say that he had been commissioned by God to preach that the people's heart would be fat, their ears heavy, and their eyes closed lest they repent and be healed (Isa. 6.10)? ... How could Christ's crucifixion be in the 'definite plan and foreknowledge of God' (Acts 2.23)?[10]

Despite all that, in the story line in Genesis, once Abraham was willing to give Isaac back, God stepped in to arrange a substitute sacrifice, a goat. That is the issue for Mark, for Jesus, for the assembled crowd. If Jesus is a beloved child of God, will "God Save" his own child as he once saved Isaac?

God the Father has already made his decision, in Gethsemane and before that in Malachi. The Father has already shown his love; the response is up to those whom He loves. The decision is in the hands of Jesus, not of God or Elijah. By dying, Jesus refuses to use miraculous resources at his command to save himself. He thus becomes the only child of God who, up to that time, has done what is necessary to be reconciled to the Father. He yields his life because it is the Father's will that he do so. Mark found that key point in Romans: "What then shall we say to this? If God is for us, who is against us? He who did not spare his own Son, but gave him up for us all, will he not also give us all things with him" (Rom. 8.31-32)? In his midrash, Mark disagreed with Paul's conclusion. God did not give up Jesus for "us all"; rather Jesus died voluntarily, consistent with the will of God, in order that he alone might be reconciled with his Father. By this strange reversal, the "I, I only" which had been temptation throughout the Gospel suddenly becomes the gospel truth. Only Jesus was reconciled to the Father by his act. Mark's implication to the reader is that this is true for everyone: each is responsible for his own reconciliation. Neither Jesus nor God will any longer function as savior because the gospel's good news is that Jesus is the exemplar to show others the way. With a loud cry, probably of mingled agony and triumph, Jesus breathes his last.

Sixth Day—The Consequences of Jesus' Death: Mk. 15.38-39

The moment such a death occurred, the Jewish temple became totally irrelevant. Patrick distinguishes between a temple-oriented Zion theology in which God was presumed to dwell in the Jerusalem temple (as in Ps. 46, 48, 78, 125, and 132) and a Deuteronomic theology in which God dwells only in heaven.[11] Mark's target was definitely the Zion theological concept of the temple. Mark symbolized the newly irrelevant status of the temple by having the "curtain of the temple" torn in two in direct response to Jesus' death. The curtain had separated a windowless room, the Holy of Holies, from the remainder of the building. It had guaranteed that the God dwelling in the room would be forever separated from the world of ordinary experience and be accessible only to a priest who entered into his presence. Jesus' death effectually eliminated that divider between an isolated God and his people. Mark midrashically adapted the rending of the temple curtain from references in The Testament of Levi and Hebrews: "Behind the second curtain stood a tent called the Holy of Holies" (Heb. 9.3); people have "a hope that enters into the inner shrine behind the curtain, where Jesus has gone as a forerunner on our behalf" (Heb. 6.19-20); "Therefore, brethren, since we have confidence to enter the sanctuary by the blood of Jesus, by the new and living way which *he opened for us through the curtain,* that is, through his flesh...let us draw near with a true heart" (Heb. 10.19-22); "Together with the rest of Israel you will sin against the law, so that [the Lord] will not bear with Jerusalem because of your wickedness, but will tear in two the temple veil" (Test. of Levi 10.3). The "temple not made with hands" (Heb. 9.11, 25) and the opened curtain are the only details in Hebrews used by Mark.

The rending of the temple curtain serves to climax the temple theme in the pattern of Passion Week. On each day there has been at least one reference to the temple. On day one, Jesus visited the shrine as a spectator. He merely looked at it and left. On day two, Jesus disrupted the priestly operation in a context which was "out of season" for those with a pro-ritual point of view. He did so to symbolize that those who forgive others directly render unnecessary the mediating function of temple priests. On day three, Jesus bested the temple leaders in their effort to trap him into a damaging contradiction and predicted that the time would come when not one temple stone would be left on top of another. He also demonstrated the inadequacy of the model from Daniel which made physical disruption of worship in the Jerusalem temple the desolating sacrilege. On day four, Judas went to the temple authorities to arrange for the betrayal. On day five, Jesus replaced the seder ritual, which traditionally had begun by killing lambs in the temple area, with a non-temple eucharistic meal. Priests sent a crowd to arrest him. On day six, still during the night, the priests tried first to frame Jesus for the crime of threatening to destroy the temple building and erect it again in three days without human hands. Failing in that, they convicted him of blasphemy and traded his life for that of the military-type messiah who had led them against the Romans. When Jesus died voluntarily, the temple apparatus was no longer relevant. Increasing antagonism to the temple and what it represented tells the story of Passion Week as a week, but not of the whole of Mark.

When Jesus dies, the Roman military officer in charge of the proceedings, seeing that "Jesus thus breathed his last," says, "Truly this man was a son of God" (Mk. 15.39). RSV's translation, "son," not Son, while correct, is based on the incorrect assumption, namely that a Roman officer, neither Jewish nor Christian, would not have been making a theological statement about Jesus as a Divine Son of God; therefore he saw Jesus as a child of God.[12] A better reason is that the statement about Jesus as a true child of God is consistent with every correct interpretation of Jesus' sonship throughout Mark. It confirms why the word "son" should be read as "son," not "Son," in Mark's opening sentence, and that the temptation in the wilderness was the attraction for Jesus to think of himself as Son when God loved him as son. It shows that everyone in the gospel is a child of God, and shows why the unclean spirits take the opposite point of view.

The point is that the centurion spoke for Mark in a way which no other one character has done in the entire book, confirming the word of God that Jesus is a beloved son of God, and that Jesus has done what is necessary for reconciliation between the Father and any one of his children.

Endnotes for Chapter Thirteen

[1]F. H. Borsch, "Mark XIV.62 and I Enoch LXII.5," *New Testament Studies*, XIV, 565-7. Borsch, on p. 566, refers to Mk. 14.62 as "a kind of *pesher*."

[2]The traditional reason for dating 1 Thessalonians as the earliest of Paul epistles has been its strong emphasis on an apocalyptic end of history, on the assumption that this began with Jesus. Now that scholars in large numbers are abandoning the latter assumption, it follows that they should also reexamine the dating for 1 Thessalonians.

[3]It is possible that Luke was doing midrash on the execution of Uriah, who was arrested in Egypt and brought back to Israel for the purpose of capital punishment.

[4]Ernest Best, "I Peter and the Gospel Tradition," *New Testament Studies*, XVI, 101.

[5]The priests who were to see Jesus at the right hand of Power were like religious leaders of the 1980s who equated true religion and national victory in the U.S.-U.S.S.R. arms race—thus indicating the continuing relevance of the issue Mark was presenting.

[6]C. L. Smith.

[7]O. J. Baab, "Concubine," *IDB*, indicates that a concubine in the Bible was a slave girl by whom the male owner had children.

[8]A. J. Mellink, "Cyrene," *IDB*.

[9]T. O. Lambdin, "Syene," *IDB*.

[10]James A. Sanders, *Canon and Community*, 57-58.

[11]Dale Patrick, *Old Testament Law* (Atlanta, John Knox Press: 1985) 100.

[12]Kee, *Community of the New Age*, 204, note #50, says that "the best manuscripts that include *uios theou* [son of God] offer it anarthrously, just as it appears in the testimony of the centurion at Mark 15.39." "Anarthrous" means "without a definite article." Kee also refers to the centurion as "a perceiving pagan," 124.

CHAPTER FOURTEEN

MIDRASH ON JACOB, JOSEPH, AND RESURRECTION

Mark, in writing a conclusion for his gospel, faced two problems. He had both to demonstrate the relevance of crucifixion to lives of those other than Jesus, and to deal with the tradition that the crucified Christ had been resurrected, as Peter and Paul had insisted. Peter spoke of resurrection in direct connection with the messiah's glorification. Paul most often interpreted resurrection metaphorically as a victory associated with crucifixion without in any sense diminishing the finality and integrity of the suffering accompanying crucifixion. In 1 Cor. 15, however, Paul spoke explicitly of resurrection appearances and envisioned a future resurrection for all believers. He said of this future resurrection that it was to be like the resurrection which Jesus had experienced. It was to be a resurrection of a kind of body different from present terrestrial bodies. Furthermore, Paul insisted that Jesus' resurrection on the third day was "in accordance with the scriptures" (1 Cor. 15.3).

Paul's repeated references to resurrection pushed Mark to create a midrashic narrative of resurrection just as he had created a midrashic narrative of crucifixion. Toward that end, Mark introduced earlier in his Gospel the concept of resurrection in a variety of contexts to prepare for his climactic treatment of it. He presented resurrection-type motifs in the revivification of Jairus' daughter, in the three passion/reward predictions, in Jesus' Mount of Transfiguration warning not to tell until he had been resurrected, in the belief of Herod that Jesus was the resurrected John the Baptizer, in the argument with the Sadducees about the meaning of resurrection, and in Jesus' prediction that after his death he would be resurrected and go to Galilee. No overall Markan definition of resurrection emerges from these because each was related only to the theme of a particular unit.

Mark's narrative about Jesus' burial and resurrection functions as an epilogue for the Gospel. It consists of three pericopes: one deals with three women whose identities and attitudes provide the meanings for the entire epilogue; a second depicts Jesus' burial; and a third tells of an angel announcing the resurrection to the three women. Some Bibles have additional pericopes after Mk. 16.8a which are well known not to have been in any of the best early manuscripts of Mark.[1] These are inconsistent with Mark's thematic development and can therefore be disregarded as an addition by some author later than Mark, in no way part of the original.

Sixth Day—The Three Symbolic Women: Mk. 15.40-41

Mark indicated that many women had come with Jesus to Jerusalem and that they followed Jesus to the cross although they were only "looking on from afar." Three of the women figure actively in Mark's narrative. Like other women in Mark, they are symbolic. They are Mary Magdalene, Mary the mother of James/ Jacob and Joses (the Greek transliteration of Joseph), and Salome ("Peace," "Well-being"). "Mary" is the Greek counterpart of the LXX's "Mariam," the sister of Moses (Miriam in Hebrew). "Magdalene" is commonly taken to mean "from Magdala," a town which is not mentioned either in the Old Testament or Josephus.[2] Mark probably intended Magdalene to sound like the Hebrew word "magdal" ("Great" or "Large"). Mary Magdalene would be "Mary the Great," the midrashic counterpart of Miriam, one of the greatest women in the Old Testament. This impression is heightened in the ensuing burial story by the identification of Mary with Rachel, the mother of Jacob and hence in a midrashic sense the mother of Israel. If the second Mary, the mother of James/Jacob and Joses, was also Mary the mother of Jesus, who had sons named James/Jacob and Joses, it is peculiar that Mary Magdalene is named before her. It makes more Markan sense if Mary the mother of Jesus and Mary Magdalene are the same person, and if Mary the mother of Joses and James/Jacob is an aspect of that same person singled out for special emphasis. Mary Magdalene's later reputation as a sinner "from whom [Jesus] had cast out seven demons" was an addition based on Lk. 8.2 and the spurious Mk. 16.9, and does not belong at all to Mark's original characterization.

Salome's name is the feminine counterpart of Solomon,[3] with both names meaning "Peace." As such, she could represent the tradition from Isa. 52.7 that the Suffering Servant messiah would appear on the mountains publishing peace, or the prediction from Isa 9.6 (Masoretic Text only, not LXX) that the messiah would be a "Prince of Peace." Isa. 57.1-2 (LXX) describes the burial of a righteous man, the Suffering Servant, in peace. Wisd. of Sol. 4.7-15 interprets Isa. 57.1-2 in terms of the death of the virtuous man who is God's son. If Mary Magdalene and Mary the mother of James/Jacob and Joses are the same person, both representing Jesus' mother, it follows that Salome should also be incorporated into that composite personality.

Burial Arrangements at Joseph's Tomb: Mk. 15.42-47

One result of Jesus' death is that a man named Joseph of Arimathea courageously offers a tomb for Jesus' burial. Arimathea is the name of a town of unknown location, but perhaps identified with one of five Jewish towns named Ramah or Rama (Height). Morton says that majority opinion holds that it was the original home of Samuel and was often associated with David.[4] A different Ramah is the traditional site of the tomb of Rachel, Jacob's mother and hence midrashically the mother of Israel. It is this Ramah which is referred to in 1 Sam. 1.1 as Ramathaim-zophim ("Twin Heights"). Mark connected "Joseph" and "Ramah" by interpreting a Jeremiah Rachel passage midrashically. The prophet said that "a voice is heard in Ramah, lamentation and bitter weeping. Rachel is weeping for her children; she refuses to be comforted for her children, because they are not" (Jer. 31.15). Rachel, the second and preferred wife of Jacob, was the mother of his two favorite sons, Joseph and Benjamin, and died in childbirth with Benjamin. Jeremiah, however, was not alluding to Rachel weeping for them. He midrashically described Rachel, in her nearby tomb, weeping for all the captives in Israel who were collected at Ramah before being taken into Babylonian exile (Jer. 40.1). She wept for these her children as she would have wept for Joseph and Benjamin, the latter of whom she had originally named Benoni ("Son of My Sorrow"). Midrashically, Joseph of Arimathea is Joseph of Ramah, the Joseph presumed to be dead and gone, thus appropriately associated with a tomb. Mary the mother of Jacob and Joses is a new Rachel, perhaps weeping for her child Jesus, and intimately related to a Jacob and Joseph (Joses) as Rachel was.

Mark also connected Joseph and Arimathea because of the "Twin Heights" etymology of Ramathaimzophim in 1 Sam. 1.1. From the beginning of Mark, "twins" has been a persistent motif. Mal. 1.1-3, with its focus on Jacob supplanting his twin Esau, generated for Mark the brothers James/Jacob and John, the disciple named Thomas ("Twin"), perhaps the surname Boanerges ("Cult of Twins" as one possibility), Iscariot ("Red Dyer" as a midrashic allusion to Esau, the ruddy twin from the red land of Edom), Rufus ("Red-Headed" as brother of Alexander whose father carried the cross for Jesus), and Mary the mother of both Joses and James/Jacob, with the latter symbolizing the resurrection. The motif is too extensive and the details too intrusive in the text for the author not to have been conscious of it. Arimathea should thus be understood as Mark's way of calling attention to twinning once more, thereby explaining to the perceptive reader the peculiar description of the woman who was on one occasion the mother of Joses and on another the mother of James/Jacob. The author of the Gospel of John understood the Joseph and James/Jacob motifs in Mark and extended them in powerfully midrashic ways.

Another midrashic source for Joseph of Arimathea, owner of the tomb, is the Gen. 50 account of Joseph, himself a highly respected official, asking permission of the ruler, the Pharaoh of Egypt, to bury Jacob in a cave-tomb which Jacob had hewed for himself beyond the Jordan. Mark's Joseph of Arimathea, "a respected member of the council," "took courage and went to Pilate" to ask permission to bury Jesus "in a tomb which had been hewn out of the rock" (Mk. 15.43-46). The Suffering Servant poem in Isa. 52-53 provides specific justification for Jesus' burial in a wealthy man's tomb: "And they made his grave with the wicked and with a rich man in his death, although he had done no violence, and there was no deceit in his mouth" (Isa. 53.9). Joseph is rich in the sense that he could afford to have an unused tomb.

Only two of the three women go to the tomb, in a sense only one-and-a-half of them. Salome ("Peace") is not there. The two who come are Mary Magdalene and Mary the mother of Joses (Joseph). At the crucifixion, she was the mother of both Joses and James/Jacob. On resurrection morning, she will be the mother only of James/Jacob; now she is the mother only of Joses. She is one character with two meanings, one for burial without hope, one for resurrection. The four sons of Jesus' mother in Mk. 6.3 are James/Jacob, Joses, Judas, and Simon. Two of those names, Judas (Iscariot) and Simon (Peter) have already been eliminated, one by betraying Jesus, one by denying him. Thinking in that way, the Judas who betrayed could be both Iscariot and a brother of the lord, and the Simon who denied could be both Peter and a brother of the lord. This would make additional sense out of Mk. 13.12's warning that "brother will deliver up brother to death, and the father his child, and children will rise against parents and have them put to death; and you will be hated by all for my name's sake. But he who endures to the end will be saved." In addition to being a statement about the future, it would be a description by Jesus of his own familial situation. Judas and Simon have already not endured to the end. Mark could have been stating this in a different way by identifying Judas with the surname Iscariot ("Red Dyer") to associate him with Esau, the prototypical brother supplanted by the beloved Jacob. Now the question is raised about Joses.

Joseph son of Jacob was saved from death by being sold into slavery; he in turn saved Jacob's family from starvation. Jacob lamented (Gen. 42.38) that Joseph was dead. The one supposed to be dead was discovered to be alive (Gen. 45.26) and became the rescuer, God turning intended evil into good so that "many people might be kept alive" (Gen. 50.20). That is precisely the scenario which is midrashically possible after the crucifixion. What if Jesus, who has five times predicted his resurrection, would emerge from the tomb to rescue his people after all? Thus "Joseph" is midrashically present at the tomb as Joseph of Arimathea, as Joses son of Mary, and as the Joseph resurrection model for Jesus. So it was that Mark introduced the name Joseph. John and Luke extended the midrash to make Joseph Jesus' father, husband of Mary, but that innovation had not yet occurred when Mark wrote.[5]

Joseph of Arimathea is assured that Jesus is really dead. Then he wraps him in a linen shroud, puts the corpse into a cave, and rolls a large stone over the entrance. He intends that the corpse remain there. Mary Magdalene and Mary the mother of Joses, coming to the tomb for the sole purpose of seeing where Jesus is laid, also accept the fact that he is dead. In the imagery of the Jeremiah quotation, these two women named Mary are the woman

Rachel weeping for her forever dead child. By their act, the "Joses" of the brothers of Jesus is symbolically eliminated from the list of those who endure to the end. He was not to be one of those who still had hope on the "third day."

Resurrection Culminating in Fear on the Third Day: Mk. 16.1-8

On Sunday morning, Mary Magdalene, Mary the mother of Jacob only, and Salome come to the tomb to anoint the corpse with spices, the Jewish equivalent of embalming.[6] Signs of hope are everywhere around them. It is the first day of a new week; the sun has just risen; Salome, "Peace," is there; the mother of Jacob, "He Who Supplants His Brother," is also present. The very large stone has already been rolled away from the cave door and the women can see in the cave a young man in a white robe. In light of the common understanding that the white-robed man is an angel, he functions as a messenger of the resurrection news, not as an supernatural personage-with-wings-and-halo. The etymology of the word *angellos* permits translation either as messenger or transliteration as angel. In the Bible, the primary function of "angels" is to be messengers. It may be relevant, because of the centrality of Malachi among Mark's midrashic sources, that the etymology of Malachi is also messenger. Mark's angel was a prophetic messenger, like Malachi, proclaiming the completed good news which had begun, according to Mark's first sentence, in a quotation from Malachi combined with one from Isaiah.

A conspicuous redundancy in Mark's account is the double emphasis on the time of day. The women came "very early" to the tomb "when the sun had risen." That feature is part of exaltation passages in the Old Testament. Joshua (Jesus) rose "early in the morning" (Josh. 3.1); "At the end of three days" the people were ordered to follow the ark of the covenant (Josh. 3.2-3); "And the Lord said to Joshua, 'This day I will begin to exalt you in the sight of all Israel'" (Josh. 3.7). The parallels of early morning, third day, exaltation in the sight of all, and the name Joshua (Jesus in the LXX) are too strong to be merely coincidental.

The lack of a resurrection appearance in Mark confirms the irony in Jesus' address to the Sanhedrin, in which he implied that they would mistakenly "see the Son of man sitting at the right hand of Power." The Joshua midrashic source would have lead to that expectation: "On that day the Lord exalted Joshua *in the sight of all* Israel; and they stood in awe of him" (Josh. 4.14). In Exod. 19.11-16, the Lord appears to people on the morning of the third day. Mark may also have followed the logic of Paul's midrash on Lev. 23.9-12, in which it was to be a "perpetual statute" that people should bring the "first fruits of your harvest to the priest." When the people brought first fruits to the priest, he was to wave the sheaf "on the morrow after the sabbath." Paul interpreted the resurrected Christ as "the first fruits of those who have fallen asleep" (1 Cor. 15.20). Thus Mark might have found additional midrashic justification in having Jesus' resurrection occur on the day after the sabbath.

A midrashic explanation for having a stone rolled away from the door of the tomb is Jacob's removing the stone from the mouth of a well so that Rachel could feed her flock (Gen. 29). Mark had previously developed a midrash on Rachel weeping for her children. Gen. 29.2-3 implies that because "the stone on the well's mouth was large," it would take all the gathered shepherds to "roll the stone from the mouth of the well" and later "put the stone back in its place." But when Jacob saw Rachel, his future bride, coming to the well, he rolled away the stone by himself (Gen. 29.10). The fact that Mary in Mark's account is the "mother of James/Jacob" adds to the relevance of the Genesis story. In addition, the circumcision of the nation on a third day led God to proclaim at Gilgal that "this day I have rolled away the reproach of Egypt from you" (Josh. 5.9). Muilenberg explains that the etymology of Gilgal is "Circle of

Stones" but says that the Joshua passage provides an "etiological narrative explaining the origin of Gilgal from the verb 'to roll away.'"[7] Another midrashic source for the detail about the stone rolled against the door of the tomb is Joshua (Jesus) 10. Three days after making a covenant with the Gibeonites, the Israelites discovered that they had been deceived but let the Gibeonites live because of the covenant. Afterward they rescued the Gibeonites from five kings, during which defense the sun stood still for about a whole day. The five kings were discovered hiding in a cave and Joshua ordered "great stones" rolled against the "mouth of the cave" (Josh. 10.16-18). Later the kings were executed, and their bodies were thrown into caves with more "great stones" blocking the entrance (Josh. 10.26-27). The combination of a covenant of life being honored on the third day and stones covering the entrance was probably sufficient to attract Mark's attention.

The effect of the appearance of the resurrection messenger to the women is that the gospel, the good news, starts over again, without warning, as in the first sentence of Mark: "The beginning of the good news of Jesus the Messiah, the son of God, as it is written in Isaiah [actually Malachi]: 'Behold, I send my messenger before thy face, who shall prepare thy way.'" Now there is a new messenger, no longer Elijah come back from the dead, but a messenger proclaiming that Jesus is alive. The end of the gospel becomes a new beginning. This ought be no surprise. Mark has written about truths which were lies as well as lies which were true, ideals which were temptations, an accurate confession of faith which was Satanic, an effort to save which was in fact a betrayal, etc. Mark has never permitted his intended readers the luxury of a simple, uncomplicated interpretation of truth. His good news has been too much like real life for that to be his message. The word from the tomb is simultaneously simple and puzzling:

> Do not be amazed; you seek Jesus of Nazareth, who was crucified. He has risen; he is not here; see the place where they laid him. But go, tell his disciples and Peter that he is going before you to Galilee; there you will see him, as he told you (Mk. 16.6-7).

Several Markan themes are included in the announcement. Jesus is "of Nazareth," i.e., still potentially to be seen erroneously as the holy one. Peter is distinguished from the other disciples, probably because Jesus' prediction in 14.28 about going before the disciples to Galilee engendered a discussion with Peter in particular. The verb "to see" is central. They are expected to see him in Galilee, but whether they will see truly or with half-healed blindness is not immediately obvious.

A trio of Markan details which are unnecessary to the message are that the messenger is "a young man" who "was sitting on the right side" and who was "dressed in a white robe" (Mk. 16.5). The particulars are likely to be midrashic on Mark's "young man" who fled from Jesus' arrest and left behind him his "linen cloth" (Mk. 14.51-52), and on the prediction that the priests would "see the Son of man sitting at the right hand of Power" (Mk. 14.62). Mark has used young people throughout his Gospel as symbols of Jesus or the Twelve. Jairus' twelve-year-old daughter represented the Twelve; the discontented mother at Tyre and Sidon functioned as Jesus dissatisfied with the Twelve; the young man fleeing from the arrest was the counterpart of the twelve disciples. Now another young man is presented as a messenger, occupying the role which the twelve were expected to be able to play. They should have been able to clothe themselves in the burial garment as a genuinely New Israel (Jacob) and thus to see more clearly what it would mean for James/Jacob and John to be at Jesus' right hand. The account is a midrashic satire on their unwillingness and that of the women.

The women react with trembling and astonishment. Nothing in the surface reading of the message should have induced their negative trembling or astonishment. They might be aquiver with excitement at the unexpected good news that Jesus was alive, but there certainly seems no reason for them to be afraid. Yet they are, as the climax of the text makes specific: "And they went out and fled from the tomb, for trembling and astonishment had come upon them; and they said nothing to anyone, for they were afraid" (Mk. 16.8). More literally, the Greek text concludes that "they said nothing to anyone, being afraid." Thus the book ends. That finale compels a search for meanings in Mark's context and in the message itself which would merit that response as Mark's last word about the good news that Jesus is the Christ and son of God.

The first clue as to why the women are afraid is that "trembling and astonishment" are internally midrashic within Mark. The woman who had been healed of a twelve-year-old hemorrhage, "knowing what had been done to her, came in fear and trembling and fell down before him..." (Mk. 5.33). When the herdsmen saw Legion, the demoniac, healed, "they were afraid" (Mk. 5.15). When Jesus calmed the first storm at sea, the disciples "were filled with awe" (Mk. 4.41). The second time they were in a storm at sea, they were at first "terrified" and then "astounded" (Mk. 6.50-51). On their third crossing of the sea, they did "not yet perceive or understand" (Mk. 8.17). The women at the tomb were not the first to react in trembling and astonishment when confronted with the news about a miracle.

A second clue is that the women were looking for Jesus of Nazareth, in Mark's sound-alike etymology, Jesus the Holy One. It was Jesus of Nazareth who had come to be baptized at the beginning of Mark and who had been tempted as a result to think of himself as the Only Son of God, the Holy One. Now, said the messenger, the women were still looking for that Jesus. "He is not here!" Had he been there as the Holy One, he would have made a direct, personal, miraculous appearance to the women. He would have been there in the way the Gospel of John later depicted him, so that the women could have touched his wounds, eaten fish with him, and clung to him. In Mark, however, there was no appearance of the resurrected Christ to excite the women. Jesus had earlier warned four of his disciples to expect that: "And then if any one says to you, 'Look, here is the Christ!' or 'Look, there he is!' do not believe it. False Christs and false prophets will arise and show signs and wonders, to lead astray, if possible, the elect" (Mk. 13.21-22). For such false Christs to "arise" could merely mean that they had appeared in history. It is more likely to mean that they would claim to be resurrected "and show signs and wonders" to lead people astray. Such Christs would be consistent with the Holy One, the Jesus of Nazareth whom the women sought, but would not be of the same nature as the resurrected Christ of Mark.

A third clue to why the women reacted with silent terror is in the words, "as he told you." After the seder, Jesus referred to the sheep being scattered after the shepherd was stricken. Then he said, "But after I am raised, I will go before you to Galilee." The immediate consequence had been to set in motion the chain of events which would lead Peter to deny Jesus three times before the night was over. The angelic messenger now repeats the instructions to go and "tell his disciples and Peter [in particular!] that he is going before you to Galilee; there [and there only!] you will see him, as he told you."

Why Galilee? Above all else, Galilee functions in Mark as the place where the route to the cross begins. The implied message of the Gospel of Mark is that no one, not Jesus or Peter or Paul or anyone, can go directly from Mk. 1.1 to the centurion's affirmation of the true child of God in Mk. 15.39 without going through the Galilee of inadequate religious models which sidetrack people from arriving at crucifixion and its reconciling effect. What the women wanted was what Paul's and Peter's epistles had promised them: a crucifixion and resurrection of Jesus which would save them and secure their forgiveness, albeit with suffering. What they did not want was the message which stunned them into silence about what occurred on Easter Sunday. This was the shocking truth that even the most prominent of Jesus' followers had to return to the beginning and work through Jesus' entire example, each one for himself or herself.

A fourth possibility is that the women's silence was Mark's midrashic reversal of Jesus having ordered people to be silent with the result that they had spread abroad what he had told them to keep silence about. Now the women are instructed by the messenger to go tell and are afraid to do so. They experience the common human dilemma that it is easy to speak the comfortable lie or support the popular illusion but difficult to confront people with the hard truth, with the reality which makes major demands upon them.

Despite all that, this was resurrection Sunday. Salome ("Peace") was there. Mary the mother of James/Jacob was there. Mary Magdalene who had confirmed the burial was there to confirm the resurrection. How could Mark at once insist that the women were wrong in what they were looking for and in their reaction to what transpired, and yet be the best witnesses to the resurrection message? The answer, as in the book of the original messenger Malachi, is that a Jacob has midrashically replaced his brother once more. Mal. 1.2 makes it clear that the Jacob act of supplanting is the proof of God's love for his people, his guarantee that he will faithfully carry the full weight of his end of the agreement to love his people whether or not they do what is necessary to be reconciled to him when they have failed him. Now, on Easter Sunday, Jacob supplants Joses as the only son of Mary who is present by being named with her. Mary who was the mother of Joses at the closed tomb is the mother of Jacob at the open one. By her being there in that role she is guarantor that the love of God lasts through the demanded voluntary death of the son, that instead of Mary being forever a Rachel weeping for her dead children, she can be a Mary coming at the break of day in a new week with "Peace" to celebrate the victorious love which is the consequence of voluntary self-giving.

The authors of the other Gospels and Acts created many midrashic variations of the victory inherent in voluntary suffering. New Testament Christianity after Mark had written could never escape his conviction that in the crucifixion itself something new had happened in history, an innovation to be added to the tradition of Israel as an extension of the core story in the Torah. When the Gospel of Mark was completed and accepted in a community of Jesus-Jews, those Jesus-Jews inherently separated themselves from Torah-Jews and Kingdom-Jews. Mark's extension of the central story of God's relationship to his people is the end of the gospel which began, as Mark saw it, in Isaiah. The central story now ends in the victory on the cross symbolized by resurrection.

Endnotes for Chapter Fourteen

[1]V. Taylor, *St. Mark*, 610, says that "it is unnecessary to examine in detail the almost universally held conclusion that xvi. 9-20 is not an original part of Mk. Both the external and the internal evidence are conclusive."

[2]E. P. Blair, "Magdalene," *IDB*. Also Bratcher and Nida, 500.

[3]E. P. Blair, "Salome," and J.M. Myers, "Solomon," *IDB*.

[4]W. H. Morton, "Ramah," *IDB*.

[5]The Gospel of John was powerfully impacted by Joseph imagery. Much of the uniqueness of John stems from the author's reading of Mark's resurrection account as a Joseph story which was to be transmuted to all aspects of Jesus' career.

[6]In the entire Bible the only references to embalming are in Gen 50, in which the embalming of both Jacob and Joseph is described. Jews did not embalm; the practice was thought of as Egyptian. So W. L. Reed, "Embalming," *IDB*.

[7]James Muilenberg, "Gilgal," *IDB*.

AFTERWORD

MARK'S MIDRASH IN THE CONTEXT OF THE NEW TESTAMENT

The evidence set before the reader makes a sufficient *a priori* case that Mark is essentially midrashic. Each pericope in the Gospel has been demonstrated to have possible midrashic sources which could explain its origin without recourse to memories of the church, whether oral or written, going back to historical events. A continuity for Mark as an integrated whole has been discovered which transforms it from seeming to be a somewhat miscellaneous collection of data about Jesus to an internally consistent interpretation of major religious themes about Jesus adapted by a midrashic genius from already existing sacred literature. Furthermore, the book has been shown to be divided into tightly written sections with a logical flow from one to the next. The combination of midrash and continuity has revealed levels of depth and spiritual insight not previously unearthed in exegeses of Mark.

An *a priori* judgment is, however, merely preliminary, the result of an initial investigation pending a more searching trial of the evidence. We were still finding new examples of Mark's midrashic sources and rejecting some we had previously entertained until the day the book was sent to the publisher. We expect that other scholars, upon turning their attention to comparative midrash, will unearth many other possibilities, with the result a few years down the line that a more definitive interpretation of Mark as midrash can be written. We also anticipate that some of our initial enthusiasms will turn out to be unsupportable and will have to be corrected. Part of that process of scholarly correction will depend upon midrashic readings of John, Luke-Acts, and Matthew which show how each of their authors read Mark.

An *a priori* case has also been established for the hypothesis that James/Jacob, 1 John, 1 Peter, Romans, 1-2 Corinthians, Galatians, Hebrews, The Testaments of the Twelve Patriarchs, the Wisdom of Solomon, and 1-2 Maccabees, in addition to the entire canonical Jewish Bible, were used by Mark as midrashic sources. The controversial part of that proposal, the early dating of the three catholic epistles, is particularly critical to the contention that Mark developed the character portraits of Peter, James/Jacob, John, and John the Baptizer from materials in 1 Peter, James/Jacob, and 1 John.

No effort has been made to prove that there was not a historical Jesus. Such a project would be fruitless. What has been accomplished is a demonstration that it is logically possible to account for most of the details about Jesus in Mark without recourse to any source other than previously existing sacred literature of Judaism. Scholars henceforth will engage in legitimate argument about how high the degree of probability is that Mark consciously intended to use any particular midrashic source, either those herein identified or those yet to be discovered. Overall, however, it is now incontrovertible that Mark was using far more midrash than previous scholarship had recognized.

An intriguing historical fact which this study has lifted up is the difference between the experience of two groups of Jews in the first century of our era, one reading the Bible in Hebrew, and the other in Greek. The former were confronted with a soon-to-be-canonized Hebrew Bible in which God had permitted his people to terminate their story with the Babylonian exile and subsequent colonial status under foreign empires. The latter were comforted with an expanded Bible, translated into Greek and with many Greek language additions, in which God had made the Jews an independent nation once more through the military victories of the Maccabees over the Greek Empire. The former was consistent with a messiah who would be a Suffering Servant or a new version of Jeremiah; the latter with a messiah who would be a Davidic conqueror. By the irony of history, it was the Jews of Palestine, with their Hebrew text, who sought military messiahs to lead them in fruitless freedom fights against the Romans; it was the Jews of the dispersion, with their LXX text, who wrote in a Greek New Testament the stories of a messiah who was much more like the suffering Jeremiah and the Suffering Servant. Logic dictates that the opposite results should have occurred. The potential for important sociological and psychological analyses of this phenomenon seems unlimited. Only after such study has been completed will the scholars of the synagogue and church be able to understand definitively the context within which the New Testament text emerged.

To the extent that the Jesus stories in Mark were written basically as midrash without need of any of the other Gospels as source materials, the case is strengthened that Mark was the original Gospel and that each of the others must be dependent upon Mark. A primary question is whether the other authors used the same type of midrashic method utilized by Mark or whether they were doing something else even while responding to Mark. From time to time in the exegesis of Mark, it has been noted that one of the later evangelists understood a Markan midrash and extended it. It remains to be determined how thoroughly each of them comprehended Mark and what was the nature of their own midrashic variations from Mark as their core source. We are already well along on the first stage of that research, demonstrating that the authors of John and Luke-Acts thoroughly understood Mark. The preliminary results not only confirm much of our interpretation of Mark but also illuminate John, Luke and Acts in new ways. Once that work has been done, the church will be in a position to reevaluate the complex origin of its faith and, hopefully, rediscover in its biblical tradition resources for contemporary living which had previously gone unnoticed.

Leland Johnson, longtime Drake University biologist, during his lifetime loved to tell the stories of great scientists arriving at their breakthrough inventions by standing on the shoulders of those who had preceded them in the scientific community. Johnson's model seems appropriate to what we are observing in the Jewish-Christian midrashic community of the first century. The new insights of Mark's Gospel were not so much the brilliant revelations of a solitary genius illuminating the darkness around him as they were the gleanings of centuries of Jewish and Greek wisdom compacted into the figure of Jesus Christ. Mark thus suggests a powerful meaning of church (or synagogue): the gradual uncovering of the deepest meanings of life by the persistent search of many scholars in a community stretching over several centuries of time. Such an insight not only illumines our perception of Christian origins, but also invites a greater appreciation of the continuing contributions of the various communities of Catholics, Jews, humanists, Protestants, and others which have brought us to where we are today.

INDEX OF AUTHORS AND TOPICS

SACRED LITERATURE INDEX
(Indexed by Chapter Numbers)

STUDIES IN THE BIBLE AND EARLY CHRISTIANITY

1. Hugh M. Humphrey, **A Bibliography for the Gospel of Mark, 1954-1980**

2. Rolland Wolfe, **The Twelve Religions of the Bible**

3. Jean LaPorte, ***Eucharistia* in Philo**

4. Peter Gorday, **Principles of Patristic Exegesis: Romans 9-11 in Origen, John Chrysostom, and Augustine**

5. Marcus J. Borg, **Conflict, Holiness and Politics in the Teachings of Jesus**

6. Watson E. Mills, **Glossolalia: A Bibliography**

7. Matthew Baasten, **Pride According to Gregory the Great: A Study of the Moralia**

8. Douglas Oakman, **Jesus and The Economic Questions of His Day**

9. John A. McGuckin, **The Transfiguration of Christ in Scripture and Tradition**

10. Raymond A. Martin, **Syntax Criticism of the Synoptic Gospels**

11. Thomas A. Robinson, **The Bauer Thesis Examined: The Geography of Heresy in the Early Christian Church**

12. John Chrysostom, **Commentary on Isaiah 1-8**, Duane A. Garrett (trans.)

13. John Chrysostom, **A Comparison Between A King and A Monk/Against the Opponents of the Monastic Life: Two Treatises by John Chrysostom**, David G. Hunter (trans.)

14. Amy-Jill Levine, **The Social and Ethnic Dimensions of Matthean Salvation History: "Go nowhere among the Gentiles..."** (Matt. 10:5b)

15. Allan Fitzgerald, O.S.A., **Conversion Through Penance in the Italian Church of the Fourth and Fifth Centuries: New Approaches to the Experience of Conversion from Sin**

16. William Lane Craig, **Assessing the New Testament Evidence for the Historicity of the Resurrection of Jesus**

17. Jack Lewis (ed.), **Interpreting 2 Corinthians 5:14-21:** ***An Exercise in Hermeneutics***

18. R.A. Martin, **Syntax Criticism of Johannine Literature, The Catholic Epistles, and The Gospel Passion Accounts**

19. Peter W. Macky, **Metaphor in *The Bible***

20. Rolland E. Wolfe, **How the Easter Story Grew From Gospel to Gospel**

21. Dale Miller and Patricia Miller, **The Gospel of Mark as Midrash on Earlier Jewish and New Testament Literature**